U.S. Foreign Policy Today

American Renewal?

U.S. Foreign Policy Today
American Renewal?

Edited by
Steven W. Hook
Kent State University

James M. Scott
Oklahoma State University

A Division of SAGE
Washington, D.C.

CQ Press
2300 N Street, NW, Suite 400
Washington, DC 20037

Phone, 202-729-1900; toll-free, 1-866-427-7737 (1-866-4CQ-PRESS)

Web: www.cqpress.com

Cover design: the designfarm
Composition: C&M Digitals (P) Ltd.
Cover image: AP Images/Susan Walsh

∞ The paper used in this publication exceeds the requirements of the American National
Standard for Information Sciences—Permanence of Paper for Printed Library Materials,
ANSI Z39.48-1992.

Printed and bound in the United States of America

14   13   12   11   10   1   2   3   4   5

Library of Congress Cataloging-in-Publication Data

U.S. foreign policy today: American renewal?/edited by Steven W. Hook, James M. Scott.
    p. cm.
  Includes bibliographical references and index.
  ISBN 978-1-60871-403-2 (alk. paper)
    1. United States—Foreign relations—1991- I. Hook, Steven W., II. Scott, James M.,
III. Title: United States foreign policy today. IV. Title: American renewal?

  JZ1480.U12 2011
  327.73—dc22

                                                                    2010043100

Contents

Part II. Policy Domains

Preface

Barack Obama ran for president at a time of acute distress in the United States. The nation's economy, which sputtered in 2007, came close to falling apart in the weeks preceding the November 2008 election. Millions of American workers had lost their jobs, homes, or both as a result of the financial crisis, which also left dozens of banks and other financial institutions on the brink of bankruptcy. U.S. troops remained mired in Iraq and Afghanistan, nuclear tensions festered with Iran and North Korea, and the United States was isolated in global public opinion. This latter problem was widely attributed to President George W. Bush's doctrine of foreign policy, which assigned a unilateral role to the world's lone superpower and seemed to grant the United States free rein in its conduct of world affairs.

During his campaign, Obama, a first-term senator from Illinois, adopted two unmistakably optimistic themes centered on the promise of *renewal*. First, his candidacy represented *hope* for a brighter future. Second, his presidency would produce constructive *change* in Washington, DC. Obama pledged to revive the U.S. economy in a way that rewarded all Americans and to renew America's membership in the international community after years of estrangement. Specifically, Obama called for non-military solutions to foreign policy problems, more consultation with allies and the United Nations, heightened attention to global warming and other global issues, and greater respect for international law. His criticism of Bush's foreign policy, often voiced from his seat on the Senate Foreign Relations Committee, translated well on the campaign trail. Once elected, however, Obama faced the task of living up to his campaign slogan, "Yes we can!"

This book examines Obama's record as he attempted to chart a new course for American foreign policy in the early years of his administration. The authors of the following chapters, all prominent foreign policy scholars, review the administration's record in their areas of expertise. Their assignment was a difficult one given the short time frame involved and the often-secretive nature of foreign policy making. Still, from their diverse vantage points the authors provide answers to a variety of questions:

- To what extent has Obama actually changed the course of American foreign policy?

- How successful has the president been in achieving his stated objectives?
- What factors account for the relative change and continuity in foreign policy?
- What lessons can be drawn from this early experience regarding the future of Obama's presidency and American foreign policy more generally?

Since the country's founding, American leaders have pursued two very different approaches to foreign affairs, each of which reflect the position of the United States within the existing balance of power (Hook and Spanier, 2010). Whereas early U.S. leaders sought *detachment* from great-power politics, once the United States became one of the world's leading powers after World Wars I and II, the nation adopted a foreign policy based on global *engagement*. The end of the Cold War left the United States with unrivaled might on the world stage, but that era also brought an array of new and unconventional threats to national security that often defied the traditional uses of power. This complex environment left the United States in search of a national consensus regarding the future of American foreign policy, a condition that persists today. As a consequence, all post–Cold War presidents have grappled with the need to chart a course through unfamiliar waters while contending with a political context characterized by partisan divisions rather than unity and unresolved tensions between domestic and global priorities. The consequences of this uncertain new era, and Obama's responses to them, comprise the central focus of this book.

Accordingly, while global developments provide the external context of these chapters, the authors pay close attentive to domestic politics, which historically have affected presidential performance as much as the global aspirations of the chief executive. American politics is well known for its fragmented centers of power, which allow multiple actors within and outside the government to influence policy. The checks and balances written into the U.S. Constitution, combined with the expansion of the national security bureaucracy after World War II, further hinder the coherent formulation and conducting of foreign policy. The problems related to domestic politics are hardly unique to the Obama era. Indeed, the high costs of domestic politics for American foreign policy were aptly described more than a quarter century ago in *Our Own Worst Enemy*:

Something is wrong with American foreign policy. . . . For two decades, the making of American foreign policy has been growing far more political— or more precisely, far more partisan and ideological. The White House has succumbed, as former Secretary of State Alexander Haig recently put it, to "the impulse to view the presidency as a public relations opportunity and to regard Government as a campaign for reelection." And in less exalted locations, we Americans—politicians and experts alike—have been spending more time, energy, and passion in fighting ourselves than we have in trying, as a nation, to understand and deal with a rapidly changing world (Destler, Gelb, and Lake 1984: 11, 13).

This bleak but accurate assessment traced the collapse of foreign policy consensus to the late 1960s and early 1970s. The "vital center" in foreign policy, which had coalesced around the strategy of communist containment, gave way to liberal critiques of the Vietnam War and to conservative attacks on President Richard Nixon's policy of détente with the Soviet Union. In the late 1970s, domestic opponents of President Jimmy Carter openly ridiculed his attempt to make human rights a centerpiece of American foreign policy, and critics of Ronald Reagan later resisted his administration's efforts to adopt a more confrontational and anti-communist stance. The partisan politics continued after the Cold War as congressional Republicans, who gained control of both houses after the 1994 mid-term elections, resisted President Bill Clinton's foreign policy of global engagement. The Republican Party's "unilateral turn" in foreign policy, though counter to mainstream public opinion (see Page and Bouton 2006), gained traction in the White House after the election of George W. Bush in 2000. His decision to invade Iraq preemptively in 2003, and the subsequent setbacks in that conflict, sapped the national unity that followed the September 2001 terrorist attacks.

Obama's election did not reflect, nor did it signal, an easing of the polarization in American politics, which had grown steadily for nearly four decades and focused largely on domestic issues (Layman, Carsey, and Horowitz 2006: 90). The trend, attributed in part to a partisan realignment in the South, left the nation's political parties more homogenous internally but less willing to compromise with each other on nearly all issues, including those related to foreign policy. As Obama confronted a skeptical Congress (despite a Democratic majority) he also faced other obstacles to change, including bureaucratic inertia, infighting among federal agencies, and constant pressure by interest groups that benefited from the status quo. Domestic demands for economic recovery further threatened to overwhelm the president's global agenda. In this context, Obama faced deeply embedded challenges to his proposed redirection and renewal of American foreign policy in 2009 and 2010. These challenges grew even sharper after the November 2010 midterm elections, which brought a majority of Republicans to the House of Representative while shrinking the Democratic Party's majority in the Senate. The outcome of these elections quickly appeared to have a spillover effect overseas as Asian leaders pushed back on the president's proposed solutions to economic problems that had long since extended far from the United States. After Obama's appeals for a united front against Chinese economic policies gained little traction at the G-20 economic summit in South Korea, it became clear that his renewal agenda faced an uphill battle at home and abroad.

This anthology is divided into two parts. The first part considers the foreign policy *process* in the Obama administration, a vital concern that highlights the actors and institutions involved in the translation of the new president's stated goals into practice. Chapters on the president and advisers (2), Congress (3), public opinion (4), and interest groups (5) highlight the complex political context and its challenges to the president's foreign policy agenda. The second part focuses on the Obama administration's *conduct* of American foreign policy in a variety of policy domains. Chapters on defense policy (6), counter-terrorism (7), intelligence policy (8), diplomacy (9), human rights (10), economic relations (11), and the global environment (12) examine the actions, challenges, successes, and failures of the administration to effect change in these areas. The references from each chapter are presented in a References section at the end of the book that is intended to serve as a comprehensive guide for further reading and research.

Taken together, the chapters reveal a great deal not only about Obama's early performance, but also about the limitations of foreign policy change in a period of political dissensus, economic strain, and public alienation. More broadly, the president's early record, detailed in this volume, has profound implications for world order (see Zartman 2009). If the years to come produce tangible signs of relative U.S. decline and balancing by rival powers, how long can Washington provide the global collective goods that preserve its own advantages along with the "constitutional" world order (Ikenberry 2001) that the United States helped create after World War II? The chapters that follow, which assess the president's successes and failures on the world stage, help us answer this and other questions at this pivot point in the nation's history.

Acknowledgments

This volume would not have been possible without the concerted effort of a large cast of characters. We first would like to thank our authors for their thoughtful and comprehensive essays that were produced under extraordinary time pressures. Our editors at CQ Press have been highly supportive along the way. Acquisitions editors Charisse Kiino and Elise Frasier approved of the project soon after it was proposed. Paula Fleming, our copy editor, skillfully handled the chapters upon their arrival and overcame our own editing deficiencies. And Lorna Notsch, our project editor, managed the production process once our work was done. Our research assistants, Tyra Blew and Jessie Rumsey, helped us meld the hundreds of references into the unified bibliography. Finally, we are thankful to external reviewers who helped us focus the volume at its inception, including Amy Below, Oregon State University; Cooper Drury, University of Missouri; Robert Hager, University of California–Santa Barbara; and Patrick Morgan, University of California–Irvine.

Contributors

About the Editors

Steven W. Hook is professor and chair of political science at Kent State University. He is author of *National Interest and Foreign Aid* (1995) and *U.S. Foreign Policy: The Paradox of World Power*, 3rd ed. (2011), coauthor (with John Spanier) of *American Foreign Policy since World War II*, 18th ed. (2010), and editor of several other volumes.

James M. Scott is professor and head of political science at Oklahoma State University. He is coauthor (with Ralph G. Carter) of *Choosing to Lead: Understanding Congressional Foreign Policy Entrepreneurs* (2009) and (with Jerel A. Rosati) *The Politics of United States Foreign Policy*, 5th ed. (2010), as well as author, coauthor, or editor of four other books and more than forty articles, chapters, and other publications.

About the Chapter Authors

Ralph G. Carter is professor and chair of political science at Texas Christian University. He is coauthor (with James M. Scott) of *Choosing to Lead: Understanding Congressional Foreign Policy Entrepreneurs* (Duke University Press, 2009) and *Making American Foreign Policy* (1994, 1996).

I. M. (Mac) Destler is professor of political science at the University of Maryland. He is author (with Ivo Daalder) of *In the Shadow of the Oval Office* (2009). His *American Trade Politics*, 4th ed. (2005) won the Gladys M. Kammerer Award from the American Political Science Association for the best book on U.S. national security policy.

Peter Dombrowski is a professor of strategy at the Naval War College, where he serves as the chair of the Strategic Research Department. He is coauthor (with Eugene Gholz) of *Buying Military Transformation: Technological Innovation and* *the Defense Industry* (2006) and coeditor (with John Duffield) of *Balance Sheet: The Iraq War and U.S. National Security* (2009).

David P. Forsythe is Charles J. Mach Distinguished Professor of Political Science at the University of Nebraska. He is the general editor of the five-volume *Encyclopedia of Human Rights* (2009) and author of *Human Rights in International Relations*, now in its third edition (forthcoming), as well as many other books, articles, and chapters on international relations and American foreign policy.

Douglas C. Foyle is associate professor of government at Wesleyan University, where he specializes in international relations and U.S. foreign policy. He is author of *Counting the Public In: Presidents, Public Opinion, and Foreign Policy* (1999).

Stuart Gottlieb is director of policy studies at the MacMillan Center for International and Area Studies at Yale University, where he teaches advanced courses on American foreign policy and counterterrorism. He formerly served as a senior foreign policy adviser and speechwriter in the U.S. Senate.

Patrick J. Haney is professor of political science at Miami University in Oxford, Ohio. He is author of *Organizing for Foreign Policy Crises: Presidents, Advisers, and the Management of Decision Making* (2002) and coauthor (with Walt Vanderbush) of *The Cuban Embargo: The Domestic Politics of American Foreign Policy* (2005).

Glenn Hastedt is a professor of political science at James Madison University. He is author of *American Foreign Policy: Past, Present, Future,* 3rd ed. (1997) and *World Politics in a Changing World* (forthcoming).

Christopher M. Jones is an associate professor and chair of the Department of Political Science at Northern Illinois University. He is coauthor (with Eugene R. Wittkopf and Charles W. Kegley Jr.) of *American Foreign Policy: Pattern and Process,* 7th ed. (2008).

Michael E. Kraft is professor of political science and public affairs and Herbert Fisk Johnson Professor of Environmental Studies at the University of Wisconsin–Green Bay. He is author of *Environmental Policy and Politics*, 5th ed. among other works.

Kevin P. Marsh is a doctoral candidate at Northern Illinois University. His research interests include American defense and foreign policy.

Jennifer Sims is director of intelligence studies and a visiting professor at Georgetown University's Walsh School of Foreign Service. She is coeditor (with Burton Gerber) of *Transforming U.S. Intelligence* (2005) and has published numerous articles on intelligence. In 1998 she received the intelligence community's National Distinguished Service Medal.

Obama Administration Foreign Policy Advisers:
Initial Appointments, 2009

Rahm Emanuel
White House Chief of Staff

National Security

Hillary Rodham Clinton
Secretary of State

Robert Gates
Secretary of Defense

General James L. Jones
National Security Adviser

Admiral Michael Mullen
Chair, Joint Chiefs of Staff

Leon Panetta
Director
Central Intelligence Agency

James Clapper
Director of
National Intelligence

Foreign Economic Policy

Timothy Geithner
Secretary of the
Treasury

Lawrence H. Summers
Chair, National
Economic Council

Ambassador Ron Kirk
U.S. Trade
Representative

Ben S. Bernanke
Chair, Federal
Reserve

Source: Images of Obama administration advisers are from official government publications.

CHAPTER 1

Seeking Renewal
American Foreign Policy in the Obama Era

Steven W. Hook and James M. Scott

CHANGE.GOV, SO PRESIDENT-ELECT BARACK OBAMA and his vice president, Joe Biden, named their transition Web site as they prepared to assume power in January 2009. Their long campaign, which had focused on ending "politics as usual" in Washington, D.C., appealed to a broad cross-section of American voters who felt anxious about the country's future direction. George W. Bush, Obama's predecessor, had left the White House—and much of the world—in a state of confusion. The United States was in the midst of a major financial crisis that threatened to engulf the global economy. While American military forces monitored a fragile peace in Iraq, others faced a growing insurgency in Afghanistan. There was no end in sight to the "global war on terror" declared by Bush shortly after the September 11, 2001, terrorist attacks. Finally, after many years of neglect of and disdain for multilateral organizations and agreements, the United States had become isolated from the international community and distrusted in global public opinion—an unlikely and unfavorable position for the world's dominant power.

President Bush's controversial policies and declining popularity contributed to electoral upheavals at home, sweeping Republicans from power and putting Democrats in the majority in Congress (2006) and in the White House (2008). The rhetoric of change reached deeply into every policy arena, with foreign policy no exception. With a view toward the unpopular—and what they regarded as ineffective and self-defeating—policies of their predecessor, the new leaders promised on their Web site to

renew America's security and standing in the world through a new era of American leadership. The Obama-Biden foreign policy will end the war in Iraq responsibly, finish the fight against the Taliban and al Qaeda in Afghanistan, secure nuclear weapons and loose nuclear materials from terrorists, and *renew* American diplomacy to support strong alliances and to seek a lasting peace in the Israeli-Palestinian conflict [emphasis added].[1]

In other venues, Obama and his running mate promised to re-engage the United States in global governance, reduce the unilateralism of the preceding administration, and restore American prestige and leadership on a host of issues ranging from security and terrorism to human rights and the global environment.

It is, of course, not unusual for an incoming administration to differentiate itself from its predecessor on foreign policy issues. During the Cold War, John F. Kennedy announced an "Alliance for Progress" with Latin American states; Richard Nixon offered a "secret plan" to end the Vietnam War; Jimmy Carter urged a commitment to human rights as the "soul of American foreign policy"; and Ronald Reagan stressed a more assertive effort to confront the Soviet Union, restore American military power, and abandon détente. In the Cold War's wake, Bill Clinton sought "engagement and enlargement [of global democracy]" in the new environment, and George W. Bush pursued a "revolution in foreign policy" focused on American military and economic power (Daalder and Lindsay 2006). It is also not unusual for a new president to exploit the rhetoric of change and progress even if his subsequent actions and accomplishments demonstrate more continuity than reform. However, the examples of preceding presidents are doubly instructive as each faced significant obstacles in changing course in foreign policy.

Historical experience also demonstrates that the domestic standing of American presidents relates directly to their credibility and political influence overseas. Obama's problems at home were clearly visible to a worldwide media audience. It was not surprising, therefore, when the Democratic Party's setbacks in the November 2010 midterm elections were followed by resistance from foreign leaders during his 10-day visit to several Asian countries. This resistance, which contrasted sharply with the previously enthusiastic response to Obama on the world stage, made it clear that he faced an uphill battle in advancing his foreign policy goals.

This volume examines the commitment of the Obama administration to a foreign policy of renewal. In the chapters to follow, a group of respected scholars explores the broad outlines of the renewal agenda and the challenges facing Obama in making it a reality. We establish the context of the administration's efforts in this introductory chapter and then explore key issues concerning policy making (Part I) and policies (Part II) in the ensuing chapters. Collectively, the contents of this volume present insights and assessments that have implications for both the general comprehension of American foreign policy making and the specific foreign policy efforts of the Obama administration.

Obama's Search for Renewal

Obama's renewal agenda, described below, called upon the foreign policy tradition of *liberal internationalism,* which was forged early in the twentieth century as the United States joined the ranks of major world powers (see Schneider 1983, 1987; Holsti and Rosenau 1984; Wittkopf 1990; and Chittick, Billingsley, and Travis 1995). In response to this shift in the balance of power, two U.S. presidents—Theodore Roosevelt and Woodrow Wilson—adopted widely varying foreign policies. Whereas Roosevelt (1901–1909) relied upon the "big stick" of U.S. hegemony and military coercion, Wilson (1913–1921) turned to normative principles and multilateral cooperation to secure U.S. interests. These contending approaches to managing U.S. great-power relations only proved effective when they were melded by President Franklin Roosevelt during World War II. His fusion of realism, based on overwhelming U.S. power, and liberalism, grounded in principles such as the "four freedoms" espoused by the president, left the United States after World War II not just with military supremacy but with credibility and extensive reservoirs of "soft power" in much of the world.

For the United States, liberal internationalism provided an appealing means to achieve its primary objective after World War II: sustaining the "preponderance of power" (Leffler 1992) the nation amassed as a result of the war. From the Truman administration through the Vietnam War, most political and economic elites agreed that the United States should establish a pervasive global presence—militarily, economically, and politically—in order to fend off potential challengers to U.S. primacy. The strategy also supported the U.S. government's secondary postwar objective: "containing" the Soviet Union and other communist governments, which, in Washington's view, threatened the United States (see Gaddis 1982).

American elites, including members of Congress, agreed that the containment doctrine, originally articulated by U.S. diplomat George Kennan, had the best chance of sustaining U.S. primacy (see Trubowitz 1998). Senator Arthur Vandenberg (R-MI), chair of the Senate Foreign Relations Committee, epitomized the mood on Capitol Hill by renouncing his isolationist world view and embracing liberal internationalism. With strong bipartisan support, presidents Harry Truman and Dwight Eisenhower created a global U.S. military presence, an unmatched nuclear arsenal, and an intelligence service that frequently engaged in covert operations overseas, some of which included forceful regime change in such countries as Guatemala and Iran. The same bipartisan consensus led to active U.S. involvement in the United Nations, the Bretton Woods economic institutions, and a variety of military alliances. In the early 1960s, President John F. Kennedy furthered the cause of liberal internationalism by creating the Peace Corps, greatly expanding U.S. foreign aid, and launching an "alliance for progress" in Latin America—all while pursuing an aggressive anticommunist security policy.

Underlying this approach to U.S. foreign policy was a longer tradition "that the nation's security is best protected by the expansion of democracy worldwide" (T. Smith 1994, 9). Early advocates of what came to be known as democratic peace theory, including presidents Thomas Jefferson and James Madison, felt the "exceptional" nature of American government and society could only be secured if the United States were not a "democratic island in a sea of tyranny"

(Hartz 1955). This perspective also applied to foreign economic relations, as early American leaders also believed the United States should restrict trade to open-market economies. These beliefs, later reinforced by the U.S. victory over fascism in World War II, carried over into its aggressive pursuit of anticommunism in the Cold War.

The domestic consensus on these points was so strong that one analyst worried that the "end of ideology" was stifling political debate (Bell 1960). His warning proved unwarranted a decade later, however, when the Vietnam War provoked unrest at home and led to charges of an "imperial presidency" (Schlesinger 1973, 2004). U.S. involvement in Vietnam shook the foundations of the Cold War consensus (e.g., Melanson 2005), and Democrats and Republicans engaged in "guns-versus-butter" debates throughout the 1970s as the United States suffered from economic recessions twice in the decade. President Jimmy Carter's attempt to make human rights the "soul of American foreign policy" faltered under these economic pressures and collapsed in 1979 amid the Soviet invasion of Afghanistan, the *Sandinista* revolution in Nicaragua, and the onset of the Iranian hostage crisis. Although Congress supported President Ronald Reagan's calls for higher military spending in the 1980s, his foreign policies were subjected to fierce partisan debates, most visibly displayed in the 1986 Iran-*Contra* scandal.

The end of the Cold War left the United States as the sole global superpower, an epochal feat that, paradoxically, proved nearly fatal for liberal internationalism. Lacking a major threat from overseas, the United States failed to establish a new grand strategy that enjoyed bipartisan and public support. Under President George H. W. Bush, many Democrats in Congress openly opposed U.S. actions in the 1991 Persian Gulf War. Later in the decade, President Bill Clinton was forced to deploy troops to Somalia (1993), Bosnia-Herzegovina (1994), and Kosovo (1999) without congressional support. Acting on its "Contract with America," the Republican-led Congress turned against U.S. multilateral engagement by suspending payments of past UN dues, refusing to ratify the Comprehensive Test Ban Treaty, and rejecting the Kyoto Protocol on climate change. As the public grew apathetic toward foreign policy (see Lindsay 2000), Congress descended into withering partisan conflict, which ensured that no unified vision of U.S. grand strategy would materialize. As Kupchan and Trubowitz (2007, 9) observed, unipolarity "loosened the political discipline engendered by the Cold War threat, leaving U.S. foreign policy more vulnerable to growing partisanship at home. 'Red' and 'Blue' America disagree about the nature of U.S. engagement in the world; growing disparities of wealth have reawakened class tensions; and political pragmatism has been losing ground to ideological extremism."

This partisan stalemate continued throughout the presidency of George W. Bush, who adopted the unilateral approach to foreign policy promoted by many congressional Republicans during the Clinton years. Even before the terrorist attacks of September 2001, Bush had rejected consideration of the Kyoto Protocol and U.S. membership in the International Criminal Court. His abolition in December 2001 of the Anti-Ballistic Missile Treaty with Russia, a product of the 1972 détente period, further signaled his intention to go it alone in foreign policy. "Neoconservatives" in the Bush administration called for a "muscular" variant of liberal internationalism that included preemptive attacks against adversaries and democratization by force in Afghanistan and Iraq (see Mann 2004). Bush's rejection of the international community, a term he found oxymoronic, left the United States isolated and widely distrusted overseas. This ill will toward Washington only increased as the Bush administration refused to honor the Geneva Conventions in its treatment of war prisoners.

To critics, the Bush Doctrine was especially troubling given its "illiberal" tactics in the war on terror and the way they were often justified by invoking liberal principles associated with the democratic peace (see Desch 2007–08). Such concerns were widely shared in domestic and global public opinion and reflected in a dramatic decline in American reputation and leadership. By the end of 2006, citizens in thirty-three of thirty-five countries surveyed believed the U.S. war in Iraq had increased the likelihood of terrorist attacks around the world (World Public Opinion.org 2006). Predictably, Bush became a lightning rod for discontent overseas. Ninety-eight percent of European Commission members and 68 percent of members in the European Parliament disapproved of his foreign policies (Centre for the Study of Political Change 2006, 6). At home, a July 2008 survey found "improving America's standing in the world" to be the general public's top U.S. foreign policy priority (Chicago Council on Global Affairs 2009).

Bush's foreign policies were greeted skeptically by citizens, the majority of whom favored constructive U.S. engagement in global affairs (see Page and Bouton 2006). Leading scholars, meanwhile, were nearly united in their calls for a U.S. return to the international community. The Princeton Project on National Security, for example, argued that the United States should create "institutions and partnerships that give liberal democracies the collective capacities to protect themselves and solve common problems, both within and alongside existing institutions" (Ikenberry and Slaughter 2006, 59). Although Bush softened his hard line toward global governance in his last years in the White House, he left office with low approval ratings at home and in most countries overseas.

According to the Obama team, the Bush White House was principally responsible for the estrangement of the United States from its allies and partners, as well as from the overall international community. Questionable policy choices were, in part, to blame, but the unilateralism, unabashed claims of predominance and disregard for international institutions, agreements, and cooperation were even more serious. In contrast to the view espoused by many in the Bush administration, Obama argued that the mailed fist of American power is best encased in the velvet glove of cooperation (Walt 2002; see also Walt 2005). His foreign policy advisers were convinced that the damage to American reputation and prestige had to be repaired if its long-term foreign policy interests were to be secured.

As noted above, armed with this perspective, Obama made a renewal agenda the core of his foreign policy. As the administration navigated its initial months and years, its commitment to this agenda took the form of enhanced efforts toward diplomatic engagement and multilateral cooperation, greater reliance on soft power, and greater concern for global problems. Public declarations and affirmations of its commitment were evident in Biden's speech in Berlin (February 2009), Obama's address to a joint session of Congress (February 2009), his address in Cairo, Egypt (June 2009), and his speech accepting the Nobel Peace Prize (December 2009). Hence the renewal agenda took shape in the policy declarations and initial actions of the Obama administration. A review of key policy declarations by Obama and Biden suggests that the key elements of this paradigm involved

- greater emphasis on global interdependence, finite resources, and collective goods;
- a broader conception of U.S. national interest, incorporating transnational concerns to a greater degree;
- a broader conception of power, including "soft" as well as "hard" forms, and reflecting an emphasis on ideas and values in foreign policy;
- a wider mix of policy instruments, especially involving diplomacy and economic statecraft to a greater degree relative to military power;
- an expanded state role in melding domestic economic development with transnational goals, particularly in the energy, transportation, and environmental fields; and
- greater involvement in multilateral institutions and support for international law.

In the administration's first national security strategy, released in May 2010, Obama laid out the rationale for his course change in American foreign policy. "Yet as we fight the wars in front of us, we must see the horizon beyond them," the president wrote in his introductory statement. "To get there, we must pursue a strategy of national renewal and global leadership—a strategy that rebuilds the foundation of American strength and influence" (*National Security Strategy* 2010, i). In a key introductory passage, the administration further framed its efforts in explicit calls for renewal:

As we did after World War II, America must prepare for the future, while forging cooperative approaches among nations that can yield results.

Our national security strategy is, therefore, focused on renewing American leadership so that we can more effectively advance our interests in the 21st century. We will do so by building upon the sources of our strength at home, while shaping an international order that can meet the challenges of our time. This strategy recognizes the fundamental connection between our national security, our national competitiveness, resilience, and moral example. And it reaffirms America's commitment to pursue our interests through an international system in which all nations have certain rights and responsibilities. (*National Security Strategy* 2010, 1)

Similarly, in August 2010, Obama (2010a) declared that

one of the lessons of our effort in Iraq is that American influence around the world is not a function of military force alone. We must use all elements of our power—including our diplomacy, our economic strength, and the power of America's example—to secure our interests and stand by our allies. And we must project a vision of the future that is based not just on our fears, but also on our hopes, a vision that recognizes the real dangers that exist around the world, but also the limitless possibility of our time.

In addition to declarations such as these, many of the administration's early foreign policy actions reflected the renewal agenda as well. These included the announced suspension of "coercive interrogations," the planned closure of the Guantánamo Bay detention facility, the "resetting" of strained diplomatic relations with Russia, and a return to more cordial relations with the United Nations. Obama also took steps to bring U.S. military actions in Iraq to an end, announcing plans to withdraw combat brigades and draw down U.S. forces while strengthening the Iraqi regime's ability to provide security for the country. Indeed, as those steps culminated in the summer of 2010, the president used a nationally televised speech at the end of August to proclaim the end of the U.S. combat role. Obama also signed an executive order requiring improved fuel efficiency of cars and trucks, organized a global summit meeting on nuclear proliferation, and dispatched Secretary of State Hillary Clinton on overseas missions of "public diplomacy" to make the case for renewed U.S. engagement in the world. These efforts paid off in global public opinion, as early surveys revealed a major improvement in U.S. approval overseas. A June 2009 survey of nearly 20,000 citizens in countries with 62 percent of the world's population found Obama was "inspiring far more confidence than any other world political leader" (World Public Opinion.org 2009a).

It remained to be seen, however, whether Obama could fully execute his shift toward liberal internationalism in the absence of a domestic consensus such as that which existed during the Cold War. As noted earlier, the United

States had become increasingly polarized ideologically after the end of the Cold War and is currently mired in partisan battles over virtually every issue facing Congress. Obama's attempts to execute this shift under these circumstances, detailed in the chapters to follow, faced a variety of obstacles that did not confront earlier presidents during the heyday of liberal internationalism.

Constraints on the Renewal Agenda

Clearly, the Obama administration embraced change and renewal in foreign policy as well as other policy domains. Nevertheless, its ability to deliver policy change has faced many challenges. As many of the contributors to this volume indicate, declaring and achieving change are not identical, and just as did its predecessors, the Obama administration has had and will have to contend with challenges and obstacles as it pursues its renewal agenda. This inescapable context has shaped its foreign policy formulation and implementation and its pursuit of the renewal agenda.

A good way to approach the counterpressures of opportunities and constraints in presidential foreign policy leadership and gain a conceptual perspective on the Obama administration's successes and failures as it pursues its renewal agenda is to understand it as embedded in a paradox of presidential power (Rosati and Scott 2010). In effect, although the president is the most powerful political actor in foreign policy, with constitutional roles and capabilities that make him central to policy making, the president also faces many constraints that limit his power. Moreover, some elements of this context strengthen the president's hand at some times and weaken it at others (see Cronin and Genovese 2004; Neustadt 1960; Pious 1979). As President John F. Kennedy understood, the president "is rightly described as a man of extraordinary powers. Yet it is also true that he must wield those powers under extraordinary limitations" (quoted in Sorensen 1963, xii).

As Obama sought renewal in American foreign policy, he was enabled by the array of powers and roles that place the president in a position of foreign policy influence. These included his role as commander in chief, chief diplomat, and chief administrator of the executive branch. The president, unlike members of Congress, also has a national constituency and can thus represent the "voice of the people." These and other sources of power and influence provided important opportunities for Obama as his administration pursued the renewal agenda.

However, like all presidents, Obama also faced a number of limitations that constrained his ability to implement the renewal agenda. First, there was the international context and legacy of inherited policies and problems. For Obama, these included the circumstances facing U.S. foreign policy upon his coming to power in January 2009. Obama, for example, was forced to manage the financial crisis that peaked in the final weeks of the presidential campaign. Triggered by reckless lending practices of American banks and mortgage brokers, the crisis spread quickly to the major economies of Europe and East Asia, many of which had adopted the same financial structures and policies as Washington. As a result, national output plunged and unemployment surged worldwide in the most severe recession since the 1930s. Millions of U.S. citizens suffered severe personal losses, and the stature of the United States as the "locomotive" of global prosperity was tarnished badly. Obama, who spent the first months of his presidency containing this damage, was forced to delay other national and foreign policy priorities. With the president's attention riveted on problems at home, a former national security adviser warned, "his grand redefinition of U.S. foreign policy is vulnerable to dilution or delay by upper-level officials who have the bureaucratic predisposition to favor caution over action and the familiar over the innovative" (Brzezinski 2010, 18).

The wars in Iraq and Afghanistan, and the decisions and prior actions of his predecessor in both situations, also demanded Obama's attention and restricted his foreign policy options in these conflicts as well as other regional trouble spots. Even as positive steps were taken to draw down the U.S. military deployment in Iraq, culminating in Obama's August 2010 declaration of the end of combat operations, American forces nearly lost control of Afghanistan, where Taliban insurgents held most provinces by the end of 2009. The insurgents renewed their ties with al-Qaeda, the terrorist group that planned the September 2001 attacks on the United States from safe havens in Afghanistan. The turmoil, which spread to neighboring Pakistan, forced Obama to deploy 30,000 additional troops to Afghanistan late in 2009. The winding down of the Iraq war, which began in March 2003, was expected to make this shift in U.S. military action possible. North Korea and Iran, meanwhile, continued to gain global stature by threatening to develop nuclear arsenals and upset regional power balances.

A second challenge was the domestic political environment. All recent presidents must contend with the increasingly partisan political arena within which foreign policy is formulated and implemented. The days of the "two presidencies," one intensely political for domestic policy and one generally bipartisan for foreign policy (Wildavsky 1966), are long gone, and the old adage that "politics stops at the water's edge" no longer applies. The Obama administration has had to contend with the increasingly partisan political environment described earlier and shifting patterns of public opinion, the activities of interest groups, and the media.

Moreover, like other presidents, Obama also has had to gain enough support from Congress to achieve his foreign policy goals, particularly those involving treaties that would require a "supermajority" of two-thirds of the Senate. The president and Congress share power; in fact, there is no constitutional power provided to the president that the Congress does not share in some way.

Therefore, while Obama can exercise great influence over the policy agenda in both the foreign and domestic arenas, Congress has been a major constraint. Moreover, Congress has become both more divided and partisan on foreign policy issues and more independent and assertive in this area as well following the Vietnam War and Watergate (e.g., Scott and Carter 2002). As the president soon discovered, even Democrats in Congress could not be counted on to support his foreign policy goals, and Republicans routinely voted unanimously in opposition. This lack of domestic consensus, as noted above, diminished the prospects that he could resurrect the liberal-internationalist foreign policies of his Cold War predecessors.

Finally, Obama faced the immediate challenge of "renewal" within the foreign policy bureaucracy. All presidents must grapple with the problem of creating a structure and process to manage and control the far-flung administrative agencies as much as possible. Obama's predecessor was widely criticized for his inefficient and ineffective foreign policy structure and process (e.g., Daalder and Destler 2009; Rothkopf 2005). Furthermore, bureaucratic "pathologies" stemming from hierarchy, specialization, and routinization—rivalries, incrementalism and resistance to change, turf wars, and bureaucratic subcultures among them—must be addressed and contended with in nearly every policy area. For Obama, among his primary challenges in this regard was coping with the challenges of the intelligence community with its decentralized structure and overlapping agencies and organizations, as well as restoring balance, trust, and cooperation between the state and defense departments, the latter of which assumed primary control of U.S. foreign policy in the Bush years. In his first year, Secretary of Defense Robert Gates, a holdover from the Bush administration, established a cordial relationship with the State Department led by Hillary Clinton. Still, tensions emerged over the role of the U.S. Agency for International Development, an arm of the State Department, which was forced to compete with the much better-funded Pentagon in managing such crises as the earthquake in Haiti. The factors outlined above have and will dramatically affect Obama's efforts, and the subsequent chapters of this volume detail his early efforts to exploit his powers as president and to overcome the constraints on his ability to achieve his policy goals.

Two other observations can be made about the trajectory of Obama's renewal agenda as we prepare for the substantive chapters that follow. First, we can distinguish between positive and negative power: positive power is the ability to initiate and implement foreign policies, while negative power is the ability to negate and to prevent others from doing something against presidential preferences. The exercise of positive power—to effect meaningful change in foreign policy—is more challenging. To initiate and implement policy, presidents must build political coalitions to support their initiatives and overcome resistance and opposition. By contrast, negation is more a question of preventing an initiative from surfacing on the political agenda or stopping it after it has surfaced, a much simpler task. The president, for example, has the ability to stifle virtually any piece of legislation he chooses through his use of the veto, which is rarely overridden.

Second, the exercise of presidential leadership tends to follow a pattern or cycle over time. Generally, presidents enter office near the peak of their power, and by the end of their term they are weaker politically and have lost some measure of public support. "Honeymoon" periods and electoral mandates provide a relatively hospitable political environment in which the president has considerable leeway to initiate new policies. Within a short period of time, however, the honeymoon is over. Congress begins to assert itself, especially if the majority party is different from the president's party; the media soon spends more time addressing the issues and critically analyzing presidential policies; interest groups and social movements descend on the policy-making process; public approval usually begins to erode. As President Lyndon Johnson observed, "You've got to give it all you can, that first year. . . . Doesn't matter what kind of majority you come in with. You've got just one year when they treat you right and before they start worrying about themselves. The third year, you lose votes. . . . The fourth's all politics. You can't put anything through when half the Congress is thinking how to beat you" (quoted in H. Smith 1988, 333).

President Obama appeared to recognize this pattern and sought to take advantage of his honeymoon and his first year in office with a flurry of political activity and policy initiatives. More generally, the opportunities, constraints, and trajectories outlined above have important implications for the ongoing pursuit of his renewal agenda. Examining the policy-making and policy domains in which that agenda are carried out constitutes the central focus of the remainder of this volume.

Plan of the Book

As noted above, President Obama took office amidst a wide range of problems facing the United States. Despite these problems, his arrival at the White House in January 2009 was met with widespread enthusiasm in the United States and overseas. High expectations included the hope that Obama would fulfill his pledge to change the direction of American foreign policy in a manner that enhanced the nation's security while reassuring the international community that the United States would "renew" its leadership role on the world stage.

The authors of the volume were faced with the difficult task of assessing Obama's early record in achieving this goal. Their analyses describe many cases that affirmed the president's foreign policies and many others in which the president had not lived up to the high expectations that he established as a presidential candidate. The chapters that follow first examine the impact of the "renewal agenda" on the presidency, Congress, public opinion, and interest groups engaged in the policy process. The second section of the book explores Obama's record in a variety of foreign policy domains, including national security, terrorism, diplomacy, economic affairs, intelligence gathering, human rights, and the global environment. While the findings of these chapters are necessarily preliminary and tentative, they shed valuable light on the capacity of an American president to change the course of foreign policy under extraordinary circumstances. A brief summary of each chapter highlights the primary concerns and findings of these authors.

Glenn Hastedt begins the inquiry by examining the presidency and advisory relations of the Obama administration. He reviews the constitutional powers of the president and then discusses the person of the president and the organization of the presidency, comparing Barack Obama and his administration to preceding presidencies. Hastedt then turns to the declaratory policies of the Obama presidency and their relationship to concrete action. He concludes that Obama entered office with good prospects for articulating a renewal agenda and impacting the "milieu" of foreign policy but faced serious domestic political constraints challenging his efforts to translate the agenda into policy.

In Chapter 3, Ralph Carter and James Scott examine the role of Congress in supporting, as well as obstructing, Obama's renewal agenda. They highlight the contentious, partisan atmosphere in Congress that greeted Obama when he entered office, even with a Democratic majority in the Senate and House of Representatives. As they find, "The policy-making environment could be characterized as very challenging, if not toxic." Their chapter then explores various models of legislative-executive relations in recent history and finds that a "strategic Congress" prevailed in 2009 in which "Congress is generally less interested in foreign policy but willing to challenge the president when it chooses to address key issues."

In the next chapter, Douglas Foyle addresses the nature, role, and impact of public opinion on Obama's renewal agenda. Making extensive use of public opinion polling, he reviews the general foreign policy orientations of the American public as well as its long-term foreign policy goals, finding significant support for internationalism and multilateralism, although at reduced levels than in previous years. Turning to more specific foreign policy issues related to the renewal agenda, Foyle highlights important areas of partisan disagreement. After touching on the reaction of global public opinion to Obama, Foyle takes up the challenges his analysis suggests for the renewal agenda. Warning that the Obama administration is likely to face continuing partisan divisions and a public preoccupied with domestic problems, Foyle concludes that the public opinion is likely to enhance the magnitude of Obama's foreign policy renewal efforts should they succeed or amplify the domestic political costs should they fail.

In Chapter 5, Patrick Haney explores the power and access of ethnic lobbies in the foreign policy domain, especially lobbies that concern Cuba, India, and the Middle East. Reviewing key groups, their roles, and their activities and influence over recent decades, Haney not only offers insights into the impact of this increasingly complex context on foreign policy and the renewal agenda but also develops the idea that interest group lobbying is a two-way street between presidents and ethnic interest groups. According to Haney, in its pursuit of the renewal agenda, the Obama administration has extended this two-way street, reaching out to cultivate relationships with key ethnic lobby groups in order to further its foreign policy aims. As Haney concludes, leveraging such social networks was a key part of the Obama strategy in the nomination and general election campaigns, so it is not overly surprising that such efforts has extended into the foreign policy arena as the Obama administration used partnerships with ethnic minority groups inside the United States to reconnect to the outside world.

Peter Dombrowski then confronts Obama's national security policy in Chapter 6. As he describes, defense analysts had concluded by 2009 that the Bush administration's "muscular" approach to foreign policy did not "represent a viable, sustainable approach to U.S. national security." Studies by the Pentagon found the strategic environment highly complex, with conventional threats such as the rise of China melding with unconventional threats that included global terrorism, weapons proliferation, and environmental and resource constraints. As Dombrowski concludes, Obama's security policy sought to accommodate both types of threats and, in so doing, continued many of the defense policies that had been pursued by the Bush White House.

In a related analysis, Stuart Gottlieb in Chapter 7 explores the Obama administration's approach to fighting terrorism. As he describes, Obama sought to shift the focus on counterterrorism from a military problem to one that could be addressed by law enforcement. In this approach, the assumption is that "terrorism is ultimately about the commission of a crime—murder, destruction of property, etc.—and in a robust constitutional democracy like the United States, the criminal justice system is more than adequate to prosecute terrorists . . . for committing such crimes, regardless of their motivations for doing so." Still, powerful forces within the U.S. government resisted this approach and forced Obama to maintain the military approach to counterterrorism while he tried to change the policy's direction.

Jennifer Sims takes up intelligence policy in Chapter 8, considering efforts to renew this troubled and controversial community in the wake of the high-profile failures of the September 11, 2001, attacks, the Iraqi weapons of mass destruction debacle, and the efforts to reform the intelligence community in 2004–05. She begins by reviewing intelligence policy—how to gather critical information on competitors and deliver it in a timely fashion—and the machinery and practices inherited by the Obama administration. Sims discusses the administration's review of existing capabilities and practical steps to improve them, as well as the substantial problems that continue to plague intelligence policy. She concludes with four recommendations for reinvigorating intelligence that range from restating key missions, shifting the responsibilities of the director of national intelligence to reduce bureaucratic friction, and improving the agility and capacity of the intelligence community to produce timely information for policy makers.

In Chapter 9, Christopher Jones and Kevin Marsh address the Obama administration's approach to diplomacy. As they explain, Obama's elevation of diplomacy as an instrument of foreign policy diverged dramatically from that of President Bush, who relied more heavily on military solutions to threats facing the United States. The authors highlight Secretary of State Hillary Clinton's efforts to restore American "soft power" by seeking to persuade allies and adversaries alike that the United States sought peaceful solutions to foreign policy problems. This shift, they argue, helped restore U.S. prestige in world politics, but it did not remove the tensions and threats facing the United States.

David Forsythe then examines U.S. policies regarding human rights in Chapter 10. In his view, the Bush administration's neglect of human rights was among the primary reasons the United States became isolated in the international community. He recounts the controversy involving the U.S. government's treatment of war prisoners, or "enemy combatants" in the lexicon of the Bush White House. He then describes both the successes and failures of Obama's foreign policy team in reviving the U.S. government's respect for human rights on this and other issues. As he finds, Obama adopted a "pragmatic" approach in which he sought to improve the U.S. record on human rights while accommodating the concerns of political opponents that, in fighting terrorism especially, national security concerns must take precedence in the conduct of foreign policy.

In Chapter 11, I. M. Destler explores the Obama administration's engagement on international economic policy. Setting the historical context shaping the machinery of the U.S. foreign economic policy structures and processes, Destler discusses the economic crises inherited by the incoming administration and the efforts to grapple with their consequences. As Destler notes, the Obama administration first set its sights on contending with the domestic economic issues it faced—the so-called Great Recession—while also coordinating a response to the global economic challenges with other countries. Destler also considers the personnel and agencies assigned to address international economic policy under Obama and reviews the administration's first steps on international policy coordination, trade, and China. He concludes that, while the renewal agenda in this arena was focused primarily on managing the economic crisis, as that issue recedes, Obama is likely to turn to trade and international economic policy as opportunities for internationalism and engagement.

Finally, in Chapter 12, Michael Kraft takes a close look at U.S. environmental policy under the Obama administration. As do other authors, he contrasts the Bush and Obama policies in his analysis and finds that "there has been no comparable shift in presidential policy positions on the environment in the last forty years." Kraft identifies the key players in the Obama administration who sought to address environmental threats such as climate change, and he details their efforts to gain congressional support for major reforms in this area. In keeping with the findings of Carter and Scott in Chapter 3, Kraft recounts the congressional opposition to many of these reforms that stymied Obama's "renewal" agenda in this vital area of foreign policy. Although the catastrophic 2010 oil spill in the Gulf of Mexico brought these issues, including U.S. energy policy, to national and international attention, Kraft argues that Obama still lacked the domestic consensus that was necessary for significant change in environmental policy.

All of these chapters identify both the advances and setbacks in Obama's renewal agenda and call upon readers to grasp the opportunities as well as constraints facing the new president after he took office. They share a central assumption that changing course in U.S. foreign policy is a formidable task due to the many domestic interests and political rivalries that make unified action difficult in the U.S. political system. Foreign policy, they find, begins at home, and presidents who come to power promising rapid change are likely to be frustrated. Still, the authors believe that Obama made considerable progress on his renewal agenda, creating a foundation for the realization of more ambitious reforms. Readers, of course, will form their own judgments as they read these chapters. Our hope is that the chapters that follow inform these judgments and prepare readers to understand the president's future efforts to "renew" U.S. foreign policy in the new era.

Notes

1. Office of the President-elect, 2009. http://change.gov/agenda/foreign_policy_agenda.

Chapter 2

Presidents, Advisers, and Future Directions of American Foreign Policy

Glenn Hastedt

In looking to determine the direction of American foreign policy, whether it involves the potential for renewal or staying the course, our attention is inexorably drawn to the White House. We look first to the president, both as a person and the institution, for clues. This said, there is nothing automatic or simple about the president's ability to set the direction of American foreign policy. As Pious (2008) observed, problems that are easily resolved do not reach the White House. Issues reach the president when no one knows what to do or they disagree strongly about what to do. They are frontier problems.

The frontier problems facing the Obama administration are many and have deep roots. Writing in the months preceding the 2008 presidential election, Richard Holbrooke (2008, 2), a former ambassador to the UN and assistant secretary of state who became special envoy to Afghanistan and Pakistan in the Obama administration, observed "the next president will inherit a more difficult opening-day set of international problems than any of his predecessors have since at least the end of World War II." Secretary of State Hillary Clinton echoed these thoughts in a July 2009 speech when she asserted that the United States could not go back to the Cold War policies of containment, twentieth-century balance of power strategies, or nineteenth-century concert of power strategies in dealing with the world. What was needed was a new global architecture rooted in partnerships.

In this chapter we will examine the extent to which the Obama administration succeeded in its initial efforts to set American foreign policy on a path toward renewal. To do so, we begin with an overview of (a) the powers given to the president by the Constitution, (b) the person of the president, and (c) the organization of the presidency. In each of these cases, we compare President Barack Obama and his administration with the preceding presidencies with a special emphasis on Obama's most recent predecessors. We will then compare the extent to which the declaratory policies of his presidency have translated into concrete action policies. In the conclusion we will speculate on the long-term prospects for Obama's foreign policy of renewal.

Constitutional Powers

The starting point for any discussion of the president's role in determining the content and conduct of American foreign policy is the Constitution. As Edwin Corwin (1957) noted long ago, the Constitution does not provide the final word on how the president and other branches of government will interact in making American foreign policy. It is the starting point, an "invitation to struggle." A review of the major areas of struggle between the president and Congress is a useful way of framing the transition from candidate Obama to President Obama as well as that from President George W. Bush to President Obama because it helps us better understand the constitutional and political context within which efforts at foreign policy renewal take place.

This struggle became increasingly volatile under George W. Bush's presidency and its embrace of the concept of a unitary presidency. According to this perspective, Article II of the Constitution gives the president the authority to govern a unified executive department. In its strongest versions, the unitary presidency theory argues that in the area of foreign policy, neither Congress nor the courts have the authority to direct or control (Yoo 2005). Bush is not the first to have acted unilaterally in exercising presidential foreign policy powers. Franklin Roosevelt issued executive orders nationalizing aviation plants, ship building companies, and coal firms; Harry Truman desegregated the military through an executive order; and John Kennedy unilaterally created the Peace Corps. However, Bush was particularly aggressive in asserting presidential imperatives.

As he assumed office, Obama did not shy away from unilateral action. He acted quickly to close the Guantánamo Bay detention facility. His administration followed this decision with the announcement that Khalid Sheikh Mohammed, the accused mastermind of the 9/11 attacks, would be tried in federal court rather than a military court over the objections of many in the Senate. Obama also followed Bush's lead in asserting the government had the right to exclude evidence in civil cases on the grounds that including it would jeopardize national security. This position reversed one taken during the campaign when Obama complained that the Bush administration had "ignored public disclosure rules" by too often invoking the state-secrets argument.

A clear sense of the constitutional stakes in the struggle over foreign policy can be obtained by taking a closer look at some of the key powers that are contested. The Constitution states that the president by and with the advice and consent of the Senate has the power to make treaties. In its first year, the Obama administration avoided direct confrontations with the Senate over treaties. This was not the case in its second year. At the time of the Copenhagen summit on global warming, expectations ran high that an environmental treaty would be negotiated, but this was not to be the case, eliminating a potential ratification battle. Prior to that summit, members of Congress had made it clear that any climate agreement had to include strong provisions that required U.S. competitors to cut emissions. According to Rep. Edward Markey (D-MA), such language was necessary to make any Copenhagen Treaty politically acceptable (Eilperin and Faida 2009), and on the eve of the conference, Senator Byron Dorgan (D-ND) urged Obama not to overpromise (Eilperin 2009b).

However, a successful treaty was negotiated with Russia in April 2010 replacing the expired START I agreement. Voices of opposition to its terms quickly emerged from Republicans in the Senate. Among the concerns they raised was its impact on U.S. verification capabilities and the U.S. nuclear presence in Europe, including the construction of a ballistic missile system. Obama was sensitive to these issues. The treaty's preamble stated it imposed no new limits on an American ballistic missile system in Europe, nor did it do away with the exchange of telemetry on missile tests. Even so, Senate ratification was expected to be a long process. Ratification of the START I negotiated by the Reagan administration had taken 430 days, and it had taken more than nine months to gain Senate approval for the 2002 Moscow Treaty negotiated by the Bush administration, despite the fact that it was only three pages long and contained no verification requirements.

Presidents have sought to limit the extent of conflicts over treaty amendments in several ways. One strategy is to attach unilateral statements of interpretation. This was done by the Clinton administration in gaining Senate approval of the North American Free Trade Agreement (NAFTA). Likewise, the signing of the April 2010 U.S.-Russian arms control agreement was accompanied by the announcement that both sides were working on unilateral statements that each would attach to the treaty. Another strategy used in trade agreements is to obtain "fast-track" authority prior to the beginning of the negotiations. This power, now formally referred to as Trade Promotional Authority, limits the Senate to a straight yes-no vote within a specified time frame on any trade agreement put before it; neither delay nor amendments are permitted.

President George W. Bush's fast-track authority expired on July 1, 2007, with several negotiated agreements stalled in the Senate due to their lack of environmental and labor safeguards. As a candidate, Obama had indicated he would not pursue fast-track authority but would replace it with negotiating criteria that emphasized such factors as a country's labor and environmental standards and the state of its civil society. Neither Congress nor the administration showed much interest in renewing trade negotiations during Obama's first year, so the issue of fast-track authority did not surface. However, this may change with the administration's emphasis on exports as a vehicle for reinvigorating the U.S. economy.

Conflict between the president and Senate does not end with the ratification of a treaty. Two perennial questions have historically arisen. First, who has the power to interpret treaty language? Reinterpretations may have effects ranging from nullifying the agreement to allowing for its continued relevance under changed circumstances. Second, who has the power to terminate a treaty? Both questions surfaced in the history of the Anti-Ballistic Missile (ABM) Treaty. In 1985 Ronald Reagan successfully reinterpreted the Anti-Ballistic Missile Treaty to permit testing of elements of his Strategic Defense Initiative. In 2002 President George W. Bush formally withdrew the United States from the ABM Treaty. Thirty-one members of Congress unsuccessfully brought legal action against the administration asserting that the president lacked the constitutional power to withdraw from the treaty. In April 2010 President Obama reinterpreted an agreement with Russia on disposing of plutonium from nuclear weapons, first signed in 2000 by the Clinton administration, by signing a new amending protocol.

Not only treaties require interpretation; so too do acts of Congress. Here presidents have responded to what they see as intrusions on their powers by issuing signing statements. Some signing statements amount to little more than claiming credit for a piece of legislation or thanking key supporters. Other times they are statements of claimed constitutional rights. The George W. Bush administration was particularly active in its use of signing statements to maintain control over foreign policy. One frequently cited example occurred in 2005 when Congress passed antitorture legislation championed by Senator John McCain (R-AZ) but opposed by President George W. Bush. In his signing statement, Bush stated: "The Executive Branch shall construe Title X in Division A of the Act, relating to detainees in a manner consistent with the constitutional authority of the President to supervise the unitary executive branch and as commander-in-chief" (G. W. Bush 2005). The effect of this statement was to claim presidential authority to ignore the McCain amendment and conduct the war on terrorism as the administration saw fit.

In spite of his criticism of Bush's use of signing statements, Obama has not abandoned the practice. In June 2009 he signed a spending bill that placed conditions on how money given to the World Bank and the International Monetary Fund could be spent. In his signing statement, Obama wrote that he would not allow this legislation to interfere with his authority as president to conduct foreign policy and negotiate with other countries.

Presidents and the Senate also spar over appointments. Presidents have systematically reduced the significance of the Senate's confirmation powers through a number of steps. One often-used strategy is to turn to personal representatives to carry out important international negotiations and for advice. A more recent variation on this theme is to create policy "czars" within the White House. These individuals do not undergo Senate confirmation, they rarely testify before committees, and they can shield information from Congress using the claim of executive privilege. Like his predecessor, President Obama was particularly active in appointing policy czars early in his administration to such foreign policy areas as Afghanistan, the Middle East peace process, cyber security, and border security with Mexico. In December 2009 Obama's special envoy, Stephen Bosworth, went to North Korea to determine that country's interest in resuming nuclear arms talks.

In acting in this fashion, Obama followed in the footsteps of his predecessor. In spring 2007, Bush had created a "war czar," who reported directly to the president. This position was created out of a sense that White House coordination of the complex political, military, and economic dimensions of the Iraq War, as well as the ongoing operation in Afghanistan, should no longer fall on the shoulders of the national security adviser. Neither the Bush nor Obama appointments of czars have escaped criticism. A common refrain is that rather than bring greater coherence, they only add another bureaucratic layer to the decision-making process, accentuating problems of responsibility and oversight (Rothkopf 2009a).

The war powers of the Constitution are the most politically volatile source of constitutional clashes between the president and Congress. The most visible instrument Congress has fashioned to control the president's use of force is the 1973 War Powers Resolution, which was passed over President Richard Nixon's veto. Presidents have unanimously maintained that the War Powers Resolution is unconstitutional. Additionally, they have routinely characterized their use of military force as lying beyond its scope. Carter, Reagan, and George H. W. Bush all argued they were engaging in humanitarian actions and did not need to consult with Congress in advance of such actions. Clinton and George H. W. Bush cited UN resolutions as justifying their actions and absolving them of the need to consult with Congress. The George W. Bush administration cited previously passed legislation and the 1991 Gulf War Resolution as providing the needed legal basis for military action.

Quite pointedly, President Obama sought no action from Congress in making his December 2009 announcement that his administration would increase the American military presence in Afghanistan by 34,000 soldiers. Instead he asserted that the post-9/11 congressional resolution authorizing the use of force against al-Qaeda and its supporters remained in effect. Just as pointedly, no voices were heard in Congress challenging his right to do so. Obama also showed his willingness to use force as he expanded military operations against targets in Yemen, Somalia, and Pakistan and authorized the use of force against Somali pirates. In a related exercise of presidential war powers, Obama reaffirmed his right to order special renditions in combating terrorism.

The President as an Individual

It has long been recognized that understanding who the president is as a person is vital to understanding how the powers of the presidency are used and ultimately what American foreign policy will look like. James David Barber's study of presidential personality (1992) remains a commonly used reference point for making such assessments. Barber defined personality in terms of three elements. The first element is world view, which he defined as an individual's politically relevant beliefs. The second element is style, which refers to an individual's habitual ways of responding to political opportunities and challenges. The third and most important component is character developed in childhood. This involves the way in which individuals orient themselves toward life and is composed of two dimensions: the amount of energy put into the presidency (passive or active) and whether the president derives personal satisfaction from the job (positive or negative).

Together these four dimensions produce four different presidential personalities. Active-positives such as Truman, Kennedy, Carter, Clinton, and George H. W. Bush are achievement oriented, put a great deal of energy into the presidency, tend to be pragmatists, and derive great satisfaction from the game of politics. Active-negatives such as Johnson and Nixon are compulsive individuals who adopt a domineering posture toward those around them and tend to get locked into rigid positions from which they cannot escape. Passive-positives do not make full use of the powers of the presidency but feel satisfied from the exercise of that power; Barber classified Reagan as such a president. Passive-negative presidents neither exercise significant amounts of presidential power nor derive much satisfaction from the office. Barber presented Eisenhower as a passive-negative president. Two problems stem from having passive presidents in office. The first is policy drift. The second is the absence of accountability.

While no unanimity exists over the placement of George W. Bush in Barber's classification scheme, most see him as an active-negative (Peleg 2009). Bob Woodward (2002, 256), who chronicled the administration's decision to go to war in Afghanistan after 9/11, noted Bush's decision-making style "bordered on the hurried. He wanted actions, solutions." Richard Clarke (2004, 287), who worked for both George W. Bush and Bill Clinton on terrorism matters, said of Bush that he "asked us soon after September 11 for cards or charts of senior al-Qaeda managers as though dealing with them would be like a Harvard Business School exercise in a hostile takeover." A negative outlook is conveyed by former White House press secretary Scott McClellan's (2009) observation that Bush often engaged in self-deception to justify his political decisions and Bush's own observation that he did not watch TV news or read newspapers other than to scan the front page because "I like to have a clear outlook. . . . It can be a frustrating experience to pay attention to somebody's false opinion or somebody's characterization, which simply isn't true" (quoted in Bumiller 2009).

Early speculation pointed to Barack Obama as being an active-positive (S. Renshon 2008) and someone likely to have the polar opposite of Eisenhower's behind-the-scenes leadership style (Greenstein 1982). He is pictured as an individual whose ambitions for higher office were "an open secret" early in his political career. Obama is portrayed as a listener who is open to the views of others while also being willing to defend his own interests and capable of doing so. Obama is seen as someone able to recognize and seize opportunities and avoid being locked into losing positions or those that carry a high price tag for victory. One of the most frequent observations is how difficult it is to determine how open Obama really is to the opinions of others, what issues he actually feels strongly about, and what positions he would "go to the mat" to defend. That said, Obama is also characterized as someone who is tough minded in defense of his personal interests.

Personality is not the only direction from which to approach the question of how the president as an individual influences the tone and direction of American foreign policy. Significant work in this area is based on the concept of operational code. As presented by Alexander George (1969), a leader's operational code has two parts. The first consists of the leader's fundamental views about the nature of politics. The second part consists of the underlying instrumental beliefs that guide a leader's choice of goals and strategies. Later researchers have conceptualized an individual's operational code less as a fundamental set of beliefs or method of political calculation than as a "state of mind" that guides how policy makers view the world and think about problems in the absence of other stimuli. The operational code is subject to change or learning as stimuli change.

George W. Bush's operational code has been analyzed using data gathered from his public speeches and prepared remarks (J. Renshon 2008). Two significant changes have been found during his pre-presidential days and his presidency. First, his view of the political universe became more optimistic and shifted from somewhat friendly to definitely friendly. Following the 9/11 attacks, his operational code shifted again. His view of the world shifted back from definitely friendly to a level lower than that which existed before he became president. He became more pessimistic, and his belief in the predictability of future political events declined significantly. In addition, Berggren and Rae (2006) argued that Bush held an evangelical presidential style, as did Jimmy Carter before him. According to their analysis, evangelical leadership is constructed around a rejection of "politics as usual," a sense of mission, a personalization of politics, and a certainty of purpose that minimizes the role of bargaining and negotiation in decision making. Bush's operational code also changed during his presidency, coming to include an increased willingness to accept risks and an increased aversion to using promises to accomplish political goals.

While it is still early in Obama's presidency, a contrast in operational codes between Obama and George W. Bush is already apparent. In contrast to moral certainty and an invocation of biblical references to guide decision making, Obama's presidential style emphasizes a greater sense of openness as to outcomes and process and a symbolism that stresses collaboration rather than the triumph of one perspective over another. Obama's operational code places great emphasis on preparation, detached analytical thinking, careful planning, and highly honed organizational skills. Issues and options, not people, are at the heart of his decision-making style. He is, one observer commented, "no accidental tourist" in making decisions. The great danger some see is that Obama will not provide enough guidance to or assert enough control over the bureaucracy to produce timely and consistent decisions (Brzezinski 2010). These concerns surfaced in the pace of his deliberations over Afghan troop deployments and his administration's continued wavering over the fate of Guantánamo Bay and a public trial for Khalid Sheikh Mohammed months after decisions on these matters were announced.

The Presidential Advisory System

As one looks at at the presidency as an institution, two convergent themes have dominated accounts of presidents and foreign policy. The first theme is the need for a National Security Council (NSC) system that maximizes the ability of presidents to obtain the information and advice they need to make foreign policy decisions. The second theme is the danger of presidential entrapment within the president's own system.

The history of the National Security Council system reveals that presidents have structured it in a variety of ways. Harry Truman was the first president to have the NSC, and he was cautious in using it. For Truman, foreign policy was the responsibility of the president alone. The NSC was to be an advisory body and nothing more. To emphasize this point, Truman did not attend early meetings of the NSC. The outbreak of the Korean War changed Truman's approach to the NSC. He started to use it more systematically and began attending its regularly scheduled meetings. Organizational changes also took place. National security issues were now to be brought to his attention through the NSC system, and the NSC staff was reorganized. An emphasis on outside consultants was replaced by having a senior staff served by staff assistants.

Institutionalization continued under Eisenhower, who transformed the NSC system into a unit that would be actively involved in making policy. A Planning Board was created to develop policy recommendations for the president, and an Operations Coordinating Board was established to oversee the implementation of national security decisions. Eisenhower also established the post of assistant for national security affairs (commonly known as the president's national security adviser) to coordinate the national security decision-making process more forcefully.

A second phase of the NSC's history began with the Kennedy administration and lasted until 1980. Under Kennedy, informal, ad hoc interagency task forces replaced the formal NSC system as the primary decision-making unit for dealing with such international problems. In Kennedy's revamped management system, the national security adviser played a key role and helped move the focus of foreign policy decision making from the State Department to the White House. Henry Kissinger, who served as Nixon's national security adviser, came to personify both the strengths and weaknesses of a national security adviser–centered, informal NSC system.

During the Reagan administration, the NSC entered a third phase. Pledging to depersonalize the system, Reagan pushed too far in the opposite direction, causing it to go into decline. The national security adviser became a "nonperson" with little foreign policy influence or stature. With no force able to coordinate foreign policy, an unprecedented degree of bureaucratic infighting and fragmentation came to characterize (and paralyze) Reagan's foreign policy.

Post-Reagan presidents sought to organize the national security council system along collegial lines, but in each case the end results were less than hoped for. The primary problem encountered in George H. W. Bush's administration was too much homogeneity in outlook. Clinton failed to make his collegial system work because he was unable to provide a constant vision to guide his team or to construct an effective division of labor among its members.

George W. Bush and his national security adviser, Condoleezza Rice, likewise sought to establish a collegial decision-making system. At its apex was an informal committee, the "War Cabinet." This group consisted of some twelve key Bush advisers on the war against terrorism, and it was this group that made major decisions regarding the wars in Afghanistan and Iraq. Instead of operating in a collegial fashion, Bush's system became highly competitive and split over how to conduct foreign policy. Secretary of State Colin Powell brought a conservative-realist perspective to the office that stressed caution in using force and the pursuit of limited objectives. On the other hand, key posts in the Pentagon and the vice president's office (and to a lesser extent at the State Department) were staffed by neoconservatives whose outlook on world affairs was firmly anchored in the belief that the United States was the world's only superpower and that it had a special role to play in transforming the world. They also held that unilateral exercise of American military power was an appropriate means of achieving this goal. One commentator describes the NSC as having become transformed from a collegial system into one of "unrestrained ideological entrepreneurship," in which pockets of officials with strongly held views competed to sell their policy preferences to the president (C. Campbell 2004).

In reviewing the history of the NSC from the Kennedy through George W. Bush administrations, Ivo Daalder and I. M. Destler (2009) concluded that there is a right way to manage the decision-making process. It lies in the creation of a deliberative process that presents presidents with a clear set of alternatives based on a careful reading of the information available. The key resources national security advisers need to balance the conflicting demands placed on them are the trust of presidents that they are being given the best advice and the trust of senior officials that their views are being presented to the president fairly.

In setting up his national security council system, President Obama acted in a fashion consistent with Daalder and Dester's (2009) recommendations. He used his first presidential directive to set up his national security system. He added the attorney general, the secretaries of energy and homeland security, and the U.S. ambassador to the United Nations to the NSC. Other advisers and officials would attend on a case-by-case basis. It was also determined that many of the functions carried out by the Homeland Security Council would be transferred to the NSC. This action was consistent with recommendations made by advisory groups in the closing months of the Bush administration. National Security Adviser James Jones was placed in charge of setting the NSC's agenda and communicating its decisions to the president and other administration officials. Below the NSC, Obama followed the basic structure of every president since George H. W. Bush and put into place a complex series of interagency committees to coordinate analysis and to review issues for consideration by more senior committees. Obama also divided presidential national security orders into two groups: policy directives and study directives.

Many predicted that a major challenge to the ability of Obama's NSC system to function as intended would be the presence of powerful figures such as Secretary of State Hillary Clinton, whom Obama defeated for the Democratic presidential nomination, and Secretary of Defense Robert Gates, who had served in George W. Bush's administration in that same capacity. Clinton's first months as secretary of state did much to dispel fears that she would not be a team player. Gates did likewise. Yet each also demonstrated an ability to take forceful stands on issues and speak more bluntly than did others in the administration.

Presidential managerial styles can be described in any number of ways (R. T. Johnson 1974; George 1980). Zbigniew Brzezinski (2007) gave the following thumbnail sketches of how the first three post–Cold War presidents managed foreign policy. George H. W. Bush had a "top-down" managerial style that placed him firmly in command of decisions. It did not mean that he or his national security adviser, Brent Scowcroft, were happy with the way the system worked. Commenting on discussions about dealing with Soviet pressure on Lithuania, Bush later said, "I was dissatisfied with this discussion since it did not point to action and I wanted to take action" (Bush and Scowcroft 1998, 381). Especially in his first term, Bill Clinton had a "kaffeklatsch" (informal coffee get-together meeting) approach to decision making. His meetings often lacked an agenda, rarely began or ended on schedule, frequently were marked by the spontaneous participation of individuals who had little reason to be there, and often ended without any clear sense that a decision had been reached. Clinton's managerial style has also been characterized as politically opportunistic and not conducive to strategic clarity. George W. Bush has been described as having "strong gut instincts" along with a "propensity for catastrophic decisiveness" and a temperament prone to "dogmatic formulations" (Hastedt 2011).

Barack Obama adopted a formalistic managerial style that contrasted sharply with that employed by George W. Bush. This can be seen in two major foreign policy decisions made early in his administration. The first was the decision to increase U.S. troop strength in Afghanistan. Some twenty-five hours of meetings and nine official review sessions spread over three months led to this decision, one that national security adviser James Jones described as a "metamorphosis" in which "none of us ended up where we started" (Kornblut, Wilson, and DeYoung 2009). Meetings were opened by intelligence briefs and covered a wide range of topics. Core participants in these sessions included Vice President Joe Biden, Secretary of State Hillary Clinton, Secretary of Defense Robert Gates, and White House Chief of Staff Rahm Emanuel, along with key intelligence, military, and diplomatic figures.

The first war review meetings took place in February and March with Biden arguing for fewer troops, Gen. David Petraeus citing lessons from Iraq, and Gates warning about creating a massive U.S. footprint in Afghanistan. These deliberations led to a decision announced by Obama on March 27 to deploy an additional 22,000 troops to Afghanistan during the spring and summer months. This would not be the end of the deliberations.

Obama and his war council met on the question of sending additional troops to Afghanistan in mid-September after Gen. Stanley McChrystal, commander of NATO forces in Afghanistan, sent a 66-page assessment of the situation to Washington. McChrystal's report was leaked to the press, and McChrystal defended its recommendations and assessment in public, calling the situation "serious and deteriorating" and urging the deployment of an additional 40,000 troops. Competing options included a Pentagon plan backed by Gates calling for 30,000–35,000 troops, a plan for sending another 20,000 additional troops that would focus their efforts on ten to twelve major population areas, and a more limited deployment of only 10,000–15,000 troops.

Obama indicated he wanted to reach a consensus on how to start over rather than simply pile in more troops. On October 8 McChrystal made a presentation via video link from Kabul to Obama's principal advisers as part of a dress rehearsal for a full meeting of the National Security Council to be held the next day. In his presentation McChrystal included a slide stating that the U.S. objective was to "defeat the Taliban." To the surprise of those in Washington, as the meeting progressed, it became clear that McChrystal took this statement, which was included in the March Strategic Implementation Plan, quite literally. In most of their minds, the truly achievable goal was reversing the Taliban's momentum and persuading supporters to abandon it. The next day Obama responded to McChrystal's presentation with the question: "This is what we told the commander to do. . . . Have we directed him to do more than what is realistic? Should there be a sharpening . . . a refinement?" (quoted in Kornblut, Wilson, and DeYoung 2009).

An October 26 meeting ended with Obama calling for a faster troop deployment than was proposed. This was followed by a November 11 meeting in which Obama was presented with a series of troop deployment schedules. One of those, Option 2A, which called for a slow downward deployment rate beginning in July 2011, would ultimately be adopted. At this meeting Obama informed Petraeus that he was looking for a surge, a deployment with a tighter timeline and a narrower mission. A meeting on November 23 focused on how to get leverage over the Karzai government. It was these discussions that produced the decision to announce a withdrawal deadline. Also in November, Karl Eikenberry, U.S. ambassador to Afghanistan and a retired general, sent two classified communiqués to Washington arguing against sending additional troops in large measure due to the weakness of the Karzai government.

Obama announced his decision to send 34,000 troops to his core group of advisers, Clinton, Gates, Petraeus, James, Emanuel, Chairman of the Joint Chiefs of Staff (JCS) Mike Mullen, and Vice Chair of the JCS James Cartwright on November 29. He announced his decision to the American public in a nationally televised address on December 1.

The second major foreign policy decision early in President Obama's presidency involved his administration's Nuclear Posture Review. Mandated by Congress and more than a month overdue, Obama's Nuclear Posture Review reversed some of the policies put in place by the Bush administration but did not set the United States out on a new nuclear path or totally "put an end to Cold War thinking," as some Democratic senators had urged him to do. It did break with Bush's nuclear policy by placing terrorists and rogue states at the center of U.S. nuclear policy, pledging to reduce the state of readiness of U.S. nuclear weapons, and stressing deterrence as the principle mission of U.S. nuclear weapons. On the other hand, it did not preclude other missions, such as retaliation for biological and chemical attack on the United States. Obama indicated only that such attacks would not be carried out against nonnuclear states adhering to the Non-Proliferation Treaty, a qualification that opened Iran and North Korea to retaliation.

As with his Afghanistan policy, Obama's Nuclear Posture Review was produced in a decision-making process that was far more structured and systematic than that under Bush, and it can easily be characterized in terms of procedural renewal at the level of presidential decision making. The week before it was released, Obama was briefed on its evolving nature, and he asked that additional intermediate options be produced between those of scaling back the U.S. nuclear arsenal and keeping it largely in its existing form. Obama also involved himself deeply in the discussions of the more radical options, such as moving away from the nuclear triad and formally adopting a no-first-use pledge (all ultimately rejected). These deliberations also gave evidence of the limits on a president's ability to redirect American foreign policy, as commentators noted the presence of long drawn-out debates over the degree to which American nuclear policy could change without alienating allies or domestic critics.

Declaratory Foreign Policy: Toward an Obama Doctrine

To this point we have examined the constitutional, individual, and organizational foundations on which foreign policy renewal takes place. We now turn to the question of to what extent renewal at this foundational level has led to a renewal in the content and conduct of American foreign policy. In answering this question, we distinguish between Obama's declaratory foreign policy and his action foreign policy.

Declaratory foreign policy is a foreign policy of words and images. It is a statement of goals and means. It provides a window into how the world beyond America's borders is defined and what America's place is in it. Especially after the onset of the Cold War, American declaratory policy has become defined in terms of presidential doctrines. The raw material for constructing them is found in presidential speeches.

In his first year in office, President Obama gave a series of speeches that touched upon the direction of American foreign policy would take in his administration, beginning with his February 24 Address to a Joint Session of Congress and ending with his speech accepting the Nobel Peace Prize on December 10. Obama's February 24 address, given in lieu of a State of the Union address, proclaimed that "a new era of engagement has begun. . . . America cannot meet the threats of this century alone, but the world cannot meet them without America," adding that the United States would not "shun the negotiating table, nor ignore the foes or forces that could do us harm" (Obama 2009a).

He spoke at some length on American nuclear weapons policy in Prague on April 5 after touching briefly on American international economic policy in his opening remarks. Obama committed the United States to creating "a world without nuclear weapons" while at the same time cautioning his audience that this goal might not be achieved within his lifetime. Reducing nuclear stockpiles, securing vulnerable nuclear material, banning global testing, and punishing those who break the rules were key components of his plan. Obama also stated that his administration would push heavily and aggressively for ratifying the

Comprehensive Test Ban Treaty and strengthening the Nuclear Non-Proliferation Treaty. At the same time, Obama asserted that the United States would maintain a safe, secure, and effective nuclear arsenal to deter aggressors and defend U.S. allies (Obama 2009i).

Soon thereafter, on June 4, Obama spoke in Cairo, Egypt, calling for an end to the "cycle of suspicion and discord" that had come to define the relationship between the Muslim world and the United States. He called for the mutual rejection of extremism and stereotypes and the formation of a partnership to address such common interests as bringing peace to the Arab-Israel relationship, controlling nuclear weapons, building democracy, ensuring religious freedom, and promoting economic development (Obama 2009o).

Obama next addressed the future direction of American foreign policy in a speech in Moscow on July 7. In it he reiterated his call for a "re-set" in Russia-U.S. relations that would move the two countries away from a zero-sum outlook on world affairs that viewed countries as pawns to be moved around a chessboard. Obama identified five areas of common interest in a new U.S-Russia foreign policy framework: reversing the spread of nuclear weapons, isolating and defeating violent extremism, increasing global prosperity, protecting human rights, and advancing international cooperation while respecting the sovereignty of states (Obama 2009l).

Later that month Obama spoke in Ghana, where he also called for a partnership among African states and the United States. In this July 11 speech, Obama identified four policy areas critical to the developing world. The first was the need to support strong and sustainable democratic governments. He noted that the United States would not seek to impose any system of government on others but that it would increase assistance to responsible individuals and institutions so as to promote good governance. The second area of concern Obama identified was providing economic opportunities for people. Tied to this was strengthening public health, his third area of concern. His fourth topic was the need to resolve conflicts and hold war criminals accountable (Obama 2009p).

To the extent that an Obama Doctrine existed at this point, it consisted of four identifiable parts. First, there was a call for a new start in U.S. relations with the world. Second, this new start was to be based on a sense of partnership that was open to all who were willing to participate. Third, it presented a list of areas of common concern in these partnerships. Finally, it recognized that success in each of these areas was a long-term undertaking. Absent in the Obama Doctrine at this point in its evolution was a more detailed statement of operational guidelines capable of guiding concrete policy decisions. Such statements began to surface in President Obama's last two major foreign policy speeches of 2009.

Speaking at West Point on December 1, Obama announced that he was sending 34,000 additional troops to Afghanistan to "bring this war to a successful conclusion." In addition to reviewing the situation on the ground, Obama turned his attention to broader questions of military strategy. Citing Eisenhower as his model, he stressed the importance of balancing means and interests in making foreign policy and citing the failure to do so, especially as it related to the health of the U.S. economy, as having been a problem "over the past several years." Obama also stressed that the United States could not rely on military might alone; it must also invest in homeland security, intelligence, and diplomacy. Diplomacy in particular was stressed since "no one nation can meet the challenges of an interconnected world acting alone." Central to success would be drawing on the strength of American values, which, according to Obama, do not lead the United States to seek world domination, claim another nation's resources, or target peoples because of their faith or ethnicity (Obama 2009n). Many commentators asserted that with this speech, Afghanistan had become Obama's war (see, for example, Balz 2009a).

President Obama accepted the Nobel Peace Prize in Oslo, Norway, on December 10, 2009, by observing that the goal of ending violent conflict will not be achieved in our lifetimes. At the center of his acceptance speech was the concept of just war. Obama argued that there have been and will be times when force must be used and is morally necessary, given the limits of human reason. He continued to say that when using force, it is essential to be clear how war is being conducted and for that reason he would close Guantánamo Bay. According to Obama, over the past six decades, the United States had demonstrated an enlightened self-interest to underwrite global security, but the United States cannot act alone. He acknowledged that getting others to act as partners required that the United States act according to the rules of the game. In looking for alternatives to violence, Obama spoke to the role that sanctions could play, emphasizing that sanctions must extract a real price and that intransigence had to be met with increased pressure. Obama concluded by noting that peace was more than the absence of violence but required the recognition of political, economic, and social rights (Obama 2009k).

Foreign Policy Action: Words into Deeds

Declaratory foreign policy rarely translates into foreign policy action on a 1:1 ratio. By the end of the George W. Bush administration, American envoys were talking to the two remaining members of the axis of evil, Iran and North Korea. At the end of Ronald Reagan's second term, some disillusioned conservatives characterized his foreign policy as "Carterism without Carter." Presidents face three major challenges in translating declaratory policy into action policy. All three quickly surfaced in the Obama administration.

The first challenge involves weaknesses in the intellectual and operational coherence of the statements that come to be taken as the president's foreign policy doctrine. Obama's speeches suggest that he is a liberal-realist. His fundamental outlook on world politics stresses patience and pragmatism. Partnerships are necessary because no one power can accomplish its goals alone. Wars cannot be ruled out because of human failings, but alternatives to military force must be found in diplomacy. Nuclear weapons must be controlled but cannot be abandoned. Friends and foes must be engaged. Sanctions must have substance to them. All of this is consistent with realist thought, but Obama's agenda extends far beyond traditional realist goals. It embraces traditional liberal international goals of economic development for the sake of people and not countries, improving human health, and respecting human rights and good governance, if not promoting democracy.

The conceptual challenge facing an Obama Doctrine is that liberal-realism constitutes a fragile outlook on world affairs. It unites two perspectives that are traditionally pictured as being in competition with one another and presents no yardstick as to when to employ force and when to seek a partnership, or when to target extremism versus promoting human rights. Realism sees foreign policies as largely being a zero-sum contest between competing national interests in which global interests matter little. Because conflict is held to be an endemic feature of world politics, considerations of power politics are paramount factors in decision making. Liberalism, on the other hand, starts from the premise that states are not condemned to operate in a world dominated by conflict. Cooperation on national and global interests is an achievable goal, given the proper conditions. Foremost among these conditions are respect for international laws, the establishment of international organizations, the promotion of beneficial trading relations, and democratic governments. The all too common result of the tension between liberalism and realism are cries of dissatisfaction from those who see too little of the liberal internationalist agenda or not enough of the realist perspective.

The Obama administration has already encountered these tensions. Obama moved quickly to reverse the Bush administration's decision to build an anti-Iran missile defense system in Poland, a largely unilateral act rooted in a realist world view that had led Russia to threaten Poland with severe military consequences for its acquiescence to the plan. Russia responded favorably to the decision, and hopes quickly rose for a new strategic arms control agreement to replace the expiring START I treaty. Yet Russia balked at signing a new agreement in hopes of extracting a pledge from Obama to forego any future construction of a ballistic missile system in Europe. Instead of seeing the United States through a neoliberal lens, Russian leaders started from a realist premise, with Vladimir Putin at one point stating that if "our partners" feel completely secure, "the balance will be disrupted, and then they will do whatever they want, and aggressiveness will immediately arise both in real politics and economics" (Barry 2009). Obama refused to accede to the Russian demand to the point of threatening to end the talks, and the demand was dropped, leading eventually to the successful conclusion of the treaty.

The inherent tension between idealism and pragmatism also surfaced in April 2010 when Obama hosted a nuclear summit that focused on the problem of unsecured nuclear-grade material. During his presidential campaign, he had pledged to secure all loose nuclear material around the world in his first term. The outcome of this conference did not match his rhetoric but rather produced nonbinding agreements to crack down on nuclear smuggling, establish standards for securing uranium and plutonium stocks, and support past UN resolutions. Although these agreements were modest in nature, defenders noted that they strengthened the foundation for the subsequent Non-Proliferation Treaty review conference and provided the United States with leverage to push states toward acting on the problem.

Outside of the nuclear policy arena, the most conspicuous policy issue where the tension between idealism and pragmatism arose was in the area of human rights. Critics in the United States accused the administration of not pursuing this part of its agenda forcefully enough, and a prime target of their concerns has been China. In their eyes Obama did not speak out in defense of political and human rights in a vigorous or compelling manner on his trip to China in November 2009, and he erred in his decision not to meet with the Dalai Lama prior to that trip. Instead of promoting a pro–human rights agenda, Obama's foreign policy to China was seen as being dominated by a concern for making China a partner in its global military, economic, and environmental policies. This same tension has been evident in his failure to characterize Turkey's early twentieth-century policy toward Armenia as genocide, something he had promised to do during the presidential campaign. Instead he defined it as "of one the worst atrocities" of the twentieth century.

Presidents also face domestic constraints on their ability to address foreign policy problems. In some cases, these constraints are self-induced. For the Obama administration, addressing the economic crisis and the health care debate has consumed its time and political resources. In other cases, these constraints lie beyond the administration's control. For the Obama administration, one such problem lies in the continuing high degree of partisanship that characterizes Republican and Democratic interactions in Congress. A case in point is the dispute over U.S. post-coup policy toward Honduras. In June 2009 the Honduran military overthrew the democratically elected government of Manuel Zelaya, a supporter of Venezuelan president Hugo Chávez, who has emerged as the leading anti-American critic in Latin America. The coup met with nearly universal global condemnation, and the new military rulers were not recognized by the Obama administration. However, Republicans sympathetic to the military government blocked two of Obama's appointments to the region in protest over the lack of support for the new government.

The debilitating impact of partisanship is not restricted to Republican-Democratic squabbles. Hard-line anti-Castro opponents and those supportive of more open ties between Cuba and the United States from both parties squared off in November 2009 over easing the ban on U.S. tourism. Obama had promised in April to begin putting U.S.-Cuban relations on a more normal footing by removing the travel ban that effectively limited visits by family members to Cuba and by allowing U.S. telecommunications firms to operate in Cuba. In constrast, President George W. Bush had threatened to veto any legislation calling for a lifting of the travel ban or easing sanctions on Cuba. Partisanship of a different sort surfaced in December when Speaker of the House Nancy Pelosi (D-CA) declared that "the president is going to have to make his case" for sending additional troops to Afghanistan. Pelosi had spoken out against the war in the past and warned the president of "serious unrest" among House Democrats on Afghanistan. In securing Democratic votes for additional war funding in June 2009, Pelosi stated she had told reluctant Democrats she would never ask them to vote for it again.

Obama's foreign policy partisanship problem extends beyond Capitol Hill. It reaches into the body of American public opinion. In late November 2009, 45 percent of Americans approved of his handling of the war, while 45 percent said the war was not worth fighting, according to a *Washington Post–ABC News* poll. Republicans were more likely than Democrats to disapprove of his handling of the war, but Democrats were more likely to think that the war was not worth fighting. Republicans favored sending more troops; Democrats favored sending fewer troops (Balz 2009b). Obama's speech left the numbers virtually unchanged as another poll, the AP-GfK poll, showed about 42 percent of the public favored the sending of more troops and 56 percent opposed it. What did increase by 10 percent was Obama's approval rating on Afghanistan, which jumped to 52 percent. Still, only 39 percent of Republicans approved of his handling of Afghanistan compared to 70 percent of Democrats (Sidoti 2009).

The fundamental international constraint on translating declaratory policy into action policy is captured by the phrase that "decision making in [fill in a country's name] does not work on Washington time." Several incidents in early 2010 highlighted the severity of this problem for a policy of renewal. First, at Copenhagen hopes for a breakthrough environmental agreement floundered on China's inability and unwillingness to play the role of partner with the United States in crafting an agreement. Instead of fashioning international rules, China was most concerned with protecting its sovereignty and deflecting responsibility to others. In April it became clear that the Middle East was not on Washington time. With Vice President Joe Biden present to signal a renewed peace offensive, Israeli leaders announced the start of new settlements in Jersualem, a move known to be opposed by the Obama administration and by Palestinian leaders. Shortly thereafter, Obama made a surprise visit to

Afghanistan. Instead of bolstering President Hamid Karzai's resolve to undertake reforms and fight the Taliban, the visit led Karzai to criticize outside powers publicly for wanting to create a "puppet government" in Afghanistan.

Conclusion

For reasons outlined in this chapter, judging the extent to which President Obama has set U.S. foreign policy on the road to renewal is an exercise fraught with difficulty. Foreign policy renewal requires more than articulating a vision and constructing a blueprint. It is not a linear process but one that involves moving multiple constituencies at home and abroad in the desired direction. At the same time, it requires flexibility in crafting a strategy to implement that vision without being trapped by one's own plans. Given the multidimensional challenges involved in a foreign policy of renewal, a variety of assessments about what has been accomplished and the challenges that lie ahead are possible.

A most positive assessment is found in the writings of Arnold Wolfers (1962), a realist, who distinguished between possession goals and milieu goals. Possession goals by their very nature are competitive and lend themselves to zero-sum logic. Milieu goals are concerned with shaping the environment within which the state operates. Competition may be present, but the international milieu cannot be possessed in a narrow sense; all will benefit from it or suffer as a result of its existence. Wolfers noted that milieu goals may be both intermediate goals in the pursuit of possession goals and ends in themselves. It is in this context that renewal offers its greatest potential rewards. The Obama administration's ability to realize specific foreign policy possession goals may be of less long-term importance than its ability to alter the shape of the international milieu in which American foreign policy is conducted through the words and images it uses and the actions it takes in victory and defeat.

A survey of citizens in twenty-eight countries conducted from late 2009 through early 2010 provides strong evidence that Obama's declaratory foreign policy strategy was bearing fruit. Only one year after his assuming the presidency, negative global perceptions of the United States had dropped by 9 points and positive perceptions had increased by 4 points, with the result that views of the United States were positive in most countries for the first time since polling began in 2005 (World Public Opinion.org 2010).

A more cautionary assessment of the potential for Obama's renewal agenda to bring about meaningful change in American foreign policy comes from Andrew Krepinevich and Barry Watts (2009). They observed that at its roots, the malaise affecting American foreign policy today is the absence of strategy. Strategies are not words or formulas. They are contingent plans of action linking all of a state's power resources and goals in a concrete and coherent fashion. Organizational, political, and conceptual barriers abound for the administration that seeks to create a strategy of renewal, just as they did for the Bush administration when it sought to create a strategy of preemption or nation building in Iraq. In 2005 Secretary of State Rice identified the Bush administration's Iraq strategy as "clear, hold, build." Yet Gen. George Casey, the commanding general in Iraq, termed this statement as little more than a bumper-sticker slogan.

A sign that Obama recognizes that foreign policy success will not be achieved simply by altering the way in which the United States is perceived abroad comes from a shift that occurred in his foreign policy strategy; he began to embrace the need to establish strong personal contacts with foreign leaders as a central step in obtaining their agreement on his goals. Where in 2009 he held a town hall–style meeting in Paris, in 2010 he had a private dinner with French president Nicolas Sarkozy. In 2009 he spoke to a crowd in Prague about the need to rid the world of nuclear weapons. In 2010, forty-six countries sent representatives to Washington, D.C., for a nuclear summit. Where the Copenhagen environmental talks featured an awkward meeting between Obama and Chinese officials, in early April Obama and Chinese president Hu Jintao spoke amicably for an hour by phone about economic problems between their two countries.

Lastly, we have what is at root a pessimistic assessment of the potential for foreign policy renewal under President Obama. From the outset, the target audience of Obama's renewal theme has been the world beyond America's borders. Missing is an equally compelling message to the American public. As Charles Kupchan and Peter Trubowitz (2007) have written, there no longer exists in the United States a center of American foreign policy public opinion that supports both power and partnership. Instead, the public has become polarized with various elements supporting one or the other. Obama was confronted with this reality in April 2010 after Arizona passed its controversial immigration law; it was noted that while immigration reform was needed, the political will to bring it about did not exist (Hsu 2010).

Absent a strong centrist base, these authors raise the specter of an American foreign policy that becomes erratic and incoherent as these two themes fight for supremacy at the expense of the other. Suggestions for restoring the center, including that put forward by Kupchan and Trubowitz (2007), generally stress the need to create a pragmatic American foreign policy around which the public can unite. What such a solution discounts is the possibility that causation does not flow from a successful foreign policy to a centrist public but from a centrist public to a stable foreign policy. If this is the case, the challenge is to rebuild the center first and then place a foreign policy upon it. A foreign policy of renewal from this perspective requires a "do-over" or "restart" of the American public's view of American foreign policy.

CHAPTER 3

Striking a Balance
Congress and U.S. Foreign Policy

Ralph G. Carter and James M. Scott

BARACK OBAMA'S ELECTION as president was widely seen as a repudiation of the basic direction of the domestic and foreign policies of the George W. Bush administration. President Bush embraced the role as "chief decider" in foreign and defense policy following the terrorist attacks on the United States on September 11, 2001, and resisted efforts by Congress to play a meaningful foreign policy–making role. The Bush administration's foreign policy agenda often caused controversy at home and put the United States at odds with many other actors in the international system. Within Congress, opposition party Democrats frequently tried to change the basic direction of U.S. foreign policy but were unable to do so. In the wake of the 2008 general election that put Obama into the White House and expanded Democratic majorities in the House and Senate, the new administration and the Democratically controlled 111th Congress appeared ready to redirect U.S. foreign policy.

However, they faced a challenging new policy-making environment. Part of that challenge was the crisis-like nature of the global economic recession that began in 2008. Rescuing the nation's major financial institutions from potential collapse, shoring up the credit markets so businesses did not fail due to a lack of short-term credit, passing an economic stimulus/jobs bill to get the unemployed back to work, and coordinating U.S. economic actions with those of the rest of the major economies in the world diverted congressional attention from many other foreign policy issues. The fact that the White House administration pressed Congress at the same time to produce a landmark health care reform bill also consumed the government's efforts for more than a year.

The ability of Congress to address any of these major initiatives was hampered by endless partisan bickering on Capitol Hill, with the leadership of each party expressing frustration with their counterparts and some rank-and-file members directing what seemed to be ill-concealed rage at the other side. Since they held a majority, congressional Democrats sought to act quickly, but following the January 2010 election of Scott Brown (R-MA) to fill the seat previously held by Edward Kennedy, Democrats lost their supermajority in the Senate. Without the 60 votes needed to prevent filibusters and force floor votes, President Obama was forced to reach out to congressional Republicans for support. After the Republican Party reclaimed the majority in the House and further narrowed the Democrats' advantage in the Senate following the November 2010 midterm elections, their acceptance of a renewal agenda was far from certain in a policy-making environment that could be characterized as challenging, if not toxic.

Yet not only did the normal annual cycles of authorizations and appropriations have to be served, but the president's ambitious agenda to renew America's engagement with others was still awaiting congressional action. So what role did the U.S. Congress play? To address this question, we first must understand the context of congressional foreign policy making and the patterns of past congressional behavior, including that during the presidency of George W. Bush. With this conceptual and historical foundation, congressional engagement and activity regarding the Obama administration's renewal agenda can be better assessed.

Interbranch Relations in Foreign Policy Making

Most accounts of foreign policy making stress the role of the president as the preeminent actor, and the conventional wisdom among scholars is that Congress seems neither prepared nor willing to challenge presidential preferences in foreign policy making, preferring instead to defer to the president (Weissman 1995). Yet the view from Washington is different. According to a longtime member of the House Foreign Affairs Committee, "Congress has a responsibility to be both an informed critic and a constructive partner of the president" (Hamilton 2002, 7). Virtually every post–World War II president at some point has shared Ronald Reagan's frustration when he pounded his Oval Office desk and told Republican congressional leaders, "We've got to get to where we can run foreign policy without a committee of 535 telling us what we can do" (Hoffman and Shapiro 1985).

In foreign policy making, the president cannot be both preeminent and hamstrung; Congress cannot be both acquiescent and an important actor that must be taken seriously. Disentangling this paradox is essential to clarifying congressional roles in foreign policy making in the contemporary era. The keys to such clarification lie in the combination of three factors: (1) recognizing the avenues of congressional influence; (2) differentiating among distinct patterns of engagement between Congress and the president; and (3) incorporating the range of actors comprising Congress, from the collective institution to its individual members.

The avenues of influence in foreign policy available to members of Congress begin with the constitutional context, which creates the possibility for interbranch competition by distributing foreign policy responsibilities across both branches. Thus an "invitation to struggle" stems from the failure of the Constitution to specify which branch is to lead in foreign policy (Corwin 1957, 171). The Constitution assigns the president powerful but numerically limited foreign policy roles, including the general executive power, commander-in-chief authority, treaty negotiation (subject to a two-thirds majority vote in the Senate), and diplomatic appointments (subject to Senate approval). The application of these powers, court decisions (see Silverstein 1994), and the growth of executive institutions under the command of the president—especially after World War II—have established important historical precedents for presidential leadership (Melanson 2005).

However, the Constitution assigns Congress more numerous and specific foreign policy powers. Congress has the power to legislate and to provide the money to pay for foreign policy initiatives. It also can set import duties, regulate foreign commerce, and articulate U.S. policies regarding international law. Further, it is in charge of the structure and regulation of the nation's military forces and has the power to declare war. Congress also makes the rules determining how foreign nationals attain U.S. citizenship, and it has the general power to make any necessary laws to carry out the above functions. This constitutional delegation of foreign policy powers to Congress is both wider in scope and more specific in nature than its delegation of powers to the presidency (Koh 1990).

Within this constitutional context, there are many ways for members of Congress (henceforth, MCs) to shape foreign policy. One can differentiate between legislative and nonlegislative actions (Burgin 1997) and between direct and indirect ones (Lindsay 1993). Legislative actions pertain to the passage of specific pieces of legislation. Nonlegislative actions do not involve a specific item of legislation. Direct actions are specific to both the issue involved and the case at hand. Indirect actions refer to those that seek to influence the broader political context or setting. Combining these two distinctions produces four broad categories: direct-legislative, indirect-legislative, direct-nonlegislative, and indirect-nonlegislative (J. M. Scott 1997). Examples of the activities that fall within each category are provided in Table 3.1. Most observers focus on direct-legislative approaches to foreign policy, while a few appreciate those actions that fall into the more indirect and nonlegislative quadrants (e.g., Lindsay 1994).

Assessing the role and influence of Congress in foreign policy also requires differentiating among types of engagement between Congress and the president. Many scholars employ simplistic distinctions (engaged-disengaged, active-deferent, assertive-acquiescent, etc.) to characterize congressional engagement on foreign policy matters, which tend to miss significant congressional foreign policy activity. For example, activity is different from assertiveness—Congress can be highly active and still be supportive of (and even deferent to) the president's foreign policy preferences. On the other hand, Congress can be

TABLE 3.1 Avenues of Congressional Foreign Policy Influence

	Direct	*Indirect*
Legislative	Legislation Appropriations Treaties (Senate)	Nonbinding legislation Procedural legislation Appointments (Senate)
Nonlegislative	Letters/phone calls Consultations/advising Hearings Oversight activities Litigation	Agenda setting Framing debate Foreign contacts

Source: Adapted from J. M. Scott (1997).

less active, but when active, it may challenge the president's policy preferences. Combining activity and assertiveness turns a one-dimensional characterization into a two-dimensional conceptualization (more or less active *and* more or less assertive). As shown in Figure 3.1, a two-dimensional activity-assertiveness model posits four models of congressional foreign policy behavior:

- A *competitive Congress,* whose greater levels of both activity and assertiveness lead it to challenge the president for foreign policy influence
- A *disengaged Congress,* whose relative inactivity and compliance with presidential preferences reflect an acquiescent Congress
- A *supportive Congress,* whose greater activity is combined with less assertive behavior, indicating a Congress cooperating with the president
- A *strategic Congress,* whose combination of less activity but greater assertiveness suggests a Congress that selects its battles carefully but is willing to challenge the president's wishes.

These four models better represent the relationship between the legislative and executive branches. *Since World War II, levels of both congressional foreign policy activity and assertiveness have varied substantially, but assertiveness has increased over time, even while activity has generally declined* (Scott and Carter 2002). Until about 1958, Congress did not assert itself so much as it cooperated with the president in the development of Cold War policy (Carter 1986), making the appropriate characterization a "supportive Congress." Between about 1958 and 1967, congressional activity declined while assertiveness grew, suggesting a "strategic Congress" uncomfortable with the logic of Cold War policy in the context of the Vietnam War overseas and domestic unrest at home. From 1968

FIGURE 3.1   Congressional Foreign Policy Orientations

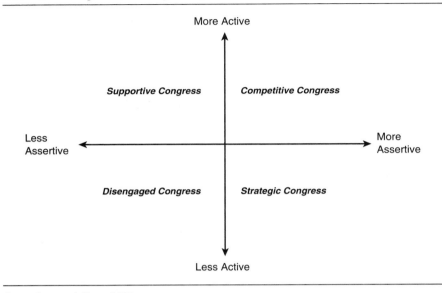

Source: Scott and Carter 2002.

through the mid-1980s, a relatively more active *and* assertive Congress emerged. This suggests a fifteen- to twenty-year period of a "competitive Congress" anxious to correct a perceived imbalance of power between the two branches and to reorient foreign policy after the Vietnam War. Finally, since the mid-1980s, the figures suggest a less active but still assertive Congress, indicating a return to the "strategic Congress" model. This pattern is consistent with the post–Cold War conception of a Congress generally less interested in foreign policy but willing to challenge the president when it chooses to address key issues.

A third clarification points to the range of actors that are actually embodied in "Congress." There is, first, the institution as a whole, frequently studied through assessments of its legislative outputs. Each chamber can also exert influence, with the Senate having a number of constitutionally provided powers. Within each chamber are the numerous standing committees and subcommittees where most policy is shaped, if not made (Loomis and Schiller 2005; Rohde 2005; Maltzman 1998). Policy is also shaped in formal and informal policy caucuses that are formed around specific policy issues or issues that affect specific regions (Trubowitz 1998; Rieselbach 1995; Hammond 1989). Party structures also play an increasingly important role both as an access point (Sinclair 2005; S. S. Smith 2005; Nokken 2000; Wright 2000) and in developing foreign policy positions (S. S. Smith 1994). "When the majority party leadership speaks for and acts on behalf of a united majority, it will continue to be a potentially formidable competitor to the president" (Sinclair 1993, 231). That challenge is more pronounced when the legislative majority party is also the opposition party to the president. Further, each chamber's floor becomes another access point, as members try to legislate via floor amendments. Conference committees also represent a final actor and access point where policy can be shaped before going to the president.

Finally, individual MCs may exert influence. Long before matters come to a vote, MCs can highlight issues, help set the governmental agenda, frame debate, introduce bills, and lobby their colleagues and administration officials for their support (Mayhew 2005; Carter and Scott 2004, 2009; Koger 2003). "Congress does not check presidential power, individuals within it do" (Howell and Pevehouse 2007, 34). From this perspective, "Congress" is really a short-hand term for those individual members who act in its name (Bax 1977), and such individuals have considerable power in a decentralized body (Hersman 2000; Kelman 1987). As one observer noted, "individualized power has come to rival institutional or structural power when it comes to congressional influence over U.S. foreign policy" (Hersman 2000, 10). From 1789 to 1988, 23 percent of such individual actions of MCs have dealt with foreign policy (Mayhew 2005).

In the context of these clarifications, a brief review of the post–World War II period and, especially, the Bush administration years suggests three factors that affect the contemporary interactions between Congress and the executive in foreign policy making: (1) the historical reaction when MCs perceive that presidents have pushed their foreign policy–making prerogatives too far, (2) the increasing impact of partisanship in foreign policy making, and (3) the types and dynamics of issue agendas.

First, MCs tend to react angrily when they think presidents have overstepped their policy-making bounds. In the 1960s, many MCs were frustrated and angry when they felt they had been misled by the Johnson administration about the war in Vietnam. The result was the beginnings of a serious antiwar effort in Congress. The excesses of the "imperial" Nixon presidency (Schlesinger 1973, 2004) created a resurgence in congressional affirmations of its foreign policy-making role (Ripley and Lindsay 1993). MCs now guard their policy-making jurisdiction from executive encroachment whenever possible.

Second, foreign policy making is a highly partisan process. Questions such as "Do I agree with the president's position?" and "Is the president from my party?" are central to congressional decision making (Asher and Weisberg 1978; Howell and Pevehouse 2007). Members of the president's party have a partisan reason to support the president or to work with or through the administration where possible (Fulbright 1966).[1] Conversely, members of the opposition party are quicker to challenge presidents and to promote their own alternative foreign policy initiatives rather than await administrative action (Burden 2007; Howell and Pevehouse 2007). Challenging the president is "good politics" for non-presidential party MCs; ideological differences can also generate substantive foreign policy disagreements with a president of the opposite party. By contrast, one would expect fewer electoral incentives or policy disagreements to prompt MCs from the presidential party to challenge the president's foreign policy agenda. Hence, with Democratic Party control of both the White House and both congressional chambers beginning in 2009, a "competitive Congress" is unlikely. Instead, "supportive" and "strategic" patterns of engagement are likely, with opposition and resistance from the Republican minority.

Third, issue types and dynamics matter. By their nature (Hermann 1969), crisis decisions generally favor the executive. The apparent necessity for quick, nonconservative actions presents Congress with a challenge for which it is structurally ill-suited, and most MCs prefer to avoid such life-and-death decisions. On the other hand, noncrisis foreign policy decisions tend to be strategic or structural in nature. For years, the conventional wisdom was that the executive branch dominates strategic decisions—those involving the basic ends of foreign policy—while Congress was more comfortable making structural foreign policy—as it dealt with the means to implement those ends (Ripley and Franklin 1990). MCs are certainly comfortable making structural foreign policy. However, the assumption of congressional avoidance of strategic foreign policy is open to question. Many MCs acting as congressional foreign policy entrepreneurs expressly seek out strategic foreign policy issues whenever they see a policy vacuum or a need for a policy correction. After 1967, the majority of congressional foreign policy entrepreneurship involved strategic issues (Carter and Scott 2009).

Issue agenda dynamics matter too. It is easier for MCs to stop a policy than to start a new one. All that may be required to stop a policy is a single person—such as a standing committee or subcommittee chair—acting as a gatekeeper, while starting a policy requires either convincing the administration to embrace the idea or convincing enough other MCs to act on it. Ironically, issues involving highly complicated matters or considerable technical expertise may at times lend themselves to easier congressional action, as other MCs will often defer to their chamber colleagues with the expertise to handle them. For years, decisions regarding complex weapons systems illustrated this tendency. Now decisions affecting complex global financial markets may begin to demonstrate similar characteristics.

Finally, the timing of the foreign policy decision matters. Presidents are typically in their strongest position shortly after their election or re-election, as their mandate from the voting public is still evident. Yet as time passes, it generally becomes easier for Congress to challenge them in foreign policy making, as presidential popularity typically declines over time and, eventually, reaches "lame duck" status.

In addition to interbranch policy-making relations, partisanship, and the types and dynamics of issue agendas, the other overarching consideration facing Congress in foreign policy making is the congressional relationship with the prior administration. Much of what the contemporary Congress does in foreign policy making is a reaction in part to what transpired during the Bush years.

Bush and the War Presidency

The relationship between Congress and the White House during the George W. Bush administration demonstrates the power of a commander in chief during wartime. Despite a number of political obstacles (his controversial selection to be president in 2000, an increasingly unpopular war in Iraq, steadily dropping public approval numbers over time, and the election of a Congress dominated by the opposition party), President Bush managed to get most of his foreign and defense policy requests approved. After the September 11, 2001, terrorist attacks, Congress authorized the use of force against the terrorists (and those who harbored or assisted them) and passed sweeping new domestic security legislation. Following the overthrow of the Taliban regime in Afghanistan, even opposition party Democrats found it difficult to oppose the president's determination to invade Iraq, and Congress authorized the use of force for that purpose. Only after weapons of mass destruction were not found there, and the military occupation of Iraq turned increasingly deadly, did MCs return to a more typical pattern whereby presidential foreign policy initiatives were challenged on Capitol Hill. Even after the Democrats won control of Congress in 2006, they still had considerable difficulty changing the basic direction of U.S. foreign policy being set in the White House. The president's congressional critics had to wait for the election of a new Democratic president in 2008 to change U.S. foreign policy.

In broad outline, the above view seems accurate, but it hides multiple efforts by MCs to influence foreign policy. These efforts set the stage for congressional behavior during the Obama administration. For our purposes, three general characteristics stand out: (1) even after the 9/11 attacks, the Bush administration did not get a blank check from Congress on foreign policy; (2) congressional activity reflected the diversity of views among MCs; and (3) signs of concern over the militant and unilateralist approach of the Bush administration were apparent and consequential.

First, although not always successfully, *MCs contended with the Bush administration across a surprisingly broad array of issues, both when the Republican Party held majorities in both chambers (early 2001, 2003–2006) and when it did not (mid-2001–2002, 2007–2008).* For example, the 2001 use-of-force authorization against the terrorists and their supporters did not give the president the authority to use force "to deter and pre-empt any future acts of terrorism or aggression against the United States," a presidential request some MCs compared to the Tonkin Gulf Resolution ("Congress OKs Force" 2002). At the same time, after 9/11 Bush got the $40 billion he requested in emergency spending for the war on terrorism—most of which went to domestic reconstruction and homeland defense, and less to the Defense Department than Bush wished ("$40 Billion Emergency Bill" 2002). In the 2003 and 2004 defense supplementals for Iraq and homeland defense, MCs gave the president virtually his entire funding request totals. Yet against Bush's wishes, Congress put most of the funds in regular line-item accounts it could oversee ("$78.5 Billion Supplemental" 2004; "$25 Billion for Iraq, Afghanistan Wars" 2005). Similar changes and restrictions were repeated in subsequent bills as well.

Another contentious issue involved the rights of detainees. In the 2005 Defense appropriations bill, Congress banned "cruel, inhuman, or degrading treatment" by Defense Department personnel. In a bargain struck to overcome an impasse, the White House backed down on its threatened veto ("Fiscal 2006 Spending Bills" 2006) and, while MCs approved Bush's request to authorize the use of military tribunals for detainees in 2006, they rejected the president's request for authority to reinterpret the meaning of the Geneva Conventions or to be able to convict detainees on the basis of classified evidence that they could not see ("Deal Reached" 2007).

Trade policy also proved contentious as the congressional fondness for economic sanctions toward targets such as Iran, Libya, Syria, and Cuba ran headlong into the president's preference for free trade. Against the wishes of the president and business groups, in 2001 MCs extended existing economic sanctions against Iran and Libya for another five years ("Iran-Libya Sanctions Extended" 2002), and in 2003 Congress imposed economic sanctions on Syria due to its unconventional weapons programs and support of terrorists in Lebanon and insurgents in Iraq. Bush eventually dropped his opposition to the sanctions due to Syria's support of the insurgency in Iraq and the fact that MCs included a provision allowing the president to waive the sanctions if needed for national security ("Congress Imposes Syria Sanctions" 2004).

Later in the Bush years, both branches could claim victories in trade policy. In 2006, Congress passed an amendment prohibiting the administration from enforcing a policy to demand cash payment in advance for any medical or agricultural sales to Cuba. President Bush backed down on his threat to veto the bill due to that amendment ("Cuba Provisions" 2007). That same year, Congress gave the Bush administration its requested authorization to waive some existing provisions on nuclear exports in the Atomic Energy Act in order to pursue a treaty with India involving the civilian use of nuclear energy. However, the authorization required that Congress get the right of approval of any final treaty, that the treaty would be automatically voided if India detonated another nuclear device or violated other nonproliferation commitments, and that the administration was required to make multiple reports to Congress regarding the negotiations and India's nuclear program ("India Nuclear Deal" 2007).

On very different issues in 2008, Congress unanimously passed a Sudanese sanctions bill despite the president's opposition on the grounds that its authorization of sanctions by states and local governments, as well as by private investors, impinged on the executive branch's foreign policy powers. Later, MCs in the House voted not to act on Bush's free trade treaty with Colombia and held up the consideration of free trade treaties with South Korea and Panama, because the administration's stance was not to send them to Congress until the Colombia treaty was approved (Schatz 2008).

Second, *congressional activity was not uniform but reflected the diverse foreign policy preferences of its members.* For instance, after 9/11, some MCs led efforts to strengthen homeland security beyond even what the administration was advocating. A good example is the creation of the Department of Homeland Security. Despite his efforts to keep it a White House office, President Bush was forced to agree to the creation of a cabinet-level Homeland Security Department subject to congressional oversight ("Homeland Department Created" 2003). Within the Homeland Security Department, in 2004 the Coast Guard was authorized about 12 percent more funding than the president requested, with a greater emphasis on counterterrorism operations ("Coast Guard Enters New Phase" 2005). In 2007 Congress increased spending for Homeland Security by about 9 percent over the Bush administration request ("Emergency Funding Softens Cuts" 2008). In 2008 Congress increased appropriations for Homeland Security above the Bush recommendations by nearly 7 percent. Virtually all sections of the department got meaningful increases (M. M. Johnson 2008).

MCs also worked to rein in administration efforts in other areas. When hastily passing the USA-PATRIOT Act in 2001, MCs rejected some administration requests and set many of the act's provisions to expire in 2005 (when another administration might be in office). After passing a temporary extension in 2005 ("Disputes Delay Reauthorization" 2006), in 2006 Congress reauthorized the USA Patriot Act but made several changes from the administration's requests. Rather than continuing all the provisions indefinitely, Congress capped provisions dealing with roving wiretaps, FBI access to business and library records, and law enforcement authority to seek warrants against individual terrorists who might not be acting on behalf of a foreign power with a four-year sunset provision ("Patriot Act Renewed" 2007). Revelations in late 2005 that the administration had engaged in warrantless eavesdropping on U.S. citizens damaged interbranch relations. Congressional outrage mounted throughout 2006. In January 2007 Attorney General Alberto Gonzales told Congress that the Foreign Intelligence Surveillance Act (FISA) Court had now approved the eavesdropping program ("NSA Program" 2007), and he said the administration would seek warrants in the future. However, other administration officials cast doubt on whether any such future warrants would be sought (Fisher 2008).

In defense policy, MCs often resisted or rejected parts of the administration's defense modernization plans. Research funds for the Army's top priority, a new generation of futuristic combat systems, were cut 7 percent, and shipbuilding funds were increased 57 percent instead. Also, the administration's request for research on a new nuclear bunker-buster bomb was denied; research funds for conventional alternatives were included ("Last-Minute Disputes" 2006). In the 2006 defense authorization bill, MCs again chose to authorize less for the administration's transformational weapons systems of the future and instead pay more for additional items deployed troops needed now, like armor to protect vehicles and personnel as well as refitting and refurbishing worn-out combat equipment ("Bush Signs Defense Authorization" 2007). Likewise in 2007, Congress gave the president virtually all the defense funding requested but changed the allocations. Among other changes, funds were again trimmed from the Army's future combat systems and from national missile defense funds in order to replenish depleted equipment in Iraq and to fund better the National Guard and military reserves ("$430.6 Billion Enacted for Defense" 2008). MCs further cut the president's request for base closures by 53 percent ("Cleaning Up the Leftovers of FY 2007" 2008).

Congress also put its complex imprint on the foreign aid program. In the 2001 foreign aid authorization bill, President Bush won his requested renewal of the Mexico City Policy (banning aid to international organizations that funded or performed abortions); in return, MCs increased international family-planning funds by almost 50 percent and cut the administration's request for antidrug operations in Colombia by 14.5 percent ("Foreign Aid Bill Sticks to Tradition" 2002). In 2003 no foreign aid authorization bill was passed. One containing the president's desired Millennium Challenge Accounts (which promoted democratization, free markets, and human rights in developing states) was derailed in the Senate by the Democrats' addition of a provision to overturn the Mexico City Policy ("Frist Pulls Foreign Relations Bill" 2004). In 2004 the foreign aid bill cut the overall foreign operations budget by 7 percent from Bush's request and cut his request for Millennium Challenge Accounts by 40 percent ("Foreign Aid Bill Rewards Allies" 2005). However the omnibus spending bill at year's end restored a portion of the Millennium Challenge Account funds cut ("Omnibus Bill Wraps Up 2004" 2005). Although MCs increased overall foreign aid funding from 2004 to 2005, in 2005 Congress cut the president's foreign aid request by 8 percent, with Bush's heavily promoted Millennium Challenge Accounts and Iraq reconstruction being targeted for heavy cuts ("Foreign Aid Enjoys Singular Boost" 2006). MCs increased funding for global

HIV/AIDS programs by 41 percent over Bush's request in 2007 ("Cleaning Up" 2008). In 2008 MCs increased funding for global HIV/AIDS programs 67 percent over Bush's request (Graham-Silverman 2008a).

Third, *concerns over the militant and unilateral foreign policy approach of the Bush administration were reflected in some congressional activity and foreshadowed some elements of congressional behavior in the Obama period.* Such concerns are reflected in a number of the examples already introduced, including resistance to unrestricted military operations, reprogramming of military aid to other purposes, and the like. In 2007, the new Democratically controlled Congress imposed deadlines for withdrawal from Iraq. Bush vetoed the bill, and the House could not override the veto ("Democrats Yield" 2008). Critics of the war had to be satisfied with creating benchmarks requiring reports to Congress on progress in the Iraq War ("President Prevails" 2008).

After 9/11, intelligence reform was high on the congressional agenda. MCs forced the president to accept the creation of an independent commission to investigate the 9/11 attacks, which he strongly opposed. The president's resistance yielded some benefits for the administration. At the administration's insistence, the commission would have relatively limited funding and would be required to produce its report in 18 months, well before the elections in 2004 ("Intelligence Bill Creates 9/11 Panel" 2003). In 2003 MCs struck back in the intelligence authorization bill by including explicit critiques of the intelligence community's performance, authorizing funds for the sharing of raw intelligence by various agencies, authorizing improvements to the counterintelligence and counterterrorism roles of the Treasury Department, and requiring the CIA to produce a "lessons learned from Iraq" report to Congress within a year ("Intelligence Bill Enhances FBI Powers" 2004). Congress reorganized the intelligence community in 2004, creating the office of Director of National Intelligence and a new National Counterterrorism Center and National Intelligence Council and making numerous other management changes within the intelligence agencies ("Intelligence Overhaul Enacted" 2005).

Many MCs found U.S. involvement in Colombia's internal affairs eerily similar to events in Indochina in the early 1960s. As noted above, the president's request for aid to Colombia was cut in 2001. In 2003 MCs prohibited U.S. troops or contractors from engaging in combat in Colombia ("Intelligence Bill Enhances FBI Powers" 2004). In 2007 Congress changed the composition of aid to Colombia. The amount funded for military aid was 21 percent less than that requested by Bush, and the amount for economic aid to Colombian farmers was 79 percent more than Bush had requested (Graham-Silverman 2008b).

On balance, President Bush won numerous major foreign policy victories over Congress. Most of these involved the war on terror in some way, and after 9/11 the commander in chief role gave Bush an extremely powerful position. However, Congress pushed back on numerous fronts, winning an assortment of victories that were significant but largely overshadowed by recovery from the financial crisis of 2008 and other pressing domestic issues.

Obama's Struggle with Majority Rule

With Barack Obama's victory in November 2008, the Democratic Party gained control of both ends of Pennsylvania Avenue. As other chapters in this volume discuss, the Obama administration promised a new approach and new priorities in U.S. foreign policy. With the White House and Congress united rather than divided, many observers expected enhanced opportunities for legislative-executive collaboration and consultation in shaping policy initiatives. However, the experiences of previous Democratic presidents with a Democrat-controlled Congress suggested that routine acquiescence would be unlikely.

President Truman worked with a Democratic Congress from 1945 to 1947 and 1949–1953. These Cold War periods featured a "supportive Congress." Yet both Presidents Kennedy and Johnson (1961–1969) worked with a "strategic Congress," as MCs were quicker to jettison Cold War perspectives applied to the developing world than were these presidents. From 1977 to 1981, President Carter faced a "competitive Congress." Carter's attempts to redefine fundamental U.S. foreign policy goals were undermined by his disdain for Congress and were poorly timed in an era when trust between the branches had largely been lost following the Watergate scandal and other outrages of the Nixon administration. Like Kennedy and Johnson, from 1993 to 1995 President Clinton faced a "strategic Congress." Democrats in Congress were not fully in step with this young president who called himself a "new Democrat" and pushed free trade as had his Republican predecessor.

With only six of these twenty years showing a Democratic Congress largely supportive of the Democratic president's foreign policy agenda, it is no surprise that the 111th Congress and the Obama administration parted ways on key foreign policy issues. Further, the House of Representatives was more polarized than before. The Republicans who left the House following the 2008 elections were more moderate in their policy views than those who remained, and in 2009 the Republican leadership in the House quickly indicated that it was quite willing to confront House Democrats over policy issues (Theriault 2009). Despite the fact that they were in the minority and did not have control of the chamber or committees, House Republicans pushed their foreign policy agendas at the expense of the Democratic administration.

How then has Congress played its role within the constraints and opportunities of the present context? The elections of November 2008 led to an initial period of Democratic support for presidential initiatives to extend the war on terror in ways that shifted its focus away from the approach of the Bush administration. Since they no longer controlled a congressional chamber,

Republicans increased their reliance on nonlegislative avenues of influence, especially framing efforts, and indirect approaches involving procedural instruments and obstruction (especially in the Senate). Moreover, the partisan landscape suggested a combination of "supportive" and "strategic" engagement, as the Democrat-led Congress worked cooperatively with the administration to address policy problems and strategically prodded the administration to address problems that MCs deemed important. At least initially, Congress was more supportive, as copartisan control (and thus heightened policy agreement), presidential popularity, and the traditional "honeymoon period" combined to lessen congressional assertiveness and channel activity (especially by members of the majority party) into less formal and less direct avenues.

For example, President Obama identified a number of key foreign policy issues on which he desired meaningful progress. These included but were not limited to the following:

- Addressing the international aspects of the global financial crisis—involving potentially difficult negotiations to coordinate multinational efforts to shore up global financial institutions, adjust currency values, and so forth;
- Addressing Mideast military operations—drawing down the number of U.S. troops in Iraq, creating a surge of troops in Afghanistan, dealing with terrorist threats or havens in Pakistan;
- Reducing U.S. dependence on imported oil—by increasing U.S. production and reducing consumption, which would likely involve U.S. participation in multinational efforts to slow the growth of fossil fuel emissions;
- Addressing the Israeli-Palestinian conflict—as it had become (rightly or wrongly) a global symbol of a lack of Western respect for Muslims and their points of view, if not an instance of outright Western imperialism to many; and
- Renewing the U.S. commitment to multilateral diplomacy to address global problems.

All of these goals engendered spirited congressional debate on the preferred means by which to address them, as well as debate on the goals themselves. In particular, the enhanced commitment to multilateral diplomacy is a response to a "renewal" agenda. Some of these debates crossed partisan lines; others have been and will be fought along partisan lines.

This pattern of partisan behavior in Congress was consistent with the general framework and context discussed earlier. Since members from the president's party are more likely to share world views (not to mention electoral fortunes) with the president (Howell and Pevehouse 2007), it is unsurprising that they have been more inclined to begin their policy-making efforts by contacting administration officials directly to press for policy accommodations, thereby relying more on indirect-nonlegislative avenues to affect policy. Consistent with the typical pattern, only when these efforts failed did majority Democrats have incentives to fill policy vacuums or make policy corrections via direct-legislative means, such as by introducing amendments or bills.

Conversely, members from the opposition party were often pushed toward indirect-nonlegislative avenues due to their lack of control of the chamber. For example, while Vice President Joe Biden was in Israel in 2010, the Israeli government angered the Obama administration by announcing new housing construction in East Jerusalem, a decision opposed by the White House. The White House showed its irritation by downplaying a subsequent visit by Prime Minister Benjamin Netanyahu. Distancing himself from Obama, House Minority Leader John Boehner (R-OH) praised Netanyahu, saying: "We all know we're in a difficult moment. I'm glad the prime minister is here so we can have an open dialogue" (Friedman and Lee 2010). In another indirect-nonlegislative effort, Capitol Hill Republicans framed early administration initiatives to close the Guantánamo prison and repudiate so-called enhanced interrogation techniques as making the United States more vulnerable to terrorists. Should such indirect-nonlegislative efforts fail, direct-legislative efforts can be expected from congressional Republicans. Even if they do not have the votes to pass, such opposition party legislative efforts can be a way to garner visibility for the issue, to frame it in favorable ways, and build potential support for the future.

While all the existing avenues will continue to be used, the "wired" nature of the new administration prompted policy advocates to pay attention to the blogosphere as a new outlet to pitch their ideas. Many liberals have embraced Internet blogs as an alternative to "talk radio" and cable news channels typically dominated by conservative points of view (Schiffer 2006, 2007). Entrepreneurial liberal MCs have increasingly pitched their foreign policy ideas on liberal blogs like Daily Kos, AMERICABlog, TalkLeft, and Crooks and Liars. Conservative MCs have responded not only on cable channels like Fox News or the syndicated Rush Limbaugh radio program but also on conservative blogs like Instapundit.com, Michelle Malkin, Power Line, Little Green Footballs, and Captain's Quarters.

Routine acquiescence proved fleeting, however. On issues such as Guantánamo, detainee trials, Iraq, and Afghanistan, fissures were already apparent in President Obama's first year. Numerous congressional Democrats joined the Republicans in opposition to these efforts (Shapiro 2010). By October 2009 the most vocal critics of escalating the number of U.S. troops in Afghanistan were Democratic MCs. Republicans generally stood behind Gen. Stanley McChrystal's request for the additional troops a more robust counterinsurgency campaign would require. Many Democrats opposed the surge due to its potential cost in lives and—given concerns about the soaring budget deficit—in dollars. Thus, the president's decision to include a deadline for the beginning of the

U.S. troop withdrawal from Afghanistan in the announcement of the troop surge was a concession to his fellow Democrats (Wilson 2009a, 2009b).

Congressional Democrats could not be counted on to do the president's bidding on other foreign policy issues, either. Moderate Democrats joined Republicans in opposing more stringent restrictions on fossil fuel emissions. Thus, after the Copenhagen Conference, when other major greenhouse gas-producing countries were pledging to cut future emissions by 20 to 25 percent, congressional opposition limited the U.S. pledge to just 17 percent, and even that figure was not assured from the Democratically controlled Congress (Eilperin 2009a, 2010). On U.S. relations with Iran, the president's dual-track approach was also jeopardized by congressional action. While the president spent much of his first year trying to engage the Iranian regime in diplomatic negotiations over its nuclear program, he often raised the possibility of later sanctions if negotiations proved fruitless. Congress did not wait on the president to act in this regard. In December 2009, the House voted 412–12 to pass an Iran sanctions bill that would penalize companies that invested in Iran's energy industry or sold Iran the gasoline it desperately needed due to its limited refinery capacity (Lobe 2010). In January 2010, the Senate passed by voice vote an even tougher Iran sanctions bill, which was sponsored by Foreign Relations Committee senior member Christopher Dodd (D-CT) and had the support of Senate majority leader Harry Reid (D-NV). The Senate bill was passed over the explicit objections of the Obama administration (Gharib 2010).

The issue agenda and broad political context also shaped congressional engagement. MCs were intensely affected—especially in the House of Representatives—by the devastating economic meltdown that began in 2008 and highly controversial issues such as the health care debate. Members' attention was often focused elsewhere—as was the administration's. As Obama's public approval fell over time, members of both parties mounted new challenges on such key issues as Afghanistan and Pakistan.

Finally, the dramatic success of the Republican Party in the November 2010 midterm elections further presaged congressional assertiveness and resistance to White House leadership. With control of the House of Representatives, the Republican majority swiftly promised an aggressive role in a variety of foreign policy issues, from the wars in Iraq and Afghanistan, efforts to confront al-Qaeda, and a whole host of other issues. In the Senate, with its majority trimmed by the loss of six seats, Democrats faced new challenges as well. For example, shortly after the November elections, Republicans signaled new and more extensive resistance to the "New START" nuclear arms treaty the Obama administration had struggled to produce as part of its efforts to "reset" U.S.-Russian relations. The divided Congress, and the divisions between Congress and the White House, promised even more challenges for the administration's efforts on the renewal agenda.

Past research shows that individual MCs will continue to press their own foreign policy agendas regardless of the president's party label (Carter and Scott 2009). At present, such congressional foreign policy entrepreneurs are now almost as likely to be found in the House as in the Senate. While they come from both parties, the more successful ones will be from the majority party—as its leaders control chamber agendas—and from the foreign policy–related standing committees—as they dominate policy making, hearings, and oversight activities (Carter and Scott 2009). As long as they are in the majority party, entrepreneurial Democrats will resist administrative initiatives that they perceive as treading on congressional or committee prerogatives—such as program authorizations, appropriations, policy oversight, and perhaps even use-of-force decisions (Carter and Scott 2009). Given the lack of a current foreign policy consensus and these trends over 60-plus years, there is no reason to expect the number of members acting entrepreneurially to diminish in the near-term future. Indeed, many members, especially Democrats, have had a sort of pent-up desire to assert policy influence given years of attempted marginalization by the Bush White House.

For example, we have already seen Speaker Nancy Pelosi (D-CA) push to get U.S. troops out of Iraq. As noted above in the case of Afghanistan, if President Obama's efforts do not go far enough or fast enough to suit her, she seems likely to act—on her own or with Senate majority leader Reid. When Israeli Prime Minister Netanyahu visited Congress in 2010, Pelosi was even more supportive of Israel than was House minority leader Boehner. Pelosi's comment to Netanyahu was: "We in Congress stand by Israel" (Friedman and Lee 2010). Pelosi's support for the president thus cannot be taken for granted, as she has been described as "a strong speaker of the House, both an ideologue and a pragmatist, who cherishes her prerogatives and guards her turf" (R. Cohen 2009).

Numerous sitting senators have long been active foreign policy entrepreneurs. Those like Dodd, Richard Lugar (R-IN), John McCain (R-AZ), Lindsey Graham (R-SC), and Arlen Specter (D-PA, formerly R-PA) will not lose their appetite to act on the issues that motivate them. Further, Democratic senators who are active entrepreneurs and now chair committees (like John Kerry [D-MA] and the Foreign Relations Committee) will want to exercise their policy-making power. Again, they will likely hold off only as long as they agree with the direction and/or pace of President Obama's policy agenda.

In sum, the lens employed here reveals predictable patterns in congressional engagement. Members must balance often competing cues stemming from the attitudes, beliefs, and values of their constituents and the public; partisan and policy factors; and policy preferences. Features of the policy and political context shape the particular balance, which ensues in predictable ways. Historically, presidents initially receive considerable leeway, and crises typically produce rallying effects and compliance with presidential leadership in the short term. However, over time members are shaped by their own policy preferences and political calculations and assert their own agendas. Ultimately, administrations either incorporate congressional policy concerns and preferences, or the situation develops into competition and confrontation.

Conclusion: Congress, the President, and the Renewal Agenda

Foreign policy making is a highly partisan business, in part because MCs from each party tend to emphasize different policy preferences regarding ends and means. Many congressional Republicans will fault President Obama's renewal agenda because they are skeptical of the value of soft power and very protective regarding sovereignty issues. Thus, a greater emphasis on engagement, public diplomacy, and multilateral negotiations will find relatively fewer supporters from the opposition party. On the other hand, Obama's pragmatic, deliberative approach toward difficult issues may leave congressional Democrats wanting more and wanting it faster. Following a presidential election that promised change, many Democrats will argue that not enough has changed—in the war on Islamic extremism, on the use of force abroad, in dealing with difficult regimes, or on the regulation of the global economy to dampen the chances of further recession.

As we have seen, the honeymoon period for the Obama administration was brief. History suggests that MCs will continue to act on their own foreign policy agendas by changing policies they see as wrong or acting to fill policy vacuums. They will be as responsive to the administration's foreign policy agenda as the president's popularity and constituent support dictate—and their own policy preferences allow. With the president's popularity declining in 2010, the public's support of his renewal agenda was, at best, mixed. By midyear no signs pointed to a "disengaged" Congress in foreign policy making. A "supportive" Congress seemed unlikely due to frequent alignments of Republicans and moderate Democrats on policies opposed by the White House. Enough liberal Democrats were in Congress, however, to prevent a "competitive" Congress from arising. As a result, a "strategic" Congress emerged in which Congress supported the White House on many issues but was also quite willing to challenge administration policy preferences. As did Harry Truman and Jimmy Carter before him, Obama quickly learned a sobering lesson: foreign policy making under conditions of unified government is still quite difficult.

Notes

1. As Howell and Pevehouse (2007) put it in their discussion of Congress and the use of force, members of the president's party are more likely to support presidential decisions because their worldviews match, they defer to the president's presumed information advantage, they have shared electoral fortunes, and they seek to curry presidential favor.

Chapter 4

Vox Populi as a Foundation for Foreign Policy Renewal?

Unity and Division in Post–Bush Administration Public Opinion

Douglas C. Foyle

What are the prospects that public opinion will support President Barack Obama's foreign policy? Surprisingly, despite dramatic changes in world politics in the past twenty-five years, the public's basic attitudes about goals, priorities, and how to interact with the world have remained remarkably stable with only a few exceptions. To be sure, the "news of the day" affects what the public worries about most, but such shifts do not change fundamental attitudes. Substantively, Americans continue in their fundamentally internationalist views of the world, with the public believing that the United States should do its part to solve international problems. To confront international problems, the public continues to favor pursuing a multilateralist approach, even if somewhat less so than in the past. At the same time, some policy attitudes have become increasingly partisan, which portends potential difficulties. This combination of stability and partisanship presents an increasingly difficult public opinion environment for foreign policymakers.

There is a different story to be told in world public opinion. Although limited by data availability, world attitudes were quite favorable toward the United States at the beginning of the Bush administration but shifted to less favorable (and even hostile) attitudes from 2002 through the end of the Bush administration. The 2003 Iraq War and the perception of the Bush administration's foreign policy as unilateralist appears to have caused world opinion to turn against the United States (Foyle 2007). Since Obama's inauguration in January 2009, many sectors of world opinion have shifted back toward a more favorable opinion due to the more multilateralist foreign policy tone in Obama's first year. This shift toward favorability emerged despite continuing opposition in world opinion to a range of substantive foreign policies that seem to have changed very little in the administration's first year (Kagan 2010b; Karon 2010).

In part, this perception reflects the reality that Obama chose to spend his first year in foreign policy addressing unfinished substantive foreign policy issues left over from the Bush administration, principally Iraq and Afghanistan, and rebuilding America's damaged international reputation. On the first two, domestic opinion supports Obama's continuation of the slow withdrawal from Iraq (begun under Bush) as well as his escalation of the war in Afghanistan. As public opinion polls from around the world suggest, Obama's efforts on the final issue have succeeded to a great extent in repairing America's image. Perceptually at least, the foreign policy renewal agenda seems to have succeeded. As the administration shifts from its second into its third year, Obama seems poised to push into new areas of foreign policy engagement, dealing with issues such as nuclear nonproliferation, especially in regard to Iran; the Israeli-Palestinian conflict; climate change; and immigration reform (White House 2010).

Unlike the "old" issues, these new priorities pose a greater potential to create controversy internationally and domestically along partisan lines (Baker 2010b; Kessler 2010). Most scholars who study public opinion's effect on foreign policy conclude that public opinion influences foreign policy at least conditionally (for a review, see Foyle 2010). One of the primary conditions for the public's influence appears to be the salience of a particular issue. In foreign policy, salience largely tracks the headlines of unexpected events, such as Arizona's signing of a new immigration law and congressional reaction to it in April 2010, potentially altering issue salience and priorities (Geman 2010). Policy failures also tend to enhance policy salience. Should the new priorities the Obama administration chooses to pursue result in foreign policy setbacks, partisan divisions within public opinion could undermine his foreign policy renewal efforts. Ironically, should Obama's efforts largely succeed, the public will support the policies but care less about them despite partisan divisions. Partisan divisions will amplify the domestic political costs should Obama's foreign policy renewal efforts fail.

This chapter's consideration of public opinion proceeds as follows: First, I consider general attitudes toward internationalism and contend that public attitudes remain fundamentally internationalist. I also argue that public opinion has been, and remains, multilateralist in its inclinations although potentially less so than in the past. Second, a consideration of the public's foreign policy goals reveals long-term continuity and large areas of partisan agreement with a few notable exceptions. Third, an examination of public attitudes on particular substantive issues regarding national security policy, international institutions, and economic issues reveals important areas of partisan disagreement. Fourth, I consider the shift in foreign policy attitudes around the world. Finally, the chapter concludes with a brief assessment of the challenges that this array of attitudes portends for the Obama administration.

International Engagement

The public's basic inclinations, in the past as well as today, suggest support for international engagement while prioritizing domestic challenges (Holsti 2004). As seen in Figure 4.1, wide majorities favored engagement throughout the last years of the Cold War, with the only discernable dip occurring during the midst of the deep 1982 economic recession. The most recent 2008 reading reported that 63 percent favored an "active part" in world affairs, which—although a small decline from post–September 11 highs—roughly tracks results from 1986 through 2000.

On the other hand, two differently phrased questions find public opinion nearing or surpassing all-time recorded highs supporting isolationism. First, although not radically different from the previous low point in 1976, for the first time a plurality now supports the United States "minding its own business" in international affairs (see Figure 4.2). Democrats more strongly favor the

FIGURE 4.1   Active Part or Stay Out of World Affairs? 1974–2008

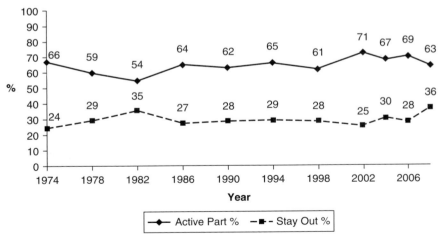

Source: Chicago Council on Global Affairs, *Global Views 2008.* "Do you think it will be best for the future of the country if we take an active part in world affairs or if we stay out of world affairs?"

FIGURE 4.2   U.S. Mind Its Own Business Internationally 1964–2009

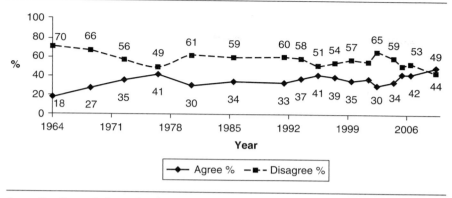

Source: Pew Research Center for the People and the Press/Council on Foreign Relations, "America's Place in the World 2009." "The U.S. should mind its own business internationally and let other countries get along the best they can on their own."

isolationist view (53 percent) than Republicans (43 percent) with independents in between (49 percent). Second, three-fourths of Americans support concentrating on national problems rather than thinking internationally (see Figure 4.3).

Although none of these polls suggests an isolationist public has returned, they seem to hint that a foreign policy renewal agenda would be best served

FIGURE 4.3   Concentrate on Own National Problems 1964–2009

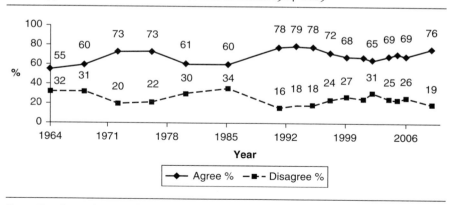

Source: Pew Research Center for the People and the Press/Council on Foreign Relations, "America's Place in the World 2009." "We should not think so much in international terms but concentrate more on our own national problems and building up our strength and prosperity here at home."

by a strong substantive and rhetorical linkage to the national self-interest and domestic prosperity. International initiatives sold as primarily benefiting non-Americans will be met with skepticism even if the costs are low. The order of foreign policy goals discussed later in this chapter also supports this notion.

Majorities continue to favor multilateral international action over a unilateralist or dominant American role. One question tracking these opinions asks, "What kind of leadership role should the United States play in the world? Should it be the single world leader, or should it play a shared leadership role, or should it not play any leadership role?" Despite dramatic changes in the world from the early 1990s to the present, the American public has expressed overwhelming and consistent support for taking a shared leadership role. For example, in November 2009, 14 percent preferred the United States act as a preeminent world leader, 70 percent wanted the United States to do its fair share, and 11 percent preferred the United States take no leadership role. Additional surveys between 1993 and 2005 show little variation across time, with shifts in the low single digits (Pew Research Center 2009a). Another long-standing question asked if the United States "should take into account the views of its major allies" when formulating foreign policy. Results found 78 percent agreeing with the proposition (14 percent disagreeing), which is very nearly the average for the period since 1964 (79.5 percent) and virtually unchanged since the 2006 poll (Pew Research Center 2009a). A majority (54 percent) in late 2008 also favored "improving relationships with our allies," while only 40 percent disapproved (figures unchanged since 2004; Pew Research Center for the People & the Press 2008a).

Another question hints that this multilateralist trend might be changing toward unilateralism. When asked whether they agreed or disagreed that "since the United States is the most powerful nation in the world, we should go our own way in international matters, not worrying too much about whether other countries agree with us or not," between 1964 and 2009 an average of 66.9 percent of the public disagreed with going it alone (with highs of 72 percent in 1968 and 1972 and a low of 57 percent in 1974). The average result since the end of the Cold War in 1991 has been 63.5 percent disagreeing. In comparison, the most recent reading from November 2009 found a precipitous drop to a recorded low of 51 percent disagreeing (multilateralism) and a rise to a recorded high of 44 percent agreeing (unilateralism). This reflects a dramatic 17-percent drop in the multilateralist position and a 16 percent rise in the unilateralist position from the previous reading in 2006. Republicans and Democrats expressed views more in tune with each other, with 50 percent of the Republicans and 45 percent of the Democrats disagreeing with the view that the United States should go its own way. Independents were more unilateralist, with 37 percent disagreeing (Pew Research Center 2009a).

If this trend continues, the Obama administration could eventually face challenges to its approach. The Obama administration's renewal agenda will require multilateral efforts across a range of issues. While most of the polls suggest consistent public support for this direction, the final question alone points to a break with the past and a more unilateralist inclination. The most likely explanation for this disjuncture is the context of the deep economic recession underway at the time of the poll. If the past inclinations continue, Obama's approach will be welcomed by the public. In the unlikely event that the general public is indeed becoming more unilateralist, however, Obama's foreign policy approach will encounter problems with domestic opinion.

Foreign Policy Goals

Any renewal agenda will need to link foreign policy to domestic priorities since regular surveys of the public consistently reveal a public preference for domestic priorities. A series of surveys commissioned by the Chicago Council on Foreign Relations (asking for the "two or three biggest problems facing the country today") revealed that as a total of all problems indicated, the percentage of responses that identified foreign policy problems varied modestly during the late Cold War: 1978 (11.1 percent), 1982 (15.2 percent), 1986 (25.9 percent), and 1990 (16.8 percent). With the end of the Cold War, public priority on foreign affairs decreased with the 1994 (11.5 percent) and 1998 (7.3 percent) surveys. Then in the 2002 CCFR survey, the priority on foreign policy rose dramatically to 41 percent after the September 11 attacks (Chicago Council on Foreign Relations 2002).

With the collapse of the American economy in fall 2008, it is no surprise that economic issues have dominated American concerns. When Obama came into office, more than 80 percent of the public mentioned the economy as the most important problem. Although that figure had dropped to 48 percent by year's end, that result was more than double the second most common problem (health care at 16 percent), and all foreign policy issues combined reached only 10 percent (Jones, Newport, and Saad 2009; Mendes 2009). One commonly posed question since early in the Clinton administration asks, "Right now, which is more important for President [Name] to focus on . . . domestic policy or foreign policy?" At no point between 1993 and late 2009 did a majority of the public indicate that foreign policy should be the focus (even in the first post–September 11 survey in January 2002). The average response during this time was 62 percent indicating a domestic policy focus (with an 86 percent high in January 1997 and a low of 39 percent in January 2007), with only 23 percent on average preferring a foreign policy focus (with a high of 40 percent in January 2007 and a low of 7 percent in December 1994 and January 1997). At only one point

(January 2007, by a 40 percent to 39 percent margin) did more Americans favor prioritizing foreign policy rather than domestic policy (Pew Research Center 2009a). Although considerable variation emerges over time, the public consistently prefers that presidents focus on domestic matters, with economic difficulties rapidly pushing foreign policy challenges down the public's priority list.

A set of recurring questions in the post–Cold War context points to fairly stable American attitudes among foreign policy priorities. A Pew Research Center and Council on Foreign Relations survey has asked whether an issue should have a "top priority," "some priority," or "no priority" at all since 1993 (See Table 4.1). With only slight variation, the absolute numbers and shifts over time largely mirror the 1974 to 2008 results of the Chicago Council on Global Affairs (2008, 7–14) survey. The changes that do emerge in both of these surveys suggest relatively modest movement rather than transformation.

Although the reports that accompanied the surveys point to an inward shift of public opinion, to a greater (Pew Research Center 2009a, 1–4) or lesser degree (Chicago Council on Global Affairs 2008, 2009, 15–16), the evidence of a shift toward isolationism appears scarce. The 2009 Pew/CFR results point to more stability over time compared to different baseline years. Compared to the eight repeated questions from 1997, five experienced less than 5 percent change, two increased in priority (protecting American jobs and strengthening the United Nations), and one decreased in priority (combating international drug trafficking). Compared to 2001, the 2009 results show that only three of the eight repeated questions exhibited a drop of 5 percent or more (protecting the United States from terrorist attacks, preventing the spread of weapons of mass destruction, and strengthening the United Nations), while two experienced a similar increase (protecting American jobs and improving the living standards in developing nations) and three changed by less than 5 percent. Compared to 2005, only three of the eleven repeated questions found a drop of more than 5 percent (addressing illegal immigration, promoting human rights in other countries, and improving living standards in other countries), while the rest remained essentially unchanged. All of the 2009 results fall within 5 points of the overall average. In terms of foreign policy goals, American attitudes reflect stability over time.

General continuity exists in the ordering of American priorities as well. The Pew/CFR results in Table 4.1 are rank ordered based on the 2009 responses, and they align with the long-term average except at the very top, where protecting jobs and preventing terrorism would swap places if the ordering were based on the overall average. At the aggregate level, Americans gave the highest priority to goals most closely associated with U.S. self-interest, with roughly two-thirds of Americans consistently prioritizing items such as terrorism, nuclear proliferation, jobs, energy supplies, and drug trafficking. Multilateral institutions and

TABLE 4.1 As I read a list of possible long-range foreign policy goals which the United States might have, tell me how much priority you think each one should be given. Do you think this should have a top priority, some priority, or no priority at all? (Percentages indicate "top priority.")

Goal	1993	1995	1997	2001 (early September)	2001 (mid-October)	2004	2005	2008	2009 (November)	Average
Protecting the Jobs of American Workers	85	80	77	77	74	84	84	82	85	81
Taking Measures to Protect the U.S. from Terrorist Attacks	na	na	na	80	93	88	86	82	85	86
Preventing the Spread of Weapons of Mass Destruction	69	68	70	78	81	71	75	62	74	72
Reducing Our Dependence on Imported Energy Sources	na	na	na	na	na	63	67	76	64	68
Combating International Drug Trafficking	na	na	67	64	55	63	59	na	56	61
Reducing Illegal Immigration	na	na	42	na	na	na	51	na	46	46
Dealing with Global Climate Change	na	na	na	na	na	na	43	43	40	42
Strengthening the United Nations	41	36	30	42	46	48	40	32	37	39
Promoting and Defending Human Rights in Other Countries	22	21	27	29	27	33	37	25	29	28
Helping Improve the Living Standards in Developing Nations	19	16	23	25	20	23	31	na	26	23
Promoting Democracy in Other Nations	22	16	22	29	24	24	24	na	21	23

Source: Pew Research Center 2009a. na = not available. Sorted in descending 2009 rank order.

transformational international objectives consistently received less than majority support. These results largely align with similarly worded questions in the 2008 Chicago Council survey except for the question of illegal immigration (where a higher percentage, at 61 percent, labeled "controlling and reducing illegal immigration" a "very important" goal). Question wording likely accounts for this difference (the Chicago Council survey added the word *controlling*). In the end, the pattern of American public preferences demonstrates remarkable consistency over time, despite great changes in the international environment over the decades. This constancy provides a firm foundation on which to build foreign policy priorities.

Some partisan differences emerged on several issues. Most politically significant are those where a majority of one party viewed an issue as a top priority and the other did not. Three issues fall into this category: reducing illegal immigration with a 17-percent gap (Republicans 56 percent, Democrats 39 percent, independents 47 percent), strengthening the United Nations with a 25-percent gap (Republicans 25 percent, Democrats 50 percent, independents 34 percent), and dealing with climate change with a 33-percent gap (Republicans 23 percent, Democrats 56 percent, independents 35 percent). As the controversy over climate change in 2009 has already demonstrated, these subjects can create significant division if the Obama administration prioritizes them. Less politically problematic are issues that have gaps but are favored by less than a majority as a top priority (a 10-percent gap in promoting human rights abroad with 23 percent Republicans, 33 percent Democrats, and 30 percent independents giving it a priority) and a 22-percent gap on improving living standards in poor nations (14 percent Republicans, 36 percent Democrats, and 25 percent independents with it as a priority). Partisan differences on the other issues were small (Pew Research Center 2009a).

National Security Policy: Terrorism, Afghanistan, and Iraq

Although American attitudes about goals have not changed dramatically, the public's attitudes on particular policies have shifted. Americans believe in a need for action to improve the American image abroad and express growing skepticism regarding military interventions in Iraq and Afghanistan.

Although Americans don't believe the danger from terrorism has greatly decreased, they appear to have soured on the ability of military force to confront it. When asked in late August 2002, "Which do you think would have a greater effect in reducing the threat of terrorist attacks on the United States?" 48 percent said "increasing Americans' military presence overseas" while 29 percent said "decreasing America's military presence overseas." The 2008 finding reversed these results, with 33 percent believing an increased military presence would reduce the threat of terrorist attack and 48 percent believing the United States needed to decrease its military presence overseas (Pew Research Center for the People & the Press 2008a).

Still, Americans continue to see terrorism as a threat and consistently favor a number of actions to address it. In late 2009, large percentages indicated "Islamic extremist groups like al-Qaeda" and the "Taliban's growing strength in Afghanistan" are "major threats" to "the well-being of the United States" (76 percent and 70 percent respectively). These figures are comparable to those seen from "Iran's nuclear program" (72 percent) and "North Korea's nuclear program" (69 percent). These threats are ranked higher than "international financial instability" (61 percent), "China's emergence as a world power" (53 percent), "political instability in Pakistan" (49 percent), "global climate change" (44 percent), and "tension between Russia and its neighbors" (38 percent). Major partisan differences among these threats exist, with Republicans seeing Islamic extremist groups as more of a threat than Democrats (a 13 point difference, 85 percent to 72 percent respectively; independents at 76 percent) and Democrats seeing global climate change as more threatening than Republicans (a 36-point difference, 60 percent to 24 percent respectively; independents at 45 percent). No major differences emerged between Republicans and Democrats on the other questions with differences of between 1 and 6 percent (Pew Research Center 2009a).

In 2008, when asked about actions that might be used to combat terrorism, the majority favored almost any action, including "working through the UN to strengthen international laws against terrorism and to make sure UN members enforce them" (84 percent), "U.S. air strikes against terrorist training camps and other facilities" (79 percent), the "trial of suspected terrorists by the International Criminal Court" (79 percent), "attacks by U.S. ground troops against terrorist training camps and other facilities" (72 percent), "helping poor countries develop their economies" (69 percent), "assassination of individual terrorist leaders" (68 percent), and "making a major effort to be even-handed in the Israeli-Palestinian conflict" (67 percent). The only option a majority opposed was "using torture to extract information from suspected terrorists" (36 percent favored and 61 percent opposed). Public attitudes on all these questions have remained essentially stable since 2002 (Chicago Council on Global Affairs 2008).

At the same time, in response to open-ended questions, terrorism does not seem to spring to mind as a pressing problem. In November 2009, when asked "What is America's most important international problem today?" only 9 percent pointed to "threats of terrorism, security problems, or international violence," which places it fourth behind economic issues (19 percent), war/ wars (16 percent), and the situation in Afghanistan (10 percent). This result reflects a drop from late 2005, when terrorism was the second most important problem (16 percent) behind only the situation in Iraq (22 percent; Chicago Council on Global Affairs 2008).

Underlying public attitudes on terrorism do not necessarily bode well for the Obama administration. First, a growing percentage of the public consider his foreign policy weak. When asked whether "Barack Obama is too tough, not tough enough, or about right in his approach to foreign policy and national security issues," 47 percent indicated in November 2009 that he was "not tough enough" (up from 38 percent in June 2009), which was more than those who thought it was "about right" (43 percent, which was down from 51 percent in June). Only 3 percent saw him as "too tough" (2 percent in June). A decidedly partisan view emerged, with 72 percent of Republicans saying Obama was not tough enough compared to 29 percent of Democrats (47 percent of independents). Sixty percent of Democrats rated his policy as about right compared to 22 percent of Republicans (41 percent of independents). Small percentages saw him as too tough (1 percent of Republicans, 2 percent of Democrats, and 6 percent of independents).

Second, the public in November 2009 saw an increased terrorist threat, with 29 percent saying terrorists have a "greater . . . ability to launch another major attack on the U.S." compared to the time of September 11. This figure was up from 17 percent in February 2009 (18 percent in September 2008 late in the George W. Bush administration). For comparison, 28 percent said they had the same ability (44 percent in February 2009 and 43 percent in September 2008), and 29 percent said terrorists had less ability to attack (35 percent in February 2009 and 36 percent in September 2008). In other words, as the Obama administration has continued, the public perceives terrorists as better able to act. As with other policies, partisanship affects these attitudes. Republicans who saw terrorists as better able to attack rose from 10 percent in February 2008 to 32 percent in February 2009 and 34 percent in November 2009. At the same time, Democratic concerns varied with 21 percent seeing an enhanced terrorist ability in February 2008 and 7 percent in February 2009, then jumping to 27 percent in November (independents went from 17 percent in both February 2008 and 2009 to 26 percent in November 2009; Pew Research Center 2009a). The failed April 2010 New York Times Square car bombing likely bolstered these concerns.

This combination suggests several considerations for the Obama administration. First, the Obama administration should expect to be supported in most of its responses to terrorism. Second, barring a successful major terrorist attack, the public will not "demand" more action. Finally, since the public feels the danger is increasing and they perceive Obama's foreign policy as "weak," the Obama administration seems uniquely vulnerable in the face of a successful attack.

Events associated with the wars in Afghanistan and, to a lesser extent, Iraq will likely have an influence on public support for the Obama administration. With the United States slated to have all its troops removed from combat operations in Iraq by the end of summer 2010 and completely by the end of 2011, it is unlikely that Iraq will present an ongoing political problem for the Obama administration. However, casualties in Afghanistan (Mueller 1973), the intervention's perceived success (Gelpi, Feaver, and Reifler 2009), and the reaction of opinion leaders (Powlick and Katz 1998) will present a different problem. If American casualties remain low, and especially if they are combined with the appearance of "success," the electoral effects of these wars will recede. On the other hand, if casualties mount, especially if associated with controversies over "success," divisions among elites will emerge and public support will wane. In that event, public support for the Obama administration's foreign policy will decline along with support for the administration overall.

Americans already have divided attitudes about Afghanistan. Polling results on U.S. efforts back to September 2006 suggest a range of support between a high of 53 percent (April 2009) and a low of 40 percent (October 2009) and opposition ranging from a high of 58 percent (September and October 2009) and a low of 46 percent (in December 2008 and May 2009). The public supports the main Obama policy of adding an extra 30,000 troops to Afghanistan by a roughly 2:1 ratio (61 percent favoring and 38 percent opposing in a CNN Poll in January 2010). Interestingly, by nearly the same ratio, the public consistently believes that the United States did not make "a mistake in sending military forces to Afghanistan" (36 percent said it was a mistake and 60 percent not a mistake in November 2009). This figure is down somewhat from August 2007 (25 percent mistake and 70 percent not a mistake) and July 2004 (25 percent mistake and 72 percent not a mistake) polls, but it does not reflect a radical shift in American attitudes. Most polls point to a small plurality disapproving of Obama's handling of the situation in Afghanistan before his December 2009 announcement of additional troops, and they point to a plurality, and even a slight majority, approving his policy after the announcement (Pollingreport. com 2010a). Barring a rise in casualties or change in the war dynamic, Afghanistan is not likely to become a salient issue.

The public's views of Iraq appear somewhat similar to those on Afghanistan although probably more negative. Asked in a series of polls by CNN whether they "favor or oppose the U.S. war in Iraq," a majority of 60 percent opposed the war while 39 percent favored it in a late January 2010 poll. These attitudes were largely unchanged since June 2006. In the same poll, the public favored the Obama policy of removing most of the troops by August 2010 and leaving a residual force of 35,000–50,000 troops by a 62 percent to 36 percent margin. In terms of the "mistake" question, Iraq mirrors Afghanistan, with 58 percent of the public agreeing that "sending troops to Iraq" was a mistake while 39 percent disagreeing in a July 2009 Gallup poll (figures that were essentially unchanged since May 2007). As for Obama's handling of the situation in Iraq, the public has consistently favored it (to greater or lesser degree) since he entered office, with a mid-December 2009 Roper poll indicating approval by a 49 percent to 40 percent plurality. Polls earlier in the year indicated a majority approving of his approach to Iraq (Pollingreport.com 2010b). In short, public attitudes support the withdrawal of American forces from Iraq. Barring a radical change in the Iraq circumstances, it will not become a salient issue in public opinion.

Large partisan gaps appear in the public's approval of Obama's handling of foreign policy issues. Predictably, Democrats are more inclined to favor Obama's foreign policy with Republicans inclined to disapprove and independents in between. In November 2009, Democratic majorities approved of Obama's handling of every foreign policy queried except for one (China at 49 percent approval). On each policy, less than a majority of Republicans and independents approved. This combination creates a major approval gap between the parties on a host of issues, including general approval of foreign policy (41-percent gap: Republicans 21 percent, Democrats 62 percent, and independents 44 percent), terrorism (48-percent gap: Republicans 29 percent, Democrats 77 percent, independents 44 percent), Afghanistan (35-percent gap: Republicans 19 percent, Democrats 54 percent, independents 31 percent), Iraq (22-percent gap: Republicans 32 percent, Democrats 54 percent, independents 36 percent), Iran (36-percent gap: 22 percent Republicans, 58 percent Democrats, and 43 percent independents), and climate change (34-percent gap: 28 percent Republicans, 62 percent Democrats, and 42 percent independents). More so than was observed on the more conceptual questions regarding internationalism, threats, priorities, and unilateralism, significant and politically relevant gaps appeared between partisans on several issues that will likely remain substantive and visible foreign policy issues throughout the Obama administration. Since this partisan gap exists across all the issues queried, this difference of opinion will likely remain politically relevant as Obama pursues his renewal agenda.

International Institutions

A common theme in Obama's foreign policy so far has been a greater embrace of multilateralism and international institutions. As with multilateralism, the public remains supportive of American engagement with international institutions, although less so than in previous periods. In response to a November 2009 question, 51 percent agreed that "the United States should cooperate fully with the United Nations," and 38 percent disagreed. Although a majority still supported cooperation, the figure is the second lowest recorded since 1964 (the lowest was 46 percent in 1976), and it is well below the average approval of 62 percent (previous high was 77 percent in 1991). A decidedly partisan division emerged, with 65 percent of Democrats and 39 percent of Republicans (47 percent of independents) favoring cooperation (Pew Research Center 2009a).

More specifically, the public supported a range of actions to expand the UN's authority, including "giving the UN the power to regulate the international arms trade" (57 percent favored and 41 percent opposed; no change in percent favoring compared to 2004), "having a standing UN peacekeeping force" (70 percent to 29 percent; 4-point drop in percentage favoring compared to 2004), "giving the UN the authority to go into countries in order to investigate violations of human rights" (73 percent supported and 26 percent opposed; 2-point drop in percentage favoring compared to 2006), "creating an international marshals service that could arrest leaders responsible for genocide" (71 percent favored and 27 percent opposed; 4-point drop in percentage favoring compared to 2006), and "having a UN agency control access to all nuclear fuel in the world to ensure that none is used for weapons production" (63 percent favored and 35 percent opposed). The one exception to public support was the response to giving the "UN the power to fund its activities by imposing a small tax on such things as the international sale of arms or oil" (46 percent favored and 51 percent opposed; 5-point drop in percentage favoring compared to 2002; Chicago Council on Global Affairs 2008). These results point to general and stable support for the United Nations.

Beyond this general assessment, Americans supported international treaties, American involvement in them, compliance with international commitments, and the expansion of international institutions across a number of issues. In a mid-2008 poll, the public supported American participation in existing and potential treaties, including a nuclear test ban treaty (88 percent favored to 11 percent opposed), the International Criminal Court (68 percent favored to 25 percent opposed), and a new treaty to address greenhouse gas emissions (76 percent supported and 23 percent opposed). All these results were essentially unchanged from previous levels of support throughout the early 2000s. The public also favored "new international institutions" to "monitor whether countries are meeting their treaty obligations to limit their greenhouse gas emissions" (68 percent to 30 percent), to "monitor financial markets worldwide and report on potential crises" (59 percent to 38 percent), to "monitor the worldwide energy market and predict potential shortages" (69 percent to 30 percent), and to "provide information and assistance to countries dealing with problems resulting from large scale migration of people across borders" (57 percent to 42 percent; Chicago Council on Global Affairs 2008). The Obama administration can expect a supportive public if it pursues its renewal agenda through existing and new international institutions.

Economics

Because of its relation to domestic politics, economics has risen in importance to the public, especially with the increasing globalization of international politics. In general, Americans express mixed attitudes toward globalization, free trade agreements, and the North American Free Trade Agreement (NAFTA). Although majorities tend to support free trade conceptually, they have more mixed ideas about the effect of these agreements. Perhaps most striking is that, in the polls taken after the 2008 financial crisis, Americans expressed attitudes more supportive of free trade rather than attitudes more negative about engagement with international economics.

Regarding globalization, a majority of Americans in 2008 (58 percent) saw globalization as "mostly good" for the United States, while a smaller percentage (39 percent) saw it negatively. The favorable attitude is in keeping with polling results dating to 1998. On the other hand, the level of opposition reflected a slow but steady rise in the view that globalization is a bad thing, up from 20 percent in 1998. At the same time, American attitudes toward the effect of globalization on particular segments of the American economy had also turned negative. The majority of Americans now believed that the effects of globalization are bad for "job security of American worker" (65 percent bad and 32 percent good), "creating jobs in the U.S." (58 percent bad and 38 percent good), the environment (52 percent bad and 44 percent bad), and the U.S. economy (51 percent bad and 46 percent good). More positive views existed on the effect on "your own standard of living" (51 percent good and 46 percent bad), American companies (52 percent good and 44 percent bad), and "consumers like you" (56 percent good and 40 percent bad). Mixed attitudes existed on the effect of globalization on "the next generation of Americans" (49 percent bad and 48 percent good; Chicago Council on Global Affairs 2008).

American ambivalence toward international economics extended to trade issues. Before the 2008 financial crisis, just under half of Americans favored an "agreement to lower trade barriers provided the government has programs to help workers who lose their jobs" (49 percent in 2008, 48 percent in 2004). When combined with the percentage who favored lower barriers while opposing worker aid programs (3 percent in 2008 and 10 percent in 2004), more than half the public at least conditionally favored free trade (62 percent in 2008 and 58 percent in 2004) compared to one-third who simply opposed these types of agreements (34 percent in 2006 and 2008; Chicago Council on Global Affairs 2008).

The 2008 financial crisis appears to have slightly strengthened American attitudes in favor of free trade agreements. When asked "In general, do you think that free trade agreements like NAFTA and the policies of the World Trade Organization have been a good thing or a bad thing for the United States?" 43 percent in November 2009 indicated it was a "good thing" (32 percent said a "bad thing"). This response represents a marked reversal from April 2008, when 35 percent said a good thing and 48 percent said a bad thing. No major partisan differences emerged. In every other repeated question, attitudes shifted to a certain degree in favor of free trade. Asked whether "these free trade agreements have definitely helped, probably helped, probably hurt, or definitely hurt the financial situation of you and your family," 33 percent in 2009 said it helped (up from 27 percent) while 40 percent said it hurt (down from 48 percent). Asked whether free trade agreements make product prices increase, fall, or make no difference, 32 percent said they made prices lower (29 percent previously) compared to 33 percent who said they went higher (39 percent previously); 20 percent said no difference (18 percent previously). Regarding wages, 49 percent believed they made American wages lower (56 percent previously), 11 percent said higher (8 percent previously), and 24 percent said they made no difference (22 percent previously). In terms of job loss, 53 percent said free trade agreements led to job losses (61 percent previously), 13 percent said they created jobs (9 percent previously), and 19 percent said they made no difference (18 percent previously). On the general economy, 25 percent said free trade agreements make the economy grow (19 percent previously), 42 percent said they slow the economy (19 percent previously), and 18 percent said no difference (17 percent previously). Across all these questions, partisan differences were slight (Pew Research Center 2009a).

While the 2009 polling results taken on their own support the notion that American attitudes toward free trade are negative, each of these polls reflected a shift toward the "pro–free trade" position. This shift is even more startling since the common view is that when economic times are tough, Americans will become more insular and protectionist. Although it is hard to explain this counterintuitive shift in public attitudes, these results provide additional evidence against an inwardly turning America.

With international economic issues at the forefront, this complex array of attitudes presents a challenge for Obama's renewal agenda. While Americans remain supportive of free trade and globalization, they are souring on its effects on major portions of the American economy. With continuing negative revelations of how investment banks operated in the era of lessened financial regulation and news of economic instability in Europe, the potential exists for a shift in American attitudes toward greater regulation of domestic and international markets.

The View from Abroad

The public outside the United States greeted Obama's presidency in overwhelmingly positive terms. In contrast with the perceived unilateralism of the Bush administration, Obama has stressed multilateralism in a number of major foreign policy speeches abroad (in Strasbourg, France, on April 3, 2009; in Prague, Czech Republic, on April 5, 2009; in Cairo, Egypt, on June 4, 2009; and in Oslo, Norway, on December 10, 2009. See Obama 2009h, 2009i, 2009o, 2009k, respectively, for transcripts). In perhaps the most visible positive reaction to Obama, the Nobel Prize Committee chose him as the 2009 Nobel Peace Prize winner "for his extraordinary efforts to strengthen international diplomacy and cooperation between peoples."

Non-American public opinion has reacted positively to the changed tone of Obama's foreign policy. The appearance of Obama's popularity clearly results in large part from the Bush administration's historical unpopularity. World opinion analyst Steven Kull observed, "There has really been no time for which we have data that shows the broad level of dissatisfaction with U.S. foreign policy that we find today [spring 2007]. . . . [This] is definitely unique. We have never seen numbers this low" (Subcommittee on International Organizations 2008, 8). This international negativity in the 2000s stemmed from real policy disagreements with U.S. foreign policies, and these significant disagreements remain (Holsti 2008; Subcommittee on International Organizations 2008, 10–16). As Obama takes action in the foreign realm on a myriad of issues such as climate change, Iran, North Korea, Afghanistan, and Iraq, among others, foreign attitudes toward Obama could change for the worse, especially if the policies align with those of the Bush administration. But, for the moment at least, Obama retains a reservoir of good will around the world.

World opinion from 2009 suggested a dramatic and positive shift in attitudes regarding the United States. First, when asked whether they had a favorable attitude toward the United States, ratings improved in most places in 2009 compared to 2008 when Bush was president (see Table 4.2). Western Europe experienced the biggest jumps, while Eastern European attitudes held steady as did attitudes in the Middle East. Asia and Africa reflected a mix of increasing and steady attitudes.

At least part of the reason for this upswing is attributable to the belief that Obama will "do the right thing regarding world affairs." Of the countries listed in Table 4.2, the average increase in confidence from Bush in 2008 to Obama in 2009 is a startling 41.5 percent. All the countries experienced a positive shift in double digits except for Pakistan (6 percent). Fourteen of the twenty countries expressed confidence that Obama would do the right thing with an average rating of 75.7 percent (including China at 62 percent). The six countries

TABLE 4.2   Favorability toward the United States

Country	2008	2009	Change
Britain	53	68	16
France	42	75	33
Germany	31	64	33
Spain	33	58	25
Poland	68	67	−1
Russia	46	44	−2
Turkey	12	14	2
Egypt	22	27	5
Jordan	19	25	6
Lebanon	51	55	4
China	41	47	6
India	66	76	10
Indonesia	37	63	26
Japan	50	59	9
Pakistan	19	16	−3
South Korea	70	78	8
Argentina	22	38	16
Brazil	47	61	14
Mexico	47	69	22
Nigeria	64	79	15

Source: Pew Global Attitudes Project 2009, 1. Question: "Please tell me if you have a very favorable, somewhat favorable, somewhat unfavorable or very unfavorable opinion of: a. The United States." Percent "very" or "somewhat" favorable.

where a majority still did not express confidence included Russia (37 percent), Turkey (33 percent), Egypt (42 percent), Jordan (31 percent), Lebanon (46 percent), and Pakistan (13 percent; Pew Global Attitudes Project 2009, 2).

Along with this increase in favorability and confidence went increasing support for the U.S. terrorism effort, belief that the United States considers their nation's interests, approval of American leadership, and approval of Obama's foreign policy. Compared to 2007 in twenty-four countries (the countries in Table 4.2 plus Canada, Israel, the Palestinian Territories, and Kenya), when only five countries had majorities supporting "U.S.-led efforts to fight terrorism," majorities in fifteen countries supported the U.S. efforts in 2009 under Obama. In these same countries, although majorities in only seven believed the United States "takes into account the interest of countries like (survey country)," the percentage had increased in eleven, fallen in four, and stayed even in nine others. Majorities approved of "Obama's international policies" in seventeen of these countries (exceptions being Russia, Turkey, Egypt, Jordan, Lebanon, the Palestinian Territories, and Pakistan; Pew Global Attitudes Project 2009, 19–20, 180). In another survey of publics from more than 100 countries regarding whether they "approve of the job performance of the leadership of the United States of America," in 84 countries where a 2008 survey existed for comparison, approval of U.S. leadership increased in 60, fell in only 3 (Indonesia, Philippines, and Vietnam), and did not change in 21. More importantly, of the 102 nations where a 2009 reading existed, majorities approved of U.S. leadership in just over half (53) and majorities disapproved in only 12 (11 falling within the Muslim world plus Serbia; Gallup Opinion Poll 2010).

Substantive evaluations of foreign policy have improved as well. When asked in an April 2010 BBC poll of nations in every global region whether the United States was "having a mainly positive or mainly negative influence in the world," a plurality of 46 percent indicated a positive influence (up from a low of 28 percent in 2007 during the George W. Bush administration) while 34 percent said a negative influence. Not only was this the first time that more respondents indicated a positive than negative influence, it represented a 4 percent increase in positive assessments from the previous year and a fall of 9 percent in those who gave negative responses. Positive assessments outnumbered negative views in twenty of twenty-eight countries surveyed (exceptions where negative attitudes largely outpaced positive views occurred in Pakistan, China, Mexico, Russia, and Turkey; BBC World Service Poll 2010).

Some troubling aspects counter the good. Of twenty-four countries surveyed, majorities in each believed the United States influenced their country a "great deal" or "fair amount." But the number saying that U.S. influence was a "bad thing" outweighed those saying it is a "good thing" in eighteen countries (with three where "good thing" was the majority and five that were essentially even; Pew Global Attitudes Project 2009, 26). In another 2009 survey, majorities in fifteen of nineteen countries surveyed (a mixture of European, Middle Eastern, African, and Asian countries) said the United States "abuses its greater power to make us do what the U.S. wants" (66 percent across all countries) rather than "treats us fairly" (only 26 percent across all countries). These publics were also split on whether the United States was "playing a mainly positive or mainly negative role in the world," with 39 percent saying positive and 41 percent indicating negative. Although 59 percent found the United States "generally cooperative with other countries" (30 percent disagreeing), the United States ran into difficulties on several substantive issues. These publics did not approve of how the United States was handling climate change (39 percent approved and 41 percent disapproved) and thought the United States used "the threat of military force to gain advantages" (77 percent agreeing to 15 percent disagreeing), and two-thirds complained that the United States promoted "international laws for other countries, but is hypocritical because it often does not follow these rules itself" (23 percent thought the United States "has been an important leader in promoting international laws, and sets a good example by following them"). And a large number (38 percent) thought the United States was not "generally respectful of human rights" (51 percent thought it was; World Public Opinion.org 2009b).

A major longitudinal survey of European attitudes largely confirms these basic positive and negative assessments, with Western Europeans being more inclined toward positive attitudes than Eastern Europeans regarding the United States (German Marshall Fund 2009).

This brief review of attitudes suggests several conclusions. First, Obama's presidency has had a noticeable positive effect on perceptions of U.S. foreign policy. Publics from around the world now see the United States in more positive terms. Second, significant concerns remain over U.S. foreign policy behavior, with large percentages of the public in the Middle East disapproving of American foreign policy. To explain this past and present dissatisfaction with American policy, researchers involved with the Pew Global Attitudes Project, World Public Opinion.org, and the German Marshall Fund surveys pointed to a combination of substantive policy disagreements (on Iraq, torture, Israel), the perceived unilateralism of American policy, and the interaction of these first two items with international perceptions of President Bush that created the intense negativity toward the United States from around the world (see the reports by these organizations in the reference section as well as Subcommittee on International Organizations 2008, especially p. 21).

Clearly, the blend of an unpopular presidential personality (Bush) pursuing policies that many in the world found troubling in a manner perceived to be unilateralist led to the historical lows associated with the Bush administration. In terms of policy renewal, Obama's election and direction addressed several of these concerns. Personally, Obama is clearly perceived in a more positive light than President Bush. His comments in major international speeches have also emphasized more multilateralist inclinations. While these first two aspects provided stylistic differences with the Bush administration, the substantive policy differences remained. Obama's foreign policies on a range of issues appeared to be substantively more similar than different from those of the Bush administration (Karon 2010). Of these three aspects, scholars suggest that policy substance affects attitudes in the long run more so than personality or style (Subcommittee on International Organizations 2008). It remains to be seen whether the positive change in world opinion will continue if policy substance does not follow the change in style.

Looking Forward: A Bipartisan Foundation or Partisan Rancor?

Scholars have pointed to the importance of political party in shaping foreign policy attitudes (Holsti 2004) and suggested that the effect of party appears to have accelerated during George W. Bush's presidency (Snyder, Shapiro, and Bloch-Elkon 2009). This chapter's consideration of public attitudes suggests a mixture of both partisan agreement and disagreement. In terms of foreign policy influence, the areas where Republicans and Democrats agree are just as important for Obama's renewal agenda as where they disagree.

For the most part, Republicans and Democrats agree on the big-picture items. Members of both parties agree on the main threats to the United States as well as long-range priorities (jobs, terrorism, nuclear proliferation, energy). The same can be said regarding unilateralism and multilateralism, which seem to split each party rather than divide the parties (though nonpartisans appear more unilateralist than members of either party). They agree substantively on how well the United States is doing against terrorism and how much of a threat terrorism poses (after a period of division early in 2009). In general, this pattern of similarities between the parties suggests that Americans of both parties largely agree with each other on the general direction the United States should pursue and the reality it confronts. This pattern could imply a firm basis on which to build a renewed American foreign policy consensus.

Despite this consensus on the fundamentals, partisan divisions exist on the day-to-day foreign policy issues, which will likely impede establishing bipartisan support for Obama's initiatives. On every issue polled, Republicans disapproved of Obama's handling of foreign policy issues while the majority of Democrats approved (except for a plurality on China policy). The majority of Republicans also saw Obama as "not tough enough" while the majority of Democrats saw his policy as "just right." Given the increasingly partisan nature of foreign policy among policy makers, these differences on policy particulars create real barriers to building a foreign policy consensus similar to the one that existed during the Cold War. With this built-in opposition to anything he does on this partisan basis, Obama is likely to find his foreign policies the subject of continuing controversy.

The array of attitudes presented by public opinion presents a challenge unlike any since the end of the Vietnam War. As indicated by the trends in internationalism, the mid-1970s represented the last time that American public opinion took a more inward-looking view toward foreign affairs. The slight drop in internationalism is accompanied by growing skepticism regarding the direction of international affairs and America's role in it. In addition, partisan divides, spurred on initially by divisions over the Iraq War, have clearly emerged over the conduct of a range of issues. The weight of the survey results considered here, especially regarding the overall stability of American attitudes on threats and priorities, suggests only a temporary downward tick in a broader trend of internationalism (as occurred after the Vietnam conflict) rather than a sea change in American attitudes.

In this context, the Obama administration seems to want to pursue a more multilateralist approach that employs more than the tools of military power. This policy will be met with both support and resistance by American public opinion. While the public prefers continued American engagement with the world and an internationalist orientation, Republicans will respond skeptically to anything Obama does. To the extent that the United Nations becomes a more important actor, Republicans (who are less inclined than Democrats to value the UN) will oppose the mechanism Obama has chosen. If these efforts are not met with substantive foreign policy success, foreign policy could become the focus of renewed partisan contention, which could spread beyond the means to the very purposes of foreign policy. This dynamic might become particularly pronounced if issues that divide the parties, such as climate change and illegal immigration, become a focal point. On the other hand, should the multilateral efforts be met with foreign policy success, foreign policy will recede as a major domestic political issue just as the Iraq war, which played such a prominent role in domestic politics from 2003 through 2008, has stopped being a front-burner issue.

As long as issues that divide the parties on both the level of threat and priority (such as climate change and illegal immigration) do not become *the* central foreign policy issues for the administration, a successful Obama foreign policy will decrease the salience of foreign policy issues and mute partisan divisions. A focus on foreign policy goals that share bipartisan support (preventing nuclear nonproliferation, protecting jobs, fighting terrorism, and promoting energy independence) will enhance the administration's prospects, especially if these efforts result in visible achievements. Success will also spur the public's attitudes toward internationalism to rebound, as they have in the past. Failed policies (for example, if Afghanistan goes badly) or a focus on divisive issues (such as climate change) will increase the importance of foreign policy and heighten potential controversy. In this case, the president might find that public opinion, rather than being a resource, will significantly hinder his foreign policy renewal agenda.

World public opinion wants Obama to succeed and hopes that he will change the direction of American foreign policy. This international goodwill and Obama's personal appeal provide a base from which to build a successful international policy. A more multilateralist foreign policy will be welcomed in Europe and parts of Asia, and positive views toward the United States might continue, especially because, on a range of substantive issues, there is more agreement among these countries than commonly acknowledged (German Marshall Fund 2009). On the other hand, major portions of the publics in key regions (especially the Middle East) oppose fundamental U.S. foreign policies, and their opposition will continue. Regardless of how U.S. foreign policy is implemented, as time passes, foreign publics will increasingly respond to what the United States does rather than the promise that Obama brought with his election. If his policies continue to present more continuity than change (Kagan 2010b; Karon 2010), world opinion could turn on the Obama administration.

Public opinion provides the Obama administration the opportunity to pursue a foreign policy renewal agenda. Internationally, a more multilateral foreign policy that engages with other nations on key international issues will be welcomed in many areas. Domestically, the general public will not oppose broader engagement with foreign policy, subject to three conditions. First, should this focus appear to come at the expense of domestic priorities, public opposition could grow. Second, as we have seen repeatedly, nothing creates public opposition like foreign policy failure. Third and related to the first two factors, opposition will begin first among Republicans, who are already skeptical of Obama's handling of foreign policy issues, and then spread to independents. A foreign policy supported by Democrats and opposed by Republicans and independents would undermine the prospects for a stable direction.

As the Obama administration looks to pursue a renewed foreign policy effort it would be wise to remember that, at least in terms of public opinion, foreign policy success breeds public indifference while failure activates public opposition. Given the difficult issues the United States faces and potential for partisan division, indifferent support might be the best that a president in the current era can hope for.

CHAPTER 5

Ethnic Lobbying in the Obama Administration

Patrick J. Haney

THE OBAMA ADMINISTRATION has set American foreign policy on a course for "renewal."[1] The purpose of this volume is to explore the ways in which the Obama administration has pursued an overarching agenda to engage with the international community after a period in which the United States became estranged from the mechanisms of global governance created, with U.S. leadership, after World War II (Hook and Scott 2011, chap. 1). Key elements of this approach include a greater emphasis on global interdependence, a conception of the U.S. national interest that incorporates transnational concerns to a greater degree than was previously the case, and a wider mix of policy instruments, including "Track 2" diplomacy to a greater degree relative to military power (Hook and Scott 2011, chap. 1). To the extent that the Obama foreign policy is marked by such goals, we would expect to see not just a significant effort to reach out to ethnic minorities and ethnic interest groups in the United States as important conduits for "renewal," but the pattern of outreach should be different than in previous administrations, particularly from the connections forged between ethnic interest groups and the George W. Bush administration. How has ethnic lobbying proceeded during the start of the Obama administration? Are the patterns any different than in the past? Here I try to track these patterns especially with respect to groups active on U.S. policy toward Cuba and toward the Middle East, but I will mention others as well. I will also try to evaluate the extent to which the Obama administration has used its relations with ethnic and diaspora groups in the United States as part of a strategy to reconnect with the world.

This chapter will explore the power and access of ethnic lobbies in the foreign policy domain, especially lobbies that apply pressure around Cuba, India, and the Middle East, drawing some comparisons between the Bush administration and the Obama administration. But there is another insight in the literature that has received far less scholarly scrutiny: lobbying is a two-way street between presidents and ethnic interest groups. Watanabe (1984, chap. 3), in particular, made the point that interest groups and policy makers often form mutually supportive, or "symbiotic," relationships. He argued that just as groups need policy makers to do something for them, policy makers need valuable resources from ethnic interest groups. These resources include help during policy debates, like information, and help during elections, like campaign contributions and votes. Watanabe (1984, 53) went on to observe that policy makers may thus "aggressively court ethnic groups and encourage their activism." This was certainly the case with the Cuban American National Foundation (CANF), as the Reagan administration actively promoted its founding and later activities so as to have help in promoting policies and to have a partner to lobby Capitol Hill (Haney and Vanderbush 1999). So while much of the literature has focused on the efforts of interest groups to push policy on Congress, here I will try to keep attention on the relationship between ethnic lobbies and the executive branch, especially during the Obama administration. Thus, in this chapter I will also try to show how the Obama administration has tried to cultivate relationships with ethnic lobby groups in order to further the foreign policy aims of the administration. Leveraging these social networks was a key part of the Obama strategy in the nomination and general election campaigns; it seems likely that the Obama foreign policy will include an effort to reconnect to the outside world by forging new partnerships with ethnic minority groups inside the United States.

Literature on Ethnic Lobbying

The standard approach in the literature to the role of ethnic lobbying in American foreign policy tends to emphasize questions of power and influence by these groups over policy (see Haney and Vanderbush 1999; Haney 2010; Rubenzer 2008b): What groups exist, and do they exert influence on policy? For example, Ahrari, in *Ethnic Groups and U.S. Foreign Policy* (1987), examined ethnic interest group activity over U.S. policy toward the Middle East, South Africa, Poland, Mexico, Cuba, and Ireland. Watanabe (1984) studied ethnic lobbying on U.S. policy toward Turkey. A similar focus drove an entire collection of essays in the journal *Foreign Policy* on "new ethnic voices," including essays by Longmyer (1985) about African Americans, by Richardson (1985) about Hispanic Americans, and by Sadd and Lendenmann (1985) about Arab Americans.

In the wake of the Cold War, the role of these societal groups in the policy process came under increased scrutiny, perhaps matching an increase in their activism in this area. The volume edited by Ambrosio (2002), *Ethnic Identity Groups and U.S. Foreign Policy,* addresses how ethnic interest groups operate today. Chapters in that volume cover a variety of issues, including support for

South Africa's apartheid regime; lobbying about Kosovo, Africa, and Turkey; and the lobbying of Latinos and Asian Americans. Paul and Paul (2009) used surveys of and interviews with policy makers and journalists to try to identify which ethnic interest groups are more influential than others and why. The survey, carried out between 2005 and 2007, identified the most powerful ethnic lobbies on U.S. foreign policy (using the survey's terms): Israeli (easily rated the most influential) and Cuban (a clear second), followed by the Irish, Armenian, Hispanic, Taiwanese, African, Greek, and Indian lobbies (Paul and Paul 2009, 137). While much of the literature sees ethnic interest groups as bit players in the policy game, many authors have come to see them as significant players; Uslander (1995, 370–373) has even argued that ethnic interest groups are now the most prominent foreign policy lobby in the United States (see also T. Smith 2000).

In terms of which ethnic lobbying groups are most powerful, the general consensus has been that the power of the American Israel Public Affairs Committee (AIPAC) dwarfs that of all other competitors, and it is often seen as an exception to the rule that interest groups are not the most important players in foreign policy making. Studies of the power of AIPAC come not just from scholars but also from political leaders, who label AIPAC as "the most effective ethnic/foreign policy lobby on Capitol Hill" (B. C. Cohen 1973; Findley 1989, 25; Fleshler 2009; Franck and Weisband 1979, 187; Goldberg 1990; Nathan and Oliver 1994, chap. 11). The publication of the controversial book *The Israel Lobby and U.S. Foreign Policy* (2007) by international relations scholars John Mearsheimer and Stephen Walt has brought new attention to the power this ethnic lobby wields over the Ship of State. Khalil Marrar tracked Arab American lobbying (2009), showing how it tries to compete with AIPAC in the post-9/11 political environment.

Perhaps the second most studied ethnic interest group has been the CANF, often seen as the second most powerful ethnic interest group in America during its heyday in the 1980s and 1990s (see, e.g., Haney and Vanderbush 1999; Kaplowitz 1998; Kiger 1997; Morley and McGillion 2002; Rubenzer 2008a; and J. C. Smith 1998). When it was led by its charismatic founder, Jorge Mas Canosa, CANF rolled off a series of policy victories during the Reagan years, including tighter sanctions on Castro's Cuba, tight links to and financing from the National Endowment for Democracy, the establishment of Radio- and TV-Marti, to name but a few (see Haney and Vanderbush 1999).

The Obama Administration, Renewal, and Ethnic Lobbying

In his inaugural address, President Obama sent a clear message of renewal and reconnection both to the world and to ethnic minorities at home (Obama 2009c):

For we know that our patchwork heritage is a strength, not a weakness. We are a nation of Christians and Muslims, Jews and Hindus, and non-believers. We are shaped by every language and culture, drawn from every end of this Earth; and because we have tasted the bitter swill of civil war and segregation, and emerged from that dark chapter stronger and more united, we cannot help but believe that the old hatreds shall someday pass; that the lines of tribe shall soon dissolve; that as the world grows smaller, our common humanity shall reveal itself; and that America must play its role in ushering in a new era of peace.

To the Muslim world, we seek a new way forward, based on mutual interest and mutual respect. To those leaders around the globe who seek to sow conflict, or blame their society's ills on the West, know that your people will judge you on what you can build, not what you destroy.

To those who cling to power through corruption and deceit and the silencing of dissent, know that you are on the wrong side of history, but that we will extend a hand if you are willing to unclench your fist.

To the people of poor nations, we pledge to work alongside you to make your farms flourish and let clean waters flow; to nourish starved bodies and feed hungry minds. And to those nations like ours that enjoy relative plenty, we say we can no longer afford indifference to the suffering outside our borders, nor can we consume the world's resources without regard to effect. For the world has changed, and we must change with it.

This message of partnership and connection—of renewal—was then echoed by Vice President Biden in the speech he gave at the 2009 Munich Conference on Security Policy. Biden argued, "America needs the world, just as I believe the world needs America." He went on to note, "In the Muslim world, a small—and I believe a very small—number of violent extremists are beyond the call of reason. We will, and we must, defeat them. But hundreds of millions of hearts and minds in the Muslim world share the values we hold dearly. We must reach them. President Obama has made clear that he will seek a new way forward based on mutual interest and mutual respect. It was not an accident that he gave his very first interview as President of the United States to Al Arabiya. That was not an accident" (Biden 2009).

This view of America's reconnection to the world, of "renewal" as the editors of this volume frame it, presented both by President Obama and Vice President Biden, also holds a particular conception of how this can be accomplished. The Obama administration seems particularly interested in developing and leveraging domestic networks to help reconnect around the world. Obama's use of social networks, often facilitated by the Internet, in the campaign is now well known, but perhaps less well appreciated is the Obama team's view of how networks of ethnic minority groups in the United States can play an important role in the American government's renewal with the rest of the world. This view of "people-to-people" diplomacy has been recast as leveraging the "networked" world in which we live by Anne-Marie Slaughter, the former dean of the Wilson School at Princeton and now head of the Policy Planning Staff at the Department of State. In a recent issue of *Foreign Affairs* magazine, Slaughter pointed out that in twenty-first-century America, "Immigrant communities flourish not only in large cities but also smaller towns and rural areas. A mosaic has replaced the melting pot, and, now more than ever, immigrants connect their new communities to their countries of origin" (Slaughter 2009, 103). She went on to argue, "The United States must learn to think of its ethnic communities as the source of future generations of 'overseas Americans'" (Slaughter 2009, 103–104). She also pointed out that as a tool of diplomacy, "the United States must recognize the necessity of orchestrating networks of public, private, and civic actors to address global problems. . . . [and] orchestrate networks of these actors and guide them toward collaborative solutions" (Slaughter 2009, 112). This is a wholesale re-visioning of America's place in the world. "It need not see itself as locked in a global struggle with other great powers; rather it should see itself as a central player in an integrated world" (Slaughter 2009, 113). In the pages that follow, I will try to sketch the early patterns of ethnic lobbying by and on the Obama administration in a few key cases.

Indian Americans

Starting in the Clinton administration and accelerating through the Bush years, the U.S.-India partnership has moved to a new level of harmony. This was marked by the 2006 nuclear agreement approved by the U.S. Congress that accepted India as a nuclear state outside of the Nuclear Non-Proliferation Treaty. As Kirk (2008) discussed, this was not only a story of government-to-government negotiations but also the story of the rise of a new and powerful domestic lobby: Indian Americans. A number of organizations among Indian Americans were formed during the 1970s and 1980s based upon religious, professional, and trade affiliations, but as Kirk (2008) showed and Lindsay (2002) predicted, what might be called "nation of origin"–based identification started to take hold for Indian Americans in the last few years. The Association of Indians in America was formed in 1967 and lobbied for a category for Indian Americans on the 1980 census form. The Indian American Forum for Political Education was founded in the mid-1980s and worked closely with some members of Congress, particularly Frank Pallone (D-NJ), to form the India Caucus in the U.S. House of Representatives in 1994 (J. Kirk 2008, 289; Kurien 2007).

In 2002 Sanjay Puri founded the U.S. India Political Action Committee (USINPAC) as a vehicle to promote more effectively the interests of the 2.6 million Americans of Indian decent. Its rise to a position of prominence, aided by some parallel lobbying by the U.S.-India Business Council and others, rivaled the speedy rise of AIPAC and CANF (Banerjee 2007; Kamdar 2007; J. Kirk 2008; Kurien 2007). On the goals of USINPAC, Puri said, "What the Jewish community has achieved politically is tremendous, and members of Congress definitely pay a lot of attention to issues that are important to them. We will use our own model to get to where we want, but we have used them as a benchmark" (quoted in Banerjee 2007). USINPAC has been widely credited with playing a major role in securing the 2006 United States–India Peaceful Atomic Cooperation Act, which permits India to buy nuclear fuel, reactors, and other technology to expand its civilian nuclear program (Banerjee 2007; J. Kirk 2008).

Groups beyond USINPAC have also been engaging in a wide range of lobbying activities. Indian trade and business groups have shown a keen interest in the U.S. concern about "outsourcing," for example. The National Association of Software and Service Companies lobbies on behalf of the Indian outsourcing industry in Washington, D.C., and "hired as its chief Washington lobbyist Robert D. Blackwill, a former senior White House adviser who served as the ambassador to India for the George W. Bush administration. As the president of Barbour Griffith & Rogers International, an arm of one of the most powerful lobby shops in Washington, he is a heavy hitter on Capitol Hill" (Giridharadas 2007; see also Kamdar 2007). During the Democratic presidential primary, the Barack Obama (D-IL) campaign tried to make an issue out of Senator Hillary Clinton's (D-NY) support for outsourcing through an "off-the-record" memo that identified Clinton as "(D-Punjab)" and that tried to suggest Clinton profited both personally and politically from the Indian outsourcing industry (Zeleny 2007; "Hillary Clinton" 2007). As the furor in the Indian American community began to rise, Obama quickly and angrily distanced himself from the memo, calling it "a dumb mistake" and "caustic" (Alfano 2007; Kamdar 2007; Prashad 2007).

While the prominence of India and Indian Americans has been rising quickly in the United States (Sewell 2009), some have noted that the Obama administration sees India from a different perspective than did the Bush administration, which concerns Indian American lobby groups. The Bush administration tended to see India as a balance against China; the Obama team tends to see India more in regional terms, relating not just to China but also to Pakistan and Afghanistan (Tharoor 2009). This was perhaps made more apparent when Obama delayed a bit before speaking with Indian prime minister Singh following Obama's 2008 election victory (Wax 2008). Sensing this movement, the Indian government mobilized to make sure that Richard Holbrooke's portfolio did not include "India" in the title. Holbrooke's title is "special representative for Afghanistan and Pakistan." "The evidence that India was able to successfully lobby the Obama transition in the weeks before it took office to ensure Holbrooke's mission left them and Kashmir out is testament to both the sensitivity of the issue to India as well as the prowess and sophistication of its Washington political and lobbying operation" (Rozen 2009a; see also Wax 2009).

Singh would later come to the White House in November 2009 for a meeting that included a large and lavish state dinner. Skepticism about the Obama administration's views of India as a major power, and of the outsourcing of American jobs, continues, while Indian Americans and groups that lobby on their behalf and on behalf of India are clearly rising in strength and prominence. Clearly aware of this, the Obama transition team and administration have worked hard at outreach to Indian Americans. Many prominent Indian Americans served on the transition and in the administration, including famous actor Kal Penn, who was appointed to a position in the Office of Public Engagement to help connect the administration to Indian Americans, Asian Americans, and Pacific Islanders, as well as arts groups (Associated Press 2009a). Likewise, Anish Goel was appointed to the position of senior director for South Asia at the National Security Council (Rozen 2010).

Cuban Americans

The rise in power and prominence of the Cuban American community as a lobbying force during the 1980s has been well documented, and its continuing clout seems to be taken as a given in the field and in Washington, D.C., journalism (see, e.g., Erikson 2008; Haney and Vanderbush 1999, 2005; Kaplowitz 1998; Kiger 1997; Morley and McGillion 2002; Schoultz 2009; Torres 2001). A string of legislative successes in the 1980s, and a very close relationship with the Reagan administration, set up the Cuban American National Foundation (CANF) and its charismatic leader, Jorge Mas Canosa, as a key voice—if not *the* key voice—on policy toward Cuba. It is sometimes less well understood that the success of CANF also helped contribute to its relative weakening through the 1990s and into today. (Mas's death in 1997 also was a blow to CANF's power).

CANF and the Cuban American community in Florida worked hard to elect a Cuban American to the U.S. House of Representatives, with Republican Ileana Ros-Lehtinen winning a 1989 special election in Miami to fill the seat vacated by Claude Pepper's death. Her campaign manager was Jeb Bush, who would later serve as Florida's governor and of course is the brother of President George W. Bush. Ros-Lehtinen would be joined in the House by other Cuban Americans: Florida Republicans (and brothers) Lincoln and Mario Diaz-Balart (elected in 1992 and 2002, respectively) and New Jersey Democrat Robert Menendez (elected in 1992). Menendez would later be elected to the U.S. Senate, and Cuban American Albio Sires (D) now represents Menendez's old district. Mel Martinez (R-FL) was elected to the U.S. Senate in 2004, having served in the Bush administration as the secretary of housing and urban development (HUD). Martinez retired in 2009.

The Cuban Americans in Congress became key leaders on Cuba policy as it ran through the Hill. While enjoying a close relationship with CANF and mostly working together across party lines on issues with respect to Cuba, these representatives and senators became more important to Cuba policy than CANF. This should come as no surprise given their proximity to power, but it is interesting that CANF's power would wane at least in part because of one of its great successes: the election of Cuban Americans to Congress. It is also worth noting, by way of background, that the Helms-Burton Act of 1996 (officially the Cuban Liberty and Democratic Solidarity Act) established the legislative backbone of the long-standing U.S. embargo of Cuba. This had two major effects. First, it tightened the embargo in a variety of ways. Second, and perhaps more importantly, it codified the embargo—which had previously existed as a series of executive orders—into law. This was a very significant step: now the embargo is a legislative status quo, and the status quo is very difficult to defeat in a legislative setting (or any setting, for that matter). For an interest group like CANF and for the Cuban American members of Congress and their many allies on the Hill, defending the status quo is a less formidable task than that facing a group who would like to ease or end the embargo.

George W. Bush was inaugurated the 43rd president of the United States in January 2001 following a very tight and contested election that drew the eyes of the nation to the state of Florida and its recount. The Cuban American community was a key asset to the Bush team in Florida, both in the election and in the recount. Gore won less than 20 percent of the Cuban American vote in Florida, well below the 35 percent that the Clinton-Gore ticket pulled in 1996. The Elián González affair, as well as candidate Bush's promises to enforce fully the embargo and Helms-Burton, turned the community strongly toward him (Schneider 2001).

Once in office, President Bush nominated a favorite of the Cuban American hard-line anti-Castro community, Otto Reich, to the top position on the Americas at the State Department. Bush also nominated Florida's Mel Martinez to head HUD. Clearly, "Bush was rewarding Florida's Cuban American community for helping him win the presidency" (de la Garza 2002). Although Reich's nomination was blocked in the Senate, he ultimately received a "recess appointment." Surprising many, given the close ties between the administration and the pro-embargo lobby, the Bush administration's first term went by with very little change to Clinton's Cuba policy. Most notably, Bush continued to waive the enforcement of a central component of the Helms-Burton law, the "right to sue," which would allow U.S. nationals to sue foreign corporations who do business in Cuba using property seized after the revolution. On the eve of the 2004 elections though, with many in the Cuban American community increasingly frustrated with the Bush approach to Cuba, and with Senator John Kerry (D-MA) making a play for the new generation of Cuban Americans who are less wedded to the embargo (but also less likely to vote, given their relative youth), Bush announced a new set of rules that would govern family travel and remittances to the island (see Lizza 2004). The new rules were far stricter, cutting the amount of money that could be sent to family in Cuba, cutting the number of times that family could visit Cuba from once per year to once every three years, and using a far more limited definition of "family" to exclude aunts, uncles, and cousins (people not part of the "nuclear family"). While these rules upset many in the community, the Bush gamble was that these tighter embargo restrictions would please the older and most hard-line Cuban Americans, who are also the most likely to vote (Nielsen 2004).

In crafting this new policy, members of the Bush administration consulted with several pro-embargo exile groups in Miami, including Junata Patriótica, Unidad Cubana, and the Cuban Liberty Council, as well as with Florida governor Jeb Bush. Interestingly, when asked about the power of the Cuban American National Foundation, which was opposed to these sanctions, a former Bush White House official told reporter Kirk Nielsen, "The Foundation, to my knowledge, has zip influence with this administration. . . . This is an organization that has zero access, zero influence in this administration" (Nielsen 2004). How times had changed for CANF! Kerry did better among Cuban Americans than Gore had done in 2000, probably closer to how Clinton performed in 1996, but still lost Florida and the election.

The evolution of the Cuban American community would gain speed as the 2008 election neared. Groups that push for a tight embargo of Cuba certainly still existed and were even joined by a new player. The U.S.-Cuba Democracy PAC was formed in 2003 in order to push for a democratic transition in Cuba aided by a strict U.S. embargo. This political action committee gives money to candidates who favor the embargo and who are opposed to looser restrictions, and it has already had some real successes (Clark 2009; Rubenzer 2008a; Swanson 2007). According to OpenSecrets.org (2010), the PAC contributed more than $500,000 to candidates in the 2006 election cycle and more than $750,000 in the 2008 election cycle. But the real energy seems to be on the other side.

As the two major parties' candidates for the presidency in 2008 approached Florida and the question of the embargo, they found quickly shifting terrain in the Sunshine State. While Senator John McCain (R-AZ) was an old favorite of the pro-embargo right, CANF interestingly gave a warm welcome to Barack Obama and his message of keeping the embargo but lifting the Bush restrictions on family travel and remittances. His willingness to meet with foreign leaders the United States might despise was less of an issue among Cuban Americans than it would have been even just a few years previously, as the community had become increasingly more open to dialog with the Cuban government (Rieff

2008). Generational change had come to south Florida. The Obama campaign tried to reach out to the new generation of Cuban Americans in a variety of ways, including through a Web site.[2] As an example of how the community's views of the embargo were changing, in 2005 the *Miami Herald* released a survey that found 62 percent of Cuban Americans wanted the embargo; just a year later, a poll by Bendixen and Associates found that number had shrunk to 53 percent. Cuban Americans were also quickly becoming more open to increased travel and remittances to the island, with younger Cuban Americans and those who had come to the Unted States more recently being the most open to these changes. A Florida International University poll in 2007 found that 64 percent of Cuban Americans wanted to return to the pre-2004 rules and a majority thought *all* Americans should be able to travel to Cuba (Cave 2008). Obama's efforts to reach out to this changing community appear to have paid dividends. He won the election, of course, and he also won Florida and, according to one exit poll, 47 percent of the Cuban American vote (Cave 2009).

Having won Florida while calling for some loosening of the embargo makes the setting for Obama quite different than for other presidents, including Bill Clinton, who won Florida in part by currying favor with embargo hardliners. Obama doesn't "owe" the embargo; quite the opposite, he's likely to want to continue to develop links to the more moderate middle and left of the Cuban American community as well as consider Cuba policy within a broader framework. Obama's key Latin America appointments are not particularly linked to Cuba. Arturo Valenzuela heads the bureau at the State Department responsible for the Western Hemisphere. Valenzuela was previously on the faculty at Georgetown and before that served at the National Security Council (NSC) under Bill Clinton. Dan Restrepo heads Latin America at the NSC staff; he had worked at a think tank started by Clinton's former chief of staff John Podesta, the Center for American Progress, and was a staffer for former representative Lee Hamilton (D-IN).

Obama didn't wait long before reaching out to the Cuban Americans who had supported him by dropping the Bush-era restrictions on family travel and remittances to Cuba (Cuba Study Group 2008). Not much else has changed, however. Bills that would end a "travel ban" for the rest of Americans seem stalled in Congress, and the impending retirements of Senators Byron Dorgan (D-ND) and Christopher Dodd (D-CT) mean that two of the embargo's fiercest opponents are about to leave Congress. Trade and business groups have become increasingly activated on the side of loosening the embargo over the last ten years, but Cuba is just one of many issues that concern these lobbies (Rubenzer 2008a). The arrest of a U.S. contractor working in Cuba to help spread "civil society" one cell phone at a time has also cast a chill on relations. It seems likely that President Obama will wait for Cuban leader Raúl Castro to take the next step before making more gestures toward a more normal relationship. The

U.S.-Cuba Democracy PAC is again contributing large sums of money to keep the embargo intact in the 2010 election cycle, when significant Democratic losses in the U.S. House of Representatives are predicted. Nevertheless, a Bendixen poll released in April 2009 found that 67 percent of Cuban Americans want to end *all* restrictions on travel to Cuba, up from only 41 percent in 2003. Only 42 percent want to see the embargo continue, down from 61 percent in 2003 (Cave 2009). The domestic context for loosening the embargo has never been more favorable and will likely continue to move in that direction; expect the Obama administration to continue to try to cultivate this part of the community and to reach out to groups who represent this interest. Since the ultimate question of the embargo is now codified as law, the ultimate target of this lobbying is Congress, which may be more resistant to change than the White House.

Arab Americans

The combination of the Bush administration's perceived tilt toward the political right in Israel, the lack of significant administration involvement in the peace process over time, and backlash against many Arab Americans following the attacks of September 11, 2001, left Arab Americans positively disposed to the candidacy of Barack Obama. Arab Americans, about 75 percent of whom are Christian, had tended to vote more Republican until after 9/11; as the Bush administration wore on, they started voting more and more for Democrats (Sullivan 2008). They supported Obama over Hillary Clinton in the primary season and heavily supported Obama over McCain. The Obama campaign included an outreach effort through the organization and website Arab Americans for Obama (http://my.barackobama.com/page/content/aahome). The first outreach coordinator, Chicago lawyer Mazen Asbahi, resigned amidst some controversy (Simpson and Chozick 2008); the group was then headed by Michigan state representative, and Lebanese American, Rashida Tlaib (AlHajal 2008).

During the transition before Obama was inaugurated, however, the Obama team hit a bit of a bump in the road when it delayed comment on the Gaza crisis (Holland 2009a). While Obama said he was sticking to the principal that there is only one U.S. president at a time, he was nonetheless criticized for his silence, both by those who saw it as a slight against Israel and those who saw it as a slight against the Palestinians. Once in office, though, Obama quickly began to address the peace process as a top priority of the administration, and he initiated a new effort to reach out to Arabs and Muslims around the world. His inaugural address, as discussed above, made an effort at outreach. Obama named former U.S. Senate majority leader George Mitchell (D-ME) as his special envoy to the Middle East. Because Mitchell is a Lebanese American (Mitchell's mother came to the United States from Lebanon), this appointment was seen by many as a sign that Obama would have a more even-handed approach to the region than did the Bush administration. Obama's first television interview was given to al-Arabiya, a 24-hour satellite network based in Dubai (*New York Times* Editorial Board 2009). And Obama's Cairo speech, titled "A New Beginning," was an effort to reach out and rebrand U.S. foreign policy in the Muslim world.

Such signals are best understood as directed not just to Arabs and Muslims abroad but to audiences at home as well, especially in light of Slaughter's 2009 essay in *Foreign Affairs* magazine about "leverage" in a networked world. The White House Office of Public Engagement hosted Arab American leaders from a variety of organizations for a two-hour briefing on a range of issues in July 2009, the second such briefing in the first six months of the administration. National security adviser Gen. James Jones and the Office of Public Engagement's Tina Tchen also spoke at the Arab American Institute's (AAI) fall 2009 Leadership Summit. Beyond highlighting what a two-way street ethnic lobbying now is, this effort at outreach was interesting for another reason. The session where Tchen spoke, a session on a "Pro Peace Agenda," also included AAI founder and president James Zogby and Jeremy Ben-Ami, the executive director of a relatively new (2008) "Jewish" lobby focused on a two-state solution in the Middle East called J Street. While progress toward the two-state solution stalled in the winter of 2010, the Obama administration continued to reach out to Arab Americans.

Jewish Americans

It's hard to talk about Arab American lobbying without also talking about Jewish American lobbying (see Marrar 2009). Jewish American lobbying has long been thought of as the near exclusive domain of the powerful lobby group AIPAC. However, the views of Jewish Americans (and Americans generally) toward the peace process and a two-state solution evolved enough in recent years that an opening arose for a different type of policy, and different type of outreach, by the Obama campaign and then transition team. The Obama campaign sponsored a dozen Jewish outreach committees in major cities and represented a real opportunity for a "new leadership to emerge" (Avishai 2008). Seeking to capitalize on "Jewish Americans for Obama" (http://my.barack obama.com/page/content/jahome), the Obama transition team met with a far wider variety of Jewish groups than those consulted by the Bush administration (Kampeas 2008). While many of these groups would try to pressure Congress on a variety of issues, including the crisis in Gaza and a two-state solution, they were also the targets of lobbying by the new Obama administration, which was trying to leverage new networks of Jewish Americans and to distance itself from groups that previously enjoyed easy access to the Bush administration, such as AIPAC.

During the transition, Jewish American groups such as AIPAC, J Street, and the Israel Policy Forum (IPF) began jockeying for position (Jaben-Eilon 2009). The Obama transition team met in December 2009 with more than two dozen American Jewish organizations representing a broad range of perspectives on the Israeli-Palestinian conflict (Jaben-Eilon 2009). Many of these groups had enjoyed little or no access to the Bush administration. The IPF "didn't set foot in the White House during the Bush Administration," for example, says its policy director M. J. Rosenberg (quoted in Jaben-Eilon 2009). The IPF was founded in 1993 following the Oslo Accords and was meant to try to balance the power of AIPAC. The Obama administration clearly sought to create space for peace-oriented groups like J Street, Brit Tzedek v'Shalom, Americans for Peace Now, and the IPF (in other words, for groups other than AIPAC).

Obama's foreign policy appointments seemed to have a little bit for everyone—which is itself a statement, since the Bush team was more closely aligned with the Jewish and Jewish American right. Dan Shapiro, who had worked on Israel-related issues for the Obama campaign and was one of the key players in the outreach effort as well as the policy effort, was appointed to the National Security Council staff on Middle East issues. Puneet Talwar, who had worked as a staffer to then Senator Biden (D-DE) and the Senate Foreign Relations Committee, joined Shapiro at the NSC staff. Talwar "has a reputation for keeping AIPAC happy" but has also worked to open up some policy space for the Obama administration (Kampeas 2009). Hillary Clinton's appointment as secretary of state brought into the center of the administration one of Israel's closest friends in the Senate and also one of the early voices for Palestinian statehood. Eric Lynn, who had worked with Shapiro on Jewish outreach for the campaign, headed to the State Department. Susan Rice, the new U.S. ambassador to the United Nations, tends to be a strong supporter of Israel. The administration also, however, includes Samantha Power (who left the Obama campaign after calling Hillary Clinton a "monster" in what she thought was an off-the-record conversation), who had been a sometimes target of pro-Israel activists because of her position that Israel's operation in Jenin included war crimes. And as I mentioned above, the appointment of George Mitchell as special envoy for the Middle East suggested the Obama administration was keenly interested in moving the process forward but also sent a signal that the administration would be more evenhanded in its approach than many saw the Bush administration as being. One appointment that didn't go through was the nomination of Charles W. Freeman to chair the National Intelligence Council, the group that oversees the production of reports from America's intelligence community. Freeman, a former U.S. ambassador to Saudi Arabia, fell victim, in his eyes at least, to heavy disapproval from pro-Israel groups and lobbyists because of statements he had made that were critical of Israel (Pincus 2009b).

J Street, and many other groups (including the Obama administration), have tried to capitalize on surveys that showed the opinions of American Jews were far more balanced toward the Middle East than those of the interest groups catered to by the Bush administration, for example. A July 2009 survey "found that American Jews opposed further Israeli settlements (by 60 percent to 40 percent), that they overwhelmingly supported the proposition that the U.S. should be actively engaged in the peace process even if that entailed 'publicly stating its disagreements with both the Israelis and the Arabs'" (Traub 2009). In July 2009, President Obama hosted a meeting at the White House of a range of Jewish American groups, including J Street and Americans for Peace Now. This was a new level of executive attention, for it was the first time J Street had met with an American president; "Numerous meetings at the White House, first meeting with the President," said J Street's director Jeremy Ben-Ami (Rozen 2009b). It is worth noting that not only are U.S. pro-Palestinian groups more welcome at the table in the Obama administration, but their efforts to reach out to American Jewish groups to work together for a two-state solution have also increased (Guttman 2009).

J Street came to a new level of public prominence in the fall of 2009 when it hosted a major conference that hosted dozens of members of Congress, politicians from both Israel and the United States, and a keynote address by National Security Adviser Jim Jones. Notably absent from the meeting was Israel's ambassador to the United States, Michael Oren, who refused to attend the conference because views would be aired there to which the Netanyahu government was opposed. Obama's efforts to engage with a wide range of groups, "including faith based and community groups [to] sustain support for his policies" (Rozen 2009b), are clearly an example of the effort at renewal. As Jon B. Alterman, director of the Middle East program at the Center for Strategic and International Studies argued, "I don't see this as the Obama administration choosing one approach or the other; I see the Obama administration as engaging broadly. There's a broad effort to speak to diverse audiences about the president's level of engagement and his desire to move this process forward" (quoted in Eggen 2009; see also Traub 2009).

Despite Obama's hope to move the peace process forward in the Middle East, progress was very slow to start. A memo from the Fatah Party in October 2009 laid the blame for this at the foot of pro-Israel pressure groups in the United States: "All hopes placed in the new U.S. administration and President Obama have evaporated." It went on to note that Obama "couldn't withstand the pressure of the Zionist lobby, which led to a retreat from his previous positions on halting settlement construction and defining an agenda for the negotiations and peace" (Teibel 2009). While this critique fails to take into account the possibility that the Obama administration might well want progress that the sovereign state of Israel is unwilling to pursue, it nonetheless underscores the widely shared sense that U.S. policy toward the Middle East is awash in ethnic lobbying, even if all groups are not yet playing on an even field.

The peace process, and difficulties thereof, also underscores how difficult pursuing a renewal agenda can be. The rest of the world does still get a vote, as it were, and in this case the Israeli government has often rebuffed the Obama administration's efforts. A very public dispute over Israeli settlements broke into the public eye in March 2010, when construction began on a settlement in the occupied territories while Vice President Biden was in Israel, even as the administration protested such construction. If the Obama approach has often failed to move Israel, neither has it fundamentally altered the dynamics in the U.S. Congress; as Traub (2009) noted, a broad-ranging debate about the Middle East has not yet broken out on the Hill. Still, I would argue that the Obama administration, in part through its efforts to reach out to groups like J Street, is trying to create political space in that direction.

Conclusion: Ethnic Lobbying and the Obama Administration

These are not the only cases of ethnic lobbying, of course. There has been some renewed attention to Iranian American lobbying, for example. In April 2008 Babak Hoghooghi became the first executive director of the Public Affairs Alliance of Iranian Americans. The goal of this group is to "enhance the political power of Iranian Americans, improve their image and protect them from discrimination" (Zeller 2008, 1457). Hoghooghi said there are approximately 1 million Iranian Americans and the first job of the Alliance is to bring his community together so that they can carry more weight in American politics. Interestingly, while he recognizes the significance of Iran as a national security issue to the United States, the focus of his group is on domestic issues like immigration and discrimination. Recognizing less consensus exists in the community about U.S. approaches to Iran as a foreign policy problem, Hoghooghi has chosen to focus his group's efforts on tasks that can help unite Iranian Americans. A more established organization is the National Iranian American Council (NIAC), founded in 2002 and headed by Trita Parsi. The NIAC mostly focuses its efforts on education and outreach and on lobbying Congress, though Parsi has deep connections to the Obama administration. He has proposed a new organization that would partner with the NIAC and lobby on behalf of Iranian Americans, but it's unclear if such a new group will emerge or not. Puneet Talwar, who was an aide to then Senator Biden, has taken up a position on the NSC staff deaing with Iraq and Iran; Talwar has previously supported engaging Iran (see Rosen 2009; Rozen 2009c).

I would argue that in the cases I discuss above, we can see significant elements of an effort at "renewal" in the patterns of ethnic lobbying that are evident in the Obama administration. To appreciate fully the Obama strategy of renewal, though, we must also see the administration's efforts at outreach to ethnic communities in the United States along the lines that Slaughter discussed (2009). On Cuba, on India, and in the Middle East, the Obama administration hoped to rejoin the world and rebrand American foreign policy. A crucial part of that effort appears to be using outreach to ethnic lobbies not just to build domestic support for the administration's agenda but also as a way to signal to those communities abroad that the United States seeks a new way forward—that is, to leverage these connections in a networked world. But does the record match the strategy?

The Obama administration moved quickly to alter the rules on family travel and remittances to Cuba, in part as a way to transition to a new relationship with Cuba (if reciprocated) and in part as a way to respond to and cultivate the changing Cuban American community. But progress there has stalled, in part because Congress seems reluctant to move further. Indian American lobbying continues to solidify and intensify, and the administration seems open to such an effort, if slightly less so than the Bush administration. The effort to alter the relationship with Iran seems to have gone nowhere so far. And prospects of a two-state solution in the Middle East appear slim at best, even while the patterns of ethnic lobbying, and administration cultivation thereof, have changed dramatically since Obama came into office and a new set of peace talks have at least begun.

A couple of other dynamics are worth pointing out. First, lobbying by foreign governments seems to be on the rise, complicating the picture and normative implications of "ethnic lobbying" even more (T. Smith 2000). Recently a lawyer, lobbyist, and Democratic Party fundraiser tried to gain permission to lobby on behalf of the outlaw regime in Sudan, for example. This effort ultimately failed, but others have not. As another example, the coup in Honduras has led to a fascinating pattern of lobbying. Honduran president Manuel Zelaya was ousted in June 2009, and since then several Honduran business groups have hired Washington, D.C., lobbyists to help make sure the U.S. government did not force Zelaya's return to power, thus keeping in power a regime more to their liking (Thompson and Nixon 2009). Lobbyists and public relations firms with ties to both parties joined others like Otto Reich, former senior official under G. H. W. Bush, Reagan, and G. W. Bush, and Senator Jim DeMint (R-SC) to pressure the Obama administration to accept a new government in Honduras.

China's lobbying has also increased markedly in recent years. In the past China had only one diplomat in Washington, D.C., who was assigned to congressional affairs; China mostly relied on others, such as the Chamber of Commerce, to lobby on its behalf. Now China has at least ten diplomats assigned to lobbying at its new embassy and has tripled the amount it spends on powerful U.S. lobbying firms (Pomfret 2010). And yet, China still gets outspent on lobbying by Taiwan. Brzezinski recognized the significance of these shifts and argued that gaining necessary domestic political support for foreign policy has become more difficult in part because of the power of ethnic lobbies: "Thanks to their access to Congress, a variety of lobbies—some financially well endowed, some backed by foreign interests—have been promoting, to an unprecedented degree, legislative intervention in foreign policy making" (2010, 28–29). The lobbying arena is now far more complicated than it used to be. And it might be about to get even more complicated. The January 2010 U.S. Supreme Court decision to allow unlimited corporate and union spending in U.S. elections (*Citizens United v. Federal Election Commission*, 558 U.S. 50 [2010]) opens the prospect that foreign-headquartered multinational corporations that operate in the United States might also now be able to spend money in American elections.

Second, it is worth remembering how complicated the arrow of causation can be when it comes to ethnic lobbying. Traditionally, we think of lobbying as an effort to capture policy, so we ask how lobby groups drive policy or fail to do so. But this focus alone misses the arrow running in the other direction—that is, the way that leaders try to cultivate ethnic lobbies for their own purposes (Haney 2010; Haney and Vanderbush 1999; Watanabe 1984). These purposes include gaining information as well as securing political and financial support. Ethnic lobbies clearly target Congress; the Indian American lobbying on behalf of the U.S.-India nuclear agreement is a classic case of this. But members of Congress also cultivate ties to ethnic lobbies. Ethnic groups target the executive branch and lobby the administration, but presidents also cultivate ties to ethnic lobbies. And the Obama approach, which includes active outreach to ethnic interest groups in part as a way to leverage these networks to reach out to the rest of the world, adds another layer of complexity to ethnic lobbying in U.S. foreign policy.

Notes

1. I would like to thank Steven Hook, Khalil Marrar, and James Scott for sharing their very helpful comments and insights and Paula Fleming for her help as well.
2. http://my.barackobama.com/page/group/CubanAmericansforObama.

CHAPTER 6

Renewing U.S. National Security Policy
Something Old, Something New

Peter Dombrowski

THE 2008 ELECTION OF PRESIDENT BARACK OBAMA was viewed by many national security experts as a potential watershed in the history of U.S. security and defense policies. By these accounts, the eight years of the Bush administration were anomalous. President Bush, especially after the terrorist attacks of September 11, 2001, had strayed from traditional U.S. foreign and security norms. The national security team selected by the new president would initiate policies and programs that would restore American legitimacy, credibility, and moral authority in the international arena. In some cases, such as American involvement with torture, the new administration was expected to distance itself quickly from its predecessor. In others, such as arms control and disarmament, it was hoped that the Obama administration would work to revitalize a long-neglected set of bilateral and multilateral initiatives, negotiations, and regimes.

Within defense policy and military circles, however, there was also wariness towards the new president. If Bush administration defense policies had swung too far in a unilateral, overly militarized direction that overstressed the American armed services, Iraq and Afghanistan still needed to be won, and new threats remained just over the horizon. Cuts in defense spending in the service of domestic priorities could undermine hard-fought gains in the war on terror and threaten plans to recapitalize, modernize, and transform the U.S. armed services.

Members of the Obama national security team, and more broadly the entire foreign policy leadership of the new administration, entered office with a relatively long track record. Many had been members of the Clinton administration, and most if not all had been prominent as participants in a virtual "shadow government," proposing alternative views on many national security issues during the Bush years. In general, their reading of the global security

environment focused less on traditional threats and more on the policy consequences of economic interdependence, finite resources, the global commons,
and collective goods. For the most part, they believed that it was simply not
effective to press U.S. national interests on the global community without taking into account the wide range of stakeholders and a broader conception of
U.S. national interest that incorporated transnational concerns. Obama administration appointees appeared to believe that leading stakeholders (as opposed
to clients or even allies) required a broader conception of power, including
"soft" and "smart" as well as "hard" forms. The appointees also reflected an
emphasis on ideas and values in foreign policy but not overly simplistic foci on
democratization, economic growth, or human rights as some critics have
charged of the Bush, Clinton, and Carter presidencies.

Working toward shared ideas and values as drivers of both policies and
actions would allow the United States to deploy a wide mix of policy instruments. Whereas Joint Chiefs of Staff chairman Adm. Michael Mullen warned
against U.S. foreign policy becoming "too militarized" in early 2008 (Pincus
2009a), the Obama administration's natural inclination was to include other
policy instruments, including economic statecraft. Moreover, given the
Obama administration's necessary focus on recovering from the rolling financial crisis affecting the U.S. as well as the global economy, "intermestic"
issues—"the domestic, intergovernmental and transnational politics of foreign policy" (Pollard 2004, 2) would be important.

The United States would now meld domestic economic development with
transnational goals, particularly in the fields of energy, transportation, and the
environment. Under these conditions, Congress would have to play a more
central role in foreign, international, and national security issues. Moreover, in
contrast to the Bush years, the Obama administration was ready if not eager to
share the burdens of global leadership with other countries by relying on multilateral institutions and the long-standing body of international law.

Further, despite election-time and partisan talk of a national security sea
change, it is important to remember that U.S. policies are often marked by
continuity following electoral change. For example, along several crucial dimensions, President George W. Bush's security policies were not all that different
from those of President Bill Clinton. On issues like preemption, the Bush
White House simply more forcefully and more publicly articulated a position
that the Clinton administration had edged toward over the course of its eight
years in office (Daniel, Dombrowski, and Payne 2005). With attacks on al-
Qaeda camps in Afghanistan and an alleged pharmaceutical plant in the Sudan
in 1998, the United States conducted preemptive strikes on the premise of self-
defense, even though it did not announce a change in strategy. Only with the
2002 National Security Strategy did Bush publicly acknowledge what had been
clear to insiders for some years: "We will not hesitate to act alone, if necessary,

to exercise our right of self-defense by acting preemptively against such terrorists, to prevent them from doing harm against our people and our country" (*National Security Strategy* 2002, III). Bush looks even less revolutionary when compared to initiatives begun but never formally adopted by his father, President George H. W. Bush. Under the direction of then Secretary of Defense Richard Cheney, I. Lewis "Scooter" Libby, and Zalmay Khalizad, among others, G. H. W. Bush proposed a draft 1992 Defense Planning Guidance (DPG) that espoused a primacist vision of the "new world order" only to have it squashed by the moderate wing of the Republican security establishment. Libby, presumably echoing the thoughts of Cheney, was not content with preventing challengers to American leadership from arising, as stated in the draft 1992 DPG, but wanted to build up U.S. military strength to the point where no challenge was feasible (Mann 2004, 209–15).

Whether the election of Barack Obama to the presidency marked a clean break from the practices of the preceding three presidents remains to be seen. Early assessments by many Democratic and centrist national security experts suggest that President's Obama's foreign and security policies have not deviated sufficiently from those of his predecessor. On the other hand, former members of the Bush national security team and some Republican candidates for Congress during the midterm election cycle have evaluated President Obama in view of how his policies have undone the work of the Bush administration, thus in their view endangering the country.

The easy debater's point to make when partisans of all stripes attack is that perhaps the president is doing something right. But a consensus exists among center-left and even center-right national security specialists that the past eight years, if not more, did not and do not represent a viable, sustainable approach to U.S. national security. The failures of the nearly twenty years since the end of the Cold War—the inability to create a durable international order, the rise of global terrorism, and festering instability in the greater Middle East—remain glaring and troubling. Partisan judgments aside, little in the first two years of the Obama administration suggests that the forty-fourth president will make more progress toward implementing a workable strategic vision than the last three. At best, it appears President Obama's first term might be viewed as a defensive or holding action: combat operations have ended in Iraq as promised, a new approach to Afghanistan—tellingly denoted AFPAK—will have been given time to succeed, and, with luck, the global economic crisis will prove not to be a "double-dip" recession.

The 2008 global economic crisis also suggests that long-standing concerns over America's decline may finally be true. Whether decline is a function of the classic argument of imperial or strategic overstretch (Cordesman 2007; Kennedy 1987), what Fareed Zakaria (2008) saw as "the rise of the rest," or of Haass's (2008) emergence of a "non-polar" system, many political analysts have jumped on the declinist bandwagon. Declinists, however, may be somewhat overeager to push their agenda, although few scholars appear ready to join Henry Nau's "myth" judgment during the last scholarly wave of declinism (Nau 1990). Even if decline is too strong a diagnosis, the strategic failures and policy debacles of the post–Cold War period may finally be catching up to the United States. It remains to be seen whether the United States will continue as the world's "indispensible nation," as Secretary of State Madeleine Albright proclaimed during the Clinton years, or whether it will sink gradually back into the ranks with other great powers.

The task for the second half of Obama's first term, a potential second term, and the terms of his successors is to renew or rebuild U.S. national security with a mix of those policies that have worked during the past two decades with new foundations more suitable to what Thomas Friedman (2006) awkwardly called the "post–post–Cold War era." Struggles to win in Iraq and Afghanistan and the growing geostrategic strength of China and even India, not to mention the long-term implications of the 2008 financial crisis, have put a premium on developing sustainable policies in an international security environment that, to many observers, appears inhospitable to American national interests today. The challenges posed by terrorism; weapons proliferation; climate change; pressures on the global commons including the seas, space, and, according to some, the cyberdomain; and shifting patterns of economic growth will remain for the foreseeable future. Only by forging a domestic consensus on the appropriate role for the United States within the global security environment and by crafting a national security strategy that combines a clear focus on U.S. interests with a recognition of the appropriate interests and roles of other countries, nonstate actors, and multilateral institutions will the United States, and thereby the global community, be able to meet these challenges.

Succeeding at this task will be difficult, not simply because of the inherent complexity of responding to diverse national security challenges in a resource-constrained environment but because the nation's Department of Defense and associated organizations are not well structured. As a study by the Center for Strategic and International Studies entitled *Beyond Goldwater-Nichols: Defense Reform for a New Strategic Era* argued:

> The Defense Department and the many organizations that comprise the national security bureaucracy are still configured primarily for Cold War era operations rather than for some of the growing threats to our national security coming from transnational terrorist groups and others. Preparing for these urgent challenges will require institutional innovations, the creation of new capabilities, and greater coordination throughout the government.
>
> Outdated organizational structures also remain a problem. . . . Duplicative procedures and often overly large headquarter staffs have created

a wasteful bureaucracy that is bogged down in protracted coordination processes. In the Executive branch, this has led to too little strategic thinking. (Murdock et al. 2004, 19)

Legacies of the Bush Doctrine

As Bush prepared to leave office in 2008, the acute sense of crisis that had affected the U.S. national security community began to wane. The high levels of violence in Iraq had subsided due to the "surge" and a temporary accommodation of the various political actors in Iraq to coping with the ongoing civil war (S. Simon 2008). This allowed the Bush administration to negotiate a Status of Forces Agreement (SOFA) with the Iraqi government and contemplate the eventual drawdown of American combat troops in Iraq. With Iraq apparently on the right track, the Bush administration turned its attention to the growing instability in Afghanistan, where a resurgent Taliban was reducing the Afghan government to a rump state in charge of little besides Kabul and marginalizing U.S. and NATO forces. Meanwhile, efforts to attack the Pakistan Taliban and remnants of al-Qaeda in safe havens across the border in Pakistan failed to have the desired effect on the overall war effort while further destabilizing a Pakistan government torn between a growing insurgency and worsening relations with its main geopolitical rival, India.

The brightening international security environment in 2008 cannot be claimed credibly as the direct result of the Bush administration's security doctrine. At best, the results can be laid to a reversal or at least de-emphasis of several of the most controversial security policies asserted by the Bush administration both before and, especially, after the 9/11 attacks. Bush and some of his advisers had fought to delay the surge in Iraq long after it had become clear to senior military leaders that such a step was necessary to foreclose an even longer and bloodier stalemate (Woodward 2008). Afghanistan had meanwhile languished as a secondary theater in the so-called war on terror as Iraq consumed the attention of U.S. policy makers and the bulk of scarce military and intelligence assets following the initial Iraq invasion. This ended when the death toll among the multinational force, civilian casualties, and rising societal chaos forced the United States and its partners to rethink the situation. As for how long the relative improvements in Iraq could be expected to last? Observers like journalist Tom Ricks have pointed to internal conflicts in Iraq that are likely to flare up as the United States reduces the number of combat forces.

Finally, a host of issues that had been left outside the Bush foreign and security policy agendas lurk just over the planning horizon. A growing body of evidence and a solidifying consensus among climate scientists suggest that global warming is real and that its implications threaten the United States and, indeed, all countries across the globe in ways that we are only just beginning to understand (K. M. Campbell 2008). Another issue, the need for arms control and potential disarmament of nuclear weapons, which had languished in the Bush White House, requires U.S. attention, in part because proliferators, including Pakistan, North Korea, and, possibly, Iran, have acquired or are on the verge of acquiring usable nuclear weapons.

Bush embraced a view of U.S. power based on the premise that the United States, as an "exceptional" world power (Spiro 2000), has a special responsibility to act to maintain peace and preserve a stable international order. It must do so even if other nations are unable and unwilling to join in America's actions. In effect, the United States reserves for itself the role of judge, jury, and executioner in the world. During the Bush presidency, the United States favored unilateral action even when it needed international cooperation to accomplish its ends. It preferred informal "coalitions of the willing" rather than more formal alliances such as the North Atlantic Treaty Organization. The Bush Doctrine justified preemptive strikes not only against terrorists but against states that sponsored or harbored terrorist groups. Not only did this expand the scope of U.S. power, it ultimately shaped international norms regarding the use of preemptive force.

By the last years of the Bush administration, multilateralism returned to favor, in part out of necessity. Particularly in the areas of proliferation and combating terrorism, unilateral approaches are often untenable. One innovation was the Proliferation Security Initiative, which employed a relatively hands-off approach in order to empower other countries to contribute to the international goal of halting the flow of weapons of mass destruction. The U.S. Navy, Marine Corps, and Coast Guard announced a maritime strategy, entitled *A Cooperative Strategy for 21st Century Seapower*, that called for gradual shifts in force structures and deployments "so that the strategic interests of the participants are continuously considered while mutual understanding and respect are promoted" (U.S. Navy, U.S. Marine Corps, and U.S. Coast Guard 2007, 2).

The Global War on Terror

In the immediate aftermath of the attacks of September 11, 2001, President Bush and his senior advisers quickly moved to launch a "war" against al-Qaeda and others held responsible. The U.S. response to the threat of terrorism both at home and against U.S. interests abroad was couched in the language of "war," with all the symbolic power and baggage the term implies. And, in a very real sense, it opened the door for President Bush to change, explicitly, how the United States would use force as an instrument of policy.

Addressing a Joint Session of Congress ten days after the attacks, President Bush (G. W. Bush 2001) stated that "our war on terror begins with al-Qaeda, but it does not end there. It will not end until every terrorist group of global reach has been found, stopped and defeated." These statements provided the raison d'être for the Bush administration's national security policies over the next seven years. It justified both the Afghan and Iraq wars, not to mention armed campaigns from the Philippines to Colombia. It changed the institutional structure of U.S. national security and the intelligence agencies while reshaping the nation's legal regime and vastly expanding expenditures on protecting America at home and abroad. One way or another, the war on terror shaped the actions of President Obama and those who will follow.

In addition, technological globalization over the previous three decades has enabled the spread of social movements and radical ideas that challenge not only specific American policies and international activities but the fundamental premises of American global leadership: capitalism and democracy. Islamist movements, among others, adopt the enablers of globalization for their own political and ideological purposes. Al-Qaeda, for example, organized its strikes at least in part through the Internet and the cellular communications networks girding the globe. In response, the United States under the Clinton and Bush administrations sought to organize a coalition of like-minded nations to combat radical movements and terrorist cells. Using financial tracking and regulations, cyber-war techniques, surveillance, and all manner of law enforcement, most states accepted the purpose if not the terminology of this "war."

Homeland Security

One of the most obvious legacies of the Bush administration was the creation of a new cabinet-level Department of Homeland Security (DHS). First announced by President Bush in a speech delivered eleven days after the events of September 11, 2001, and given institutional life in a serious of legislative acts and executive orders, the new department was created to remedy perceived shortfalls in the nation's ability to guard against threats to U.S. territory, including both citizens and infrastructure (U.S. Department of Homeland Security 2008). The new organization brought many independent agencies under centralized management, including U.S. Customs and Border Protection, the newly created Transportation Security Administration, the Coast Guard, the Federal Emergency Management Agency, and the Secret Service. By the time Obama took office, DHS included more than 200,000 employees and had a budget of more than $50 billion. By some accounts, the creation of DHS was the largest government reorganization since the National Security Act of 1947.

From the start, DHS has been controversial. Criticisms ranged from the purely political—such as who should take credit or blame for the department's creation—to the organizational: Can such a large and diverse organization fulfill its mission effectively and efficiently? More telling, substantive and conceptual challenges have emerged. As DHS, through its subagencies, expanded immigration and airline security, it became a focal point for debates over the tradeoff between civil liberties and security. As it sought to rationalize and centralize homeland security programs, it also ran afoul of long-standing tensions over federalism. Namely, to what extent could the national government override state and local authorities in the name of national security? Still later, DHS and the Bush administration came under fire because critics claimed that the inadequate national response to Hurricane Katrina could be traced to the implicit downgrading of disaster management and relief in favor of preventing terrorist attacks. Regardless of the controversies over the origins and impact of DHS, the department will in all likelihood remain a permanent feature of the U.S. national security bureaucracy. No president or Congress would want to send the symbolic message that protecting the nation against terror is no longer a priority (see Kettle 2007; Noftsinger, Newbold, and Wheeler 2007).

The Militarization of U.S. Foreign Policy

Spurred by his advisers, Bush frequently sought military solutions to problems that were social, political, or economic in nature (Priest 2004). The Bush administration's own ideological and bureaucratic tendencies further exacerbated the problems with plenty of help from Congress and the other agencies charged with foreign affairs responsibilities. With ongoing wars and dire threats to the American homeland, it became relatively easy to appropriate funds and add missions to the military services. The net result of the militarization of U.S. security policy is that the armed services are increasingly overwhelmed by the variety of tasks they have been assigned. Meanwhile, the resources of civilian units such as the U.S. Agency for International Development (USAID) eroded or were shifted elsewhere to support goals related to U.S. national security. The State Department remains underfunded and undermanned both relative to its responsibilities and to other instruments of power, especially the Pentagon and the intelligence agencies.

Militarization presents a skewed view of American power and interests. American military leaders became wary of foreign and security policies with blurred missions, none more so than Secretary of Defense Robert Gates, who served Bush as well as Obama. Admiral Mullen raised the issue in a February 2009 speech at Princeton University when he argued that "we need a whole-of-government approach" (Mullen 2009). Of course, whether the Joint Chiefs of Staff, the secretary of defense, or other military leaders would accept a reallocation of defense funds to nondefense expenditures such as foreign assistance seems highly unlikely.

Planning the Future of U.S. Security

For many Obama supporters, the long and arduous campaigns against both Senator Hillary Clinton (D-NY) and Senator John McCain (R-AZ) in the

2008 election campaign represented rolling referenda on the Iraq War that revealed and reflected wider dissatisfaction with America's role in the world. Contrary to the claims of the Bush White House, the American public supported international engagement, multilateralism, and even the much-maligned United Nations. Majorities feared the potential impact of global climate change and were willing to support efforts by impoverished countries to engage in "sustainable" development.

It appeared to many experts at least that by voting for Obama, the American public had indicated it wanted change in security policy. With Obama's election, however, painful realities quickly set in. Change would be halting, and the parameters of a new approach to national security would be limited by circumstance. First, the 2008 global financial crisis and its domestic implications occupied much of the time and attention of the new administration. Second, the practical difficulties of disengaging from Iraq or Afghanistan were soon clear. Third, many national security issues ignored or put lower on the national priority list by Bush—including energy dependency and climate change—were not amenable to quick or easy solutions. Most of Obama's proclaimed reforms involved not substantive changes in American policies but re-engagement with an international community. The "renewal" of American leadership, while welcomed in many quarters, was not a magic elixir but rather a necessary catalyst to spur other improvements in the security environment.

By early 2010, as required by statute and tradition, the Obama administration issued the first set of strategic planning documents required of a new administration: the Quadrennial Defense Review (QDR), the Nuclear Posture Review (NPR), and the National Security Strategy (NSS). All three outlined the strategic vision of President Obama, including the principal objectives of his administration, its interpretation of the international security environment, and its sense of the challenges facing the United States in the future.

The QDR addressed three sets of changes facing defense analysts: changes in U.S. national interests, changes in the material and political ability of the United States to pursue these interests, and changes overseas that determine how the United States will pursue its objectives (U.S. Department of Defense 2010b). Since the 2006 QDR, little has changed in terms of U.S. national interests, which are not subject to changes of administration or even the vagaries of global politics. When a new presidential administration assumes office, the new national security leadership adjusts policies and programs, often minimally, and focuses on the means for achieving long-standing national objectives.

The global security environment, however, has changed greatly since the previous QDR was completed by the Bush national security team. The 9/11 terrorist attacks shook the United States to its core and revealed that the American homeland was no longer safe from attack. The response of the United

States to the attacks, including the launching of wars in Afghanistan and Iraq, reshaped the security environment of all nations. At home, however, the United States faced serious problems that, according to the report, threatened its ability to achieve its regional and global security objectives.

As the 2010 QDR asserts, the major national security driver of the Obama administration involved the the global economic crisis, which presents an enormous challenge to national governments worldwide. The crisis, however, does not alter the tectonics of global security structures or power relationships within the system itself. Yes, the crisis potentially weakens the overall resource base from which the U.S. government maintains its world power. The United States, however, remains capable of sustaining its defense spending and global commitments indefinitely. While the economic crisis may make the management of global conflict more difficult and may stress existing failed states, there is little direct evidence to date that the overall level of conflict, internal or external, has increased in recent years. Still, the QDR signaled a number of shifts in U.S. policy, especially with regard to the means for achieving strategic ends. For example, the QDR stressed the importance of global collaboration, capacity building with friends and allies, and ensuring homeland security (U.S. Department of Defense 2010b).

The *Nuclear Posture Review Report,* also unveiled in 2010, took a bold step by stating that the overall purpose of U.S. nuclear forces "is to deter nuclear attack on the United States, our allies, and partners" (U.S. Department of Defense 2010a, vii). Although this may seem obvious, previous strategic documents dating back to the origins of the nuclear age rarely made this simple case because strategists and policy makers in the United States often envisioned other diplomatic, political, and military purposes of nuclear weapons. Previous presidential administrations, for example, refused to rule out the use of "tactical" nuclear weapons in war-fighting scenarios.

Obama's NPR, however, called for increased funding for modernizing of the nuclear weapons complex. This step may help quiet congressional supporters of nuclear weapons while ensuring that the U.S. nuclear industrial base will have the ability to produce new weapons in the uncertain future. However, it also called into question the president's commitment to "nuclear zero" as embodied in his statement in Prague calling for "the peace and security of a world without nuclear weapons" (Obama 2009i). Why would President Obama devote resources to modernizing facilities and human capital while promoting global zero? The answer lies partly in the domestic politics of nuclear weapons policy in the United States: to win political support for new cuts in nuclear stockpiles, the president had to demonstrate real concern for the state of the nuclear arsenal, which some critics in Congress claimed was being neglected.

Finally, the National Security Strategy adopted by the White House was perhaps best known for the delays that preceded its release in the spring of 2010.

High-level officials within the Obama administration were preoccupied with short-term concerns in the first twelve months of the new government. Specifically, much of 2009 was spent crafting a strategy to withdraw from Iraq, prevail in Afghanistan, and cope with the domestic and international ramifications of the 2008 global economic crisis. Obama's focus on domestic issues such as health care reform further distracted him from devising a national security strategy that would implement the sweeping changes he had called for during the presidential campaign.

White House officials tried to characterize the 2010 NSS as a sharp break from its predecessors released by President Bush. Skeptics, however, argued that the report was "Bush lite" in that it diluted but did not disavow Bush-era themes, including unilateralism, military primacy, and the need to wage war against extremists. Certainly, the NSS language was less provocative and more self-aware of how earlier strategies that had stressed military predominance had damaged U.S. legitimacy with allies and adversaries. On the other hand, the NSS, like the QDR, was clearly a wartime document stressing the need to win current conflicts and not weaken the domestic strengths that had fueled the rise of the United States to the status of a global superpower after World War II and the preeminent power after the Cold War. Indeed, the focus of the NSS was on managing the greater complexity of global security in the new era of "asymmetric" warfare, a concern that focused on the means rather than the ends of U.S. security policy.

Key Issues for the Obama Administration

Regardless of official strategy, the future of U.S. national security under Obama is and will be dominated by a number of issues, only some of which made appearances within the three reports discussed above. This section provides an introduction to these issues in part by contrasting future options and challenges with those facing past presidents.

Searching for Answers in Iraq and Afghanistan

Obama entered office with two shooting wars in progress, a heavy burden for any incoming commander in chief. Beyond domestic political considerations, the United States must support these costly operations half a globe away in order to protect its global reputation as the preeminent military power. Even organizing orderly withdrawals is complicated, time consuming, and expensive, that is unless one considers the American evacuation of Saigon in 1974 a viable model.

Although the political debates of the late Bush years and in the 2008 presidential campaign focused on how to "win" the two conflicts, the arguments seem sterile relative to the strategic and security policy issues at stake. Winning in the unambiguous manner understood in the Civil War or the two world wars has become increasingly rare. Now the United States appears to focus on "exit strategies" regardless of whether stated political or military objectives have been achieved. Moreover, unlike the mass demobilizations that followed America's wars prior to the Second World War, the United States will maintain a standing, professional, volunteer military at a relatively high level of combat readiness. Thus, if winning in Iraq and Afghanistan, given the objectives set out by the Bush administration, seems no longer possible, the Obama administration will search for a politically acceptable compromise. In all likelihood, both Obama and his successors will continue to base U.S. troops either in Afghanistan and Iraq themselves or in facilities nearby.

With regard to Iraq, the Obama administration was fortunate in that the Bush administration helped create the conditions that would allow for a reduced military commitment by the United States before the midterm elections in 2010. By suppressing the worst violence during the "surge," negotiating a status of forces agreement, and helping to establish an Iraq government, no matter how vulnerable, the Bush administration set the stage for President Obama to claim he had fulfilled an important campaign promise. Of course, whether the Iraqi government can meet its internal and external security challenges on its own, with greatly reduced support from the United States or other coalition members, is an open question. Even as American combat operations "ended" in August 2010, more than 50,000 American troops remained on the ground, many with combat missions; in addition, high levels of Iraqi-on-Iraqi violence continued, and Iraq's politics remained "deeply dysfunctional" (Pollack 2010). In the long run, Iran remains an external threat and may even be capable of undermining Iraq's sovereignty through its influence on domestic groups within Iraqi society. If the United States no longer "owns" a broken Iraq, to play off Colin Powell's memorable phrase, it continues to rent at a very high price.

On December 1, 2009, Obama outlined his core national security goal in Afghanistan: to "disrupt, dismantle, and defeat" al-Qaeda and Taliban insurgents and to prevent their return to either Afghanistan or Pakistan. To meet this objective, the president committed an additional 30,000 U.S. troops to Afghanistan. Operationally, military leaders sought to target the insurgency, break its momentum, and better secure population centers. In effect, in consultation with his political, diplomatic, and military advisers, Obama decided to replicate the "surge" strategy that had stabilized Iraq (see Reidel 2009). The prospects for this strategy, however, worsened in 2010 as insurgents maintained control of most regions. As dissension among military leaders in June spilled into the news media, Obama was forced to replace Gen. Stanley McChrystal as commander of Afghan troops with Gen. David Petraeus, the architect of the Iraqi surge strategy.

Even as the Obama administration phases down the war in Iraq, conducts a surge in Afghanistan, and seeks to deter terrorist attacks, it has downplayed the "global war on terror" declared by Bush. As noted in the following chapter, Obama favors an approach to counterterrorism that combines military with legal mechanisms, relying more on law enforcement and prosecution of suspected terrorists in civilian courts than his predecessor. Unfortunately, the fundamental issue of protecting the American homeland remains uncertain. In December 2009, the aborted effort of the so-called underwear bomber to blow up an airliner bound for Detroit refocused public attention on this broader conflict and on homeland security. Meanwhile, Obama's campaign promises to shut down Guantánamo and thereby regain international legitimacy and credibility have foundered on legal, bureaucratic, and political realities. In this sense, Bush's global war on terror remains a central part of Obama's national security strategy.

Arms Control and Disarmament

As noted elsewhere, Bush did not make arms control or disarmament a priority. One of his most prominent foreign policy decisions was to abrogate the Anti-Ballistic Missile (ABM) Treaty unilaterally with Russia, the other signatory to the agreement. At the same time, the Bush administration provoked skepticism abroad by working with the nuclear industrial complex, proponents within the military, and Congress to develop a new class of so-called bunker-buster nuclear weapons designed to destroy hardened or buried weapons of mass destruction (WMD) facilities. Bush also supported efforts to maintain "replacement" nuclear warheads in addition to those officially listed as part of the active nuclear arsenal. Each of these positions undermined U.S. credibility on nuclear arms control, disarmament, and nonproliferation within much of the international community.

Obama staked out a strong position on nuclear issues during his first hundred days in office and took numerous concrete steps to initiate arms control talks with Russia. He chose Prague, capital of the Czech Republic, as the venue for making his first major speech on nuclear arms and arms control (Obama 2009i). Obama asserted America's commitment to seek the peace and security of a world without nuclear weapons, and he called for a global summit on nuclear security to be held in 2010. His administration's ongoing negotiations with Russian leaders led to a new agreement announced April 8, 2010. While this agreement lowered the levels of nuclear weapons on both sides, it remains to be seen how far Obama will be able to push toward "nuclear zero." Even ratification of the so-called New START agreement remained uncertain in the fall of 2010, as congressional leaders delayed hearings, much less a vote, in the face of political miscalculations by the treaty's supporters and political posturing by arms control critics (Rademaker 2010).

Defense Budgets under Fiscal Austerity

Defense analysts, including those working for the Pentagon, widely believed that Obama's election would eventually lead to reduced defense spending. In truth, even with the spending increases since 9/11, U.S. defense spending is nowhere near its historic highs as a percentage of U.S. economic output. As Benjamin Fordham (2007, 396) concluded, "there are many reasons for questioning contemporary U.S. national security policies, but the fiscal and economic consequences of military spending are not among them." From a political or electoral perspective, this judgment may be less relevant in the wake of the global financial crisis and subsequent expenditures by Washington to prop up the ailing financial services industry and cushion the effects of the recession on the American public.

Obama's first defense budget contained little surprising or new. As one respected budget analyst argued, "the Fiscal Year 2011 defense budget request does not signal a significant change in direction for the defense program" (Harrison 2010). Deeper reductions in defense spending may be in the works, especially as federal deficits balloon and the American public becomes more concerned for the economic future. To date, under Obama major defense programs such as the Future Combat Systems and the Air Force's F-22 fighter program have borne the brunt of cancellations, thus allowing the administration to pay for continued expenses in Iraq and Afghanistan. Otherwise, the defense budget of more than $700 billion is not significantly different than that adopted during the Bush years.

Another factor militating against large decreases in defense spending is the need for modernization of U.S. forces in the wake of the two wars. Even if the Obama administration manages to extricate more troops from Iraq and wind down the Afghanistan conflict, the U.S. military will feel the aftershocks of the wars far into the future (Duffield and Dombrowski 2009). Wars chew up people and machines. Weapons and other military equipment have degraded rapidly in the harsh terrain of both countries and must be replaced. Although the U.S. Army and U.S. Marines have done a remarkable job of replacing equipment while fighting the war, most experts expect a wave of repairs and replacements for everything from helicopters to Humvees.

Indeed, even modest steps to rein in defense spending under the Obama administration have met with bipartisan complaints from members of Congress and political commentators. As though following the famous political axiom that "only Nixon could go to China," President Obama had Bush administration holdover and longtime Republican secretary of defense Robert Gates to make the case in late summer 2010 for defense spending cuts in the face of widening federal budget deficits. Beginning with several high-profile program cuts, including, for example, ending F-22 fighter production and scaling back the Army's Future Combat Systems, and continuing with a modest slowdown in the growth of spending rather than actual cuts, Secretary Gates fought all comers—members of Congress protecting districts and jobs, lobbyists promoting companies and programs, and, not least, the military services hoping to save their own total budget authority ("War Within" 2010). Obama may yet tame the post-9/11 growth in military spending, but a return to the "hollow force" period of the 1970s or the "peace dividend" years of the early 1990s is unlikely.

Confronting the Rise of China

Two-plus decades into the most recent re-emergence of China on the world stage, the United States does not have a coherent policy for adjusting its regional and global strategies to accommodate a new great power. American policies toward the People's Republic of China (PRC) are deeply conflicted. On the economic side, U.S. policy makers are pleased to encourage the import of cheap Chinese goods into the United States and the massive flow of private investment that moves in both directions. American defense analysts, however, are deeply concerned about China's rise. What they see is a country determined to acquire military and political power commensurate with its economic weight. As a consequence, officials have watched with alarm as Beijing has undertaken both conventional and nuclear modernization programs. More worrying still is the aggressive posture that Chinese forces have taken in the region and increasingly farther afield, as in the planned deployments of peacekeepers on the African continent.

The Obama administration will have limited room to maneuver in its relations with the PRC, which is projected to have a larger economy than the United States by midcentury. Further, due to China's conventional and nuclear modernization programs of the past decade, by even cautious estimates the regional balance will have tipped against the United States. China may even see itself, and be viewed by others, as part of a bipolar balance of world power. The open question is how the United States chooses to respond to this development, especially since it is clear that it cannot stop or even greatly slow China's rise without damaging its own economic well-being. With the PRC holding billions of dollars in U.S. treasury bills, its leaders realize they have the upper hand in the bilateral relationship, at least financially.

For nearly two decades, American politicians have lurched from accommodation to fear with regard to the PRC. Yet, with the possible exception of Taiwan, there are few natural differences between U.S. and Chinese national interests. Both countries depend upon a vibrant global economy for their domestic economic prosperity. Both see stability as the means of ensuring the continuation and consolidation of the globalization process that brought both to the forefront of the international community. These common interests provide the United States and others with a firm foundation for keeping relations with China peaceful and productive.

But between most great powers in history, and in a classical sense between the status quo power and the rising power, friction may be inevitable (Johnston 2003; Christensen 2001). What is not inevitable is that these differences must be played out through military competition or contrasting visions of regional and global security. The shift of the Obama administration toward a more multilateral, less militarized, and more issues-oriented foreign policy may ensure that military conflicts between the two nations can be avoided. Then again, it remains to be seen whether China will be satisfied with some variation of the status quo whereby the U.S. Navy operates freely in Asian waters.

Securitizing Climate Change and Energy

In little more than a year, the Obama administration has moved beyond the positions of its immediate predecessors to include climate change and energy under the broad rubric of national security policy. Under President Clinton, the United States signed but did not ratify the Kyoto Treaty. The Bush administration explicitly rejected efforts to draw the United States into international renewed negotiations over climate change. In an interesting example of U.S. armed services getting out ahead of national policy, toward the end of the Bush administration the U.S. Navy helped sponsored several projects that asserted the importance of climate change for U.S. national security because climate change could potentially destabilize affected regions across the globe.

Institutional proof of the elevation of climate change was the creation of a Center on Climate Change and National Security by the Central Intelligence Agency in 2009. In effect, the United States is increasingly adopting a more comprehensive definition of what constitutes the appropriate scope of national security that includes nontraditional threats such as global warming and securing the nation's energy future in the face of declining supplies and rising prices for petroleum products. Borrowing from the language of constructivist scholars of international relations, it could be argued that this phenomenon represents an example of "securitization" (Weaver 1995). Identifying climate change and energy with national security effectively raises their profile and, more important, makes them higher priorities (Booth 2007, 163–69). Even as the Obama administration has de facto securitized U.S. responses to climate change and national energy security, the majority of activity takes place outside the control of traditional agencies concerned with national security and defense policy. The Department of State, the Department of Energy, and, of course, the U.S. Congress remain the most important players in crafting a national response to these challenges. It remains to be seen whether President Obama and his national security team will succeed in addressing climate change and energy insecurity in the context of national security rather than as issues of "low politics" associated with domestic issues.

Prospects for Obama and Beyond

Official forecasts of U.S. defense planners and the public discussions of national security specialists seeking to prepare for the coming decades envision a multi-polar world in which the United States has relinquished its primacy due to the rise of other powers and the decline of its own political, economic, and military capabilities. Alternative futures proposed by government agencies are both notoriously inaccurate and often ignored by security and defense agencies charged with developing budgets and acquiring new weapons and intelligence systems. One would be hard pressed to trace actual programs back to the generic scenarios developed to prepare for the uncertain future. Yet the musings of the intelligence analysts, planners, and scholars who contribute to the Joint Operating Environment and the various planning documents of the armed services do provide parameters for thinking about the future. This is important because many government actions—from current deficit spending to large, long-term acquisition programs for buying satellites and ships—only come to fruition or enter into the strategic calculus in the intermediate to long run. Today's choices reverberate far into the future.

For defense planners, pessimistic scenarios are a boon. Many government strategists believe that the post-unipolar world projected by the National Intelligence Council will be more conflictual even than the present. Nations with more equal capabilities will compete, even militarily, to extend national control into the global commons (Posen 2003) and seek to secure critical resources under their control (Klare 2002). In this event, the United States must, necessarily, maintain or increase the capabilities and readiness of its military forces. Multilateral defense and security policies may be hard to maintain when states are highly competitive over material gains. The world might return to a bloc-like order in which geopolitics or clashing values lead to the creation of anti-American alliances at the regional or global level.

Defense planners often believe these pessimistic forecasts in part because worst-case planning is rewarded. Especially within the individual military services, careers are not enhanced by arguing that peace is breaking out all over. After all, such an analysis might lead to force reductions, decreasing budgets, and fewer opportunities for individual advancement. The "military-industrial complex" warned about so famously by President Eisenhower feeds on potential threats and the need to expand U.S. defenses further. In addition, military planners are instinctively cautious and embrace the maxim "better safe than sorry" when it comes to U.S. national security.

The lessons of the last decade in Iraq, Afghanistan, and elsewhere suggest that military and defense policies, programs, and operations represent only one part of the answer to keeping American secure. "Whole-of-government" approaches that emphasize the "soft power" of ideas as well as the "hard power" of military force may result in an evolution of U.S. security policy that combines something of the militarized past with a fresh appreciation for diplomacy; economic leverage; and the benefits of working with allies, friends, and even potential adversaries. While Obama's security strategies have explored these alternative futures at length, their more immediate and pressing concern is for the present. As the president's experience has thus far demonstrated, solutions to long-term security challenges cannot be found while the United States remains mired in the here and now.

CHAPTER 7

Change and Continuity in America's Counterterrorism Strategy under Obama

Stuart Gottlieb

AS WITH OTHER KEY AREAS OF FOREIGN POLICY and national security, Barack Obama campaigned for president and entered office promising significant change from his predecessor in the area of counterterrorism. According to Obama, the overly aggressive policies of George W. Bush following the terrorist attacks of September 11, 2001, led the United States to "act contrary to our traditions," severely damaging America's standing in the world and harming the overall fight against al-Qaeda (Obama 2009o). Having stated repeatedly that he rejected "as false the choice between our security and our ideals," Obama assured America and the world that his administration would reverse the Bush excesses and craft new counterterrorism policies "consistent with our values and our Constitution" (Obama 2009q).

And to great fanfare, on January 22, 2009, his second day in office, President Obama signed executive orders that mandated the closing of the U.S. prison camp at Guantánamo Bay, Cuba, within one year; eliminated secret Central Intelligence Agency (CIA) prisons around the world; and required all interrogations of terror suspects in American custody to follow the noncoercive guidelines of the U.S. Army Field Manual (Priest 2009). In addition, the Bush administration's military commissions system to try enemy combatants was suspended, and the label *enemy combatant* was retired. The term *war on terrorism* was dropped, and the word *terrorism* itself was to be rarely, if ever, uttered.

Despite the bold promises and initial high-profile changes in policy and terminology, Obama's counterterrorism initiatives during his first term as president have closely mirrored those of the prior Bush administration. Obama has adopted, and in some instances bolstered, many of Bush's most hard-line

Obama similar to Bush's counterterrorism

policies, including targeted killings of suspected terrorist leaders abroad, "rendering" captured terror suspects to third-party countries for interrogation and detention, and justifying the administration's refusal to release court-ordered information in terrorism cases against the U.S. government on the grounds that it would compromise state secrets (Savage 2009).

Indeed, while banishing the term *war on terrorism*, Obama has significantly stepped up America's military efforts against al-Qaeda and its Taliban allies in Afghanistan and Pakistan and has ordered air strikes and U.S. Special Forces ground assaults against al-Qaeda operatives and affiliates in faraway lands such as Somalia and Yemen. The Obama administration has also fought successfully to maintain controversial Bush-era Patriot Act provisions, and it tacitly supports the Bush Justice Department argument that the president has the right, as commander in chief, to engage in wireless surveillance inside the United States and the right to indefinitely detain terror suspects anywhere in the world without formal charges (Wills 2009).

Such continuity, however, is far from the full story. Though maintaining many of the Bush administration's post-9/11 counterterrorism policies, there has been a marked effort by the Obama White House to break from the prior administration's approach toward fighting terrorism in two crucial ways: by rebranding of America's overall global counterterrorism strategy and by returning antiterrorism to a more constitutional "rule of law" footing rather than a war footing. The results of these endeavors toward meaningful change have been mixed.

The rebranding of America's global counterterrorism strategy has been the more consistent and arguably more successful of the administration's efforts to break from the past (Goldsmith 2009). Indeed, softening America's rhetorical approach toward counterterrorism, particularly vis-à-vis the Arab and Muslim world, has been a core component of the Obama administration's overall macro foreign policy strategy to steer America in a new post-Bush direction in foreign affairs, with multilateral engagement and the use of diplomacy and soft power taking precedence over hard-edged rhetoric and military-heavy hard-power tactics. At its core, terrorism is a propaganda-fueled phenomenon—an ongoing battle to win hearts and minds and entice new recruits to fight for the cause. By reversing Bush's "bring it on" and "smoke 'em out" rhetoric, and instead making it clear to the world that his administration's efforts will be based on enlightened principles and robust engagement, Obama has taken important steps toward building greater legitimacy—and thus greater effectiveness and sustainability—into America's global counterterrorism efforts.

The second area of visible change—emphasizing a criminal justice approach to fighting terrorism, particularly with regard to the treatment and legal status of terror detainees—has had less certain results. Although "returning to constitutional values" in counterterrorism was a key campaign promise of Obama's—and is an important component of his efforts to rebrand America's overall counterterrorism strategy—these efforts have often conflicted directly with the practical realities of governing. During Obama's first year in office, there were more "terrorism-related events" (plots and foiled plots) inside the United States than in any year since 2001 (Jenkins, quoted in Ghosh 2009). With the threat level remaining high, and the American people increasingly concerned about terrorist attacks, many of Obama's core promises regarding constitutional values have fallen by the wayside ("Another War President After All" 2010). Indeed, the administration's continuing struggle to appear to accede to the "rule of law" in the face of terrorism has led to glaring contradictions and inconsistencies, such as the administration's decision to delay closing the Guantánamo Bay detention center and to try some terror suspects in federal civilian courts and others in (resurrected) military tribunals, while holding yet others indefinitely without any charges at all.

Thus, while changes in the rhetoric and packaging of America's counterterrorism strategy have in large part taken hold, many of the most important promised changes in tangible policy have not. And where Obama has tried to clearly break from Bush—such as efforts to criminalize detainee issues—the administration has found itself politically vulnerable to charges of inconsistency from the left and of dangerous naïveté from the right. Bridging the gap between the rhetorical promises of change that have helped boost America's global image and popularity over the short term with the practical realities of keeping the nation safe from terror attacks over the longer term remains a vital challenge for Obama and his national security team.

This chapter details the substance of American counterterrorism strategy under President Obama, with a specific focus on how it fits within his administration's overall goal of renewing America's role in the world. It does so by placing the Obama administration's counterterrorism policies in the context of America's traditional approaches to fighting terrorism and through comparing the practices of this administration with those of prior administrations. Part I provides a brief background of American counterterrorism policy from the 1970s through the attacks on September 11, 2001. Part II reviews the counterterrorism policies enacted under George W. Bush following 9/11. Part III presents President Obama's counterterrorism approach and policies. Part IV concludes with an assessment of how Obama's counterterrorism policies have impacted (and have been impacted by) his administration's broader foreign policy goals and what the future likely holds for American counterterrorism policy.

Counterterrorism and U.S. Foreign Policy: An Overview

Although fighting terrorism has been an obvious priority in U.S. foreign policy since the 9/11 attacks, the fact is America had been tangling with terrorism, both foreign and domestic, for decades prior to 2001. In the 1970s, the Palestinian Liberation Organization and its affiliated groups orchestrated dozens of high-profile international terrorist attacks, often impacting American lives and interests. The 1980s witnessed the rise of an even graver international terrorist threat—Iranian-backed groups, such as Hezbollah, that engaged in suicide attacks, including one in 1983 that destroyed the U.S. military barracks in Beirut, Lebanon, killing 241 U.S. Marines. Other state sponsors of terrorism also emerged in the 1980s, including Libya, which was behind the 1988 downing of Pan Am Flight 103 over Lockerbie, Scotland, killing 270, including 189 Americans.

In the 1990s, the tangible threat from al-Qaeda and other Islamic radical groups grew precipitously. Deadly attacks included the 1993 World Trade Center bombing; the 1996 attack on U.S. military personnel stationed in Khobar, Saudi Arabia; the 1998 attacks on the U.S. embassies in Kenya and Tanzania; and the 2000 attack on the U.S.S. *Cole* in Aden, Yemen. In 1995, the United States suffered its worst domestic terrorism attack in history when Timothy McVeigh, inspired by America's Christian militia movement, set off a bomb at the Murrah Federal Building in Oklahoma City, killing 168.

With terrorism rising as both a threat and a challenge in the years prior to 9/11, the United States was compelled to develop counterterrorism strategies. These strategies employed a variety of counterterrorism tools and tactics and were shaped by several guiding principles.

Counterterrorism Tools and Tactics

At its core, the goal of counterterrorism is to weaken the strike capacity of terrorist organizations and undercut their bases of support. Elements of both "hard power" and "soft power" will play a role in any comprehensive counterterrorism strategy (*National Strategy for Combating Terrorism* 2006; Nye 1994).

There are essentially five traditional tools, or instruments, that the United States has utilized for combating terrorism (Pillar 2004):

1. Diplomacy (persuading foreign governments to cooperate on mutual issues relating to terrorism)
2. Law enforcement (capturing and prosecuting terrorists)
3. Military force (physical strikes against terrorist groups and their supporters)
4. Intelligence (the vital "eyes and ears" of counterterrorism)
5. Financial controls (cutting off terrorist funding)

It is important to note that the manner in which these five tools are employed (i.e., their tactical use) is determined in large part by the guiding principles of counterterrorism strategy. These guiding principles have varied from era to era, and from administration to administration, as based on changing assessments of terror threats and each administration's philosophy regarding what it deems the most effective ways to fight terrorism while limiting the negative impact on American society.

Guiding Principles of Counterterrorism

From the 1970s through the mid-1990s (and arguably through 9/11), American counterterrorism policies were oriented almost exclusively around efforts overseas to isolate and punish so-called state sponsors of terrorism (U.S. Department of State 2009, chap. 3). This makes sense when considering that although terror attacks were steadily increasing overseas, there was little perception of a direct threat to the homeland. It also makes sense when considering the many controversies and difficulties inherent in trying to combat terrorism within the borders of a robust democracy like the United States, which jealously guards its delicate balance between civil liberties and security. It would take a clear and dire threat to create a context for aggressive domestic counterterrorism measures, as witnessed after 9/11.

What little domestic counterterrorism there was in the quarter-century or so prior to the 9/11 attacks fell primarily under the rubric of traditional law enforcement. Terrorism was considered a crime, and terrorists were considered criminals. The rising threat of domestic terrorism in the early to mid-1990s—as seen with the 1993 World Trade Center bombing and the 1995 Oklahoma City bombing—did little to change this general perception, and the Clinton administration met it with an almost exclusively criminal justice approach.

For example, between 1993 and 1999, the number of Federal Bureau of Investigation (FBI) agents working on terrorism rose from 550 to nearly 1,400, and the proportion of the FBI's budget devoted to counterterrorism increased from 4 percent to roughly 10 percent (Pillar 2004, 80). The successful federal criminal prosecutions of terrorist conspirators from the 1993 and 1995 attacks were viewed by many as important victories in fighting terrorism. All the while, however, the Clinton administration placed increasing restrictions on the ability of FBI intelligence agents to engage in preventative surveillance inside the United States or to share information with other divisions within the FBI or with the CIA (National Commission on Terrorist Attacks Upon the United States 2004). Clinton's criminal justice approach to fighting terrorism also extended overseas, where the FBI became increasingly involved in working with foreign governments to locate and arrest wanted or indicted terrorists. Meanwhile, the CIA's budget for its covert "Special Activities" division was cut significantly. Strict prohibitions were placed on the ability of CIA agents to recruit spies with unsavory or criminal records, as that was thought to violate American laws and values (Gertz 2002; National Commission on Terrorist Attacks Upon the United States 2004, chap. 3).

In fact, what emerged from the 1980s and 1990s was dueling guiding principles for U.S. counterterrorism strategy—the traditional criminal justice approach, as embodied by the Clinton administration, versus an evolving "warfare" approach, which rested on the assumption that combating the rising threat of global terrorism required more than successful prosecutions (Laqueur 1999).

The cornerstone of the criminal justice approach to fighting terrorism is the notion that terrorism is ultimately about the commission of a crime—murder, attempted murder, destruction of property, etc.—and in a robust constitutional democracy like the United States, the criminal justice system is more than adequate to prosecute terrorists (citizens and noncitizens alike) for committing such crimes, regardless of their motivations for doing so (Cole and Dempsey 2006).

By contrast, the warfare approach rests on the notion that modern terrorism is actually a revolutionary form of international warfare, requiring a broader national security rather than a primarily law enforcement response. Particularly in an age of catastrophic terrorism, the argument goes, simply responding to terrorist events after they occur with criminal indictments and prosecutions is not sufficient: the goal must be to prevent attacks from occurring in the first place, and that requires a far greater use of national, especially presidential commander-in-chief, powers (Posner 2006).

Internationally, every U.S. administration since the 1970s tapped into elements of the warfare approach to combating terrorism. For example, in 1986, the Reagan administration ordered air strikes against Tripoli in retaliation for the Libyan government's alleged role in the 1985 bombing of a disco in Germany. In 1993, the Clinton administration ordered missile strikes against Baghdad in retaliation for the Iraqi government's alleged involvement in a plot to assassinate former president George H. W. Bush during a visit to Kuwait. In 1998, following the U.S. embassy bombings in East Africa, the Clinton administration bombed a private pharmaceutical plant in Sudan on suspicions that the owner had ties to al-Qaeda and might supply the group with chemical weapons (Leffler 2004).

Domestically, however, the criminal justice approach to counterterrorism remained dominant in every administration prior to the attacks on 9/11.

Counterterrorism and U.S. Foreign Policy under George W. Bush

George W. Bush entered office in 2001 with an overall foreign policy goal of scaling down America's global commitments, centering its focus on narrow national interests as opposed to what it considered the multilateral excesses of the Clinton administration (Krauthammer 2001). Yet just eight months into his first term, the 9/11 attacks would redefine both Bush's presidency as well as America's role in the world for the better part of the next eight years.

It is instructive to recall that the immediate aftermath of the 9/11 attacks was defined by a tremendous coming together of the world community. "We Are All Americans," read the headline of the French daily *Le Monde* on the morning after 9/11. On the evening of September 12, 2001, and for the first time in its history, the North Atlantic Treaty Organization invoked Article 5, the alliance's collective defense clause.

There was also a swift recognition by the Bush White House that what lay ahead would need to be a global endeavor. Two days after the 9/11 attacks, former president George H. W. Bush, a close personal adviser to his son, said, "Just as Pearl Harbor awakened this country from the notion that we could somehow avoid the call to duty and defend freedom in Europe and Asia in World War II, so too should this most recent surprise attack erase the concept in some quarters that America can somehow go it alone in the fight against terrorism or in anything else for that matter" (G. H. W. Bush 2001). In his September 20, 2001, address to Congress, President George W. Bush said, "This is not, however, just America's fight. This is the world's fight. . . . We ask every nation to join us. . . . We will need the help of police forces, intelligence services, and banking systems around the world. . . . Perhaps the NATO Charter reflects best the attitude of the world: an attack on one is an attack on all" (G. W. Bush 2001).

But there was also a strong belief among the Bush national security team that America's overall approach toward fighting terrorism in the decades leading to 9/11 had been inadequate—that the "terrorism as crime" model had failed catastrophically. With nearly 3,000 Americans dead in New York, Pennsylvania, and Virginia, both the U.S. Congress and the federal courts deferred to the executive branch to respond, leaving the Bush administration essentially free to craft America's approach virtually any way it chose. Indeed, it would not be until June 2004—in the *Rasul v. Bush* and *Hamdi v. Rumsfeld* cases—that the U.S. Supreme Court would render its first decision on Bush's post-9/11 antiterror policies. It would be longer still before Congress played any meaningful role in counterterrorism oversight.

Birth of the "War" on Terrorism

Within four months of the 9/11 attacks, President Bush had publicly issued 22 Presidential Executive Orders or Proclamations related to the event, and more than two dozen new measures proposed to Congress by the administration had become law (Donohue 2004, 313). This included the September 18, 2001, Joint Resolution of Congress authorizing the president to "use all necessary and appropriate force" against those who committed or aided the attacks and in order to "prevent any future attacks of terrorism against the United States." The measure passed by 98–0 in the Senate and 420–1 in the House of Representatives. It also included the USA Patriot Act, which was signed into law on October 26, 2001, after passing by 98–1 in the Senate and 356–66 in the House. The Patriot Act was the most significant domestic counterterrorism law since the passage of the 1978 Foreign Intelligence Surveillance Act (FISA), which restricted the ability of FBI intelligence agents to spy on American citizens or persons residing inside the United States or to share such information with the FBI's criminal division and the CIA. The Patriot Act significantly lowered the threshold for antiterrorism surveillance in the United States and dismantled much of the "firewall" between domestic and international intelligence gathering and between intelligence and law enforcement.

Though congressional approval was viewed by the administration as an important show of unity, the administration was in fact operating under a different paradigm: that the United States was now "at war" and the powers of the president as defined by Article II of the Constitution, particularly the commander-in-chief clause, permitted—indeed obligated—the president to do whatever he deemed necessary to protect the nation (Yoo 2010b). What followed in the weeks and months after 9/11 was a series of secret Executive Orders authorizing aggressive action on a range of issues, including the creation of secret CIA prisons to house and interrogate captured terrorists overseas; the permitting of "enhanced interrogations" of captured "high value" terrorists; the dramatic expansion of the CIA's renditions program that had begun under the Clinton administration in the mid-1990s; a secret domestic terrorism surveillance program operated by the National Security Agency that existed outside the bounds of both FISA and the Patriot Act; a secret program to search private international banking transactions in search of al-Qaeda financiers; and a directive for the U.S. military and CIA to engage in covert targeted assassinations of terrorist leaders (Mayer 2008; Wittes 2008; Goldsmith 2007; Tenet 2007; Suskind 2006).

In addition, along with secret CIA prisons and U.S. prisons in Afghanistan (and later Iraq), the U.S. military base at Guantánamo Bay, Cuba, was designated as a primary destination to detain individuals captured in counterterrorism operations. The administration argued that such detainees, as nonstate, nonuniformed "unlawful enemy combatants," were not covered by international law or the laws of war and could be held at the sole discretion of the president (Yoo 2004). The administration instead developed its own military commissions system to determine the status and punishment of detainees.

While much of the "war on terrorism" was overt—such as U.S. military operations in Afghanistan (Operation Enduring Freedom) and the creation of the prison camp at Guantánamo—much was deeply secretive. American values, some in the Bush administration argued, would need to take a back seat if the United States were effectively to meet and defeat this ruthless enemy. On

September 16, 2001, Vice President Richard Cheney (NBC News's *Meet the Press* 2001) said that along with a broad range of military operations, the United States would "have to work, though, sort of the dark side, if you will. We've got to spend time in the shadows of the intelligence world. A lot of what needs to be done here will have to be done quietly, without any discussion, using sources and methods that are available to our intelligence agencies, if we're going to be successful. That's the world these folks operate in, and so it's going to be vital for us to use any means at our disposal, basically, to achieve our objective."

Counterterrorism Tools and Tactics under Bush

With an aggressive "terrorism as warfare" philosophy guiding the counterterrorism strategy of the Bush administration after 9/11, the manner in which the traditional tools of counterterrorism were employed underwent significant changes.

Diplomacy. Prior to 9/11, the State Department had led nearly all international efforts relating to counterterrorism, such as garnering cooperation against states on the "state sponsors" list and crafting international extradition agreements to allow the transfer of captured terrorists to the United States to stand trial. After 9/11, with the United States on a war footing, international cooperation and coordination became a vital tool for many other agencies, as directed by the White House—for example, the Defense Department worked with NATO allies and dozens of other countries on overt and covert military operations, the Treasury Department crafted new international cooperative efforts to stanch terrorist financing, the Transportation Department worked with other countries on airline security, and the CIA and other U.S. intelligence services forged new alliances with intelligence agencies around the world. The Bush administration also endeavored to use diplomacy to address root causes and "hearts-and-minds" issues related to terrorism by, for example, setting up the Millennium Challenge Account to help bring economic opportunity and good governance to less-developed and at-risk countries, as well as other creative uses of foreign aid (Radelet 2003). Later in the administration, democracy promotion in the Arab and Muslim world became a leading diplomatic exercise.

Law Enforcement. After 9/11, and as codified by the Patriot Act, domestic anti-terror law enforcement was no longer focused primarily on indicting and prosecuting terrorists but on aggressively infiltrating plots and preventing attacks through aggressive search and surveillance measures. Terrorists captured and detained both domestically and internationally, including American citizens, were presumed to have no constitutional rights.

Intelligence. Prior to 9/11, restrictions were placed on aggressive and morally questionable "human" intelligence-gathering activities overseas, and far greater

[handwritten margin note: agencies working together]

emphasis was placed on less (though not un-) controversial electronic and "signals" intelligence gathering using, for example, spy satellites, eavesdropping devices, and decryption technologies. After 9/11, CIA human intelligence activities were significantly stepped up, as noted by Cheney. Enhanced interrogations, renditions, and other aggressive measures were utilized in the name of learning about al-Qaeda and its affiliates and acquiring "actionable intelligence" to prevent future attacks. The CIA also became the lead agency in identifying suspected terrorists abroad and directing covert assassinations using its fleet of unmanned "drone" aircraft armed with precision-guided missiles.

Military Force. After 9/11, military force in counterterrorism was no longer limited primarily to retaliatory strikes in response to terrorist attacks or commando raids to free hostages held by terrorists. Under Bush, military operations in the name of counterterrorism and counterproliferation ranged from full-scale war (Afghanistan and Iraq), to U.S. Special Forces operating on the ground in dozens of countries, to covert air strikes using the military's own fleet of "unmanned aerial vehicles" or drones. Indeed the administration introduced a new doctrine of military "preemption" in its 2002 National Security Strategy, arguing that in the post–Cold War world, and in light of 9/11, it had an urgent calling to prevent attacks in ways that may sometimes require acting militarily against "emerging threats before they are fully formed" ("National Security Strategy" 2002). This was the primary justification for the Iraq War in 2003 (Woodward 2004; Perle 2002).

Financial Restrictions. Prior to 9/11, there was diplomatic trepidation regarding aggressive action toward states that helped finance international terrorist organizations (some of which did so openly). There was also little political wherewithal for aggressively investigating charities or other legitimate and semi-legitimate economic enterprises that were suspected of having links with terrorism, such as the Muslim Holy Land Foundation, based near Dallas, Texas. After 9/11, the United States became far more aggressive in imposing sanctions on and freezing assets of states suspected of financing terrorist groups and in prosecuting charities and businesses. For example, just weeks after the 9/11 attacks, the Holy Land Foundation's assets were frozen and five of its leaders were indicted on charges of materially supporting terrorism, for which they were convicted in November 2008 (Kovach 2008).

Foreign Policy Effects of Bush's "War on Terrorism"

Both George W. Bush and his father were right when they said in the days after 9/11 that fighting a global terrorist movement like the one led by al-Qaeda would need to be a global endeavor with global partners. One of the ironies of the Bush presidency is that there was a tremendous degree of bilateral and multilateral cooperation in fighting terrorism during both of his terms in office—with European allies, as well as with China, Russia, India, and many Muslim countries, all of whom worked closely with the United States to combat mutually threatening radical Islamic movements. Due to the increasing global unpopularity of Bush and America—following the opening of Guantánamo prison, the initiation of the Iraq War, revelations from Abu Ghraib, reports of torture, etc.—most governments publically distanced themselves from the Bush administration and denied such cooperation, even as they quietly maintained it. Another reason for such denial was undoubtedly due to the controversial nature of many of the cooperative initiatives. A good example of this was the outrage in Italy over the public disclosure of a CIA rendition in Milan in 2003, which led to the indictment and prosecution in Italy of 23 CIA officers (in absentia). During the trial, it was embarrassingly revealed that the head of Italy's military intelligence agency (and likely the prime minister's office) was involved with the rendition (Donadio 2009). More to the point, the initial global goodwill following 9/11 and the continuing behind-the-scenes counterterrorism cooperation did little to paper over the fact that America's aggressive approach to fighting terrorism under Bush had, in the eyes of much of the world, lost its credibility.

Polling tells the story, as Douglas Foyle details in Chapter 4. In 2000, the year before Bush came to office, the favorability rating of the United States was 78 percent in Germany, 62 percent in France, 52 percent in Turkey, and 75 percent in Indonesia, as Douglas Foyle details in Chapter 4. In 2003, a little more than one year into the "war on terrorism," U.S. favorability was down to 45 percent in Germany, 42 percent in France, 15 percent in Turkey, and 15 percent in Indonesia (Pew Global Attitudes Project 2009). In 2004, one year after the invasion of Iraq, another survey (Pew Global Attitudes Project 2004) found that U.S. favorability in the Arab and Muslim world had cratered into the single digits in many countries; in some, the public gave al-Qaeda leader Osama bin Laden a far higher favorability rating than George W. Bush (e.g., Morocco, 45–8; Jordan, 55–3; Pakistan, 65–7). These numbers followed Bush and America throughout his second term in office—by 2007, U.S. favorability was 30 percent in Germany, 39 percent in France, 9 percent in Turkey, and 29 percent in Indonesia; and only 24 percent of the British, 28 percent of Canadians, and 7 percent of Spaniards had "confidence in U.S. global leadership" under George W. Bush (Pew Global Attitudes Project 2007).

Granted, the United States was dealt a difficult hand on 9/11, and even its most clearly justified aggressive responses (e.g., the war in Afghanistan) were unlikely to garner long-term support from much of the world, particularly the Muslim world. Nonetheless, the combination of a more generalized warfare approach, along with a unilateral "with us or with the terrorists" message and public relations disasters like Abu Ghraib, had taken its toll on America's leadership and moral standing in the world.

Domestically, the Bush administration's unfettered terrorism-as-war approach also came under increasing strain, both constitutionally and politically. Beginning with the June 2004 decisions in *Rasul v. Bush* and *Hamdi v. Rumsfeld,* through the June 2008 decision in *Boumediene v. Bush,* the Supreme Court increasingly issued rulings on the side of the rights of foreign and American-born terror detainees to challenge their detention in U.S. civilian courts, as well as rulings on the inadequacies of the Bush administration's military commissions system.

Beginning with the 2004 presidential campaign, Democrats and others opposed to the Bush administration's approach to fighting terrorism began speaking out more aggressively against the Iraq War, the treatment and legal disposition of terror detainees in Guantánamo prison and elsewhere, as well as other hard-line policies. They were especially critical of the way such policies had in their view harmed America's standing in the world, hindering America's overall foreign policy objectives and the fight against al-Qaeda itself. This was the primary foreign policy message of Democratic presidential nominee John Kerry and his campaign for president in 2004. Specifically, Kerry promised to close Guantánamo, apply Geneva Convention protections to all current and future terror detainees, rescind the Patriot Act, and end domestic warrantless wiretapping; these promises were later adopted by most 2008 Democratic presidential candidates, including Barack Obama.

Little recognized is the fact that the counterterrorism policies of George W. Bush evolved in a more moderate and constitutionally grounded direction during the course of his presidency. Much of this could be traced to Supreme Court rulings, congressional push-back, and disclosures of secret programs in the news media (Baker 2010c). But it was also representative of the natural tendency throughout American history for presidents to seize tremendous authority in times of acute national security crisis, with power slowly ceding back to the other branches when the immediate crisis fades (Yoo 2010a; Stone 2004). Indeed, by the time Bush left office, harsh interrogation tactics, including waterboarding (simulated drowning), had been halted for years; secret CIA black-site prisons had been ordered emptied; and the NSA's domestic surveillance program and Pentagon's military commissions system had been restructured and approved by Congress. Bush even declared his desire to close Guantánamo and released or transferred more than 500 Guantánamo detainees before leaving office. Finally, many of the hard-line tactics that continued throughout Bush's tenure—such as renditions and targeted killings—had become generally accepted by Congress and the American people as necessary evils in the global campaign against al-Qaeda and its affiliates.

Upon winning a presidential election in 2008 in which being Barack Obama was of comparable importance to not being George W. Bush, broadly promising to undo the policies of the prior administration certainly had political cachet. It was equally clear, however, that in the area of counterterrorism, many of the effective and accepted practices developed under Bush were not going to be easily "reversed," nor arguably should they have been.

Counterterrorism Policy under Barack Obama

To say that Barack Obama entered office in January 2009 with a plate full of challenges is a dramatic understatement. The worst economic recession in decades, a financial system teetering on the brink of collapse, two increasingly costly and unpopular wars overseas, and the continued threat of global terrorism were among the challenges Obama inherited from his predecessor. In domestic policy, Obama approached the challenge with an ambitious strategy to restructure the "foundations" of the U.S. economy, introducing robust reform initiatives specifically targeting education, energy, health care, and the banking system. In foreign policy, the strategy, described on the Obama campaign's and White House's Web sites, was no less ambitious: to "restore America's leadership and moral standing" in the world through a policy of "renewed American diplomacy" centered on aggressive outreach toward allies and adversaries alike.

The importance of reformulating U.S. counterterrorism strategy as a key component of the broader foreign policy program of the Obama administration cannot be overstated. During and after the presidential campaign, the Obama team was clear in its assessment that the hyper-aggressive manner in which the Bush administration had prosecuted its "war on terrorism" was largely responsible for the diplomatic ditch the United States had fallen into in recent years. As such, an early commitment was made to create a whole new counterterrorism "paradigm." This new paradigm, which continues to guide the counterterrorism polices of the administration, was based on changing the macro-messaging of counterterrorism strategy, reaching out to the Arab and Muslim world (including traditional adversaries like Iran), and positioning antiterrorism policies within the bounds of constitutional "rule of law." Hard-line policies would be maintained as necessary, but they were to be downplayed in favor of the important symbolism of diplomacy and constitutionalism.

Generally speaking, the new paradigm was about lowering the thermostat on terrorism so it could take its "proper place" as one of many foreign policy challenges, not the only one. To the Obama foreign policy team, overreacting to the threat of terrorism—by word or deed—played directly into the hands of terrorists by elevating their stature and by undermining America's broader foreign policy endeavors (Brennan 2009).

Changing the "Mood Music": Unraveling the Rhetorical War on Terror

By far the biggest change the Obama administration has made to counterterrorism is what one former Obama adviser called the "mood music"—choice of language, outreach to Muslims, rhetorical fidelity to the rule of law, and a shift in tone from the all-or-nothing days of the Bush administration (Baker 2010a). During the presidential campaign, Obama vowed to "turn the page"; he said that the hard-line approach of the Bush administration "compromised our most precious values" as a nation and provided fuel to the belief that the United States was "at war with Islam." Obama promised that as president he would "author" an entirely new narrative through broad outreach to the Muslim world and follow through on important policy promises to ban torture, close Guantánamo, end military commissions, and apply Geneva Convention protections to all terror detainees (Obama 2007b).

And upon entering office, Obama quickly made good on his promise to begin changing the tone: on January 27, 2009, less than a week into his presidency, Obama tellingly chose the Arabic satellite television station al-Arabiya for his first televised Oval Office interview, where he called for a "new partnership" between America and the Muslim world "based on mutual respect and mutual interest." This interview was followed by major speeches to Muslim audiences in Turkey and Egypt, where Obama quoted verses from the Qur'an and promised Muslims worldwide that the United States would "listen carefully, bridge misunderstanding, and seek common ground" (Obama 2009j; Obama 2009o). In the meantime, aggressive diplomatic outreach was extended to Iran—a member of the former Bush administration's "axis of evil"—including a video released in March 2009 in which Obama wished the Iranian people a "happy Persian new year" and offered a "new beginning" for relations between the "Islamic Republic of Iran" and the United States.

Key to these outreach efforts was the notion, as Obama told the al-Arabiya audience, that "the language we use matters." Thus the rhetoric of the prior administration such as "war on terrorism" and "jihadist" was scrubbed from the executive branch nomenclature, and the use of the word *terrorism* itself was to be played down. This led to embarrassing, almost comical, efforts to go to the other extreme, as when a member of the administration advised senior officials across the federal bureaucracy to replace the term "global war on terror" with "overseas contingency operation" (Erdbrink and Kessler 2009). And Homeland Security Secretary Janet Napolitano absorbed much criticism for replacing the word *terrorism* during her Senate confirmation hearing with the term *man-caused disaster*. She said this was done to help the country "move away from the politics of fear" (quoted in Kamen 2009). Nonetheless, the new language initiative fit well with Obama and his national security team's view that its efforts should be directed specifically against al-Qaeda, not against abstract notions like "terrorism" nor through the use of vague concepts like "war on terrorism" or with words loaded with nuance and sensitivity in the Muslim world like *jihad*.

Underpinning his new administration's efforts to craft a new narrative, Obama also quickly signed a series of executive orders "reversing" major parts of Bush's counterterrorism policy. Guantánamo prison would be closed within one year. Torture was banned "without exception or equivocation." Secret CIA prisons would be shuttered. The treatment of terror detainees held at home or abroad would be protected by the Geneva Conventions or the U.S. Constitution. "Bush's 'War' On Terror Comes to a Sudden End," exclaimed a *Washington Post* headline just two days after Obama was sworn in as president (Priest 2009).

As Chapter 4 described, to the administration's credit, these early moves can be viewed as having worked precisely as intended: the new messaging and symbolically important policy changes contributed to a swift and positive effect on America's image in the world. In July 2009, six months into the Obama presidency, an average of 71 percent of those surveyed in nearly two dozen countries had "confidence" in America's handling of world affairs, as compared with just 17 percent one year earlier when Bush was president. More specifically, those with confidence in U.S. foreign policy rose from 13 percent in 2008 to 91 percent in 2009 in France, from 14 percent to 93 percent in Germany, from 2 percent to 33 percent in Turkey, and from 23 percent to 71 percent in Indonesia. According to a poll conducted by the Pew Global Attitudes Project (2009), the overall improvements were "driven much more by personal confidence in Obama than by opinions about his specific policies." This clearly shows the power of the early rhetoric and symbolic moves of the administration.

And yet, to be fair, this early period also represents what can be considered the easy part of changing counterterrorism strategy. The hard part was going to involve efforts to follow through on the exceedingly ambitious policy promises. It is here—in the nuts and bolts of actual counterterrorism policy making— that the devil can be found in the details and that tensions between the desirable and the possible would be most glaring.

A War by Any Other Name . . .

Whereas the Bush administration stated clearly and—for better or worse— operated consistently under the "terrorism as warfare" paradigm, the Obama administration has tried to create a hybrid "criminal justice–national security" counterterrorism model based on three components: (1) a firm reliance on rhetoric and outreach consistent with its promise to "turn the page" on the prior administration; (2) showcasing to the world the power of American values and ideals by, whenever at all possible, placing counterterrorism decisions under the rubric of constitutional "rule of law"; and (3) all the while quietly maintaining the aggressive warfare practices and policies it believes were effective and necessary under Bush (Benjamin 2010). While this model surely requires some fancy political and public relations footwork (as discussed below), what it also requires is a strong wartime president.

Indeed, after years of accusing the Bush White House of using the war on terrorism as "an excuse for unchecked presidential power," in his inaugural address on January 20, 2009, Obama admitted more forcefully than at any point during his campaign that "our nation is at war against a far-reaching network of violence and hatred" (Obama, 2009c). It was apparent from that day forward that the promises of the campaign to rein in executive power, and the efforts of the administration to reshape the macro-messaging of counterterrorism strategy, would often find themselves at loggerheads with the president's own sworn commitment to "preserve, protect, and defend" the nation during this time of war.

For example, celebrations by civil liberties groups and others over Obama's early executive orders overturning key Bush policies quickly turned into questions over the sincerity of his administration's commitment to the new direction (Savage 2009). In fact, each of the supposed "reversals" of Bush policy contained important caveats and loopholes that protected the flexibility of the president to act aggressively and unilaterally in combating terrorism using wartime powers of the commander in chief.

So while torture was technically outlawed "without exception," the administration quietly reserved the right to use "additional or different" secret interrogation methods outside the bounds of the noncoercive guidelines of the Army Field Manual should "special circumstances" arise (Mazzetti 2009b). The terror suspects the administration would shuttle to third-party countries under its expanded renditions program could continue to be interrogated with little or no assurance they would not be abused (Schmitt and Mazetti 2009). And while Guantánamo and secret CIA prisons were ordered closed, and promises were made to provide all terror detainees with baseline habeas protections, the practice of detaining suspects indefinitely without any charges continued in alternative detention centers. These included the U.S. prison at Bagram airfield in Afghanistan, with the Obama administration using the September 18, 2001, congressional "Use of Military Force" resolution to justify the president's unilateral right to do so—the exact same claim Bush had made (Richey 2009; "Backward at Bagram" 2010).

Further, after initially promising to end military commissions, the Obama administration has revived that system, and after railing against the secret NSA spying program and the most controversial Patriot Act provisions during the presidential campaign, the administration has maintain them in virtually their original forms (Perine 2010). The White House's use of the state-secrets privilege to defy court orders demanding information in counterterrorism-related cases continues seamlessly from the days of Bush ("State-Secrets Privilege" 2009). Finally, few policies are as blatantly contradictory to Obama's promise to craft new counterterrorism policies "consistent with our values and our ideals" as his expanded covert drone-strike assassinations initiative against

Obama kept military commissions & the Patriot Act provisions

suspected Taliban and al-Qaeda operatives in Pakistan, Afghanistan, and else-where that have also killed or maimed hundreds of women and children and other innocent bystanders (Gottlieb 2009). Perhaps no other policy runs as contrary to the administration's overarching goal of improving relations with the Muslim world (Kilcullen and Exum 2009).

Benefits and Costs of Obama's Counterterrorism Tactics

As shown, while taking a vastly different approach toward diplomatic outreach and messaging, the Obama administration has maintained many if not most of the "terrorism as warfare" tactics developed by the Bush administration after 9/11. And in some instances the Obama White House has expanded upon them, as with stepped-up renditions and drone strikes as well as with the increased U.S. troop commitment to Afghanistan that the president announced in December 2009. According to Bradford Berenson, who helped craft counterter-rorism policy as a White House lawyer in the Bush administration, "the glass is eighty-five percent full in terms of continuity" between hard-line Bush and Obama counterterrorism tactics (quoted in Mayer 2010).

It is clear that once in office, President Obama recognized that balancing security and ideals, a trade-off he repeatedly decried as "false" during the cam-paign, was in fact necessary. Indeed, the challenge the administration has faced has not been with the prudence of its security-first policies. Drone strikes, for example, have been tremendously successful in killing senior leaders of al-Qaeda and its affiliates in Central Asia, East Africa, and the Arabian peninsula and have weakened the central command structure of al-Qaeda. And aggressive Patriot Act provisions were credited with helping to disrupt a major plot target-ing New York City in 2009 that was described by some as a planned "Mumbai on the Hudson" (Bergen 2009).

Instead, the challenge the administration continues to face is with its perennial struggle to reconcile the obvious disconnect between the compo-nent parts of its counterterrorism model—that is, how to "turn the page" on the prior administration, whose counterterrorism approach Obama and his senior advisers have repeatedly denounced as illegal, unconstitutional, anti-American, and fundamentally flawed—while maintaining their core policies (Greenwald 2009).

A thoughtful argument can be made that Obama has struck just the right balance—that maintaining many of the effective (but politically contentious) tactics of his predecessor while rhetorically disassociating himself from them, or attempting to resell them as constitutionally grounded, is a way to build new legitimacy into America's counterterrorism strategy. And there is little doubt that this is the most practical way for the administration to justify its continu-ation of Bush's hard-line policies. But it is equally plausible that the inherent contradictions involved are harming America's credibility, particularly in key regions of the world, and may undercut U.S. long-term counterterrorism efforts along with its broader foreign policy goals.

For example, the disconnect between messaging and tactics in Obama's counterterrorism strategy may help explain why the Arab and Muslim world has been far less receptive to Obama's presidency than have other parts of the world. After all, when looking beyond the speeches and promises, what the Muslim street sees is an administration that has ramped up the war in Afghanistan; is killing scores of Muslim civilians with drone strikes; continues to detain many hundreds of prisoners at Guantánamo, Bagram, and elsewhere; and has maintained America's virtually unconditional support of Israel. This is not to critique any or all of these policies but to point out that they certainly do not match the raised expectations of the Muslim world. And it helps explain why even after Obama's speeches in Turkey and Egypt in 2009, "opinions of the U.S. among Muslims in the Middle East remain largely unfavorable" with "animosity toward the U.S." continuing to run particularly "deep and unabated in Turkey, the Palestinian territories, and Pakistan" (Pew Global Attitudes Project 2009). Perhaps more startling, between May 2009 and May 2010 the number of Middle Eastern Arabs expressing optimism in the Obama administration's approach toward the region had dropped from 51 percent to just 16 percent, and those who described themselves as "discouraged" by Obama's presidency rose from 15 percent to 63 percent, according to The Brookings Institution (2010).

The Criminal Justice Approach and Its Discontents

Whereas the continuation of many of Bush's hard-line counterterrorism tactics has caused consistency problems for Obama's macro-messaging strategy, there is one area where the administration has made a sincere effort to break from the past: emphasizing a constitutional criminal justice approach in the handling of terror suspects and detainees ("War on Terror's Legal Battle" 2010). This was seen most notably with the administration's first-year decisions to close Guantánamo; ban harsh interrogation techniques; investigate allegations of past interrogation abuses by CIA officers; and put Khalid Sheikh Mohammed (KSM), the alleged mastermind of the 9/11 attacks, on trial in a federal civilian court in New York City rather than before a military tribunal (Baker 2010a).

On the one hand, these decisions can be viewed as part of the "turn-the-page" symbolism vital to the Obama counterterrorism model. For example, closing Guantánamo prison has, by the administration's own admission, more to do with what the prison negatively symbolizes to the world than with any substantive new rights that will be bestowed upon the prisoners themselves. In fact, the administration's proposal to transfer Guantánamo detainees to a prison facility inside the United States has been roundly criticized by leading human rights groups as simply "moving [Guantánamo] prison onto U.S. soil" (Human Rights Watch 2010). And the purported global public relations benefits of the proposed KSM civilian trial were clearly of paramount consideration: KSM had already admitted his guilt and requested the death penalty before a military tribunal in 2008 (Glaberson 2008).

On the other hand, it is equally clear that Obama deeply believes that the U.S. criminal justice system should serve as a cornerstone of fighting terrorism; he has repeatedly lauded the civilian courts for effectively trying and convicting terrorists both before and after 9/11, and he has vowed to create a legal process for all detainees "that adheres to rule of law, habeas corpus, basic principles of Anglo-American legal system" (quoted in Bruce 2009). And while Obama has tempered his universalist view on the rights of detainees—he has admitted that some terror suspects in Guantánamo and elsewhere would need to be held indefinitely without charges—he has remained committed to a greater criminal justice approach to counterterrorism, despite the political risks involved.

This was perhaps best seen in Obama's decision to defer key counterterrorism judgments to the Justice Department under Attorney General Eric Holder, a decision seized upon by Republican critics to boost their charges that Obama had a "September 10th mindset" (Cooper 2008) and that his administration was hewing too closely to a pre-9/11 "terrorism as crime" model (Cheney 2009). Though these charges may have been overblown—the Bush Justice Department tried hundreds of terrorists in federal court—Holder did little to stem the tide of criticism, and the hybrid "criminal justice–national security" counterterrorism model appeared to begin skewing heavily toward the "criminal justice" side.

For example, on the same day in November 2009 that Holder announced his decision to try KSM in federal court, he also announced his decision to try Abd al-Rahim al-Nashiri, the alleged mastermind of the U.S.S. *Cole* bombing in 2000, in a military tribunal. Part of his reasoning for the different venues was that al-Nashiri had attacked a military target abroad, while KSM directed his attacks against civilians inside the United States—implying that international terrorists who slaughter civilians in an American city may be treated as common criminals with all of the constitutional rights of an American citizen, while terrorists who attack military assets overseas are unlawful enemy combatants deserving of a lower standard of justice (Krauthammer 2009).

Holder's decisions in the aftermath of the failed al-Qaeda bombing of an airliner over Detroit on Christmas Day 2009 sparked further accusations of over-criminalizing counterterrorism. Not only was the suspected bomber, Umar Farouk Abdulmutallab, charged criminally and read his Miranda rights after only 50 minutes of questioning, but Holder approved this without consulting the administration's national security chiefs, including the secretary of defense, the director of national intelligence, and the director of the FBI. In subsequent Senate testimony, Dennis Blair, the director of national intelligence, said he believed greater efforts should have been made to extract intelligence from Abdulmutallab, even if that meant delaying formal charges (Blair 2010).

In the weeks and months following the Christmas Day incident, Obama found himself under heavy fire from critics accusing his administration of being soft on terrorism and leaving the country vulnerable to attack (Sherman 2010; Allen 2009). On the face of it, this was an unusual charge considering that Obama had maintained or bolstered most of Bush's hard-line counterter-rorism policies. And yet it was clear that the administration had lost control of its own narrative. With public opinion militating against the administration—in February 2010, 68 percent of Americans said captured terrorists should not receive constitutional protections, and 76 percent said the Christmas Day bomb suspect should have been held as an enemy combatant, not a civilian criminal (Quinnipiac University Polling Institute 2010)—the White House was forced to recalibrate. The closing of Guantánamo was put on indefinite hold. The New York City civilian trial of KSM was cancelled. And the White House took back the reins from the Justice Department on legal issues related to coun-terterrorism (Kantor and Savage 2010).

Readjusting the Thermostat on Terrorism

In fairness to Eric Holder, his decisions to try KSM in civilian court and to treat Abdulmutallab as a civilian criminal were fully consistent with the Obama administration's broader effort to "lower the temperature" on the issue of ter-rorism, an effort based on the belief that overstating and overreacting to terror threats cost the United States dearly during the Bush years (Hsu and Warrick 2009). Treating captured terrorists as criminal "miscreants" rather than "100 feet tall" global warriors was all part of Obama's plan to bring a more measured approach to counterterrorism (Brennan 2010). However, just as we learned under Bush that overstating and overreacting to the threat of terrorism can create a context for counterproductive outcomes—rushing into the Iraq War, Abu Ghraib, etc.—so too can understating or underreacting to the threat. Herein lies the ongoing challenge of any counterterrorism strategy: finding an approach not so strong that it rallies your enemy and helps its recruiting, but also not so soft that it gives the appearance of letting down your guard (Gottlieb 2008).

And it is here that the Obama administration has paid a price for overlearn-ing the lessons of the past: despite its reliance on hard-line counterterrorism tactics, the administration's near obsession with "lowering the temperature" on terrorism via softer and more nuanced rhetoric and a law enforcement approach to detainees left it—fairly or not—vulnerable to charges of complacency the moment tangible terror threats re-emerged (Taylor 2010). Other clear examples of the administration trying to lower the temperature include its decision not to refer to the mass shooting at Fort Hood in November 2009 as a terror-related event, despite the fact that the shooter, Army doctor Maj. Nidal Malik Hasan, an American-born Muslim, had spoken out in favor of violent jihad and had multiple contacts with a leading al-Qaeda recruiter. It also included Obama's initial reaction to the failed Christmas Day bombing, when the president referred to the suspect as "an isolated extremist" despite his direct ties to al-Qaeda. And after acknowledging in his Inaugural Address that America was "at war" with al-Qaeda, it would be nearly a year before President Obama would again use the term *at war* to describe America's relationship with al-Qaeda—only after the near miss on Christmas Day. Most explicitly, the administration remains steadfast in its unwillingness to describe the primary current threat as "Islamic terrorism" or discuss the impact (or even existence) of "radical Islam." Indeed, its 2010 National Security Strategy replaces such terms with the nondescriptive "violent extremism," exposing itself to charges of counterproductive "political correctness" in its approach (Hirsh 2010; Lamb 2010). If the effort was intended to help soften the American people's concern with Islamic terrorism, it appears to have backfired: in August 2010 fewer Americans held a favorable view of Islam (30 percent) than five years earlier during the Bush administration (41 percent), with more Americans (35 percent) saying Islam encourages violence more than other religions than in 2002 (25 percent; Pew Research Center for the People & the Press 2010).

In practical terms, aggressive efforts to downplay the threat of terrorism may have had deleterious effects on policy. It may help explain, for example, the failure to prevent the 2009 Christmas Day would-be bomber from boarding an airplane to the United States, despite his being on a terrorism watch list (Shane 2009). It may also help explain why, nearly a year after outlawing coercive interrogations, the administration had still not created its promised alternative, a High-Value Interrogation Group (HIG), and seemed to be caught flat-footed by the capture of mass-casualty terrorists on American soil. And it may help explain how the administration could have so overestimated its ability to close Guantánamo and appeared blindsided by the political uproar over efforts to transfer Guantánamo detainees to U.S. prisons.

Following the string of high-profile terror events in late 2009 and early 2010, the Obama administration began changing its rhetoric along with its policies. As Obama went about revising his plans to hold civilian trials for KSM and other Guantánamo detainees and ordering a complete overhaul of the overseas terrorism watch-list program, the language out of the White House began more closely resembling that of the Bush administration. "We've been reminded again of the challenge we face in protecting our country against a foe that is bent on our destruction," Obama (2010b) said two weeks after the 2009 Christmas Day incident. "We are at war against al-Qaeda, a far-reaching network of violence and hatred . . . that is plotting to strike us again. And we will do whatever it takes to defeat them."[1] The thermostat on terrorism had, by practical and political necessity, been forced back up.

Counterterrorism Lessons Learned—and to Be Learned

Like President Bush before him, President Obama has undoubtedly come to recognize that fighting terrorism is much more art than science—that crafting a sturdy counterterrorism model based on a logical framework only takes you so far. The strict "terrorism-as-warfare" approach employed by the Bush administration, though understandable in the immediate aftermath of the 9/11 attacks, ultimately required significant course corrections along the way. Likewise, the clever "criminal justice–national security" hybrid approach adopted by the Obama administration, with its heavy emphasis on symbolism and rhetorical promises of change, has also required significant fine-tuning.

Such adjustments have less to do with any inadequacies of either approach and more to do with the fact that any effective counterterrorism strategy requires a tremendous amount of flexibility, including the flexibility to question underlying assumptions. Terrorism is a threat that emanates from asymmetric actors whose behavior and actions are literally defined by their innovation, adaptability, and lethal creativity. This is particularly true regarding al-Qaeda and its affiliates. The key to combating such actors is likewise to maintain a highly adaptable approach that is both clear-eyed as to the threats and candid as to the difficult trade-offs that may often be required to defend against them. In other words, fighting terrorism will remain a perennial work in progress.

Foreign Policy Effects of Obama's Counterterrorism Strategy

President Obama's refreshingly diplomatic approach to the world helped spark a sea change in positive perceptions of America's global image and global role (Graham and Indyk 2010). This is certainly an important contextual change for the operation of American foreign policy, one that should pay dividends for years to come. And yet, the administration has often struggled to translate such international goodwill into tangible accomplishments regarding its top foreign policy priorities, most of which are directly related to the administration's broader goal of combating terrorism.

For example, despite Obama's sky-high personal approval ratings in Europe, he has been rebuffed in his efforts to resettle a significant number of Guantánamo prisoners in Europe, and America's NATO allies remain unwilling to contribute more combat troops to the vital mission against Taliban and al-Qaeda forces in Afghanistan. And despite Obama's formal "resetting" of U.S. relations with Russia and China, both countries remain opposed to the president's call for "crippling" sanctions against Iran over its nuclear program in the United Nations Security Council. Obama's personal appeals to Israelis and Palestinians to restart peace talks has also underwhelmed, having taken almost two years to coax the two sides even to begin meeting face-to-face. Nabil Fahmy, a former Egyptian ambassador to the United States, says he was initially impressed by Obama's efforts to bring Israelis and Palestinian together, "but nothing tangible came of it. Now he's seen by Arabs as a nice guy who can't deliver" (quoted in McManus 2010).

These examples show both the wildly unrealistic nature of the expectations for the Obama presidency overseas as well as the limitations of personal popularity on foreign policy more generally. But they also show the stubborn nature of many of America's global challenges and the eternal difficulty in fashioning robust multilateral solutions. This is particularly true with regard to America's top foreign policy and counterterrorism priority of improving relations with the Muslim world, which will require more than just a change in American presidents. It will require a great deal of patience and mutually responsible cooperation—as noted by Secretary of State Hillary Clinton during her appearance at the U.S.-Islamic World Forum in February 2010 (Landler 2010).

The fact is many of the foreign policy challenges Obama faces, including the ongoing struggle against Islamic extremism, were decades in the making. It is unrealistic to expect the Obama administration to single-handedly resolve these issues in a single term in office. But it is reasonable to expect it to begin laying the foundation for future achievement, and it is in this regard that the administration has been effective.

Tone Matters

Both in foreign policy in general and counterterrorism strategy in particular, the Obama administration's commitment to changing the diplomatic tone in the relations between America and key regions of the world through increased engagement and other soft-power mechanisms has shown impressive results.

For one thing, a new positive context exists for nations to cooperate openly with the United States, after nearly eight years in which such cooperation often came with a highly negative stigma. This does not mean nations of the world will always support America's foreign policy initiatives, but it does mean the pathway for cooperation has been broadened. Equally important, the change in diplomatic tone has provided cover and credibility for the Obama administration to engage in hard-line policies when it deems them necessary. For example, the administration faced criticism for its unsuccessful year-long effort to engage directly with the leaders in Iran over its nuclear program. However, such patient efforts have effectively rallied America's European allies to work together on a more aggressive stance toward Teheran. Regardless of whether China or Russia (or the United Nations) ultimately come along, the legitimacy required to take even more aggressive action against Iran has been created. The same principle applies for counterterrorism policy in general: the "turn the page" rhetoric and aggressive outreach of the Obama administration provided it with the credibility and legitimacy to engage in many of the same tough measures that caused criticism and condemnation to rain down upon President Bush.

Such leeway, however, cannot last forever. Every administration will ultimately be judged not by its words but by its actions. As did Bush, Obama recognizes that America's fight against terrorism will be a generations-long endeavor. Achieving success will require consistent candor regarding the specific nature of the threats and necessary responses, as well as clear delineations of how counterterrorism fits more broadly within American foreign policy.

The "Trumanization" of America's Counterterrorism Strategy

Setting aside differences in style and rhetoric, the fact remains that the Obama administration has co-opted and codified nearly all of the Bush administration's second-term counterterrorism policies. This is certainly not widely touted by administration officials—many of whom continue to insist that Obama has reversed course from Bush on counterterrorism—and it does not sit well with many administration supporters. There is, however, a historical precedent for the successful continuation of necessary, though politically contentious, foreign policy: President Dwight Eisenhower's continuation of President Harry Truman's containment policy.

When Eisenhower ran for president in 1952, Truman was the most unpopular president in modern American history, in large part due to his handling of foreign affairs. The Eisenhower campaign used strategic failures, such as the fall of China to communism and the bloody stalemate in the Korean War, to discredit Truman's approach to foreign policy—with Eisenhower pledging to reverse Truman's signature containment policy, which he accused of appeasing communism. Once in office, however, Eisenhower maintained the broad outlines of Truman's containment policy—not because it was popular (it wasn't)—but because there were no viable alternatives to the complex challenge of fighting communism. According to historian Walter Russell Mead (2010), "By the end of the Eisenhower administration, containment was the basis of a bipartisan consensus [in foreign policy] that lasted, more or less, for another generation."

Obama's evolving approach to counterterrorism can be viewed in a similar fashion. After promising to reverse President Bush's hard-line policies, the complex reality of fighting terrorism has compelled the Obama administration to maintain the core of Bush's approach. The prudent adjustments Obama has made—and will continue to make—to Bush's policies and to his own initial approach will likely serve to refine an effective counterterrorism template to be used by future generations of policy makers and presidents.

Notes

1. Compare this with Bush's rhetoric in an address to a Joint Session of Congress a few weeks after the 9/11 attacks: "How will we fight and win this war? We will direct every resource at our command . . . to the destruction and to the defeat of the global terror network" (www.washingtonpost.com/wp-srv/nation/specials/attacked/transcripts/bush address_092001.html).

CHAPTER 8

U.S. Intelligence Policy
Where Do We Stand?

Jennifer Sims[1]

SEPTEMBER 11, 2001, has joined Pearl Harbor (1941), Moscow's first thermo-nuclear test (1953), and the collapse of the Soviet Union (1990–1991) in the American portfolio of big surprises. Reflecting on what these cases teach us, most experts have urged Americans not to expect more from intelligence than it can realistically deliver (Betts 2007; Lowenthal 2009). Public expectations are hard to moderate, however, when the price tag for intelligence remains more than $40 billion a year and growing. After the 9/11 Commission found flaws in the way intelligence had been handled, the victims' families' demands for change resonated broadly with Americans and on Capitol Hill. In December 2004, Congress delivered on its promises. The Intelligence Reform and Terrorism Prevention Act represented the most radical restructuring of the U.S. intelligence establishment since its creation in 1947.

Then, Americans were surprised again—and it was a near miss. Exactly five years after the 2004 reforms, Umar Farouk Abdulmutallab attempted to ignite explosives hidden in his underwear aboard a jetliner en route to Detroit (Leahy and Hsu 2009). President Barack Obama reacted quickly, describing the plot's near success as "a mix of human and systemic failures" on the part of U.S. intelligence (Obama 2009f). Obama went on to say, "I will accept that intelligence by its nature is imperfect, but it is increasingly clear that intelligence was not fully analyzed or fully leveraged. That's not acceptable and I will not tolerate it" (quoted in Zeleny and Cooper 2010). Public reaction to the failed attempt suggested that many Americans agreed: intelligence, properly implemented, can and does reliably prevent surprise, and the U.S. system was not working well.

Most intelligence experts, however, still disagree. They argue that intelligence cannot stop every attack and that the U.S. record has been good overall.

After all, U.S. intelligence is tracking thousands of suspected terrorists, supporting operations in Iraq and Afghanistan, and stopping al-Qaeda recruits in Pakistan. Although Abdulmutallab almost succeeded, others have not (Eddy 2008).[2] While U.S. intelligence needs to evolve to fit the changing nature of international politics, real reform cannot be accomplished, according to this view, when only the failures get publicity. Much about how intelligence works is classified, so public debates about how to do it better inevitably miss both the worst vulnerabilities and the secret successes. The bottom line: leave intelligence reform to the insiders.

The question is: Who is right? Has U.S. intelligence been working, or is it still riddled with structural and heuristic impediments to success? This question begs others: What is the objective for intelligence in democracies, and how should success be measured? In his best-selling book *The Black Swan* (2007), Nassim Nicholas Taleb suggested that building a new intelligence structure in the emotionally shattered 9/11 environment may have been politically necessary but was not strategically smart. Taleb's arguments about risk and probability are complex, but their significance for U.S. intelligence boils down to two key observations. First, poor heuristics—not just poor information and analysis—underlies almost every surprise. Assessing the nature of swans based on the white ones that show up day after day, for example, is bound to lead to surprise when a black one arrives. This is a fault of inductive reasoning, which sets up expectations about the future based on what happened yesterday (with 9/11 being, figuratively speaking, yesterday). Second, people tend to account for such surprises by creating stories based on a retrospective sifting of facts and causal inferences. Such narratives about past surprises generate prescriptions for remedies that allow everyone to relax in the belief that the problem has been solved. That comfort can be deadening and literally deadly; it usually sets up the next surprise.

In this chapter, we will explore U.S. efforts to renew its intelligence endeavor, evaluating progress in the context of the broader sensibility Taleb suggests. We will be judging performance not only in the context of the stories we have told ourselves about the causes of intelligence failure on 9/11 but in light of what must be done to avoid Taleb's metaphorical Black Swan. The chapter begins with the politics of the issue. Intelligence policy—decisions about how to gather critical information on competitors and deliver it in time to win—has become a hot topic in national politics. Certainly such policy questions as the propriety of renditions, secret detention or methods of interrogation, and the role of the Central Intelligence Agency (CIA) were on the minds of incoming officials of the Obama administration. They did not have the luxury of designing the intelligence community they wanted; they had to work with what was there. And this required a fresh look at existing capabilities and the practical steps that could be taken to improve them. We will then examine the perspectives and policies of the Obama administration in its first year in office. The chapter concludes with a reflection on the problems of renewal from a theoretical perspective, generating four practical recommendations for reinvigorating intelligence.

The Setting for the Obama Administration: Grading the 2004 Reforms

From the vantage point of 2010, the 2004 reforms seem hasty, though also politically essential. After the 9/11 Commission finished its review, Congress rapidly proposed the legislation, catching most experts by surprise. After all, the new law was drafted before the Commission on Weapons of Mass Destruction in Iraq had reported its findings. Politicians were eager to respond to public pressure for change. They were ready consumers of even the most contentious ideas for reform and expressed their determination to implement many of them.[3] Thus, Congress quickly took sides on issues that had been hotly debated for years: the creation of an intelligence "czar" (what has become the director of national intelligence, or DNI) to sit above all 16 intelligence agencies; the demotion of the CIA from its role as coordinator of worldwide intelligence operations in support of the White House to its current role as, principally, a home for spies; the breaking down of intelligence "stovepipes" to encourage intelligence sharing; and creation of a national counterterrorism center for joint analysis (U.S. Congress, Senate, Select Committee on Intelligence 2004). The overall idea was to create a strong chief at the top who could end turf fights and help agencies focus on their common mission—the prevention of terrorist attacks.

Two years after issuing its report, the 9/11 Commission analyzed the government's progress in fixing the government's intelligence deficits. Two commissioners, former congressman Lee Hamilton (D-IN) and former New Jersey governor Thomas Kean (R), had asked some of the staff to monitor results, and by the end of 2005, they offered grades: many Ds and Fs and an overall average grade of C– (9/11 Public Discourse Project 2005). The one bright spot seemed to be intelligence sharing, where good steps had been made under the auspices of the new deputy DNI for analysis. Still, as 2006 came and went, many intelligence experts seemed to agree with the commissioners' low grades but to disagree about the missteps that had earned them.[4]

According to one view, the 9/11 Commission and legislators had overlooked the importance of intelligence operations outside of Washington and, by demoting the CIA and disrupting its sensitive relationships with foreign liaison partners, had put these operations at risk (Rosenbach 2008; Sims 2005). U.S. soldiers, customs agents, and law enforcement officers were fighting terrorism in foreign countries like Afghanistan and Iraq, along U.S. borders, and in major U.S. cities. To the extent that domestic operatives were winning, it seemed largely because of innovations in intelligence at the state and local level; overseas it seemed due to the ongoing work of chiefs of station, troops using human terrain teams, and restored capacities for human intelligence within the Army. Bureaucratic changes brought about by the 2004 reforms, such as relocating the principal locus for counterterrorism database management from a CIA center (before the reforms) to a DNI center (after the reforms) or realigning the relationships among intelligence agencies' headquarters in Washington, seemed to have little to do with operational successes.

Even the apparently successful disruption of domestic plots in places such as New York, Florida, and Illinois had arguably less to do with the 2004 law than improved cooperation among newly empowered federal investigators and law enforcement officers in the field.[5] Cities, importing ideas from Britain, had introduced the innovation of intelligence-led policing, which was bringing good results in Chicago, New York, and elsewhere. Los Angeles had created the first fusion center for federal and local law enforcement well before 9/11, an innovation the U.S. Department of Homeland Security (DHS) quickly adopted and replicated nationwide.[6] The New York Police Department (NYPD) developed a capability for strategic analysis, publishing in 2007 a landmark study on the process of radicalization among Muslim youth (Silber and Bhatt). Ignoring Washington's opposition, the NYPD deployed officers in 11 foreign cities where they could respond to incidents, learn from them, and help to rapidly bolster urban defenses (Kelly 2009).[7]

In April 2009, NYPD commissioner Raymond Kelly illustrated the federal problem for an audience at the Council on Foreign Relations: whereas NYPD agents in Madrid were able to report from the scene of that 2004 bombing almost immediately, the first federal report on the incident took 18 months to arrive (Kelly 2009). Cooperation with federal agents was getting better, but in Kelly's view it had more to do with Federal Bureau of Investigation (FBI) director Robert Mueller's acquiescence to an expanded NYPD role than to a scaling back of his mission and an augmentation of capacities in Washington. By mid-2007, it seemed as if all the NYPD wanted from Washington was money and noninterference.[8] Indeed, with the approval of Commissioner Kelly, Deputy Commissioner David Cohen and his colleagues had created a worldwide information exchange with fellow law enforcement officers that, in a moment of candor, Kelly described as "a Council on Foreign Relations with guns" (Kelly 2009).

Another set of critics focused less on the glacial movement of federal bureaucracies than on the role of the DNI as they graded the performance of the intelligence community and estimated what the new president would do with it (J. M. Simon 2010; Lowenthal, pers. comm. January 2010). Their grades were equally harsh. Part of the problem was that the legislation did little to increase the DNI's budgetary powers.[9] The Defense Department continues to control 80 percent of the U.S. intelligence budget. Also, whereas under the old system, the director of central intelligence (DCI) could use his bureaucratic base in the CIA to influence other agencies, under the new system, the DNI cannot. The reform legislation specifically removed the "czar" from any single intelligence bureaucracy so that the intelligence community could be coordinated from above. Yet the means the DCI had often used for influencing the 16 agencies before the reforms—methods such as managing the worldwide network of stations and bases, running liaison relations and ground operations through station chiefs, and controlling operational risks, including the management of covert action infrastructure worldwide—were mostly left beyond the DNI's reach.

The position's inherent weakness was so obvious that the Bush White House struggled to fill the position and keep it filled. The first DNI, Ambassador John Negroponte, had left in fairly short order to become deputy secretary of state, a position of supposedly lesser stature. Adm. Michael McConnell, Negroponte's successor, attempted to build and consolidate his power by revising Executive Order 12333, the directive that establishes the distribution of authority within the intelligence community. But his hard-fought effort only confirmed for observers that the position was inherently weak and perhaps even fatally flawed. These critics believed that, at the very moment the 2004 legislation had created him, the "czar" had been neutered.

By the time President Obama came into office, the plan to create a director of national intelligence who could be both detached from all intelligence agencies, yet capable of commanding them, seemed to be on the brink of failure. Whereas some critics saw this weakness as a problem of execution, others saw it as a problem in the 2004 statute itself. As a practical matter, both DNIs had spent most of their time preparing and delivering the president's daily briefings, leaving little time to build relationships with chiefs of station and liaison services, review functional budgets that allocate resources across agencies, or evaluate expensive collection systems. In such circumstances, the job had turned out to have both less power and more responsibility than advertised.

As President Obama took office, pledging to take up the fight against terrorism, reinvigorate diplomacy in the Middle East, and reintroduce serious arms control negotiations, it seemed possible that the U.S. intelligence infrastructure was too plagued with problems to support his ambitious agenda. Of the three major structural changes the 2004 legislation had introduced—the czar, the demotion of CIA, and the creation of the National Counterterrorism Center (NCTC)—only the last, the central nervous system for federal counterterrorism operations, seemed to be bringing expected results. So when the Christmas Day terrorist failed in his mission—not because of his timely capture but instead because of his incompetence and the bravery of other passengers—the intelligence community was in trouble yet again. The question was: How to fix it?

The Obama Administration's Intelligence Agenda

Repairing the intelligence community had been on President Obama's mind from the moment he took office. The incoming administration knew the challenges ahead were serious ones. Threats to the homeland from terrorism and cyber attacks were on the rise. The CIA, already suffering morale problems from its lowered bureaucratic stature, was coping with press reports on interrogation methods used during the prior administration, including allegations of torture against suspected terrorists. Incoming officials knew intelligence systems would need bolstering, but presidential attention for the job of fixing these institutions would be scarce. Domestic issues such as health care, the financial crisis, and the state of the U.S. economy seemed more pressing. The goal was to set things right but to do so quietly and professionally.

Settling Questions of Authority

The nomination of Leon Panetta as head of the CIA was, in this context, a surprise. Obama's widely anticipated choice for CIA director, John O. Brennan, had far more extensive intelligence experience. But his role in the controversial detention and interrogation programs of the Bush administration forced him to withdraw from consideration (Mazzetti and Huse 2009; R. J. Smith 2009).[10] In choosing Panetta for the CIA post, the president cited the nominee's record of opposition to harsh interrogation methods, political connections, personal integrity, and management experience (Holland 2009b; Mazzetti and Huse 2009). Officials also reportedly believed that the nominee's gravitas and close ties to the new president would help in bureaucratic negotiations with the Pentagon (Mazzetti and Huse 2009).

For close observers of intelligence policy, however, the added power for the CIA threatened to undermine further the position of the DNI. Although aides to the president described Panetta's nomination as part of an effort "to bring clarity to the division of responsibilities among American intelligence agencies, and in particular to end the current disputes between the offices of the C.I.A. director and the director of national intelligence," exactly the opposite also seemed possible (Mazzetti 2009a). The Senate confirmed Panetta as director of the CIA on February 12, 2009; in less than a year, the bureaucratic infighting rose to a new level (Pincus 2009c).

The problem was not that Obama's selection for DNI, widely respected Adm. Dennis Blair, seemed of lesser stature or that he got a late start. Indeed, the U.S. Senate had confirmed Admiral Blair's nomination as DNI on January 28, 2009 (Klonsky 2009). Prior to becoming DNI, Blair had served as commander, U.S. Pacific Command, director of the Joint Staff, and the first associate director of Central Intelligence for Military Support at the CIA. From 2003 to 2006, he was president and CEO of the Institute for Defense Analyses

(U.S. Office of the Director of National Intelligence [ODNI] 2009a). John Lehman, former Navy secretary and member of the 9/11 Commission, reportedly called Blair's nomination "a very logical choice" (Eisler 2009). But others seemed skeptical (Baer 2008). Like Panetta, Blair had no significant connections to the contentious intelligence policies of the Bush administration, but he also did not have the close connections with the White House that Panetta seemed to enjoy (Eisler 2009). And since the DNI's power depends so much on such connections, given that the position was created to be a stand-alone office, some analysts wondered why the nominees weren't switched.

The tension between the DNI and the director of the CIA came to a head in 2009 when disagreements emerged regarding, among other things, the appointment of chiefs of station as DNI representatives overseas and the designation of officials attending high-level domestic meetings (Pincus 2009c). The CIA's chiefs of station have long been intelligence counterparts to ambassadors overseas, responsible to chiefs of mission for coordinating all intelligence activities in the countries to which they are assigned. Their roles on embassy country teams have been critical to effective execution of policy and the management of trusted relationships with foreign intelligence services—a role that demands interpersonal skill and a nose for deceit and bluff. For the CIA, the issues of chief of station (COS) authority and management go to the core of the human intelligence business, for which the CIA, as manager of the national clandestine service, has long been accountable. The right to designate attendees at Washington meetings was a nonissue by comparison. For the DNI, the COS matter was one of fundamental authority. Unless the DNI had a direct relationship with Washington's intelligence authorities in the field, the DNI's position as head of U.S. intelligence would be effectively neutered.

The issues were brought to national security adviser Gen. James L. Jones and Vice President Joe Biden for mediation in November 2009. The White House sided with the CIA: station chiefs, appointed by the CIA, would continue to serve concurrently as DNI representatives. Blair, however, would have the right to name the intelligence community representative to National Security Council (NSC) meetings (Pincus 2009c).

The CIA claims of victory underscored the now widely held view that the creation of the DNI had also created a new and thorny set of bureaucratic issues—issues that were absorbing scarce White House attention. Covert action was one such issue. As part of the November 2009 mediation between the DNI and director of the CIA, General Jones reportedly decided that "on covert actions and their oversight, the CIA would continue to deal directly with the White House but must report oversight findings also to the DNI" (Pincus 2009c). Blair, when requested by the White House, would have responsibility for strategic oversight. Not surprisingly, the CIA viewed this decision, too, as a victory (Pincus 2009c).

Coupled with the decision concerning chiefs of station, the choice on covert action effectively confirmed the CIA's role as central manager of the intelligence community's worldwide presence. In a memorandum the following week, DNI Blair said, "The DNI's responsibilities include assessment and evaluation of the effectiveness of sensitive operations in meeting national policy objectives, as requested" (quoted in Gerstein 2009). Yet, as one U.S. intelligence official noted, "Covert action is ordered by the president and carried out by the CIA. That relationship, which involves a single, direct line of command and communication between the White House and the agency, isn't changing" (Miller 2009b).

Reconciling Intelligence Sharing and Counterintelligence

Another area that had preoccupied legislators in 2004 was the matter of intelligence sharing. Critics of the intelligence community's operations before 9/11 were nearly unanimous in faulting intelligence agencies for failing to pass intelligence to those analysts who needed it (National Commission on Terrorist Attacks 2004). To fix the problem, Congress mandated a new ethic of collaboration, defined by DNI McConnell as a proactive "responsibility to provide" (ODNI 2008).[11] His deputy for analysis, Thomas Fingar, introduced far-reaching changes in collaboration across agencies by improving analysts' access to each others' work and helping senior managers find formerly hidden pockets of expertise prior to his departure in January 2009 (Fingar 2008; Shaughnessy 2008). These initiatives led to substantial progress in information sharing among agencies. Congress also created, as mentioned earlier, a National Counterterrorism Center (NCTC) reporting to the DNI on intelligence collection but directly to the president on sensitive operations, including covert action. Although the NCTC made good progress on strategic planning and database management, it was also widely regarded as an intelligence clearinghouse in which information flowed in more readily than it flowed out, and its relationships with both the FBI and DHS seemed uneven at best (DeYoung 2006a; DeYoung and Leahy 2009). Its anticipated role overseeing overseas operations was limited by the dominance of military missions and its lack of proximity to field-based operations.

Moreover, with all this emphasis on information sharing, concerns began to mount concerning the intelligence community's counterintelligence capabilities (Sims and Gerber 2009). Sound intelligence policy involves careful balancing of initiatives to improve sharing and dissemination of information with protection of those sources or methods by which it is acquired. Indeed, prior to 9/11, arguably the biggest U.S. intelligence failures concerned foreign penetration, treachery, and the loss of sensitive sources. The commission that, during the 1990s, was investigating the espionage of CIA traitor Aldrich Ames, criticized the CIA for sharing too much information in house, not too little. Ames gained access to material about which he had no need to know, including highly sensitive information on agents working for the United States overseas. He became rich by sharing what he learned with Moscow, which then used its knowledge to capture and kill U.S. agents. Similarly, FBI traitor Robert Hanssen made ample use of his wide access to databases when working for the Russians. For intelligence professionals with long memories, the new emphasis on "obligation to share" was an understandable reaction to 9/11 but also worrisome. In a world in which the productivity of espionage and the ethics of the profession rest on protecting the lives of agents, the new policy raised both a moral quandary and the specter of loss.

Both the intelligence community and the FBI obviously appreciated the importance of counterintelligence, but their differing orientations meant the two communities were not smoothly integrated. Whereas collection agencies saw the problem primarily in terms of protecting U.S. collection efforts (operational security), the latter saw it primarily in terms of disrupting foreign ones—particularly those taking place on U.S. soil. The culture of the first was built around cover and secrecy; the culture of the second was built around law enforcement. Not surprisingly, the mix felt like oil and water to those responsible for managing overall counterintelligence strategy.

That responsibility fell, at least in theory, to the national counterintelligence executive (NCIX), a position folded into the office of the DNI as a result of the 2004 intelligence reform. The position had been plagued with problems since its creation. None of the powerful counterintelligence entities that were directly responsible for protecting lives and countering serious threats wanted top-down interference in their work. Successive DNIs had too much on their plates to tackle the complex set of issues a joint approach would require.[12] By 2008, the new mantra of openness and sharing running rampant at senior management levels of the intelligence community made the office of the NCIX a backwater. Rather tightly leashed by the DNI's office on the one hand and the FBI on the other, Joel Brenner, the NCIX during McConnell's reign as DNI, found his best traction in the issue of cyber threats. Brenner's hot pursuit of the cyber issue, while commendable, also illuminated the broader terrain he was unable to cross.

The incoming DNI, Admiral Blair, was attentive to the problem in counterintelligence and immediately established a task force to advise him on what to do about it. At least one of the participants had been heavily involved in the Defense Department's reorganization of counterintelligence under the under secretary of defense for intelligence, Gen. James Clapper. The task force recommended, among other things, a new emphasis on offensive counterintelligence and better integration of intelligence and counterintelligence planning. Blair took the advice. His new *National Intelligence Strategy* made counterintelligence a major mission area. Moreover, after considerable

deliberation, he made one of the members of the task force, former FBI deputy director Robert "Bear" Bryant, the new NCIX. Bryant took the job in
September 2009 (ODNI 2009b). He was chosen, according to the ODNI, for
his "many years of investigative, operational and management experience in
counterintelligence, counterterrorism and law enforcement" (ODNI 2009b).
This was, if anything, an understatement. Bryant's past accomplishments
included the investigation and prosecution of Aldrich Ames, Earl Pitts, and
Harold Nicholson; oversight of the Oklahoma City bombing and Khobar
Towers bombing investigations; and the resolution of the Montana Freeman
standoff (ODNI 2009b).

The counterintelligence community seemed, at least on the FBI side, to
support the choice. The question remained whether, even with his vast experience, Bryant would be able to work with the CIA to bring counterintelligence
into service as a tool of strategy, not just a tool for security and defense.[13] Such
innovation would require the trust of policy makers and CIA case officers—
people whose jobs involve political outcomes and, in the latter case, breaking
laws overseas. For a senior law enforcement officer like Bryant, this would be a
tough new mission (Gertz 2009).[14]

There were, however, plenty of signs that the new administration was ready
to place greater emphasis on counterintelligence than some had anticipated it
would, especially after candidate Obama had sharply criticized the NSA's
aggressive domestic surveillance program conducted secretly on behalf of the
Bush administration. Candidate Obama had argued that this program ignored
key provisions of the Foreign Intelligence Surveillance Act (FISA), which had
established secret court procedures for wiretapping suspected spies and terrorists (Murray 2008; Vargas 2008). Once in office, however, the Obama administration demonstrated a willingness to support laws bolstering federal powers in
this domain, including renewal of three controversial provisions of the USA
Patriot Act that were due to expire: section 206, which allows roving surveillance of targets who take measures to thwart FISA surveillance; section 215,
which authorizes the FISA court to compel the production of "business records";
and section 6001, which effectively permits a "lone wolf" to be treated as an
agent of a foreign power under FISA (Weich 2009).[15] As Suzanne Spaulding
(2008) noted in her testimony before Congress on the matter, this latter provision provides a large loophole in the protections FISA was meant to provide
ordinary U.S. persons, because it takes away the requirement that secret wiretaps be used only in the case of foreign operations conducted on U.S. soil, not
against people without such overseas connections. The administration argued,
however, that such tools are needed to disrupt terrorist plots; establishing connections to foreign powers might not always be possible in time to prevent an
attack and would be pointless when investigating homegrown terrorists. Congress ultimately agreed with the administration and extended these provisions,

though the debate reminded everyone that civil liberties and domestic intelligence remain sensitive matters for the public.

The Matter of Civil Liberties: What Boundaries for Intelligence in the Post-9/11 Era?

The new administration's policy on counterintelligence methods should not have been all that surprising since it was in line with Obama's July 2008 Senate vote in support of expanding FISA, including legal immunity for the phone companies that cooperated in the NSA wiretapping program (Johnson and Nakashima 2009). To civil libertarians, however, the new policy appeared to be contrary to statements the presidential candidate had made during his campaign. As a candidate, Obama had indicated that he opposed the Bush administration's aggressive domestic surveillance programs and that he would resist further compromises to civil liberties. Once in office, however, the new president seemed willing to invoke the executive branch's prerogatives with regard to secrecy in court proceedings and proved unwilling to prosecute CIA officials who likely engaged in practices that, although approved by the Justice Department, nonetheless fit legal definitions of torture. Such decisions raised concerns on the political left that Obama would strike no new balance between intelligence and civil liberties but would instead adhere to the one his predecessor had established (Johnson and Nakashima 2009).

As the year progressed, however, evidence seemed to indicate that the new administration would take a deliberative approach to these issues and might become more flexible than its predecessor. More in line with the expectations of civil libertarians was the new president's decision on matters of detention and prosecution of suspected terrorists. On January 22, 2009, the president issued executive orders requiring the closure of the Guantánamo Bay detention center, banning the use of controversial interrogation techniques, and creating Special Task Forces to review interrogation guidelines and detainee policy (Obama 2009b). By August, the Task Force had concluded that the Army Field Manual, which prohibited waterboarding and similarly aggressive procedures, should guide interrogation methods for U.S. intelligence agencies (U.S. Department of Justice 2009).[16] It also advised that the United States create a High-Value Detainee Interrogation Group (HIG), which would "bring together the most effective and experienced interrogators and support personnel from across the Intelligence Community, the Department of Defense, and law enforcement" (U.S. Department of Justice 2009). In late August 2009, the Obama administration endorsed the Task Force's recommendation to create such an elite interrogation unit (Miller 2009a).

The administration also decided, however, not to prosecute those who had conducted waterboarding authorized by Alberto Gonzales, President Bush's attorney general, and the Department of Justice's Office of Legal Counsel (OLC). While releasing OLC memoranda that detailed interrogation tactics used against terrorism suspects and condemning the harsh interrogation techniques described in them, Obama wanted "to assure those who carried out their duties relying in good faith upon legal advice from the Department of Justice that they will not be subject to prosecution" (Johnson and Tate 2009; Obama 2009r). Furthermore, he explained that "the exceptional circumstances surrounding these memos should not be viewed as an erosion of the strong legal basis for maintaining the classified nature of secret activities" (Obama 2009r). Such decisions, together with later backpedaling on closing Guantánamo and prosecuting 9/11 terrorists in civilian courts, suggested that the administration intends to restore confidence in U.S. moral authority but not at the expense of damaging the trust and effectiveness of the U.S. intelligence community.

What Should Americans Expect: Swans on the Potomac?

This White House approach and the 2009 record suggest more commitment to intelligence renewal than to ongoing reform. As the administration seeks to increase these agencies' effectiveness, how well has the balance been struck between civil liberties and aggressive operations? The issue of metrics remains: after all the intelligence reforms and expense, how do we know whether we are any better off? Was the failure to preempt the Christmas Day terrorist really a sign of continued weakness or just another indication that intelligence can never be perfect?

The Black Swan's (2007) author, Nassim Taleb, might say that the various commission reports and a host of other publications have created a lulling narrative about why 9/11 happened: a dual-hatted spy-chief, ingrained cultures, stovepipes, and the like. The problem is that this story could be a highly biased narrative that infers phantom causes. The 9/11 narrative Americans now widely accept ignores the silent evidence against it, such as the disasters that did not happen perhaps because intelligence actually worked pretty well before 9/11. If the CIA was crippled by poor capacities for espionage and a dual-hatted chief, how did it manage to be "first in" against the Taliban in Afghanistan immediately after the 9/11 attacks? How did an agency that "lost" on 9/11 help win the initial battles against al-Qaeda and the Taliban in one of the most forbidding environments on earth? How certain are we that flaws in U.S. intelligence agencies, particularly those addressed by the 9/11 Commission in its rushed recommendations, were the ones really responsible for the surprise of 9/11?

Consider, for example, the momentous change that occurred in international politics as the 1980s folded into the 1990s. A multiethnic superpower, bristling with nuclear weapons, suddenly collapsed. Setting aside the question of why so few people (including major players such as Mikhail Gorbachev) foresaw the exact timing of particular events, it is worth noting that, despite myths to the contrary, U.S. intelligence had steadily and accurately tracked the Soviet Union's serious economic decline. As noted by an expert commission charged by congressional overseers with reviewing the CIA's record,

> Most reports [from 1979] through 1988 on the course of the Soviet GNP and on general economic developments were equally satisfactory: accurate, illuminating and timely. . . . These reports regularly reported the steady decline in the Soviet growth rate and called attention to the deep and structural problems that pointed to continued decline and possibly to stagnation. (House Permanent Select Committee on Intelligence 1991, quoted in MacEachin 1997, 57–58)

More important, as the empire imploded, strategic nuclear war did not occur. Nor was there even a "minor" conventional war in Europe. This relatively peaceful evolution of the bipolar international system into a unipolar one full of weak states constitutes a historical surprise for which intelligence might be credited. After all, the unraveling of the Austro-Hungarian Empire in the late 1800s led directly to World War I. It seems likely that war was avoided in 1989 because, among other things, the intelligence services both in Moscow and Washington made the chain of events—particularly military moves—relatively transparent to the key decision makers, thus staving off defensive or opportunistic impulses and the escalating tensions that could have led to war. Whether this hypothesis is true or not, the lack of systematic attention to why this good thing "happened" in 1989–90 (or why a bad thing did not) should lead us to conclude, according to Taleb (2007), that we really do not know.

If one adopts Taleb's (2007) sensibility when looking at the evidence about intelligence community performance, recent "fixes" not only seem less certain to stop the next bad event, they may actually abet it. Indeed, we have already seen that attentiveness to the problem of intelligence sharing may have blinded intelligence policy makers to the dangers of too much of it—dangers amply illustrated by the prosecution of Aldrich Ames but subsequently overlooked. There are other, similar concerns. For example, developments in robotics (mechanical spies), nanotechnology (phones that smell germs), and optics (invisibility cloaks) pose new challenges to the traditional craft of intelligence that have nothing to do with organizational change or the distribution of authorities so hotly debated at the time of the 2004 legislation. And the issue of terrorism will likely not always be our top priority. Iran may be our next nuclear state. North Korea has already tested a nuclear device and is now on the cusp of another change in leadership. China holds so much U.S. debt that international stability may depend more on a steady hand in Beijing than in the damping down of insurgencies in Iraq and Afghanistan.

The point is, staring at 9/11 will not tell us how to adapt the large intelligence institutions of the Cold War to an era in which failed states may dominate; rogue states may clandestinely pursue biological or nuclear weapons; and, as the *Economist* ("Third-World Mobile Telecoms" 2008) reported, more than half the world's population will own vulnerable cell phones, many of them linked to the critical infrastructure of the United States. This is a world in which Google is attacked by China and retaliates, Georgia and Russia conduct a war they find difficult to terminate because of the persistence of private Internet attacks, and pirates pose real threats to shipping off the coast of Africa. Yet, with 9/11 as our political reference point, critics and defenders of U.S. intelligence still think mostly about countering terrorists and fixing bureaucracies in Washington to do better at it. In this sense, the 2004 legislation has us in an intellectual lockbox.

The message that Taleb's (2007) analysis delivers is not that U.S. intelligence is necessarily worse than before 9/11, though it may be; it is rather that measuring intelligence performance is difficult, especially when afflicted by myth and hearsay. We can measure how far we have come in implementing the recommendations of past commissions, but we do not really know if we are better off for it.

Re-evaluating U.S. Intelligence

A good place to start in evaluating U.S. intelligence is to define what intelligence is supposed to do and compare these requirements to contemporary American performance. In this way we set aside past failures and reforms to take a more holistic approach. Although Taleb (2007) might think of this as storytelling at a higher level of generality, it at least breaks analysis free from the incrementalism that has plagued U.S. reform efforts in the past.

To begin such "out-of-the-box" thinking, one must first identify the box, which has been surprisingly difficult to do in the policy domain but is making substantial headway in scholarly circles. Blue-ribbon panels and commissions mentioned so far have mostly defined intelligence as, essentially, whatever intelligence agencies do. This view tends to bias analysts towards a focus on secrets. Although secrecy is often important to sound intelligence practice, such a traditional view is, according to recent scholarship, largely misguided (Mercado 2004; Sands 2005; Sims 2005; Steele 2001). Crucial sources of intelligence exist outside the secretive intelligence community, such as the Department of State's Foreign Service, which gathers information on foreign governments' perspectives and decision-making processes not available through other media. This department's relative poverty among national security agencies has led to a significant drop in such reporting over the past twenty years, forcing clandestine agencies to fill the gap and making the gathering of intelligence by secret agencies more difficult and probably more expensive than it once was.

Although the decline in State Department reporting escaped notice by the 9/11 Commission, there are signs the Obama administration has recognized the problem. Secretary of State Hillary Clinton has argued strenuously for more resources and appears to be getting them. Recognizing the importance of Foreign Service reporting reminds us that intelligence is about gathering information that helps dissuade or defeat adversaries, regardless of whether the entity that does these functions has "intelligence" in its name. To perform this function well, U.S. intelligence needs to take steps the 9/11 Commission never mentioned. In addition to the issues the Obama administration has already identified, five areas seem most important: accountability for decentralized decision making, trust and oversight, warning, collection management, and counterintelligence (Sims 2009).

Accountability: The Policy Makers' Responsibilities

The first requirement of intelligence is timely delivery of relevant information to decision makers. To accomplish this mission, decision makers must understand how intelligence works, take responsibility for investing in it, and share their strategies and tactics, specifying what they need and when. For its part, to assist in gaining advantages over adversaries, intelligence has to focus on delivering enough information for the decision, not necessarily comprehensive knowledge. Intelligence that is complete can also be useless if it arrives after the battle has been fought. In this sense, President Obama was right to be dismayed over the intelligence community's performance with regard to Abdulmutallab, the would-be Christmas bomber. Information about Abdulmutallab's radicalization, provided by the terrorist's father to a senior U.S. official in Nigeria, should have been enough to trigger a decision to pull the son's multiple-entry visa to the United States. Instead, his name was transferred to a central database in Washington so all-source analysts could make a more well-rounded determination.

From the standpoint of modern requirements for agility and decentralized support of decision making, this focus on centralized data processing seems old-school. During the Cold War, all-source analysis centralized in Washington seemed more important than the processing and exploitation of single sources for tactical decision making overseas. When missteps might have brought about strategic nuclear war, caution ruled. International politics moved slowly; decisions were made on the basis of intelligence pieced together over relatively lengthy periods.

Now, the reverse may be true. Adversaries, such as drug and weapons traffickers, terrorists, and pirates are more mercurial, hit-and-run specialists. Intelligence policy needs to take greater risks for better tactical performance against them, much as the military is doing in Iraq and Afghanistan. It is not clear, though, that the fault for flat-footedness in the Abdulmutallab case rested with the intelligence community and not policy makers. Risk taking is something most intelligence professionals are willing to do, provided policy makers will back them up—witness the controversy over the CIA's acquiescence to the Bush administration's support for waterboarding. To make the no-fly list amendable by chiefs of station or ambassadors and thus more all-inclusive would have been, and remains, a political decision, not an intelligence one. If the threshold needed to be lowered or decision making delegated to allow the station chief to add Abdulmutallab to the list or the ambassador unilaterally to revoke his visa, then policy makers should have done it and the president should have said so.

Strategic Analysis, Trust, and Oversight

The point is, if intelligence is about gaining advantages—that is, advancing one's own interests through the process of informing the design, building, execution, and termination of winning strategies—then intelligence must be married to strategy to succeed. And for policy makers to reveal sensitive strategies to intelligence colleagues requires trust. When the two work well together, policy and intelligence almost seem to merge in the decision-making process, raising the temptation of politicization, which must be resisted. This is also why covert action is often confused with the intelligence function itself. Although the conduct of secret policy (covert action) is conceptually distinct from the pursuit of an information edge (intelligence), in practice, covert action is usually conducted by intelligence services because those who topple governments or manipulate perceptions need secret information and effective counterintelligence to do so successfully. Operatives who put their lives on the line depend so much on those who are identifying their targets that policy execution and intelligence support become almost indistinguishable. The same is true for military operations; uniformed intelligence officers cannot provide situational awareness unless they have intimate knowledge of the mission. When Gen. Michael Flynn released his devastating assessment of intelligence support of the war effort in Afghanistan, he made this point: intelligence designed to stop terrorist attacks does not provide effective support to a mission that is seeking to build trust and community (Flynn, Pottinger, and Batchelor 2010).

As discussed above, the moment such trust is lost between decision makers and intelligence providers, problems with timeliness and relevance will emerge. Commanders who do not trust the intelligence service may begin to withhold their strategic intent and the details of their intended next moves. Intelligence providers are then unmoored from the intimate aspects of the competition and are doomed to gathering information commanders may not want or need, which, in a vicious loop, only confirms their uselessness to those whom they are trying to serve.[17]

To repair damaged trust, effective oversight is essential, because it promises the risk takers that, if they follow the law, policy makers will have their backs. Unfortunately, policy makers have not provided this kind of support for intelligence professionals for some years.

Congressional oversight practices had been strong from the late 1970s to the late 1990s, but they declined precipitously as political infighting broke out after 9/11. By the time reform legislation was up for consideration in 2003, the intelligence oversight committees had lost their traditional role, and the Government Affairs Committee took the lead in holding hearings and drafting the legislation. Not surprisingly, the 2004 legislation did not offer prescriptions for making congressional oversight more effective, and little has been done to improve the relationship between the Hill and intelligence agencies. In fact, during 2009, tempers flared between new CIA director Panetta and Speaker of the House Nancy Pelosi (D-CA) over the extent to which the CIA had briefed congressional leaders—commonly referred to as the "gang of eight"—about sensitive operations that, while never carried out, might have involved planning for the assassination of terrorists.[18] In an atmosphere of such tension and mistrust, intelligence professionals inevitably recalibrate the risks they are willing to take.

Although oversight is essential to sound intelligence performance, substantial research has suggested that trust can also be improved through analytic tradecraft (Davis 1995; Lowenthal 2009, pp. 146–149, 187–192; McLaughlin 2008; Treverton 2008). Analysts should focus not only on how to reduce uncertainty but, perhaps more important, how to convey both knowledge and uncertainty to decision makers so that they can gain the strategic and tactical advantages they need. This does not mean telling them what they *want* to know; it means telling them what they *need* to know. Deriving meaning from knowledge for the use of decision makers under pressure is at the core of the analytic art; one cannot do it without some degree of intimacy with them.

Of course, intimacy with decision makers can doom an intelligence service, an outcome Americans know well and have long sought to avoid. Historians have, for example, documented the famous relationship between Gen. George B. McClellan, Civil War commander of the Army of the Potomac, and the head of his intelligence apparatus, Allan Pinkerton. The latter knew his boss so well that his overinflation of enemy numbers was usually in the same ballpark as McClellan's own inflated estimates. The result: dithering, delay, and loss. Yet improving the objectivity of intelligence need not involve detaching from the decision maker's problem or ignoring the frame for his or her choices. Even Sherman Kent, a strong advocate of objectivity in analytic tradecraft, advised that, if forced to choose between objectivity and relevance, the wise analyst chooses the latter (Kent 1949). In this sense, the U.S. debate on intelligence reform has probably overemphasized politicization at the expense of constructive intimacy. "Speaking truth to power" is a misleading mantra, since truth and power reside on both sides of the intelligence policy–making divide. The more apt imperative is to enable advantage by lubricating choice.

Warning

That an intelligence service must convey intelligence to key decision makers in time seems so obvious as to be elementary, but even the elementary becomes difficult when it conflicts with past practices. For example, it would seem elementary to expect intelligence to collect information policy makers do not believe they need to know in order to provide warning of the unexpected and thus prevent surprise. Intelligence must serve as the angel of commanders' better intentions. Its practitioners must sometimes collect what commanders do not want to know in order to spare them surprises. For this reason, a good intelligence service—one less vulnerable to surprise—will have a capacity for independent action. Decisions about what to collect will flow from the bottom up, as well as from the top down.

Yet as James Simon, a former senior intelligence official and now Microsoft executive, has pointed out, U.S. intelligence collection is still dominated by a top-down requirements system that gives intelligence agencies little latitude to collect against the possibility decision makers are wrong or against targets that have not yet captured the interests of policy makers (J. M. Simon 2005). Even if the U.S. intelligence system were optimized against the terrorist threat, this would provide no guarantee that it would perform well against the next threatening adversary. Indeed, with the NCTC now at the top of the intelligence architecture, it seems less likely than before that new threats will get the attention they deserve. Recently, the National Intelligence Council established a National Intelligence Officer for Warning, though the position remains unfilled as of this writing. In the view of Charlie Allen, an intelligence professional widely regarded as an expert in the warning problem, creating the position was necessary but is hardly enough (pers. comm. February 26, 2010). The problem is, it is hard to justify resources on the basis of what agencies do not know and policy makers do not expect. Building in a reserve capacity for collecting against the unknown and unexpected is a hard sell in Washington; after all, funds run short for known priorities on a regular basis. No bureaucratic reforms seem likely to make warnings of this kind easier for the top U.S. intelligence officer. Improved collection, however, might work.

Improve Collection

Collection is best when it is speedy, wide-ranging, and a bit redundant. After all, if you want collectors to take risks to get good, meaty information, they have to have backup so a loss of one source does not lead to larger failures. All this seems pretty straightforward, but it is deceptively so. The thought is often that one needs more spies, satellites, liaison relationships, or listening devices to get more intelligence. But it is really not that simple. A spy usually needs a disguise, travel documents, communications, and a base out of which to work (which is also part of his or her disguise). In fact, every intelligence sensor needs communications, a platform, a way to process the information, and a way to get the information from its collection point to someone who can use it. Just multiplying sensors can create more problems than it solves if these other pieces are not also integrated, coordinated, and managed. The faster you want your collection to work (say, getting a spy to chase a terrorist through many countries), the better integrated your logistical support must be.

What most Americans do not realize is that this logistical tail is not "stovepiped" at all for most modern U.S. intelligence collectors—quite the opposite. Unlike in the nineteenth century, when the military provided its cavalry and balloon corps with integrated logistics, modern national intelligence collection is a complicated, multiagency enterprise. This is why the Defense Department resists ceding budgetary or management control over collection to the DNI; national intelligence collection relies on the military services' communications systems, airplanes, ships, and vehicles, many of which are integral to operations of deployed troops. This problem is not, moreover, exclusive to the Pentagon. Other agencies outside the intelligence community are involved in the collection of national security information, including the Department of State and the Department of Energy, which has important laboratory capabilities for data exploitation.

The result is that intelligence collectors, such as the CIA and NSA, conduct overseas operations for which someone else owns the modern equivalent of these operators' uniforms, horses, communication gear, and travel documents. Not only is it difficult for CIA spies to be agile, it is nearly impossible for them to exercise independent initiative, except in quite rare circumstances and at high risk. This lack of independence is why countering surprise has become so hard that we are beginning to define intelligence as something that cannot much help with it, which is silly. But to build independence, one must have trust, which takes us back to the issue of oversight and the thorny problems of secrecy and deceit.

Remembering Counterintelligence

The fifth key ingredient of an excellent intelligence capability is a capacity for counterintelligence. Although there is more to the business than denial and deception, these capabilities are critical. They include keeping secrets and snookering opponents. Somewhat surprisingly, most Americans believe we are not very good at either of these skills, even though they also perceive Washington as thick with both. The United States protects massive amounts of data in its classification system—one that even includes multiple categories of "sensitive but unclassified" information whose growth and ambiguous status would have Senator Daniel Patrick Moynihan (D-NY), once Congress's most ardent critic of rampant secrecy, turning in his grave.

The problem for the United States is not so much its capacity to keep secrets as its capacity to do so selectively, a task that is at the heart of an effective counterintelligence strategy. Deny the opponents everything you think they might want, and you become easily manipulated; your opponents can drive you to financial ruin, stimulate domestic opposition, deny your freedom of action, and slow you down. The key to successful counterintelligence is to use secrecy to conceal and reveal as necessary, thus confusing and deceiving the opponent.

A superior intelligence service has a capacity for secrecy but exercises it selectively in the interest of gaining and retaining tactical and strategic advantages, including source protection or deception. Although deception usually involves a lie, the lie is apt to be close to the truth, and in any case, it is conveyed through the opponent's most trusted channel for collecting information, usually its intelligence service. When secrets no longer serve such objectives, they need to be released. Needless to say, the U.S. system is constipated with secrets. We are a long way from where we need to be: agile, cunning, and accountable.

Intelligence Policy: An Agenda for Reform

The foregoing evaluation of U.S. intelligence would be unlikely to satisfy Taleb, but as a rough overview of U.S. strengths and weaknesses, it suggests progress has been uneven at best. While comparing current efforts to ideal ones might suggest a better institutional arrangement than the United States now has, we are ultimately a nation of laws, and the Intelligence Reform and Terrorism Prevention Act of 2004 is one of them. If overhauling the structure set up by the 2004 Act is a political nonstarter, which it probably is, then the issue for President Obama is not what an ideal intelligence system would look like but rather how to work with what we have. These are the boundaries within which President Obama's new DNI, Gen. James Clapper, and CIA director Leon Panetta now work too. They should take four principal steps.

1. Restate the mission of intelligence, and press decision makers to see their critical role in it. Intelligence production for policy makers should be less about preparing the "Golden Books" of secrets on countries or functional issues for broad dissemination than about disseminating only the products that offer information advantages over competitors, both present and future. Intelligence production should not be an industrial enterprise but rather a tailored, custom, and surgical one. And if the products deliver advantage, as they properly should, then those products should be classified even if the sources and methods used were all unclassified, There are, of course, rare exceptions: the urgent delivery of a message in a competition where the utility of advantage is fleeting and timeliness trumps all else. But in general, the advantage delivered by an unclassified product will gain no advantage at all if it is given away and will likely box in policy makers rather than assist them.

This point has ramifications for intelligence sharing. The emphasis on sharing makes good sense, unless it masks lack of intimacy with decision makers or the hiring of undereducated analysts. The breadth of circulation of intelligence products is no measure of the value they contain—quite the contrary. Value depends, instead, on competitive advantage, an advantage that is put at risk each time the information is shared unnecessarily. Highly sensitive intelligence should not be used for raising the baseline knowledge of civil servants or junior analysts. Policy makers should be responsible for learning their portfolios through open means and using intelligence for gaining traction on the issues of national interest with which they are entrusted. The idea that intelligence, funded through secret means, should go beyond this highly specialized role to educate more broadly is a dangerous one in a democracy.

Morale among intelligence troops should improve once those troops understand that they are not responsible for "truth" in every instance but for competitive advantage.[19] They succeed when they deliver better information than that available to opponents and competitors. DNI McConnell accepted this more nuanced mission, as evidenced by his release of *Vision 2015* (DNI 2008) shortly before leaving office. The approach should be institutionalized, but carefully. The temptation to deliver intelligence en masse, just because one believes 9/11 mandated more sharing and because one can do so using modern technology, does not make it right; indeed it would seem to negate the essential notion of decision advantage, which implies intimacy and specialization. The danger is that all-source analysis will become homogenized and decision advantage lost should sharing inside the intelligence world take precedence over intimate and interactive sharing across the policy-making divide. The two are not always compatible, as former policy makers and foreign liaison partners have been quick to point out (Davis 1995).

2. Relieve the DNI of day-to-day responsibility for briefing the president on all-source intelligence. This job should be delegated to the chair of the National Intelligence Council and, when available, the CIA's station chiefs worldwide. Station chiefs, who are senior, field-based officers, should be encouraged to contribute all-source analysis from the field, brief it when they are in town, and use it to target new opportunities for collection. The National Clandestine Service, which conducts most U.S. covert action, needs to work with an analytic team that has knowledge of strategy and the context for its work. Cleaning up the visual lines on an organization chart should not be a priority if it is achieved at the expense of good decision support to the president and the cabinet, which, in this case, requires all-source analysts and collectors to mix things up more, not less. The DNI should sit in on any morning briefings, using them and the president's queries to orchestrate methods for closing gaps in collection and moving resources against emerging targets, whether or not they are apparent to others managing day-to-day collection. With this more circumscribed but still critical set of responsibilities, the DNI's staff could become the president's first responders for impending intelligence problems that individual agencies cannot afford to solve alone or that involve multiple agencies. Regarded as such, they would have the power of the White House behind their initiatives and find less resistance from the collection agencies—a point elaborated on below.

3. Empower the DNI by limiting his mission. Three steps will accomplish this goal. First, instead of "taking on" the Defense Department, bolster the DNI's relationship to it by institutionalizing the practice of designating the same individual as both deputy to the defense secretary and to DNI. Such was the role played by Gen. James Clapper for Robert Gates and Dennis Blair until Blair stepped down and Clapper was named as his replacement. While he served both agencies, the relationship appeared to work; there is no reason not to build on it. Second, balance this strong partnership with an equally strong partnership with the Department of State using a similar mechanism. This will aid the integration of collection and the management of ground-based intelligence operations worldwide. Ambassadors could then play a more effective coordination role overseas with their defense and intelligence counterparts.

This Washington-based triumvirate of the DNI, the Defense Department, and the State Department would then be in a position to take the third step: backstopping fast-paced field operations by ensuring that budgeting, programming, and logistics are coordinated across agencies. Thus, the DNI could orchestrate the logistical tail for overseas intelligence collection with half his current staff while driving agility and efficiency into the process in ways that actually help the principal collection agencies instead of stepping on their toes. It would also improve the DNI's ability to influence the "nonintelligence" sources of intelligence problems, such as the underfunding of the Department of State's Foreign Service reporting.

Of course, the same logic holds on the home front. Forcing a Washington intelligence presence at the state and local level is often counterproductive. State and local police are crafting a balance between policing and counterintelligence that varies across state and municipal boundaries, which is not necessarily a bad thing. Encouraging the DHS's new under secretary for intelligence, Caryn Wagner, who begins her job with already strong ties to the intelligence community, to bolster her connections to state and local law enforcement while working collaboratively with the FBI should obviate the need for a U.S. counterpart to Britain's MI-5—a whole new federal agency created exclusively to conduct domestic intelligence collection.

4. Find ways to achieve more agile and selective secrecy. The DNI, working through the NCIX, needs greater presidential authority to orchestrate worldwide counterintelligence operations, subordinating security chiefs to the formulators of intelligence policy. Sometimes keeping secrets will be necessary; sometimes it may be more useful to give them away—strategies the FBI should never be asked to formulate and execute. The kind of artful security, deception, and redirection that saves citizens' and soldiers' lives arises more often from sudden secrecy and revelation than it does from the more predictable kind of classification process that comes with highly bureaucratized systems. Offensive counterintelligence is anathema to those responsible for law enforcement, locks, and safes because it complicates their work. Putting intelligence policy makers truly in charge of strategic counterintelligence through the office of the DNI and its national counterintelligence executive may not be something with which law enforcement agencies are comfortable. That is as it should be. In the intelligence business, there should be limits to "jointness" and interagency collaboration.

5. Enhance the prospects for successful warning by hiring a more diverse workforce, increasing the DNI's reserve funds for discretionary operations (to include R&D and HUMINT deployments worldwide), and improving the mechanisms for oversight. Top-down requirements systems invite surprises like 9/11. Our systems should encourage somewhat greater independence in operations so that Washington officials learn what they need to know, not just what they want to know. A corollary of this recommendation is the need for greater tolerance for risk. Risk will only be acceptable to intelligence officers if they are allowed to foster a culture and esprit de corps that instills and reinforces a compatible operational ethic. In this sense, "culture" is a good thing and should not be discouraged. In fact, multiple cultures in an intelligence community, properly managed, actually prevent the kind of group-think that led to faulty analysis of Saddam Hussein's weapons of mass destruction prior to the 2003 war. Of course, as explained above, increased risk taking will only be acceptable to policy makers if oversight is strengthened in useful ways. Although changing congressional practices will be a long and uncertain endeavor, the oversight authorities of ambassadors (over intelligence operations overseas) and chiefs of station (over intelligence operations of all agencies) should be reinvigorated and their direct access to the president assured when necessary.

Implicit in these recommendations is the central premise underlying Admiral McConnell's *Vision 2015:* greater involvement and accountability for decision makers, both in Congress and in the executive branch, in the wake of national security disasters (DNI 2008). If intelligence is to serve policy well, it must provide "decision advantage" for strategists, but it must also be freed from responsibility for policy makers' inattention, errors of judgment, and leadership failures. Intelligence may be able to provide advantages, but it is still the decision makers who choose and therefore bear ultimate responsibility for their policies.

Notes

1. I owe great thanks to my graduate research assistants at Georgetown University, Wesley Jenkins, Gregory Thompson, and Allison Wright for their excellent work conducting research, editing drafts, and providing general support for this article.
2. Plots have reportedly been disrupted in Lackawanna, New York; Bly, Oregon; Lodi, California; Torrance, California; Iredell County, North Carolina; Miami, Florida; Toledo, Ohio; and Syracuse, New York.
3. Those experts included Bruce Berkowitz and Alan Goodman, authors of the prescient volume *Best Truth: Intelligence in the Information Age* (New Haven, Conn.: Yale University Press, 2000), and Amy Zegart, whose book *Flawed by Design: The Evolution of the CIA, JCS, and NSC* (Palo Alto, Calif.: Stanford University Press, 1999) pointed out organizational defects built into the U.S. intelligence establishment.
4. A 2007 book by Zegart, *Spying Blind: The CIA, the FBI, and the Origins of 9/11* (Princeton, N.J.: Princeton University Press), essentially agreed.
5. The chair of the U.S. Senate Select Committee on Intelligence, Diane Feinstein (D-CA), worried openly about renegotiating the terms of the Patriot Act in the midst of the Zazi incident. This act, passed in 2001 to permit roving wiretaps and other forms of domestic intelligence collection, provided many of the tools that law enforcement agencies needed to investigate and prosecute the Zazi case.
6. As of July 2009, DHS had created 72 fusion centers, of which 27 had the Homeland Security Data Network for accessing information held by the new National Counterterrorism Center and communicating secret-level intelligence. See U.S. Department of Homeland Security, "State and Local Fusion Centers," September 16, 2009, www.dhs .gov/files/programs/gc_1156877184684.shtm (accessed September 13, 2010).
7. In April 2009, Commissioner Kelly said that the NYPD Intelligence Division maintained relationships with law enforcement agencies in Abu Dhabi; Amman; London; Léon and Paris, France; Madrid; Montreal; Toronto; Singapore; Tel Aviv; and the Dominican Republic (Kelly 2009).
8. Author's interviews at NYPD, July 11, 2007.
9. Legislation concerning the intelligence community is considered not only by the intelligence committees in Congress but also by the powerful armed services committees. These latter committees in both the House and Senate oversee the Defense Department but also defend its interests, making significant change in authority for the distribution of power and resources for intelligence-related agencies very difficult.
10. John O. Brennan, coleader of Obama's intelligence transition team, was reportedly under serious consideration for the position of CIA director in late 2008. Brennan had been chief of staff to then CIA director George Tenet from 1999 to 2001 and director of

the National Counterterrorism Center from 2004 to 2005. Brennan was later chosen as top adviser to the president on counterterrorism—a position that does not require Senate approval.

11. Thanks to Georgetown University student Philip Cherry for this reference.

12. Before 2009, the DNI published a National Intelligence Strategy quite separately from the National Counterintelligence Strategy—an odd circumstance that nonetheless reflected the lack of joint effort at that time.

13. Counterintelligence, which watches how adversaries spy and thus can acquire clues to their interests and objectives, ideally supports policy making; to do so, it must recognize critical intelligence and provide it to political leaders, not just to those who decide when to arrest and how to prosecute those who are caught.

14. Two other candidates for the position had been eliminated before Bryant was chosen. Suzanne Spaulding, who had previously worked for the House Intelligence Committee and the CIA, was reportedly the Obama administration's first choice. Retired Army Maj. Gen. Robert A. Harding, a former director of operations at the Defense Intelligence Agency, was reportedly also considered for the position.

15. In September 2009, Assistant Attorney General Ronald Weich submitted a letter to Congress in which he, with the backing of the Obama administration, recommended reauthorization of three Patriot Act provisions.

16. The Special Task Force on Interrogations and Transfer Policies, established pursuant to Executive Order 13491, issued its recommendations in August 2009. The Task Force also made recommendations regarding the transfer of individuals between countries.

17. Whatever one thinks about Under Secretary of Defense Douglas Feith's reputed "cherry-picking" of intelligence prior to the Iraq War, his assertion that he was convinced that CIA intelligence analyses were biased is evidence of the deep rift that had emerged between intelligence providers and their policy partners by 2003. Regardless of who deserves the greatest blame, at that moment, intelligence had failed, and both policy maker and analyst had a responsibility to fix it.

18. The "gang of eight" includes the minority and majority leaders of the House and Senate and the chairs and ranking members of the Senate and House intelligence oversight committees.

19. Obviously, the importance of "truth" depends on the type of decision being made. Pilots need accuracy (factual truth) about a target's location. Truth about Iranian intentions or the meaning of the toppling of the Berlin Wall for the residents of East Berlin is, however, elusive at best. The problem for intelligence—the only problem—is gauging how any of these matters might affect the strategies of nation-states in ways that are significant for U.S. policy makers.

CHAPTER 9

Conducting Diplomacy

Christopher M. Jones and Kevin P. Marsh

"Diplomacy is concerned with the management of relations between states and between states and other [international] actors. From a state perspective, diplomacy is concerned with advising, shaping, and implementing foreign policy" (Barston 1988, 1). This important tool of statecraft encompasses many tasks, such as official representation abroad, explaining and defending national policy, negotiating treaties, reporting on significant developments overseas, preparing major policy initiatives, fostering cooperation to address transnational challenges, and reducing tension and conflict between states. At its most fundamental level, of course, diplomacy is designed to advance a state's national interests, and its purpose and use are reflective of the strategic choices that leaders make.

President George W. Bush pursued a national strategy of primacy in which his administration sought to preserve U.S. hegemony through unilateralism, preemption, democracy promotion, and maintenance of a military beyond challenge. Diplomacy was employed to serve national security objectives in Iraq and Afghanistan, from cobbling together "coalitions of the willing" to ensuring access to foreign bases and supply routes to waging joint counterterrorism operations. Diplomatic activity also produced some important accomplishments beyond the military sphere, such as the U.S.-India nuclear agreement, disarmament talks with Libya, and a strategic dialogue with China. However, the underutilization of diplomacy was a more dominant pattern throughout the eight-year period. The Bush administration opposed a range of international treaties, showed little enthusiasm for working with intergovernmental organizations, and resisted the idea that fruitful outcomes would emerge from serious dialogue with adversaries. The use of U.S. diplomacy to achieve major breakthroughs on intractable international issues such as the Israeli-Palestinian conflict was not a major priority. Overall, the Bush era was marked by war, global estrangement, and the militarization of foreign policy, an environment not conducive to ensuring the centrality of diplomacy in U.S. foreign policy making.

President Barack Obama signaled a different strategic choice well over a year before he was elected. As Obama (2007a, 4, 11) observed long before his election, "the security and well-being of each and every American depend on the security and well-being of those who live beyond our borders. The mission of the United States is to provide global leadership grounded in the understanding that the world shares a common security and a common humanity. . . . To renew American leadership in the world, I intend to rebuild the alliances, partnerships, and institutions necessary to confront common threats and enhance common security." During the first year of his presidency, Obama delivered major speeches in Prague, Ankara, Cairo, and at the United Nations (UN), as did Vice President Joseph Biden in Munich and Secretary of State Hillary Clinton in New York. These addresses gave further definition to a new cooperative security strategy designed to "renew" U.S. engagement in the global community. With an emphasis on promoting shared interests, accepting international institutions and treaties, and reversing controversial policies from the Bush era, this multilateral approach elevated diplomacy to a far more prominent role in U.S. foreign policy making.

This chapter begins with an examination of the conduct of diplomacy during the first year of Obama's presidency. The discussion seeks to uncover how the new administration has sought to implement an agenda of renewal and re-engagement in the international community. It places an emphasis on the initiatives, policies, and gestures that have facilitated a new diplomatic tone in U.S. foreign relations. The study then probes the issue of who conducts U.S. diplomacy in the Obama era. This section illustrates the president's strong engagement, the nature and extent of Secretary Clinton's role, and the substantial diplomatic activity that occurs beyond the Foreign Service, the nation's traditional diplomatic corps. The chapter concludes with some consideration of the diplomatic capabilities available to support the Obama administration's global posture and priorities. Attention is devoted to the U.S. Department of State's budget, staffing levels, and diplomatic skill set.

Setting a New Diplomatic Tone

During their first nine months in office, the president, vice president, and secretary of state wasted little time in distancing the new administration from the foreign policy of its predecessor. They delivered major speeches that articulated a foreign policy direction designed to counter the international perception of the United States as an arrogant, unilateral superpower bent on actively spreading its values, policies, and military influence without concern for the interests of others (see Biden 2009; Clinton 2009a; Obama 2009c, 2009i, 2009j, 2009k, 2009o). This approach embraced three dimensions: shared or common interests within a multipartnered world, strong support of multilateral institutions and frameworks, and a reversal of controversial U.S. policies from the Bush era. Overall, this worldview and cooperative security strategy placed diplomacy at the center of Obama's foreign policy.

The first two dimensions of Obama's approach—shared or common interests within a multipartnered world and strong support of multilateral institutions and frameworks—are exemplified by a re-engagement with the UN. In a shift from the Bush administration, the president restored the U.S. ambassador to the UN to Cabinet-level rank, which was the status the position enjoyed during the Clinton administration. The United States also paid its UN membership dues, including hundreds of millions of dollars in arrears, successfully negotiated stiff UN Security Council sanctions against North Korea, and rejoined the UN Human Rights Council. In September 2009, Obama became the first U.S. president to chair a session of the UN Security Council. During that meeting, the council voted unanimously in favor of a global disarmament and nonproliferation resolution. In the words of the U.S. ambassador to the UN, Susan Rice, "The United States has dramatically changed the tone, the substance and the practice of our diplomacy at the United Nations" (quoted in Jha 2009).

Beyond the UN, other actions further illustrated the Obama administration's commitment to multilateral frameworks and a "common-interests" perspective. Secretary of State Clinton was the first senior U.S. representative to participate in the annual Members Conference of the Comprehensive Test Ban Treaty (CTBT). Also, Stephen Rapp became the first U.S. government observer to the International Criminal Court (ICC). Although the United States remains outside both the test ban treaty and the Rome Statute, these symbolic actions were significant given the Bush administration's unflagging opposition to both agreements. In another policy area eschewed by its predecessor, the Obama administration devoted effort toward a climate change treaty to succeed the Kyoto Protocol. Other multilateral actions included the president's efforts to work with G-20 states to forge a coordinated international response to the global financial crisis, U.S. support of both an international food security initiative and the Millennium Development Goals, and the signing of the Convention on the Rights of Persons with Disabilities. The United States was also a visible presence at the annual meeting of the Association of Southeast Asian Nations (ASEAN) in summer 2009 and signed the organization's Treaty of Amity and Cooperation. It was the first time a U.S. president participated in the ASEAN summit.

As noted, the third dimension of the new administration's worldview and strategy is a reversal of controversial U.S. policies from the Bush era. In this direction, Obama jettisoned the terms *long war* and *global war on terrorism* (GWOT) in favor of *overseas contingency operation* with a near exclusive focus on al-Qaeda and the Taliban. He prohibited the use of torture and authorized the closing of the Guantánamo Bay prison. These developments were accompanied by a presidential call to move toward a nuclear-free world and the articulation of a dense arms control agenda, including the need to strengthen the Nuclear Non-Proliferation Treaty, secure U.S. ratification of the CTBT, and pursue an international pact to end the production of fissile material for nuclear weapons (see Obama 2009i). A serious commitment to arms control was also the basis for improving or "resetting" U.S.-Russia relations and a major diplomatic success. The Obama administration backed away from its predecessor's decision to build a missile defense system in the Czech Republic and Poland, which had been a major irritant to Moscow, and instead concluded the START follow-on agreement. If approved by U.S. and Russian lawmakers, the arms reduction pact signed by President Obama and Russian president Dmitry Medvedev on April 8, 2010, would ensure significant cuts to both countries' nuclear warheads and launchers.

Undoubtedly, the most dramatic shift was the willingness to enter into dialogue with adversaries shunned by the Bush administration. Over the course of his first year in office, Obama followed up on his inaugural speech pledge to "extend a hand if you are willing to unclench your fist" (see Obama 2009c). He agreed to exempt Syria from U.S. sanctions on a case-by-case basis (see Otterman 2009) and return an American ambassador to Damascus for the first time since February 2005. With Burma, the administration decided to maintain sanctions, yet at the same time, it initiated new, high-level engagement with the repressive Southeast Asian regime. In a controversial move, Obama warmly greeted Venezuelan president Hugo Chávez at the Summit of the Americas in April 2009. The two countries subsequently restored their ambassadors in Caracas and Washington. The new administration also signaled a willingness to rethink Cuba policy with a decision to lift restrictions for Cuban Americans on travel and remittances to Cuba.

Most notably, Obama sought to engage North Korea and Iran, both of which are considered rogue states and nuclear weapons threats. The White House dispatched special envoy Stephen Bosworth to Pyongyang in December 2009 and raised the prospect of establishing a U.S. liaison office in 2010 as a step toward the normalization of relations (Herskovitz 2009). With Iran, Obama delivered a conciliatory video message to the Iranian people and government in March 2009 (on Nowruz, the traditional Persian New Year) in which he said, "We have serious differences that have grown over time. My administration is now committed to diplomacy that addresses the full range of issues before us, and to pursuing constructive ties among the United States, Iran and the international community. This process will not be advanced by threats. We seek instead engagement that is honest and grounded in mutual respect" (Obama 2009s). Months of secret negotiations over Iran's low-enriched uranium stockpile followed. According to one source, the president "weighed in" at least three times in an effort to move the process forward (Calabresi 2009). Eventually, the result, aided by the head of the International Atomic Energy Agency, was the first set of direct meetings between U.S. and Iranian officials in three decades and a tentative agreement in October 2009. The deal, which ultimately fell apart, called for Russia to receive and enhance Iran's low-enriched uranium and then return it to Iran for peaceful purposes.

The Obama administration's substantive policy adjustments and initiatives were complemented by some rather dramatic diplomatic gestures. Most significantly, there was the new president's impressive attempt to reach out to Islamic countries and their peoples in June 2009. In a well-crafted and received speech in Cairo, Obama declared, "I have come here to seek a new beginning between the United States and Muslims around the world; one based upon mutual interest and mutual respect; and one based upon the truth that America and Islam are not exclusive, and need not be in competition" (Obama 2009o). In a marked departure from the past, Secretary of State Clinton also admitted that failed U.S. drug policy and American citizens' strong demand for illicit narcotics play a role in Mexico's violent drug war (see Sheridan 2009). When Obama visited China in the fall of 2009, he diverged from long-standing U.S. practice and deliberately avoided the subject of the Chinese government's human rights record. Even diplomatic protocol has been affected. The president bowed before the king of Saudi Arabia and the emperor of Japan, acts that many but not all of his predecessors have avoided with handshakes or mere nods. In fact, not only did the president bow to the emperor, but it was such a pronounced bow that some observers complained it manifested subservience (see Associated Press 2009b).

These gestures, coupled with the Obama administration's pursuit of shared interests in a multipartnered world, a strong commitment to multilateral institutions and frameworks, and a reversal of controversial Bush era policies, clearly set a new diplomatic tone. For his efforts, Obama was awarded the Nobel Peace Prize for "creat[ing] a new climate in international politics" and for instilling confidence in people around the world (Norwegian Nobel Committee 2009; see also Kull et al. 2009). This global transformation in U.S. credibility and global appeal marked the new administration's central foreign policy accomplishment during its first year in office.

However, the Obama administration's cooperative security strategy and diplomatic approach were not without criticism. The symbolism of the ceremonial bow raised the concern that the Obama administration has displayed too much deference in international affairs. In an effort to distinguish itself from its predecessor, it may also be too eager to reach out and deal with adversaries. As Tom Malinowski (quoted in Wilson 2009c) observed, "There's an appropriate reaction to the crusading moralism of the Bush administration, but [Obama's approach] sometimes goes too far in the direction of hoping that reasoned and quiet persuasion will convince cynical and self-interested authoritarian governments to change their ways." Others expressed disappointment with the lack of tangible progress on human rights. According to the executive director of Human Rights Watch (quoted in Roth 2010), "President Obama recognizes the importance of redeeming America's reputation on human rights after the dark Bush years. But it will take more than impressive rhetoric to succeed. Words must be followed by deeds."

The absence of significant policy achievements during the administration's first year in office was another criticism. Critics charged that, despite attempts to court adversaries, there were no breakthroughs with Iran, and North Korea and Syria made no concessions to the United States when the White House decided to post an ambassador in Damascus. In other areas, NATO allies resisted increasing their troop commitments in Afghanistan; merely a nonbinding political statement emerged from the Copenhagen environmental policy summit; and Obama was unsuccessful in persuading France, Germany, and other states at the G-20 (Group of 20) summit to pledge funds for an additional stimulus package. Lastly, some charged the administration with embracing adversaries and strategic competitors at the expense of allies and complained that relations with some friends had worsened rather than improved under Obama (e.g., Kagan, 2010a).

Generally, the Obama administration's early defense of such criticisms took two directions. On the issue of reaching out to adversaries, Secretary of State Clinton remarked, "We cannot be afraid or unwilling to engage. . . . Negotiations can provide insight into regimes' calculations and the possibility—even if it seems remote—that a regime will eventually alter its behavior in exchange for the benefits of acceptance into the international community" (Clinton 2009a). With respect to the concern that Obama's gestures and substantive policy actions did not generate significant results, senior presidential adviser David Axelrod (quoted in Scherer 2009b, 18) noted that "these are things that will pay off over time." It is also evident that domestic and international financial crisis diverted the White House's priorities and attention. It will take the remainder of Obama's term to determine whether the many efforts to set a new tone during the first year constituted a solid foundation for future achievements or the emergence of a pattern in which the renewal of U.S. foreign policy was largely restricted to inspiring rhetoric and conciliatory gestures.

Who Conducts America's Diplomacy?

At one time the oldest executive department in the U.S. government was also one of the most influential. From its inception as the Department of Foreign Affairs under the Articles of Confederation until the Second World War, the U.S. Department of State was the nation's leading foreign policy organization.

The growth of America's role within the international system and the subsequent dawn of the Cold War, however, marked the beginning of the State Department's diminishing stature within the U.S. foreign policy-making process. The strategy of containment prompted greater presidential interest in foreign affairs, a burgeoning national security bureaucracy, and a new reliance on military and intelligence capabilities at the expense of diplomacy. By the 1970s and 1980s, the organization's position relative to other actors had weakened to such a point that numerous studies emerged to explain its "creeping irrelevance" (Pringle 1977–78; also see Acheson 1971; Destler 1974; J. F. Campbell 1975; A. M. Scott 1975; Rockman 1981; Rubin 1987; Sorensen 1987–88; D. L. Clarke 1987, 1989; and Abrams 1989). On the one hand, these analyses portrayed State as its own worst enemy, plagued by weak leadership, poor internal management, superficial analysis, excessive caution, and limited creativity. On the other hand, the institution's loss of primacy was attributed to circumstances beyond its control—negative images of the U.S. Foreign Service subculture, presidents eager to direct foreign policy from the White House, assertive national security advisers and staffs, larger bureaucracies with greater resources, and a weak domestic constituency.

While these many factors coalesced to erode the State Department's policy-making influence, one scholar wrote at the time that it was reasonable to expect that the institution would remain central to the implementation of foreign policy and the conduct of traditional diplomatic functions. "In the diplomatic arena the department and the Foreign Service possess unique experience and talent" (D. L. Clarke 1987, 142). However, several developments in the post–Cold War and post-9/11 eras have challenged the diplomatic primacy of the State Department. The conduct of foreign policy and, more specifically, diplomacy during the first year of the Obama administration were consistent with this trend. The president, White House foreign policy advisers, secretary of state, and bureaucracies beyond the State Department all played important roles.

Despite his inexperience in international affairs and the need to address a host of serious domestic problems, President Obama wasted no time in embracing his role as the nation's chief diplomat. His first foreign trip, an eight-day visit to Europe in spring 2009, included six countries, three international summits, twenty-five scheduled meetings with global leaders, twenty-two occasions in which he delivered public remarks, two town hall meetings, five press conferences, and a brief stop in Iraq before returning home. The European trip also demonstrated the new president's propensity to do real diplomatic work. An example was his instrumental role in forging a deal that resulted in Turkey abandoning its attempt to derail the selection of Anders Fogh Rasmussen as NATO's secretary general (Scherer 2009a, 23). More recently, Obama convened a two-day Nuclear Security Summit at the White House in April 2010. Forty-seven countries participated, making it the largest international gathering organized by a U.S. president since 1945 (White House, Office of the Press Secretary 2010). Another instance arose at the Copenhagen climate conference in December 2009. Obama and Clinton unexpectedly attended a private meeting of leaders from Brazil, China, India, and South Africa and proceeded to negotiate language for the summit's three-page accord on pollution-reduction goals. One journalist (Crowley 2009) noted, "Whether he is shaping the White House's message on Iran, or personally cajoling Asian leaders to crack down on North Korea, or brokering power deals among NATO allies, Obama has, in effect, been his own national security advisor and secretary of state."

Obama quickly emerged as the administration's principal diplomatic spokesperson. In his major foreign policy speeches, he not only articulated his vision and goals but introduced a new U.S. foreign policy lexicon encompassing shared interests, mutual respect, engagement, partnership, and multilateralism. These speeches were supplemented by numerous statements that reinforced the administration's desire to renew America's relationship with the world. Many times the president communicated this message directly to foreign leaders and peoples. During his first year in office, he traveled abroad more than had any other U.S. president, visiting twenty-one countries and spending more than five weeks outside the United States. To place Obama's global presence in perspective, his five predecessors only traveled to an average of nine countries during their first twelve months. In fact, Obama's first-year total could be counted as twenty-five foreign trips, given that he visited Denmark, France, Germany, and Mexico on two separate occasions (Thomma 2009; Zoll and Layton 2010).

Due to the president's strong level of engagement in international affairs, it was not a surprise that the White House emerged as the hub of the Obama administration's foreign policy and diplomatic apparatus. According to Leslie Gelb, president emeritus of the Council on Foreign Relations, "You ask people who've been in government for a long time, and they would say this is one of the most centralized policy-making operations ever" (quoted in Landler and Cooper 2010). Clear signs of this centralization were the expansion of the National Security Council (NSC), the expansion and reorganization of the NSC staff (including the establishment of a new Global Engagement Directorate to integrate diplomacy and national security goals), and the increased authority of the national security adviser (see Obama 2009g; DeYoung 2009). Another key development was the June 2009 decision to move Dennis Ross, a leading Middle East expert and experienced Israeli-Palestinian negotiator, from the State Department to the White House. Most key foreign policy decisions were closely controlled by the president and a small group of advisers, including Vice President Joe Biden, National Security Adviser James Jones, Chief of Staff Rahm Emanuel, senior adviser David Axelrod, Deputy National Security Adviser Tom Donilon, and National Security Council Chief of Staff Denis

McDonough. In addition, Mark Lippert (until his resignation as chief of staff of the National Security Council in October 2009), UN ambassador Susan Rice, and White House liaison to Congress Jim Messina enjoyed influence within this small circle (see Crowley 2009; Richter 2009; A. Klein 2010; Landler and Cooper 2010). One observer pointed to the White House decision to post a U.S ambassador in Syria without consulting the State Department or demanding anything from the Syrians in return as an example of the group's willingness to sidestep bureaucracies that may possess useful expertise on certain issues (see A. Klein 2010).

Most notably, this core foreign policy group did not include Secretary of State Clinton over the course of the administration's first year in office. It was not that Clinton was completely frozen out of the inner circle as Colin Powell was during the Bush administration (see C. M., Jones 2006). By all accounts, she steadily developed a good working relationship with the president and Obama's foreign policy decision-making approach was consistent with Alexander George's "collegial" presidential management model (see George 1980). For instance, national security adviser James Jones (quoted in Crowley 2009) remarked, "The process is extraordinarily inclusive. No one gets left out." However, factors associated with Clinton's governmental position inevitably limited her time and influence with the chief executive. She traveled extensively overseas during her first year of service, but rarely with the president. She was also compelled to devote time and energy to overseeing a State Department bureaucracy of nearly 50,000 employees—11,500 Foreign Service officers, 7,400 Civil Service officers, and 31,000 Foreign Service nationals (U.S. Department of State 2010). Clinton did not have unfettered access to the Oval Office, something that many of her predecessors had enjoyed. The primary conduit for personal interaction between Obama and Clinton in 2009 was a regularly scheduled weekly meeting (Meacham 2009). Of course, Clinton had other avenues at her disposal, from e-mail messages to telephone calls to formal NSC meetings. Yet these channels did not offer personal access to the president and his foreign policy advisers situated in the White House on a daily basis. In short, location affects relative influence, and Clinton's operating environment was not especially unique. The few exceptions have been secretaries of state who have had personal friendships with the president. Examples include James A. Baker III and George H. W. Bush and Condoleezza Rice and George W. Bush. Hillary Clinton and Barack Obama do not fall into this category.

Given the president's high level of foreign policy and diplomatic engagement and a White House–centered advisory system, what role has been left for Hillary Clinton to play? Evidence suggests the secretary of state fulfilled two primary functions beyond her administrative tasks. First, she served as the "bad cop" of U.S. diplomacy. As President Obama sought to renew America's place in the international community with positive, uplifting speeches and new policy positions, Clinton was the administration official who delivered the tough messages to adversaries, such as Iran and North Korea, and partners, such as Afghanistan and Pakistan (see Ghattas 2009; Henderson 2009; Tully 2009; Zengerle 2009). Second, Clinton was an active practitioner of public diplomacy. That is, she used her global celebrity status and interpersonal skills not only to push substantive policy positions but also to promote good relations with average foreign nationals. For instance, one journalist described her tour of Africa in August 2009 as "eleven days, seven countries of friendly, engaging, edifying talk" (Gettleman 2009). Whether in Asia, Europe, or the Middle East, Clinton frequently bypassed the mainstream media in favor of large town hall meetings, television appearances, and events designed to connect with the public, especially young people. Within these venues, she was quizzed about her musical tastes, personal life, and how to balance work and family. In an effort to help transform international perceptions of the United States, Clinton also fielded critical questions by less than polite audience members and admitted when she thought past U.S. policy had failed. Whether addressing an easy or difficult question, her responses were often informal, blunt, and undiplomatic for a sitting secretary of state (see Dilanian 2009a; Gettleman 2009; Kessler 2009a, 2009b; J. Klein 2009; Landler 2009c). Overall, the realm of public diplomacy was an area in which Clinton distinguished herself by moving away from her predecessors' nearly exclusive focus on interactions with foreign leaders and media.

With Clinton engaged in foreign travel, people-to-people diplomacy, "bad cop" diplomacy, and leadership of the State Department, significant portions of the day-to-day, high-level management of challenging policy areas were often left to special envoys during the first year. The two most prominent examples were former senator George Mitchell's responsibility for issues tied to Middle East peace and former ambassador to the UN Richard Holbrooke's oversight of U.S. relations with Afghanistan and Pakistan. However, Mitchell and Holbrooke were by no means the only two. In fact, eighteen other individuals were designated to oversee and coordinate major regional, substantive, or functional issue areas. Beyond Mitchell and Holbrooke, there were four other regional appointments, including a special envoy for Sudan and three envoys to cover different aspects of policy toward North Korea. As discussed, Dennis Ross, who was to serve as a special envoy to Iran, was reassigned to the White House during the early months of the administration. In terms of substantive policy, there were eight appointments related to security issues: climate change, international energy affairs, Eurasian energy, threat reduction, conventional armed forces in Europe, nuclear nonproliferation, nonproliferation and arms control, and the closure of the Guantánamo Bay detention facility. There were also envoys named to manage nonsecurity matters and functional areas: global women's issues, Muslim communities, Holocaust issues, monitoring and combating of anti-Semitism, global partnerships, and global intergovernmental affairs. As one scholar (Fullilove 2009) observed, "envoys are a recurring feature of U.S. foreign policy—but Obama is resorting to them unusually early and often. The contrast is especially striking with the Bush administration, which had a prejudice against envoys that reflected President George W. Bush's general lack of interest in diplomacy." In just his first eight months as president, Obama appointed half as many special envoys as Bush did in eight years (Ward 2009).

Special envoys, who can hold a range of titles (e.g., special representative, special adviser, special coordinator, and ambassador-at-large), represent the president and secretary of state and, therefore, the United States, on specific foreign policy issues. Often, prominent individuals or recognized experts are tapped for these high-level positions, which do not have to be confirmed by the U.S. Senate. The wisdom of the Obama administration's extensive use of special envoys is open to debate. On the positive side, special envoys signal to foreign actors that a particular issue is a top priority of the president and U.S. government. In speaking about the Mitchell and Holbrooke appointments, the president stated the appointments "convey our seriousness of purpose" (quoted in DeYoung and Kessler 2009). Foreign governments view these emissaries as authoritative and influential and assume that they possess considerable high-level access at home. Whether that access is to the president or the secretary of state largely rests with the official's portfolio. In either case, the assumption is that the envoy, as a political appointee rather than a career diplomat, will be more responsive to the administration's perspective, priorities, and direction.

Special envoys also have the time to concentrate intensely on a single policy matter, allowing the secretary of state to choose when and how to get involved in the envoy's area of responsibility; the capacity to gravitate to other issues; or the ability to focus on overall strategy and "the big diplomatic picture." Given the scope of U.S. foreign relations and Obama's challenging global agenda, one can argue that the reliance on envoys is a reasonable way of dealing with an enormous international workload that the president, secretary of state, and the traditional diplomatic corps cannot hope to handle effectively on their own. Lastly, when they are seasoned practitioners, special envoys become a means of enriching an administration's foreign policy expertise and professional diplomatic experience. This is an important consideration when one takes into account the backgrounds of both Obama and Clinton as well as the strained resources of the State Department (discussed below).

On the negative side, special envoys add more players to an already crowded U.S. foreign policy–making process. This reality raises the concern that some foreign states will wonder who really speaks for the United States— the envoy, the ambassador and embassy team, State Department officials in Washington, representatives of other bureaucracies, the secretary of state, the NSC and White House foreign policy advisers, or the president. The prospect that inconsistent messages will be conveyed to international actors increases. The proliferation of special envoys also intensifies the challenge of and the need for effective coordination across multiple individuals, agencies, and jurisdictional lines. When such coordination is deficient or absent, it becomes more challenging to prevent political battles over the substance and conduct of policy. Then there is the matter of circumvention. Will special envoys respect the authority of the secretary of state or seek to deal directly with the president and White House officials? Even if the secretary of state is able to maintain control over these special envoys, what will be the effect of their presence on other State Department personnel? It is very likely that special envoys and their support staff will encroach upon and diminish the role and influence of assistant secretaries and State Department bureaus in Washington as well as ambassadors and Foreign Service officers posted overseas. If that is the case, there can be a negative effect on institutional morale, which can undermine bureaucratic buy-in for a policy orchestrated by the envoy. This is an important consideration given it will be the career bureaucracy, not the special envoy, that implements the policy.

Collectively, an internationally engaged president, a White House–centered foreign policy system, a globetrotting secretary of state, and the expanded use of special envoys have limited the involvement of U.S. ambassadors and Foreign Service officers in matters of high-level diplomatic importance. Thus, a reasonable assumption would be that State Department personnel stationed at more than 260 diplomatic posts in more than 180 countries are responsible for the conduct of routine, day-to-day diplomatic activities. And, of course, they are to some extent. However, the reality is the State Department is not the sole practitioner of U.S diplomacy. Instead the power to conduct U.S. foreign relations is shared by a number of departments and agencies playing active roles in other countries. State Department "diplomatic personnel, not including support staff, occupy 42 percent of positions overseas—a plurality, not a majority" (Zeller 2007, 21). In fact, "representatives of more than 30 federal agencies are stationed in U.S. embassies where they manage and advance their organization's agenda based on instructions from [their Washington] headquarters" (Peck 2007, 29).

Interestingly, the agencies that are increasing their representation are not a part of the traditional foreign policy or national security bureaucracy. As State struggles to staff its embassies and consulates, departments associated with domestic affairs—Justice, Treasury, Transportation, Health and Human Services, Homeland Security, and others—are steadily expanding their global presence. This development diminishes the role and influence of the State Department, not merely because ambassadors have always had difficulty reining in personnel from other organizations but because official U.S. relations are being conducted less frequently by Foreign Service officers. Even when diplomats take the lead overseas, they are often compelled to consult with a growing number of agencies, which insist their priorities be reflected in policy. This phenomenon is further intensified by the expanding international activity of U.S. companies, nongovernmental organizations (NGOs), and state and local governments. Many of these institutions have established foreign offices to advance their own agendas. Overall, the proliferation of actors and interests overseas places into serious question the State Department's capacity to serve effectively as the nation's leader and coordinator of diplomatic affairs.

The challenge to State's centrality does not stop there. More established members of the U.S. foreign and national security bureaucracy have also become increasingly visible and active in areas that were at one time dominated or controlled by the State Department. The Department of Defense's growing global role offers some of the best examples. In an effort to reduce or eliminate interservice rivalry, the Pentagon maintains ten combatant commands headed by a four-star general or admiral, who is responsible for exercising unified command and control across all military forces in a functional or geographic zone of operations. Of the ten unified commands, six are regionally focused and, therefore, span numerous countries. With broad authority, large support staffs, control over tens of thousands of troops, and substantial budgetary resources, these regional combatant commanders enjoy notable stature and wield considerable influence with foreign governments. In fact, "the combatant commander has the authority to fund military cooperation agreements with governments in his area of responsibility. . . . That prerogative alone gives the commanders enormous prestige with host governments at a time when their civilian counterparts, from ambassadors on down, have been pauperized by spending cuts that date back to . . . the 1990s" (Glain 2009).

The diplomatic role and influence of combatant commanders and the Department of Defense itself have been enhanced through the Pentagon's global "mission creep" (see Patrick and Brown 2007; Capps 2009). Through funding, staffing, and program implementation, the Defense Department has become significantly engaged in humanitarian assistance, economic and social development, public diplomacy, and other noncombat areas of responsibility. "In Iraq and Afghanistan, the military is carrying out traditional State Department functions, such as funding local school-reconstruction projects, as well as information programs, such as running Web sites and producing radio and television broadcasts" (Pincus 2009a). One journalist notes, "[The State Department] relies on Pentagon funding and even personnel for basic operations central to its mission. . . . In Somalia, for example, the State Department's budget for public diplomacy is $30,000. The Pentagon's is $600,000" (Armstrong 2009). Another observer writes, "Despite the Foreign Assistance Act's stipulation of State Department authority, the Pentagon accounts for nearly a quarter of America's budget for overseas direct assistance—up from near zero a decade ago—while the U.S. Agency for International Development's share has declined to 40 percent from 65 percent during the same period" (Glain 2009).

Much of the Defense Department's greater diplomatic role and influence has been tied to counterterrorism and the ongoing conflicts in Iraq and Afghanistan. In the midst of the Iraq War, the Pentagon was granted the authority and funding to carry out stabilization operations. According to Department of Defense Directive 3000.05, stability operations are defined as "military and civilian activities conducted across the spectrum from peace to conflict to establish or maintain order in states and regions." That same directive, which was released in November 2005 and reissued as an instruction in September 2009, explicitly stated that such operations are as important as combat operations and assigns U.S. military personnel to the task of promoting the development of an "indigenous capacity for securing essential services, a viable market economy, rule of law, democratic institutions, and a robust civil society" (U.S. Department of Defense 2005, 2009). In a related development, under Section 1206 of the National Defense Authorization Act, the Pentagon was authorized to use more than $1 billion (FY 2006–FY 2010) of its own budgetary resources to train and equip foreign armed forces to conduct counterterrorism or stability operations (Congressional Research Service 2010). Traditionally, such a program would fall under the purview of the State Department, yet the law only requires the Pentagon to "coordinate" with State Department officials.

In addition to the Directive 3000.5 and Section 1205 authorities, two other important developments have enhanced the Pentagon's expanding role in the diplomatic affairs sphere. First, the Commander's Emergency Response Program (CERP), which was established in 2003, has allocated billions of federal dollars *in cash* to U.S. commanders on the ground in Iraq and Afghanistan to fund small humanitarian and reconstruction projects that immediately help local populations. Examples have included small public works projects; restoration of basic services; repairs to education and health care facilities; and payments to civilians for deaths, injuries, and property damage caused by U.S. and coalition forces. However, CERP funds, which were to finance pressing needs valued under $500,000, have frequently gone to much larger and more expensive projects, such as water and sewage treatment plants, health clinics and schools, and jobs programs for young men. The money has also funded more questionable expenses, such as $600,000 for dolls and action figures that look like local security forces, $14,250 for "I Love Iraq" T-shirts, and $12,800 for pools to cool animals at a Baghdad zoo (Hedgpeth and Cohen 2008; also see Martins 2005 and Commander's Emergency Response Program 2008).

Second, the Defense Department took the lead in instituting Provincial Reconstruction Teams (PRTs), first in Afghanistan in 2002 and then Iraq in 2005. PRTs are interagency teams in which soldiers and specialists from the State Department, USAID, and the Department of Agriculture work side by side to promote stabilization. In Afghanistan, they have sought to strengthen security, reconstruction, and the central government by "disarming militias, training police forces, building roads, and supporting elections" (Patrick and Brown 2007, 6). However, these PRTs have been predominantly military in composition and operational focus. In Iraq, PRTs have encompassed more civilians and are headed by State Department officials, but military personnel play a significant role here as well (McNearney 2005; Patrick and Brown 2007).

The Limits of Diplomatic Capabilities

Beyond the global war on terror and the conflicts in Iraq and Afghanistan, the central reason for the Defense Department's greater diplomatic role and influence has been the perennial underresourcing of the traditional diplomatic establishment. In short, the State Department and USAID are underfunded and understaffed, creating a major resource gap that the Pentagon has filled. It was previously noted that the Defense Department's share of U.S. overseas direct assistance has skyrocketed in recent years, while USAID's portion has plummeted. However, the situation is much worse when total institutional resources are taken into consideration. A former ambassador and president of the American Foreign Service Association wrote in *Foreign Affairs* in 2009:

> The number of lawyers at the Defense Department is larger than the entire diplomatic corps [of 11,500 Foreign Service Officers], there are more musicians in the military bands than there are diplomats, and the Defense Department's 2008 budget [including supplemental appropriations for the wars in Iraq and Afghanistan] was over 24 times as large as the combined budgets of the State Department and USAID ($750 billion compared with $31 billion). A mere $7.5 billion went to the State Department's diplomatic and consular programs, including its large operations in Afghanistan and Iraq and 265 other diplomatic posts around the world. In fact, the Pentagon spends more on health care for its military personnel than the U.S. government allocates for diplomacy and foreign assistance (Holmes 2009, 150).

It is important to underscore that during his tenure as secretary of state (2001–2005), Colin Powell revitalized the State Department as an organization. He improved relations with Congress, secured more funding, addressed crumbling infrastructure, invested in information technology, strengthened public diplomacy efforts, and built a larger and better trained diplomatic corps (see C. M. Jones 2006). On the last point, Powell's Diplomatic Readiness Initiative led the Foreign Service to grow by about 1,200 positions above attrition. However, this gain was undermined by two developments. First, there was the pressing need for several hundred diplomats in Iraq and Afghanistan. In fact, the personnel requirements were so great that "when State couldn't fill 350 civilian positions in Iraq and 300 positions in Afghanistan, Defense filled the gaps" (Capps 2009, i). Second, Secretary of State Rice (2005–2009) failed to build on Powell's organizational legacy. Instead of devoting high priority to staff resources, it was not until the final year of the Bush administration that she pushed for a sizeable increase in new diplomatic positions. This inaction has been compounded by the reality that a significant portion of State Department and USAID employees are "baby boomers" who are nearing retirement and are not especially eager to serve at dangerous hardship posts where they are needed most (e.g., Afghanistan, Iraq, Pakistan, and many African countries). These conditions have left many U.S. embassies and consulates with vacant positions. In fact, as of June 2009, "nearly 20 percent of regular positions in embassies and in the State Department [were] unfilled" (Kissinger et al. 2009). Thus the State Department entered the Obama era with a significant shortfall in Foreign Service officers, which does not bode well for an administration that is committed to using diplomacy to renew America's relationship with the world.

In the absence of an adequate number of State Department and USAID employees, there will be no choice but for the Obama administration to continue to rely heavily on the Pentagon to implement diplomatic-related tasks, from foreign assistance to development to public diplomacy. The situation has become so serious that senior Defense Department officials have called for more budgetary support and personnel for the State Department and even gone so far as to suggest that some funds be transferred from the Pentagon. Secretary of Defense Robert Gates and chairman of the Joint Chiefs of Staff Adm. Michael Mullen have been motivated by their concern over the increasing militarization of U.S. foreign policy and the use of overstretched armed forces to cover overseas missions normally performed by civilians (see Gates 2007; Tyson 2008; Armstrong 2009; Mullen 2009, 2010). Their uneasiness with the current state of affairs seems especially well placed given Obama's desire to change the global perception of the United States and its policies. That objective becomes more challenging if the international face of the United States is that of a soldier rather than a diplomat. A State Department or USAID program implemented abroad by military personnel will be perceived by many foreign nationals as a military program. Moreover, one has to question whether soldiers have the requisite training and skill sets to accomplish diplomatic and foreign aid tasks effectively.

Given the foregoing discussion, it is not a surprise that Obama pledged to strengthen the State Department with the appointment of Clinton as secretary of state. John Naland, the president of the American Foreign Service Association, remarked in January 2009, "[State Department] employees are ecstatic that we now have a secretary of state who is going to fight for the resources that we need. For three years, there were no requests for additional staffing and resources" (quoted in Landler 2009a). The belief was that Clinton would act more like Powell than Rice and her pre-established relationships on Capitol Hill from eight years of service as a U.S. senator would be an important asset as she sought to secure a larger budget for the State Department. Clinton also hired an experienced government finance expert, Jacob "Jack" Lew, to serve as her deputy for Management and Resources. Lew had served as director of the Office of Management and Budget during the Clinton administration and took the lead in persuading Congress to increase State Department funding. With the backing of a powerful constituency of eight former secretaries of state (six Republicans and two Democrats), Obama, Clinton, and Lew enjoyed success during the administration's first year. They requested a $53.9 billion international affairs budget for FY 2010, which constituted a major 27 percent increase compared to funding levels in FY 2008 and FY 2009. Congress appropriated $51 billion, falling less than $3 billion short of the president's proposal. A key portion of this money was targeted for the hiring of 1,300 new Foreign Service officers and moving toward Obama's goal of doubling U.S. foreign aid by 2015 (Abott 2009; Dilanian 2009b; Glain 2009; and Williams 2009).

Despite this infusion of resources and the Obama administration's continuing commitment to invest in the core diplomatic capabilities of the State Department, there remain real challenges tied to a legacy of underfunding and understaffing, not to mention a new era of expanding needs. For instance, Admiral Mullen has remarked publicly that the State Department and other civilian agencies are "a good decade away" from being in a position to take over some of the roles that military personnel are fulfilling in Iraq, Afghanistan, and other strategically important places (see Mullen 2009). Other observers have contended that it will take far more than 1,300 new Foreign Service officers to make the State Department a more capable and influential global actor. For instance, one expert has argued that the chronic underresourcing of the past and present demands require Obama and Clinton to "double the number of the FSOs [currently at 11,500], increase the number of specialists at the State Department by 50 percent, and boost USAID's Foreign Service staff by 150 percent" (Holmes 2009, 160). Adding such a large number of employees would necessitate a major, multiyear, executive-legislative commitment and, if successful, still would not cover the loss of personnel created by anticipated retirements in the coming years. On the budget side, there is the question of whether the presently understaffed State Department can even absorb and use the money that Congress allocates it, especially if there is a sustained period of budget growth. If it can, it is almost certain that Pentagon personnel and private contractors would have to play significant roles in delivering better funded State and USAID programs.

The State Department's challenges are not restricted to merely the number of dollars and diplomats available to it in an era of international renewal and engagement. There is also the matter of ensuring its employees have the professional capabilities to support twenty-first-century diplomacy. Certainly, State Department officials will continue to represent U.S. interests overseas, draft daily and annual reports on a range of subjects, issue passports and visas, provide travel warnings, sponsor educational and cultural exchange programs, and negotiate international agreements. These necessary, often mundane, diplomatic tasks will not disappear. Yet, as one experienced foreign policy analyst recommended, "the State Department needs to transform itself to deal with new challenges. . . . A new breed of diplomat with new skills and new career expectations is needed. This diplomat needs to know how to negotiate, represent, and report, but he or she also needs to know how to shape, implement, and evaluate a foreign assistance program; how to reach out to the public overseas; how to oversee humanitarian assistance in a crisis; and how to support another government as it rebuilds" (Adams 2008).

These tasks will require solid knowledge of transnational issues (including economics), mastery of critical foreign languages and public diplomacy, a stronger understanding of non-Western cultures, training in areas typically associated with business and public administration degrees (e.g., budgeting, management, strategic planning, program evaluation, etc.), and the ability to partner effectively with other governmental and nongovernmental actors. On the last point, Anne-Marie Slaughter, head of the State Department's policy planning staff, argues that "diplomats are going to need to have skills that are closer to community organizing than traditional reporting and analysis. New connecting technologies will be vital tools in this kind of diplomacy" (quoted in Rothkopf 2009c).

The State Department must make a commitment to developing recruitment strategies and training programs that create and sustain a workforce with these essential skills. It is a daunting challenge when one considers, for example, that "25 percent of public diplomacy officers abroad do not meet language requirements. In Arab countries, 36 percent of U.S. public diplomacy officers assigned do not speak Arabic at the designated level" (Hughes 2009). Of course, it will take more than simply finding qualified individuals with the right skills or the potential to acquire such capabilities. It will necessitate a shift in organizational culture. There will need to be broad institutional acceptance that the aforementioned new skills set is truly welcome alongside traditional diplomatic duties. In addition, the State Department would be wise to treat all its diplomatic career tracks or "cones" (management, consular, political, economic, and public affairs) as equally important and ensure its personnel receive training and experience across these functional areas.

Lastly, America's oldest cabinet department needs to embrace strategic planning. State's attempt in this regard is the Quadrennial Diplomacy and Development Review (QDDR). It is modeled after the Pentagon's Quadrennial Defense Review (QDR) process, which has existed since 1993 (see Chapter 6).

In announcing the QDDR process in July 2009, Secretary of State Clinton explained the final report or strategic blueprint "will provide us with a comprehensive strategy for organizational reforms and improvements. . . . [It] will give us the strategic guidance we need to help us allocate our resources more efficiently and deploy people where they will have the most impact. I think it's a new way of doing business that will give us the dynamism and that we should have and better equip us to deal with the accelerating rate of change that we confront" (Clinton 2009b). It will take time to determine whether the new QDDR can meet such expectations.

Diplomatic Continuity and Change in an Era of Renewal

This volume explores the Obama administration's "renewal" of U.S. engagement in the global community following eight years of estrangement. No policy area has been more central to this process than the conduct of diplomacy. With an emphasis on promoting shared interests, embracing multilateral institutions and agreements, and reversing controversial policies from the Bush era, Obama's approach to world politics has elevated diplomacy to a far more prominent role in U.S. foreign policy making. The result has been a new American diplomatic tone and a substantially improved international climate.

Whether these changes will lead to significant foreign policy achievements, however, remains to be seen. Despite a lack of foreign policy expertise, the president has been a highly engaged chief diplomat supported by a broad array of diplomatic practitioners, from his secretary of state to a cadre of special envoys to traditional and nontraditional foreign policy bureaucracies. This crowded diplomatic playing field, which constrains the relative role and influence of the Department of State, continues a long-standing trend in U.S. foreign policy making. The dominance of the military in diplomatic-related activities, which emerged in the Bush years, will continue for several years out of mere necessity given the longtime underresourcing of the diplomatic establishment relative to the Department of Defense. Knowing strong diplomatic capabilities are essential to its overall foreign policy approach, the Obama administration is committed to rebuilding and expanding the State Department's budget and personnel. With the support of the Congress, Obama and Clinton enjoyed early success in this regard, securing a major increase in the international affairs budget. The question is whether such a funding level, which has begun to facilitate new hiring and stronger foreign policy programs at State and USAID, can be sustained over time. A greater number of diplomats and dollars, however, are not enough to make the State Department a more viable and influential actor with the realm of foreign and diplomatic affairs. It will also require a better trained workforce and a commitment to transforming an organizational culture that is more conducive to supporting twenty-first-century diplomacy.

CHAPTER 10

Protecting Human Rights

David P. Forsythe

AMERICAN LEADERS have long talked about the country as an exceptional nation, a shining city on a hill whose divinely blessed destiny was to lead the world to greater freedom and democracy (see Ignatieff 2005; Lipset 1996; T. Smith 1994). This constructed self-image of American exceptionalism, however, did not preclude periods of isolationism and self-restraint. Moreover, this exceptionalist self-image, at least rhetorically linked to the notion of personal freedom, did not preclude the ethnic cleansing if not genocide of Native Americans, slavery and segregation, the Alien and Sedition Acts to suppress dissent, the internment of innocent Japanese Americans during World War II, U.S. support for various dictators during the Cold War, and various other manifestations of morally dubious and illiberal policies. But, as various authors have sagely noted, nationalism and especially chauvinistic nationalism require a great deal of selective memory and belief in things that are just not so (see Gellner 1998; Hobsbawm 1990; Renan 1996; and Anderson 1991).

American exceptionalism is alive and well in the Obama era. His election gave new life to the belief, held not only in much of the United States but also in certain circles abroad, that America is indeed exceptional in its ability to reinvent itself, overcome past errors of judgment, and move progressively toward a more perfect union at home and a more enlightened foreign policy abroad. Obama's inauguration speech appealed to this notion of American exceptionalism when he talked about a return to traditional American values that would not be sacrificed on the altar of security concerns and when he identified the country as interested in the fate of all individuals everywhere (Obama 2009c). No less than Ronald Reagan or Franklin Roosevelt, Obama sought to rekindle American confidence in itself as a leader for progressive change at home and abroad, including a renewed commitment to internationally recognized human rights.

At the end of the Obama administration, an important question will be whether the president and his foreign policy team were able to break clearly from President George W. Bush's legacy in foreign policy. In particular, analysts will want to know if Obama was able to renew U.S. engagement with the international community after eight years in which Bush pursued a foreign policy of "revolutionary unilateralism" (Daalder and Lindsay 2006). For other observers as well, the Bush legacy contains a very strong strain of misguided and even arrogant unilateralism (Bacevich 2008; Hoffmann 2003).

The so-called Bush Doctrine of unilateral preemptive use of force was central to this legacy. But the Bush record also involved unilateral steps to reject the Kyoto Protocol on global warming, reject and try to undermine the International Criminal Court, abrogate an arms control treaty with Russia, resist the regulation of trafficking in light arms, reinterpret the UN Convention against Torture and the 1949 Geneva Conventions, and refuse to participate in the new UN Human Rights Council. More than a few Bush officials were united in viewing international law and organization, and even the idea of international punishment for war crimes, in a negative light (Goldsmith 2007). Suspicion of international law and organization was a hallmark of the so-called neoconservatives (Fukuyama 2006).

A leading scholar held that this Bush version of American exceptionalism, precisely because it took the form of American *exemptionalism* (from global institutions and laws), was unsustainable in a globalized world (Ruggie 2006). This latter view suggests that Obama would necessarily move toward "renewal" of engagement with the international community.

Thus, an important question is whether Obama can renew U.S. engagement with multilateral global governance, meaning primarily international regimes for the cooperative management of transnational problems. To be sure, some authors consider U.S. unilateralism, based on responsible primacy, to be a form of global governance itself (Mandelbaum 2005). And on certain issues like management of the Internet, the world may indeed be content to let the United States remain in the central position rather than risk transferring management to an international regime that might become politicized to the detriment of values like freedom of opinion and speech. But in general, the so-called neoconservative push to free the United States from the restraints imposed by weaker states through their use of international law and organization was not well received in the rest of the world. With some exceptions—namely Great Britain and Denmark—many other governments found the Bush administration considerably less virtuous than advertised. Obama's campaign speeches made clear he understood the decline of U.S. standing in parts of the world, especially the Islamic world.

The human rights record is an important component of the Bush legacy, and it is clear it will be an important arena for Obama. In a short analysis such as the present one, an author has to be selective in coverage of human rights. The international law of human rights is vast, and just the International Bill of

Rights alone contains at least thirty basic normative principles, with perhaps three times that number of specific rights at issue (Donnelly 2007). A detailed proposal regarding what Obama should do to improve the U.S. record on a series of human rights requires a book (see Schulz 2008). Moreover, we have at the time of writing only a year or so of evidence about the Obama team, with much of that time devoted to domestic questions. What follows, therefore, is a summary of important human rights questions bequeathed by the Bush White House to the Obama team and a further discussion of prospects for change as the latter administration considers renewed engagement with multilateral governance.

The central argument here is that Obama's changes in the field of protecting human rights will likely turn out to be modest and incremental due to three factors:

1. The president's tendency toward pragmatic bargains rather than sweeping crusades
2. The weakened economic situation in the United States and overstretched military forces, which mandate some scaling back of objectives
3. The strength of illiberal pressures at home

This chapter will explore U.S. human rights policies in both administrations. Of particular concern are the policies of the United States with regard to the treatment of prisoners in the "global war on terror," a term coined by Bush but later avoided by Obama in favor of less sweeping language. The chapter will then turn to developments regarding global governance, specifically the Durban I and II conferences on racism and the U.S. role within the United Nations Security Council.

Abuse of Enemy Prisoners

The central human rights issue for the United States is the question of torture as an element of its counterterrorism strategy. We should be clear that torture and other forms of severe cruelty became policy under the Bush administration (Pfiffner 2009; Warshaw 2009; Mayer 2008; and Forsythe forthcoming). And we should understand that domestic political pressures to avoid attacks similar to the ones on September 11, 2001, will weigh heavily on the Obama administration.

The seriousness of the question merits a brief review. The terrorist attacks of 9/11 led to a widespread view that the country faced an existential threat, that is, to its very being (Mayer 2008; Brysk and Shafir 2007). Whether this was a case of "threat exaggeration" is still debated. To a considerable extent, competing values and concerns were sacrificed on the altar of a quest for perfect homeland security. This was certainly true regarding human rights in national emergencies and, in particular, respect for the internationally recognized rights of enemy detainees.

As a matter of policy, led by Vice President Dick Cheney, the Bush team authorized state kidnappings, forced disappearances, extraordinary renditions to other states well known for torture and other brutalities, prolonged administrative detention with little serious attention to due process, and cruel interrogations that sometimes rose to the level of torture (Gellman 2008; Savage 2007; Mayer 2008; Goldsmith 2007; Suskind 2006). A few trials were attempted in military commissions in which information from coerced confessions was permitted and defendants had no right to see the evidence or witnesses arrayed against them. Whereas President Franklin Roosevelt had authorized similar commissions on a small scale (O'Donnell 2005), the Bush team failed to understand how much American and international legal culture had changed in the intervening years and how much opposition would arise to various aspects of Bush detainee policy. Jack Goldsmith, head of the Office of Legal Counsel in the Bush administration's Justice Department, did understand, with considerable unhappiness, that stronger human rights culture (Goldsmith 2007).

Authorized interrogation procedures, cleared at the highest levels of the Bush administration and sometimes directly supervised by high officials, resulted at times in torture, at other times in cruel, inhuman, and degrading treatment (CID), and at other times in lesser forms of coercive techniques in the quest for actionable intelligence. There were four suicides at the U.S. military detention facility at Guantánamo Bay (GTMO), Cuba, protesting unlimited detention without a clear legal framework. Some prisoners were beaten to death at U.S. military detention facilities in Afghanistan and Iraq. The International Committee of the Red Cross (ICRC) was prohibited from conducting its traditional prison visits in the secret prisons run by the Central Intelligence Agency (CIA).

The ICRC has existed since 1863 and is mandated by the 1949 Geneva Conventions to visit prisoners detained in international armed conflicts (see Forsythe 2005). Various prisoners were hidden from the ICRC at various times at GTMO and in Afghanistan and Iraq. The Federal Bureau of Investigation (FBI), meanwhile, withdrew from certain interrogations rather than be complicit in what was transpiring. The pattern of prisoner abuse was broad, consisting both of tightly controlled and supervised coercion and less precise actions that evolved in Afghanistan and Iraq amid ongoing armed conflict and U.S. occupation.

Given that the United States had ratified the International Covenant on Civil and Political Rights; the UN Convention against Torture and Other Cruel, Inhuman, or Degrading Treatment or Punishment; and the 1949 Geneva Conventions, the first step for the Bush administration was to supervise its lawyers

[handwritten margin note: The Bush team authorized :]

in the making of secret and unilateral interpretations of these documents. In effect, this amounted to tearing down the international legal framework that had been constructed over the years to protect prisoners in armed conflict and other situations of national emergency. The Bush team had to worry about the U.S. War Crimes Act of 1996, which criminalized torture, CID, and grave breaches of the laws of war. Until changes mandated by the Republican Congress in 2006, humiliation of detainees was also a war crime in U.S. law. *[War Crimes Act]*

Overriding the objections of the ICRC and the American Bar Association, among other groups, the Bush administration declared that no one at GTMO, the supposed primary holding facility for enemy detainees that had been opened in January 2002, was protected by the Geneva Conventions. The U.S. Supreme Court held this interpretation to be incorrect, ruling in 2006 that the United States was obligated to apply, at a minimum, Common Article Three from the four Conventions of 1949 since it pertained to nonstate parties as well as states and since, in the opinion of the Court, it had become the minimum humanitarian baseline in all wars, including the so-called global war on terrorism. While the judgment was directed to the issue of military commissions, it clearly implied that neither torture nor cruel, inhuman, or degrading treatment could legally obtain at GTMO. The Bush administration also refused to provide a hearing by an independent authority as to the proper status of questionable detainees, as called for by the Geneva Conventions. Refusal to classify a prisoner of war as such is a war crime.

The Office of Legal Counsel (OLC), which pronounces definitively on legal matters for the executive branch, declared that harsh interrogation techniques were not prohibited under the UN Torture Convention unless severe damage approaching "organ failure" transpired (see Greenberg and Dratel 2005). The OLC also held that if an interrogator did not have intense pain as an objective, then the fact of intense pain as a by-product of interrogation measures would not result in prohibited behavior. These arguments were so at variance with the wording of the Convention and its legislative history that a subsequent Bush-appointed head of the OLC eventually withdrew them in an unprecedented move (Goldsmith 2007). These and other relevant memos were designed to give the administration a blank check for detention and interrogation (see P. Sands 2008).

In Iraq, for a considerable time after the U.S. invasion in March 2003, U.S. attention to lawful detention and interrogation was lax and confused. The Abu Ghraib prison scandal of 2003, publicized in 2004, entailed photos of various acts of depravity and degradation by U.S. military personnel visited upon Iraqi prisoners. This situation was the result of a more general practice by high U.S. civilian and military officials of denigrating the legal and humane standards normally relevant and then issuing vague documents that left lower-ranking military personnel unsure as to the relevant guidelines (U.S. Senate Committee on Armed Services [Levin Report] 2009; Independent Panel to Review Department of Defense Detention Operations [Schlesinger Report] 2004). Secretary of Defense Donald Rumsfeld tried to suppress information about the mistreatment of prisoners at Abu Ghraib and the broader policy context in which it occurred by commissioning a series of reports that excluded any review of high officials (Jones and Fay 2004; *Article 15-6 Investigation of the 800th Military Police Brigade* [Taguba Report] 2004; Schlesinger Report 2004). The myth was advanced that the problem stemmed primarily from "bad apples at the bottom of the barrel" (see Feith 2008).

It is now quite clear Vice President Cheney and his primary lawyer on the question, David Addington, disliked the relevant national and international laws existing on the subject and sought a free hand for "coercive" interrogation. They created a legal war counsel composed of John Yoo and James Bybee in the Justice Department, Timothy Flanagan and Alberto Gonzales in the White House, and William Haynes in the Pentagon to devise legal interpretations allowing the abusive and unlawful treatment of many prisoners to go forward in many places.

Cheney in particular believed in going to "the dark side" after 9/11 (Mayer 2008) and often cut out of the policy-making process Secretary of State Colin Powell and National Security Adviser Condoleezza Rice, their primary legal advisers, and others who might have had different views on the abuse of enemy prisoners (Gellman 2008). In particular, State Department and military lawyers never had a chance to influence early policy because the legal team persuaded Bush to sign off on key decision papers before other interested parties in the administration knew that decision time was at hand. Controversial legal interpretations were made by a group of politically appointed lawyers in an irregular policy-making process. Rice and her NSC team were not inclined to oppose what Bush wanted due to pressure from Cheney and Rumsfeld (Bumiller 2007; Graham 2009; Daalder and Destler 2009). Powell, who thought the al-Qaeda threat did not merit abusive interrogation and who believed the al-Qaeda threat was exaggerated, nonetheless chose not to resign over the issue (DeYoung 2006b).

As for the CIA, ICRC interviews with prisoners at GTMO in 2006 indicated systematic torture and CID, according to a report leaked to the press (International Committee of the Red Cross 2007, published 2009). That report, in addition to legal memos from the Bush era released by the Obama team, made clear that more than a dozen so-called high-value detainees had been seriously abused as authorized and supervised by Bush officials. The ICRC report characterized treatment as sometimes torture and sometimes CID, both prohibited by international law, as was forced disappearance itself.

Given this brief and necessarily incomplete version of events, it is little wonder that GTMO became a symbol of harsh unilateralism by the Bush administration in much of the world. The exposure of abuses at Abu Ghraib in

2004 fueled the controversy over proper treatment of enemy detainees. Congress responded with the Detainee Treatment Act (DTA) in 2005, which mandated humane detention and interrogation by both the CIA (when operating in military installations) and the military. The DTA, however, decriminalized humiliating detention and interrogation and provided amnesty to Bush operatives who might be charged with war crimes. The U.S. Supreme Court in 2006 ruled that core parts of the laws of war applied to U.S. policies toward detainees, and in 2008 it ruled that GTMO prisoners had the right of habeas corpus and could challenge their detention in federal courts. In this context there was a delayed, but somewhat effective, domestic push-back against these policies.

Upon taking office in January 2009, Obama saw things mostly but not entirely differently. During his first week as president, he issued executive orders to close GTMO within a year, to shut down the secret CIA "black sites" where prisoners were held and interrogated, to forbid interrogation methods that went beyond the revised U.S. Army Field Manual, and to make null and void all executive branch legal memos on detention and interrogation matters since 9/11. He rejected the Bush concept of "unlawful enemy combatant," which implied that international laws of war were not relevant in military conflicts with the Taliban and al-Qaeda and many other fighters or suspected fighters after 9/11. While it proved impossible to close GTMO by Obama's self-imposed deadline, other policy changes appeared to have taken effect.

The military had already reversed course, prodded by the Supreme Court's 2006 decision as well as by self-reflection in several important circles. Gen. David Petraeus, a leading Army expert on counterinsurgency who was placed in charge of Iraq before moving to higher command, had stressed the importance of humane interrogation as part of a "hearts-and-minds" campaign in Iraq, the Arab-Muslim world, and beyond. Petraeus's view fit with the statements of other U.S. military officials who said that GTMO and Abu Ghraib in particular had fueled violent opposition to the U.S. presence in Iraq. A number of military officials argued that the "juice was not worth the squeeze"—that information gained from coercive interrogations was not worth the resulting negative U.S. image and mobilization of anti-American extremists.

Obama's early steps in this domain were strongly supported not just by liberals, civil libertarians, and human rights advocates but also by a distinguished group of high military officials and many State Department career officials. (President Obama received a standing ovation at the State Department when he announced his curtailment of the harshest interrogation measures). On the other hand, Obama's opponents in Congress were not enchanted at the direction of change. Senate Republicans held up the confirmation of Attorney General Eric Holder after he stated that "waterboarding," a tactic of interrogation that brings detainees to the brink of drowning, constituted torture. In general, those who had supported the Bush administration's views on detention and interrogation believed that Obama was moving too fast and too soon, without a careful study of security needs.

While publicly opposed to abusive interrogation, Obama backtracked on some campaign statements in this issue area. As president, he proposed not the elimination of military commissions to try certain detainees but rather their reconstitution to afford more procedural due process. He also continued extended administrative detention for certain GTMO prisoners who, in his view, could not be tried because of tainted evidence (e.g., obtained through torture) or because of strong but incomplete evidence of enemy status that might not stand up in court. He wanted to move most remaining GTMO prisoners to a site in Illinois, but congressional opposition to the plan and other factors meant that GTMO was not closed by early 2010 as Obama had pledged. The Obama team also continued controversial renditions of terror suspects to foreign governments for detention and interrogation but pledged closer supervision of their treatment to ensure compliance with humane standards.

The question of possible criminal prosecution for past abusive interrogations proved vexing. It was clear that Obama did not want to move in this direction. He had promised to reach out to Republicans and end the spirit of intense partisanship in Washington. He wanted Republican support for his domestic legislative agenda on economic recovery, health reform, and other issues. He also understood that some low-level officials had acted in good faith once the Justice Department had issued memos authorizing harsh interrogation methods. (George Tenet, director of the CIA, had been careful to get written approval for what he was being asked to do regarding the treatment of enemy prisoners.)

There was a movement for judicial accountability among some Democrats and nongovernmental lawyers, but many conservatives in and out of government argued for impunity in the name of national security and cohesion. In *Rasul v. Myers* (2009), the Obama legal team urged the Supreme Court not to review charges of torture by former GTMO detainees. On other judicial matters, such as the argument that further release of photographs of abuse would harm U.S. security interests, Obama's decisions mirrored Bush policy positions.

On the subject of personal legal liability, or command responsibility, a possible compromise position was the creation of an independent or bipartisan commission, similar to the 9/11 Commission, in lieu of judicial proceedings. This idea, however, gained little traction in Washington, despite early support from Leon Panetta, Obama's head of the CIA. The Senate Armed Services Committee, however, issued a report holding Rumsfeld responsible for much of the prisoner abuse that occurred in military facilities (Levin Report 2009). The report, however, failed to address the question of criminal prosecutions or other follow-up options.

Even the question of legal justice for Islamic militants and their supporters proved controversial within the country. When on Christmas Day 2009 a Nigerian with militant training in Yemen slipped through security procedures and tried to blow up a Delta airliner as it landed in Detroit, the Obama team handled the would-be suicide bomber via regular criminal justice procedures. This angered critics, who claimed the terrorist should have been turned over to special procedures and eventually tried in a military commission.

Likewise, when the Obama administration indicated an intention to try Khalid Sheikh Mohammed, the self-proclaimed mastermind of 9/11, in federal court in New York City, the push-back was so intense that Obama and Attorney General Holder cancelled those plans. They chose this reversal rather than face charges that they were endangering security and being excessively concerned about the rights of alleged terrorists.

Regarding policy about enemy prisoners, it was clear that the Obama White House was much more sensitive than the previous administration about the U.S. government's reputation in the world. It was also more attentive to the fit between U.S. detainee policies and relevant international treaties and other standards. Obama officials sought a comprehensive and defensible legal framework for the handling of terror suspects rather than the ad hoc executive authority utilized by the Bush administration. In this sense, early signs indicated that Obama's attempt to renew engagement with international human rights and humanitarian regimes would have some positive consequences, if not achieve all of the reforms sought by the president regarding the treatment of enemy prisoners.

Human Rights at the United Nations

The Bush legacy of assertive unilateralism was also clear regarding certain human rights issues at the United Nations, although Bush's overall UN policies were less unilateral than sometimes pictured. The United Nations is actually a sprawling family of agencies in which important decisions might be made by governments speaking for states or by international civil servants, especially agency heads, claiming to speak for either the organization or the international community. This complex reality makes analysis and generalizations difficult. If we explore a few examples, we find that Obama had to deal with the aftermath of Bush unilateralism regarding the new UN Human Rights Council and the UN World Conference against Racism, Racial Discrimination, Xenophobia and Related Intolerance (Durban I) but also with a more engaged Bush policy in the UN Security Council concerning a series of human rights issues intertwined with security concerns. Some information about Bush policies, and their fate, is required in order to place Obama decisions in proper context.

Human Rights Commission to Council

The Bush administration was highly critical of the UN Human Rights Commission, the center of traditional UN debate and diplomacy on human rights from 1947 through 2005. The White House's central argument was that the commission was politicized and engaged in blatant double standards, spending a vast amount of time and energy on regimes disfavored by a majority of member states in the developing world. Bush's second ambassador to the UN, John Bolton, a neoconservative skeptical of international law and organization, often noted the commission's failure to confront egregious violations of human rights in places like Idi Amin's Uganda.

Bolton, however, failed to address similar double standards in the U.S. approach. For example, Washington devoted far more effort to lambasting Fidel Castro's human rights record in Cuba than to engaging the Commission in a serious review of human rights violations in pro-U.S. states such as Saudi Arabia. Careful studies eventually showed that the Commission's record was not as bad as most governments and many human rights groups claimed (Lebovic and Voeten 2006; Forsythe 2009). Still, in 2006 the General Assembly voted to create a new UN Human Rights Council reporting directly to the Assembly.

The United States opposed this action and sought a body restricted to "genuine" democracies. This was unacceptable to a large number of postcolonial states, which chafed when, in their view, the West lectured the rest, disregarding its own human rights defects. More than a few non-Western states thought that poorer states that had emerged from colonial exploitation recently should be given considerable time to get their human rights house in order. In fact, a number of developing countries did have poor human rights records and thus were not keen on rigorous review by a UN body.

The European and other democratic states, seeing this split between the United States and many developing states, opted for mediation and engagement. They decided to support the new Council even though its authority and membership were not drastically different from those of the old commission. In a deal brokered by Jan Eliasson of Sweden, the General Assembly president, they decided to make the new Council work as well as possible. Bush, however, remained opposed to the Council even after its creation was approved. The Bush administration then boycotted the Council while criticizing its double standards as it continued to devote far more attention to Israel than to comparable human rights violations in the Democratic Republic of Congo and the Darfur region of Sudan.

Beginning in 2009, Obama and Secretary of State Hillary Clinton faced the question of whether to follow the European lead and re-engage with the Council, working from the inside to make it as dynamic and balanced as possible, or to continue to criticize its defects from the outside. Obama decided that the United States would indeed stand for election to the UN Human

Rights Council and gained a seat in May. In keeping with his renewal agenda, Obama opted for renewed engagement.

Durban I and II

A similar unilateralism could be seen in Bush's reaction to the UN Conference against Racism held in Durban, South Africa, in August 2001. Given the persistent criticism of Israel by a number of Arab and African states in the run-up to the meeting and the actual conference itself, the United States and Israel walked out in protest. Other democracies did not, choosing to stay engaged and fight for preferred language in conference documents. These states also could record their votes and exercise their explanations of vote at the end of the process. But a walk-out dramatized unhappiness and played to various supporters at home.

The Bush team was sufficiently unhappy with Mary Robinson, the UN high commissioner for human rights and the UN official in charge of the conference process, that the administration pressured UN secretary-general Kofi Annan not to renew her contract. Robinson had been publicly critical of the Bush policies in its war on terrorism, outlined in the previous section of this chapter. She also engaged in open criticism of Israel's treatment of Palestinians. Annan complied with Washington's wishes. Regarding the first Durban conference, Robinson's position was that the gains of the conference outweighed the potential pitfalls.

As Durban II approached in April 2009, with a mandate to revisit the status of racism and xenophobia, some of the previous trends were evident—namely an attempt by certain Arab and African states to label Israel a racist regime. There was also an attempt by Islamic states to insert language in conference documents that to most Western parties seemed to limit freedom of speech in order to ensure that there was no criticism of religion, particularly Islam. The Obama team, coming into office several months before Durban II, needed to decide either on a policy of engagement or repeat the Bush walkout of 2001. Such decisions were intertwined with broader considerations about U.S. foreign policy in the eastern Mediterranean. If the Obama team was considering pressing Israel for significant concessions on the Palestinian question, should it reassure Israel of basic support in the UN Human Rights Council, such as by boycotting Durban II?

The Obama team decided to boycott Durban II, thus displaying considerable continuity with the Bush administration. The conference itself turned out to be a rather tame affair, and the concluding document contained almost no wording that could possibly offend Israel or any other concerned state. It was impossible to say definitively whether the strong opposition by Bush to Durban I had provoked more moderation in the policies of various parties, whether the

Obama team was using its boycott of Durban II to demonstrate its support for Israel, and/or whether many states wanted to make a new beginning with the Obama administration and avoid controversy on the issues associated with Durban I.

In the Security Council

As is well known, the United States has one of the preferred positions in the UN Security Council, being one of the five permanent members and thus possessing a veto. Unlike the Soviet Union during the Cold War, the United States has never walked out of the Council in protest since, as the Soviets discovered, a boycott by a permanent member does not stop Council business but merely leads to the loss of the veto power.

The Bush administration was centrally engaged in Council deliberations about how to mitigate human rights violations, humanitarian law violations, and human suffering in places like the Darfur region of Sudan and did not pose an obstacle to UN attempts to manage these situations. In Sudan, the primary obstacles to progress came from the central government, as backed by its Chinese allies, and from a reluctance by states in the African Union to take muscular and timely action to stop the violence.

In a remarkable development, in March 2005 the Bush administration abstained on, and thus did not veto, a council resolution authorizing the prosecutor of the International Criminal Court to open an investigation into war crimes in Darfur. Although contested by Sudan, the resolution was presented as legal both according to the UN Charter, which is authorized to make binding decisions regarding security questions, and according to the Rome Statute of the ICC, which gave a general grant of authority to the Council to make such referrals. For the Bush administration, which had been trying to kill the ICC for some years, this abstention reflected a policy shift. The president appointed a special envoy on Darfur, and it seems likely that the president's concern with the humanitarian emergency, stimulated by lobbying for action by Christian conservatives in the United States, finally outweighed his initial determination to make the Court stillborn.

The Obama team has yet to take a definitive position on the ICC. Several statements by Obama officials indicated a less hostile attitude toward the court, and the United States has attended ICC meetings as an observer. There was no move either to re-sign the Rome Statute or to seek Senate consent to ratification, as this would provoke strong reaction from many Republicans in particular. All of this indicates a tendency toward further engagement with global governance in the field of human rights alongside awareness of domestic opposition to the ICC. Obama suggested that further diplomacy should be tried with regard to Sudan and that, if progress were forthcoming, the United States might rethink the issue of prosecuting President Omar al-Bashir and other indicted Sudanese officials. Obama's willingness to engage diplomatically with Sudan, along with China and other repressive states, triggered criticism that he was selling out human rights (Stephens 2009; Landler 2009b).

As for the Democratic Republic of the Congo (DRC), the very size and complexity of the problems in that large and fragmented country impeded easy management. At times, almost a dozen outside states have intervened in the country, driven by a quest for various political objectives along with economic gain from a variety of valued natural resources. Bush supported the deployment of a UN security field mission principally for the Ituri region and stayed persistently involved in UN efforts to cope with a horrific situation that had taken the lives of a quarter of a million persons and had featured systematic rapes, among other atrocities.

Having other priority concerns, the Bush team was in favor of avoiding unilateral intervention in the DRC. The administration was bogged down in Iraq and Afghanistan, was concerned about Pakistan and India, and was trying to make sure that al-Qaeda did not operate out of the failed state of Somalia and the weak state of Yemen. Similar concerns impeded deep involvement in this conflict by Obama, not the least of which was the worst recession the United States had seen in decades. While cutting back military involvement in Iraq, Obama had escalated U.S. military force in Afghanistan. The latter ensured no U.S. unilateral intervention in Africa despite the humanitarian disasters taking place in many countries there.

The Obama administration inherited these and other agenda items in the Security Council. Multilateral engagement per se was not the issue. Even with a good-faith effort at global governance, the specific problem was how to get proper, decisive, muscular action without provoking a veto from other permanent members. To the extent that enforcement action was considered in the Security Council, persistent questions were: Which countries would agree to put their military personnel in harm's way, and which countries would agree to mandatory economic sanctions that hurt the supporters as well as the target? These questions further forced Obama to modify his renewal agenda regarding human rights, and in his first year there were no radical changes in the politics of the UN Security Council in this area.

Conclusion

This short and limited review suggests first of all that, with regard to human rights in emergencies, Obama has been only partially inclined to make U.S. security policies fit better with the international legal framework concerning human rights and humanitarian law. He did take important steps to end torture, forced disappearances, and the previous strained legal interpretations of international law, and he effectively transferred many suspected terrorists to federal courts for trial.

On the other hand, Obama opted for continued administrative detention and military commissions and refused to prosecute or extradite for prosecution those Americans involved in the mistreatment of prisoners as required by international law. Obama continued to send suspected terrorists to foreign regimes associated with abuse of prisoners with only diplomatic assurances that they would not be mistreated. Clearly on some of these issues Obama elevated pursuit of bipartisanship and consensus, and his domestic agenda, over vigorous implementation of international rights obligations.

The nearly successful terror attack on a civilian airliner arriving at Detroit on Christmas Day 2009, noted already, caused the Obama team to talk tough about security and slow the release of remaining prisoners at GTMO. These and other actions further hindered progress on human rights by the United States. Likewise, Obama's policies at the UN showed change but not a radical break with the previous administration. Continuity with Bush was most clear concerning Durban II, as Obama continued the Bush boycott of meetings. Change was most evident in regard to the Human Rights Council. Obama's decision to join the Council reflected his preference for engagement, which contrasted with the old policy of isolated protest. In general, differences in U.S. policy in the Security Council in the Obama era are likely to be of degree, not of kind.

It would be difficult for any analyst to see the Obama team as more unilateralist than the record compiled by Bush. Hence, one would expect a continuation of greater sensitivity to international law and organization, including in the area of human rights. Clearly, however, there was to be no crusade for human rights after the 2008 election, whether in the very different molds of Jimmy Carter or George W. Bush. Despite speeches by Secretary of State Clinton pledging fidelity to human rights, the administration's early record was such that leading groups like Amnesty International and Human Rights Watch expressed deep concerns (Colvin 2009).

Times of insecurity and economic distress usually correlate negatively with advances in human rights. Still, the centrist and pragmatic Obama team did not abandon human rights in foreign policy. But those rights were far from constituting a cornerstone of the president's foreign policy. Emphasizing the need to restore the health of the U.S. and global economies, scaling back U.S. involvement in Iraq, and managing the "surge" in Afghanistan were all indicative of the fact that human rights were but one of many foreign policy issues for Obama, and far from being the most important.

CHAPTER 11

"First, Do No Harm"

Foreign Economic Policy Making under Barack Obama

I. M. (Mac) Destler[1]

IT WAS THE FIRST FULL WEEK of the Obama presidency. On Monday, January 26, 2009, U.S. businesses announced plans to lay off more than 55,000 workers—a huge economic hit for a single day. On Tuesday, the president journeyed to Capitol Hill for nearly three hours of meetings seeking support from congressional Republicans for massive economic stimulus legislation. On Wednesday, the House passed its $816 billion bill, with zero Republicans voting in favor. Thursday brought front-page news that that bill contained a provision requiring projects that it funded to use made-in-America steel, posing a frontal challenge to U.S. trade policy. On Friday, the Commerce Department reported that the U.S. economy had declined 3.8 percent in the fourth quarter of 2008, the worst performance since 1982, with expectations of an even greater decline for the first quarter of 2009.[2] That same day, the president was forced to telephone Chinese president Hu Jintao to disown a statement, submitted by his tax-embattled Treasury secretary nominee during confirmation hearings, that the new administration had concluded that Beijing was "manipulating" its currency for trade advantage. Meanwhile, multiple global leaders—notably the premiers of China and Russia—were denouncing, at the world economic forum in Davos, Switzerland, the U.S. role in precipitating the worst international economic crisis since the Great Depression.

All in all, it was a rugged week.

To address these matters, Obama had been assembling his own high-powered team, which would lead the eclectic welter of U.S. trade and economic policy agencies in some form of policy renewal. Yet his early presidency would exemplify a paradox. As a person, he was the epitome of globalization:

father from Kenya; childhood years in Hawaii and Indonesia. Yet in the economic sphere, his focus was overridingly domestic. The international economic issues he would address in his first fifteen months were, by and large, not issues that he chose but issues that were thrust upon him.

And his responses to these issues were minimal. He took care not to move backwards, not to seriously impede present and future international cooperation. In the words commonly attributed to the ancient Greek physician Hippocrates, Obama would "first, do no harm." But he would not embark on the type of bold new initiatives that were otherwise characteristic of his early presidency. To put Obama's challenge in context, we must go back into history, into how the United States came to have the government he inherited for the conduct of international economic policy. At least four historical imperatives generated today's official institutions.

The Institutional Prologue: Depression, War, and Economic Challenge

The first imperative was represented by the Bretton Woods Conference of 1944, where officials from Allied nations met to build the basis for the postwar international economy. To avoid a repeat of the economic malaise of the interwar (1919–39) period, they agreed to create two global institutions: the International Monetary Fund (IMF) and the International Bank for Reconstruction and Development (now "the World Bank"). In the implementing legislation, the Department of the Treasury was assigned the task of representing the United States at these two institutions, a responsibility it has retained to this day. There was a subsequent conference at Havana that sought to establish a parallel body, the projected International Trade Organization. This proved stillborn when Congress failed to ratify its charter. But an "interim" organization, the General Agreement on Tariffs and Trade (GATT), proved surprisingly effective in establishing rules within its sphere in the half century after World War II, until at last the World Trade Organization (WTO) opened its doors in January 1995.

The second U.S. imperative was essentially domestic—to legislate policies and institutions aimed at preventing a recurrence of the Great Depression. Reflecting the new doctrine of Keynesian economics, the Employment Act of 1946 made it the responsibility of the federal government to "promote maximum employment, production, and purchasing power." To propose policies to achieve this, the Act established a three-person Council of Economic Advisers (CEA) in the Executive Office of the President, which would report annually to a Joint Economic Committee of the Congress also established in the legislation. Both institutions were just advisory, and a more potent role in achieving this objective would be played by the Federal Reserve Board (the Fed) and its chair. But the Employment Act laid down a marker: Americans would henceforth hold the federal government responsible for keeping the economy running at full steam.

The third imperative began as a response to the postwar economic crisis in Europe. Faced with a continent ravaged by war and a particularly cruel winter in 1947, the United States responded with the Marshall Plan, a uniquely far-sighted program that put resources in the hands of Europeans, provided they joined in a coordinated reconstruction effort. Abroad, this sowed the seeds of what would eventually become the European Union (EU). For the United ＊ EU States, it established a new policy sphere under the generic label of "foreign assistance." The Eisenhower and Kennedy administrations shifted priority to the developing nations—with bilateral programs under what became the U.S. Agency for International Development (USAID) and multilateral aid through the World Bank and the United Nations.

Fourth, and particularly important for the evolution of U.S. foreign economic policy making, there was the challenge posed by the nations that became our economic competitors. First it was the uniting Europe, then Japan, then East Asia more generally. In the early postwar period, U.S. manufacturing had been globally dominant, and the U.S. economy was remarkably self-contained. In 1950, U.S. imports and exports were each about 5 percent of domestic goods production. But this would rise, using rough figures again, to 9 percent in 1970, 20 percent in 1980, and 29 percent in 2000.[3] The political response would rise also. U.S. producers thought it acceptable for international economic policy to be a handmaiden of foreign policy—as long as they were not overly affected. However, the internationalization of the U.S. economy led logically to greater domestic concern over, and influence on, U.S. economic transactions with the world.

An early harbinger came in 1962, when President John F. Kennedy sought expanded statutory authority to negotiate reductions in trade barriers, particularly with Europe. Legislators were reluctant to grant this if State Department officials continued to lead the negotiations, as they had done since the Reciprocal Trade Agreements Act of 1934. Those diplomats were competent enough, said House Ways and Means Committee chair Wilbur Mills (D-AR), but they didn't understand U.S. industry and were not sensitive to its needs. So Kennedy agreed, reluctantly, to the creation of a "special representative for trade negotiations" in the Executive Office of the President to lead the negotiations. The office would expand over the years—gaining Cabinet status in 1975 and a more permanent-sounding name in 1980—United States trade representative (USTR). It would also become, over those same years, more and more responsive to U.S. domestic economic interests.

A bit later began a parallel trend—the movement of responsibility for coordinating international economic policy away from the National Security Council (NSC) to institutions created to give priority to the economic side of these issues. The dollar crisis of 1971, highlighted by President Richard Nixon's decision to abandon our currency's link to gold, led to establishment of the Cabinet-level Council on Economic Policy (CEP) under Secretary of the Treasury George Shultz, which operated parallel to Henry Kissinger's NSC. Subsequent administrations established comparable Cabinet-level committees. Bill Clinton renamed and elevated this function by establishing the National Economic Council (NEC) in 1993 (Destler 1996), and his successors retained that organization. Its focus was domestic as much as international, but both institutionally and practically it highlighted the economic policy links between the two and diluted somewhat the links between international economic policy and international security.

So by the time Obama came to office, authority over foreign economic policy was being exercised by an eclectic set of institutions and actors—and only one of the primary actors (Treasury) was a department headed by a "Secretary." Interestingly, this meant relatively little attention to Obama's economic appointments by a press fixated on who would be named to the fifteen "Cabinet" positions.

But Obama did not just inherit institutions—he also inherited what was arguably the worst economic situation confronting any new U.S. president since Franklin D. Roosevelt.

The Subprime Prologue

The crisis had been years in the making. Among its broader causes was a global credit explosion, fueled by undersaving in the United States and oversaving in East Asia. The United States ran huge trade deficits, requiring foreign capital to finance them. China and Japan in particular provided this capital, which was generated by their large international surpluses. This mass of capital needed specific destinations, vehicles where it could be placed and rest secure and/or earn good returns. U.S. Treasury bills met part of this need. But private financial institutions rushed into this market also by developing higher-yield securities. They also developed instruments that allegedly protected investors from loss, such as the now-infamous "credit default swaps" pioneered by the insurance giant American International Group (AIG).

A particularly creative area for new investment vehicles was real estate. Rapid appreciation of U.S. home prices through the mid-2000s generated unprecedented demand for investment in home mortgages. Banks and financial houses responded by packaging mortgages in securities that they marketed worldwide. To expand the market further, lenders lured financially marginal buyers by offering initially low, "subprime" interest rates, which would typically rise sharply after a few short years. Some loans were truly egregious—dubbed "Ninja loans" by industry insiders since the recipients allegedly had "no income, no job." But because these loans were packaged together and marketed to unsuspecting investors, those who originated them did not bear the risk.

The securities were solid only if prices continued to rise. But in the second quarter of 2006, U.S. home prices peaked. They declined moderately for the next year, then more severely.[4] This put holders of mortgage-based securities at risk. By late 2007, the market was facing serious problems. The Federal Reserve responded aggressively. It reduced the federal funds rate by a full 1 percent in the last four months of that year and an additional 1.25 percent in the single month of January 2008. It also poured money into banks and investment houses—this action capped perhaps by the government takeover of AIG in September 2008. Congress passed a $168 billion stimulus bill in February, and when bank credit froze in September, it enacted, reluctantly, a financial rescue package of $700 billion aimed at saving banks whose balance sheets were laden with bad mortgage debt.

The George W. Bush administration had responded aggressively (if somewhat belatedly) to the crisis, with Treasury secretary Henry Paulson in the lead, but its economic stewardship was discredited nonetheless. In the three presidential debates, the cool and cerebral Obama gained support vis-à-vis his more impulsive and less informed adversary, Senator John McCain (R-AZ), and the Illinois senator rode to a decisive 365–173 electoral victory in November. He also became the first Democrat in the past ten presidential elections to carry a majority of the popular vote. Obama set to work immediately to assemble a strong Cabinet and White House staff, with particular emphasis on the economy. And he engaged selectively in influencing policy during the 76-day transition period.

Still, Obama entered office under the bleakest economic circumstances confronting any president since the Great Depression. And what started as an *American* crisis centered on *finance* had become a deep global economic downturn, as it turned out that many foreign banks had been similarly egregious in making unsafe real estate-based investments. The IMF would report that the world's "advanced economies experienced an unprecedented 7½ percent decline in real GDP during the fourth quarter of 2008" (IMF 2009, xv).

Each nation necessarily viewed the Great Recession first and foremost in terms of its own dire situation, of course. And national measures were aimed primarily at turning things around at home. But there was broad recognition of the need for international cooperation. It was not just Ben Bernanke, economic historian of the Depression years and now chair of the Federal Reserve Board, who recalled the "lessons" of the 1930s—the Smoot-Hawley Tariff and its foreign emulators; Franklin Roosevelt's torpedoing of the London Economic Conference of 1933. Both were viewed, with benefit of hindsight, as "beggar-thy-neighbor" efforts of nations to fuel recovery at others' expense—through new trade barriers and manipulation of exchange rates that ended up making world recovery harder. Obama's predecessor had recognized this when he invited twenty heads of state and government to Washington in November 2008 to consult and coordinate their responses. Obama would play a lead role in two such G-20 meetings in 2009—the London conference of April and the gathering in Pittsburgh that he hosted in September.

The new president faced other serious international economic challenges as well. The Doha Round of international trade talks, launched in 2001 under the auspices of the WTO, remained stalled, notwithstanding eleventh-hour efforts by the Bush administration to break the impasse. There were also three bilateral free trade agreements, controversial within Obama's Democratic Party, which the Bush administration had signed but Congress had not ratified. This unfinished business came after a year when public anxiety over globalization appeared on the rise and support for trade liberalization seemed to be waning—a Pew Center poll the previous year had found that 48 percent of Americans believed free trade agreements to be a "bad thing" for the country, the first time a plurality had taken that position since Pew began asking the question in 1997 (Pew Research Center for the People & the Press, 2008b).[5] Reflecting this chilly political climate, the advisory report of a twenty-two person advisory group convened by C. Fred Bergsten, director of the Peterson Institute for International Economics, a group that included two former U.S. trade representatives, highlighted "the political backlash against further trade liberalization" caused, in part, by "the lack of a national strategy that responds effectively to economic dislocation." The recommended response gave priority to measures in pursuit of such a strategy: not until page 9 (of its 12-page report) did the group address the specific topic of trade policy (Trade Policy Study Group 2008).

Looking Homeward

Like the typical Democratic presidential candidate, Barack Obama emphasized the domestic impact of trade policy during his campaign. Mainly in response to an opponent, Hillary Rodham Clinton, who had broad appeal to labor unions and globalization skeptics, he expressed opposition to Bush's free trade agreements in their present form and called for renegotiation of the North American Free Trade Agreement (NAFTA). He did not emphasize trade once he secured the nomination, however, and his Republican opponent, John McCain, was not able to use his earlier statements against him. But the world was wary. The problem, however, was not that Obama would prove to be a "protectionist." Rather, it was where trade and international economic policy would rank on his list of priorities. His first purported choice for U.S. trade representative, House Ways and Means Committee member Xavier Becerra (D-CA), withdrew with the unhelpful but revealing observation that for Obama this policy issue "would not be No. 1, and perhaps, not even priority No. 2 or 3" (interview with editorial board of *La Opinion,* quoted in "Becerra" 2008).

Hence, unlike his two Democratic predecessors—Jimmy Carter and Bill Clinton—Barack Obama did not begin his presidency with a strong focus on *foreign* economic policy. He had, during his campaign, pledged a renewal of American global leadership, with an emphasis on multilateralism. But the spotlight had been on Bush administration unilateralism in diplomacy and international security—Bush had in fact embraced multilateralism on trade. Obama recognized, of course, that the crisis he inherited had become global. But his first duty was to Americans, and that was his focus.

The big appointments were Timothy Geithner, president of the New York Federal Reserve Bank, as secretary of the Treasury, and former Treasury secretary Larry Summers to head the NEC as Obama's assistant for economic policy. Both were controversial. Summers's outspokenness on sensitive issues had led to his resignation in 2006 as president of Harvard University. Geithner carried two burdens—participation in pre-Obama economic rescue efforts that were criticized as overly generous to banks and a mishandling of income on his tax forms, which became a prominent issue during the confirmation process. Both, however, quickly became the dominant administration figures for this key policy sphere. Both were internationalists by conviction, but both necessarily gave priority to the domestic side. Other important economic appointments included Peter Orzsag, then head of the Congressional Budget Office, to direct the Office of Management and Budget, and Berkeley economist Christina Romer to be chair of the Council of Economic Advisers. She would prove to be exceptionally good at public articulation of economic policy issues. And towering over them all, perhaps, was Fed chairman Ben Bernanke, whose bold rescue efforts would later win him recognition as *Time* magazine's "Person of the Year" for 2009 (Grunwald 2009).

"The Fed" is normally thought of as an overridingly domestic policy institution, and its mandate—to be sure—is to protect and enhance the *U.S.* economy. But it operates in an era when the markets that it targets are globalized. When Bernanke collaborated with Bush's Treasury secretary, Hank Paulson, and then New York Fed president Geithner to rescue AIG in September 2008, a key decision (much criticized later) was to make whole the assets of those institutions that had unwisely placed their bets on the insurance giant. These included "nearly every major financial institution in the world . . . *Societe Generale,* the big French bank, had $4.1 billion at stake" (Wessel 2009, 192). To allow AIG to fail, Bernanke told Congress in March 2009, would have been "devastating to the stability of the *world* [emphasis added] financial system" (Wessel 2009, 195). To limit action to American holders of these assets would have been neither pragmatic nor effective. While taking these steps, in October 2008, with the crisis deepening and spreading, the Fed chair was also orchestrating a coordinated interest rate cut by the world's major central banks and winning, through Paulson, a commitment by the Group of Seven finance ministers to protect and restore financial markets worldwide.

These and the broad range of bold Bernanke measures were taken in 2008, prior to the Obama presidency. The Fed chair devoted 2009 to consolidating and extending these actions—maintaining the zero-to-0.25 federal funds rate set by the Fed's Open Market Committee during the presidential transition; targeting provision of credit to markets that weren't functioning, such as housing, student loans, and consumer credit. The magnitude and scope of these actions, taken largely on Bernanke's own authority (albeit in cooperation with administration leaders), turned the spotlight on the enormous power the Fed possessed. And though a strong case can be made that he deployed this power with extraordinary courage and effectiveness—keeping the Great Recession from becoming a second Great Depression—he also exposed the institution to political attack and potential congressional action to curb its powers. Hadn't the end result been to reward the bankers who had caused the catastrophe—Wall Street—while on Main Street, unemployment grew to 10 percent? To his many admirers, this seemed like the fulfillment of an old Washington rule: "No good deed goes unpunished." But he took more heat than any Fed chair in decades, placing his institution clearly in harm's way.

For the Obama administration, these political problems were unwelcome to say the least. Through 2009 and into 2010, frustration over the economy grew, and it became less and less useful and effective to blame the Bush administration. Bernanke worked well with the new team, Geithner in particular: they had gone together through the fire of fall 2008 and established deep mutual respect and trust. But trust between central bankers could only reinforce public suspicion that the rich of Wall Street had been saved while Main Street continued to suffer. (Bernanke took to the public media to rebut this argument: the only reason for the rescues had been to prevent a financial collapse far more devastating to Main Street than what had occurred.) His relationship with Summers was necessarily more complicated for one simple reason: his four-year term would expire on January 31, 2010, and Summers was generally thought of as the most likely choice if Obama decided to make a change. This created what must have been a certain tension between the two until the president resolved the matter with his August announcement that he would renominate Bernanke to a second four-year term.

The public controversy continued into January, and there was a day or two when opposition to Senate confirmation seemed to grow. The incumbent was attacked by Socialist Bernie Sanders (D-VT) and populist Russ Feingold (D-WI) from the left and by Richard Shelby (R-AL) and James DeMint (R-SC) on the right. But in the end Bernanke won broad bipartisan support: 77–23 to break the filibuster against his nomination and 70–30 to confirm.

Solid majorities of both parties voted in favor, though the number of "nays" was the largest in the history of the office.

The G-20 Summits

One place where the president had to address international economic policy was at the meetings of the leaders of the world's major economies convened to address the global crisis. The first of these had been hosted by President Bush in November 2008, shortly after Obama's election victory. The second came on April 2, 2009, in London. Obama arrived there as the United States ended its worst economic quarter in decades, with GDP shrinking at a 6.4 percent annual rate. In his London press conference at the meeting's conclusion, he acknowledged the dire situation:

> The global economy is contracting. Trade is shrinking. Unemployment is rising. The international finance system is nearly frozen. Even these facts can't fully capture the crisis that we're confronting, because behind them is the pain and uncertainty that so many people are facing. We see it back in the United States. We see it here in London. We see it around the world: families losing their homes, workers losing their jobs and their savings, students who are deferring their dreams. So many have lost so much. Just to underscore this point, back in the United States, jobless claims released today were the highest in 26 years. We owe it to all of our citizens to act, and to act with a sense of urgency (Obama 2009e).

He then went on to underscore how the recession was a world event, reflecting the fact that "our economies are more closely linked than ever before." Nations had "prolonged and worsened" the Great Depression "by turning inward." But "we've learned the lessons of history" and "rejected the protectionism that could deepen this crisis." He then highlighted the steps states were taking and had agreed to take: to stimulate their economies, to deal with toxic assets still held by banks, and to enhance IMF funding to help developing countries navigate the crisis (Obama 2009e).

The G-20 summit was Obama's first major international conference as president and, hence, his debut on the global stage. He would go directly from there to the NATO summit in Strasburg, France. He was preceded, of course, by the extraordinary European reception to his election—"Obamamania" had swept the continent (Meunier 2010, 41).[6] Deploying the remarkable global public standing his campaign and election had brought him, he effectively allayed concerns about the depth of his internationalism. He benefited from the fact that he was *not* George W. Bush. But he benefited also from another fact: that, as the months passed and the crisis deepened, nations and peoples began to recognize that their own financial institutions had been willing accomplices—the crisis was not simply "made in America." And Obama's words in fact echoed those in the communiqué signed by all participants. In response to "the greatest challenge to the world economy in modern times," the leaders committed to measures that would "constitute the largest fiscal and monetary stimulus and the most comprehensive support programme for the financial sector in modern times." The aim was "restoring growth and jobs" and "strengthening financial supervision and regulation" to avert a future crisis. The language on trade was briefer, but the leaders promised "to refrain from raising new barriers to investment or to trade in goods and services," and they declared themselves "committed to reaching an ambitious and balanced conclusion to the Doha Development Round" (London Summit 2009). By joining in these sentiments, the Obama administration bought time to focus primarily on other matters, as noted above.

Still in his honeymoon period, Obama could gain points abroad by using the right language in communiqués and press conferences and then return to his preoccupations at home. The same was true, to a somewhat diminished extent, when the president hosted the next G-20 summit in Pittsburgh the following September. But the Obama administration accomplished more there.

The "Leaders' Statement" began by declaring the world to be "in the midst of a critical transition from crisis to recovery," a nice recognition that economies were beginning to bounce back. A particular achievement for Obama economic officials was the inclusion of a new "Framework for Strong, Sustainable, and Balanced Growth": a commitment, at least in principle, to a more balanced pattern of growth and trade among the major nations. As spelled out in the Annex, "All G-20 members agree to address the respective weaknesses of their economies.

- "G-20 members with sustained, significant external deficits pledge to undertake policies to support private savings and undertake fiscal consolidation while maintaining open markets and strengthening export sectors.
- "G-20 members with sustained, significant external surpluses pledge to strengthen domestic sources of growth. According to national circumstances this could include increasing investment, reducing financial markets distortions, boosting productivity in service sectors, improving social safety nets, and lifting constraints on demand growth" (*Leaders' Statement: The Pittsburgh Summit* 2009, Annex 2).

In addition to this global rebalancing, the statement also included commitments to coordinated regulation of financial institutions—less detailed and firm than some Europeans would have liked but significant nonetheless. And the leaders made formal and permanent the demise of the old G-7/G-8, dominated by advanced industrial economies and grossly overrepresenting Europe—by "designat[ing] the G-20 as the premier forum for our international economic cooperation" (*Leaders' Statement: The Pittsburgh Summit* 2009, Preamble 19). They announced plans to meet in Canada in June 2010 and Korea in November 2010, with annual meetings thereafter beginning with France in 2011.

The international summits—and the ongoing domestic economic trials—put Obama's economic advisers at the center of his policy process. Presidential economic adviser Larry Summers was less in the public eye, but his role remained central. Always controversial, and sometimes fueling the controversy with smart but ill-considered comments, he nevertheless retained the president's confidence. Treasury Secretary Geithner, of course, was essential to both issues—to developing and defending internationally the U.S. position on bank regulation and to shaping, explaining, and defending the financial "rescue" to hostile home audiences. Alone among Obama's team, he had been central to the actions taken in 2008 as well as 2009. The "bailout" of the banks had always been virulently unpopular. And he was vulnerable to challenge on details—like paying back AIG's bank creditors 100 cents on the dollar. He had to balance efforts to limit end-of-the-year bonuses paid by financial firms with concerns of principle (not abrogating contracts) and limits on his power. It didn't help that he looked boyishly younger than his 47 years and that his brilliant public service career was largely in "insider" positions that had ill prepared him for the rough-and-tumble of public politics. He had warned Obama, prior to his appointment, that his 2008 engagement could prove a liability to the administration (Lizza 2009). And so it seemed to be, even as he employed the crisis—and his particular powers at Treasury—to make a series of tough decisions: developing "stress tests" for the banks, encouraging them to pay back their government loans, standing firm against the calls of influential experts for nationalizing them (Solomon 2010). By early 2010 he was rebuffing Republican calls for his resignation, arguing that administration actions had in fact brought the economy back from the brink. But the fact that Geithner was *perceived* to be losing power owing to his unpopularity could not but hurt him. And this view seemed reinforced when President Obama endorsed, in the wake of the surprise Republican capture of Ted Kennedy's Massachusetts Senate seat, proposals by former Fed chief and now presidential adviser Paul Volcker to limit the trading activities of large banks (Paletta and Weisman 2010). Geithner had been reported to be skeptical of some elements in the proposal.

And trade? Obama was not unique in making the United States trade representative one of his later cabinet-level appointments—most of his predecessors had also. And his choice—former Dallas mayor Ron Kirk—had a certain promise. The first African American to hold the post, he had political skills of the sort that had built success for USTRs like Robert Strauss under Jimmy Carter and Bill Brock under Ronald Reagan. But lacking both trade policy and Washington experience, he would depend particularly on a strong mandate from the president. Before Kirk was confirmed on March 18, 2009, after resolution of some minor tax problems, Obama would face his first serious trade policy challenge.

"Buy American"—and "Health Care"

One of the less-noticed impacts of the Great Recession was its sharply negative effect on trade. Beginning in August of 2008, and continuing through April of 2009, the value of U.S. exports dropped 26 percent, and the value of U.S. imports plunged 35 percent.[7] (U.S. Census Bureau 2010). Unlike some of the trade decline during the 1930s, this was not the product of "protectionism" or of any trade policy actions at all. Some of the import plunge grew out of the sharp drop-off of oil prices from their mid-2008 peaks. But the rest was simply a product of the fall in U.S. and global demand (and some adjustment in the value of the dollar).

Obama came to office with a plan that would help reverse this decline, not a trade policy measure but his economic stimulus legislation. With the economy still shrinking, Summers had prepared a fifty-seven-page transition memo to the president addressing the full range of economic challenges Obama would face. This served as background for a December 16, 2008, meeting at Obama's transition headquarters in Chicago, orchestrated by Summers, in which the president-elect's main economic and political advisers assessed the depth of the economic threat, the appropriate magnitude of the U.S. response, and the limits of the size of a stimulus bill Congress could be expected to swallow. None of the economic challenges highlighted in the Summers memo was international. He knew that territory well—his first position in the Clinton Treasury had been under secretary for international affairs, and he had recently been named chair of the Advisory Committee at the Peterson Institute for International Economics. But he also knew the president's—and the nation's—priorities.

With enhanced Democratic majorities in both House and Senate, the administration put forward a $825 billion package (reduced by Congress to $787 billion) of enhanced government spending and tax cuts. It was enacted expeditiously—Obama signed it exactly four weeks after his inauguration—with no Republican votes in the House and just three in the Senate.

Before it was enacted, however, the stimulus bill would provide Obama with his first trade policy test. House members added to the legislation passed on January 28 a restrictive "buy-American" provision, specifying that governments receiving the funds must buy only iron and steel products made in the United States. A Senate draft extended this restriction to all U.S. manufacturers. There was an immediate international uproar, particularly from Canada, whose factories had long supplied inputs to construction projects in northern U.S. states. And the United States had international obligations under WTO agreements to open certain procurement to international bidding. The issue was more complex than it seemed—there were other U.S. "buy-American" laws already in place, other nations frequently employed the same practice, and U.S. international obligations in this sphere were limited if real. It was also true that such provisions would make projects more expensive and subject them to procedural delays related to enforcement of the provisions. And they were unlikely to save very many American jobs (Hufbauer and Schott 2009).

Obama had an overloaded agenda and wanted to defer trade policy, but he could not duck this one. He declared in several early February interviews that the United States could not replicate its protectionist response to the Great Depression 79 years earlier: "I think it would be a mistake . . . at a time when worldwide trade is declining for us to start sending a message that somehow we're just looking after ourselves and [are] not concerned about world trade" (Obama 2009d). The Senate modified its draft language to require observance of international trade agreements, though it rejected a McCain amendment to remove the buy-American provision entirely. The Canadians were still adversely affected. A year later, however, Kirk was able to negotiate a deal that opened more U.S. procurement to firms north of the border in exchange for greater access for U.S. firms to procurement by Canadian provinces (Office of the U.S. Trade Representative 2010).

As Norman Ornstein has noted, the Obama stimulus bill itself contained a plethora of notable legislation—more than a typical administration will achieve in a typical year (Ornstein 2010). In the trade-specific area, for example, it included a far-reaching expansion of Trade Adjustment Assistance, the program for workers displaced by import competition. Among other reforms, it extended eligibility to service workers, to workers producing an input to a final product whose market was hurt by trade, and to workers whose employers had shifted production to any foreign country. It also extended the allowed time for retraining programs during which the trade-displaced worker could receive a stipend, raised the percentage of health insurance premiums the government would fund for such a worker, and removed or loosened a number of restrictions that had undercut the effectiveness of the program. Ironically, this reform went largely unnoticed, though a prominent reason why free-trade liberals had long supported such action was that it would alleviate worker anxieties over trade's impact on jobs.

The stimulus included a range of other major policy reforms: "green energy" was among the big winners, and funds contained in the bill enabled Secretary of Education Arne Duncan to launch a new competitive process to encourage school innovation across the nation. This legislation alone should have been a source of pride for the president and the 111th Congress. However, the administration's legislative ambitions went much further: to an energy/climate bill (which passed the House in June), reform of financial regulation, and—above all—the issue that would dominate the second half of 2009. In August, as this author was preparing to fly to Australia to address a conference on Obama's trade policy, he asked an expert colleague what he should say. The answer? "You should say two words: 'health care.'"

The Democrats had won seemingly healthy congressional majorities in the 2008 election. In the House, they expanded their margin to 256 to 178. To increase their margin, they had accepted ideological diversity—courting relatively conservative candidates to run in swing districts where liberals were not likely to triumph. The result was a Democratic caucus with a preponderant majority to the left but with a healthy number of centrists as well. In the Senate, Democrats moved from tenuous control (51 votes, counting socialist Bernie Sanders [VT] and independent Joe Lieberman [CT]) to 58 after the election, 59 in April when Arlen Specter (PA) switched parties, and then 60 at the end of June when the Minnesota Supreme Court declared Democrat Al Franken the winner in the bitterly contested Senate race there. In a Senate where the minority party increasingly employed "extended debate" to block measures it opposed, the 60 votes gave Democrats a "filibuster-proof" majority—provided they could stick together. But it also inflated the power of moderate Democrats and independents on controversial legislation, for if the Republicans stuck together, the Democratic leadership needed the support of every member of its flock to prevail. And Republicans in both houses had settled on a policy of noncooperation. This was part tactical political decision and part substance—overall, the parties had become quite distinct ideologically (Binder 2003). The annual *National Journal* congressional vote ratings for 2009 would find that over the year "long-standing ideological divides" persisted, and in some respects "even deepened" (Cohen and Friel 2010).

With Republican support unlikely, Obama, Speaker of the House Pelosi (D-CA), and Senate majority leader Harry Reid (D-NV) had to keep their somewhat fractious troops in line. This meant concentrating on the top-priority issues and deferring any that might inflame intraparty divisions. Trade policy was such an issue, particularly within the House Democratic Caucus.

After the 2006 elections, the Bush administration had sought to broaden its support base on trade by accepting, in a May 10, 2007, agreement, long-standing Democratic positions on the inclusion of labor and environmental standards in free trade agreements (Destler 2007). This had sufficed to win approval of the Free Trade Agreement (FTA) with Peru in November—but buried in the 285–131 margin was the fact that a plurality of Democrats (116–109) had voted no, even though organized labor had acquiesced. Labor was vehemently opposed to the pending agreements with Colombia and South Korea, and the House Democratic leadership was unwilling to take it on. When in April 2008 President Bush sent the implementing legislation for Colombia down anyway for the up-or-down vote required under House rules, Pelosi responded by orchestrating a change in those rules—deleting the 90-day time limit as it applied to approval of that agreement. And the Democrats newly elected to Congress in 2008 were, on average, no more trade-friendly. The Obama administration needed to keep the allegiance of these trade-skeptical House Democrats—and that of labor—through the compromises with House and Senate moderates that would be necessary to get the top-priority health care legislation through. So the FTAs stayed on the shelf.

The strategy succeeded. Pelosi won a historic House victory, passing health care legislation by a 220–215 majority on November 7. In the Senate, Reid managed to combine bills from two committees, add and subtract provisions as needed, and win (by identical 60–39 margins) a November 22 vote to take up the bill and a December 22 vote on final passage.

The plan to go promptly to Senate-House conference was derailed by the surprising victory of Republican Scott Brown in the race to fill the seat of the late Senator Edward Kennedy (D-MA). This cost the party its 60-vote majority and unsettled Democrats nationwide. So health care moved temporarily from likely enactment to the endangered list. Obama responded by shuffling the political deck. First he invited Republicans to a bipartisan health care summit. When that failed (as expected) to produce agreement, he set forth his own substantive proposal. Pelosi got it through the House on March 21 in two dicey stages—first accepting the Senate version (so it could go directly to the president), by 219–212, and then passing a "reconciliation" measure, by 220–211, approving a set of budget-related changes that the Senate rules allowed to be enacted by a bare majority. The Senate did so by 56 to 43.

"Time Out" on Trade

All this time, the administration was inactive on trade. This made life hard for USTR Ron Kirk—lack of a serious administration agenda made it difficult for him to build a credible role. By giving priority to other issues, Obama was carrying out, in practice, the "trade time-out" called for by Hillary Clinton during the primary campaign. His administration did make gestures to respond to critics of its inaction. In July 2009, Kirk initiated a two-month comment period on the Colombia and South Korea FTAs, inviting affected interests to express their views and signaling to those in favor that this was their chance to strengthen the agreements' prospects. But expiration of the comment period did not lead to further action.

One ongoing negotiation where the USTR *was* engaged was the unfinished Doha Round under the WTO. Launched in November 2001, the talks had long been stalemated over the issue of agricultural protection and subsidies. The targets were the advanced nations. Europe made modest concessions, but the cumbersome EU decision-making process made it hard to do more. The United

States had tried to unblock the negotiations in fall 2005 by raising its offer and suggesting it could do more if others reciprocated with barrier reductions on products important to U.S. trade. But the gesture yielded little in return, so Kirk's predecessor, Susan Schwab, had refused to go further, saying the United States "would not negotiate with itself." She participated in several high-profile principals-level negotiations, the most recent in June 2008, aiming for a break-through. And her deputies made eleventh-hour forays to rising trade powers like China and Brazil, seeking sufficient assurance on specific barrier reduc-tions. President Bush, moreover, would have liked very much to conclude his presidency with a global trade agreement. But Schwab was convinced that unless she could bring home more market-opening concessions from U.S. trad-ing partners, there would not be the votes in Congress to approve any Doha deal. So the matter was left to the Obama administration.[8]

Kirk picked up where Schwab left off—but without the presidential push to close a deal. Substantively, the U.S. position was essentially unchanged: the terms currently available were insufficient to serve U.S. interests and win the support of key constituencies—particularly agriculture and organized business. Procedurally, however, Kirk resisted the efforts of some trading partners and WTO director-general Pascal Lamy—newly re-elected to a second term with-out opposition—to move toward addressing Doha at a full-blown ministerial-level meeting. He saw this as a recipe for failure until adequate groundwork was laid in the form of new export opportunities for the United States. Instead, U.S. officials made the rounds of advanced developing nations, conducting what were labeled "bilaterals" to exchange ideas on potential concessions. This in turn irritated some of the parties, including, reportedly, the Chinese. But while all continued to declare their commitment to the round's success, no nation, including the United States, appeared ready to change its negotiating stance in a way that would give it new life.

Meanwhile, there was a surprise shift in U.S. public opinion. As noted earlier, April 2008 had brought a sharp plunge in support for free trade agree-ments. But April 2009 saw a rebound, Great Recession notwithstanding. Compared to the prior year's margin of 48–35 percent of respondents to a Pew Research Center poll viewing such agreements as a "bad thing" rather than a "good thing," in 2009 the numbers were essentially reversed: 44 per-cent said "good thing," and 35 percent "bad thing" (Pew Research Center for the People & the Press 2009b). Other surveys—by Gallup, Times/CBS, and CNN/Opinion Research—found similar upticks in support for free trade (Gresser 2009).

Normally, protectionist sentiment rises during recessions and with height-ened unemployment. Philip I. Levy of the American Enterprise Institute declared, "This one is hard to explain." The only reason he could come up with was that the 2008 number had been driven down by Democratic presidential candidates who were trashing trade (Levy 2009). Edward Gresser of the Progressive Policy Institute stressed the positive side: Obama's early 2009 statements declaring protectionism a threat to recovery might have swayed Democrats (Gresser 2009). Overall, the recovery of the numbers to recently normal levels suggested that, whatever the position of organized groups, the American public was permissive if not enthusiastic about trade.

China

One trade relationship remained visible and controversial—that with the People's Republic of China. The U.S. merchandise trade deficit with that country had risen from $84 billion in 2000 to $268 billion in 2008. Moreover, U.S. purchases of Chinese goods were consistently five to six times the value of Chinese purchases of American goods—an imbalance far greater than that with any other large, non-oil-exporting nation. One clear contributor to the bilateral imbalance—and China's large global trade surpluses—was the exchange rate of the renminbi (RMB, or yuan, the Chinese currency). Alone among major trading nations, China did not allow its currency to float but maintained a fixed "peg" tied to the dollar. Moreover, to stimulate the growing levels of manufacturing employment Beijing saw as essential to political stability, China kept that peg at a rate well below what other nations saw as reasonable or fair. As early as 2005, 67 U.S. senators had backed a proposal by Charles Schumer (D-NY) and Lindsay Graham (R-SC) to impose a 27.5 percent surcharge on imports of Chinese products, reflecting the range (15–40 percent) of expert estimates of how much the RMB was undervalued. Shortly thereafter, Chinese authorities began a cautious, step-by-step appreciation, which brought the value up from 8.3 to the dollar in July 2005 to around 6.8 three years later. But this was halted once the Great Recession began to have a serious impact—as of late June 2010, the rate remained at 6.8. Meanwhile, China had been running larger and larger trade surpluses with the world as a whole, as its relative productivity continued to grow. The recession reduced these surpluses somewhat, but they remained a serious concern.

Congress had required, in its 1988 trade legislation, that the Treasury Department issue a semiannual report on other countries' exchange rate practices and that it name specific countries that it found to be "manipulating" their rates for trade advantage. The George W. Bush administration had declined to so name China, though it conveyed its concerns, and Obama had suggested in the primary campaign that he would take a tougher approach. But as president he proceeded cautiously. When Geithner, in written response to Senate questions during his difficult confirmation process, repeated the campaign statement alleging manipulation, the White House backed off. The Treasury reports of April and October 2009 would follow the Bush practice of stopping short of so naming China.

212 I. M. (MAC) DESTLER

Two reasons apparently account for this decision: concern that such naming would be counterproductive and the need for Chinese cooperation across a range of global issues—Iran, North Korea, and the global economy. Beijing had criticized the United States for its role in precipitating the crisis, but it did its part in fulfilling the London and Pittsburgh summit commitments with a large domestic stimulus package. And when China emerged from the downturn with surprising speed, this was a further contribution to the global recovery that all were seeking. So the policy appeared to pay off. In the words of *National Journal* reporter Bruce Stokes, who asked China experts in early 2010 to "grade" the Obama White House on specific aspects of its China policy, "Washington and Beijing get high marks from analysts for their close cooperation at both the G-20 summit in April 2009 and the Pittsburgh meeting in September." Working together at the G-20, moreover, "dovetailed nicely with the Obama team's thinking on how best to nudge China into assuming greater global responsibilities" (Stokes 2010, 23).

There were, however, specific trade issues that the administration could not avoid. Obama and Kirk had, in the early months, placed particular emphasis on "enforcement" of existing trade agreements—partly to buy time, partly to build a record for toughness and hence a political base for possible future action (R. Kirk 2009). And part of the argument for enforcement was the assertion that this administration's predecessor had neglected it. A case in point was an obscure legal provision, Section 421 of the Trade Act of 1974, as amended. As a condition for its accession to the World Trade Organization in 2001, China had agreed to a special "safeguard," effective through 2013, that allowed the United States to impose restrictions if it found that imports of a specific product in "increased quantities" had caused or threatened to cause "market disruption." Under the law, an industry or union could file a case. The U.S. International Trade Commission (USITC)—an independent regulatory body—would determine whether "market disruption" existed and, if so, would propose a remedy. The matter then went to the president, who could adopt, reject, or modify the USITC recommendation.

Four Section 421 cases had gone to President George W. Bush. Four times he had rejected an affirmative USITC finding and refused to impose protection. In the summer of 2009, Obama was confronted with his first case, involving Chinese tire imports. The USITC had found disruption and recommended a stiff penalty: a tariff for three years, beginning at the rate of 55 percent, descending thereafter. Moreover, the statutory timetable required Obama to make his decision by September 17, a week prior to the Pittsburgh summit.

In law, Obama had lots of leeway—he could do anything from applying the full USITC remedy to rejecting it entirely. In practice, rejection was difficult—because of his prior stress on trade enforcement and because of the need for union support on health care. So he decided to impose descending tariffs beginning at 35 percent. Beijing was warned in advance, and the Chinese response seemed vociferous. The PRC spoke of taking the decision to the World Trade Organization, asserting (incorrectly, it appears) that the decision was inconsistent with WTO rules. And it announced it was launching investigations of imports of U.S. automobiles and poultry to see if these products were being subsidized by the U.S. government or otherwise sold unfairly. In practice, however, these actions were moderate and limited, signaling that the two nations were able to manage and contain such conflicts.

This incidence of trade protection did not prevent good bilateral cooperation at the Pittsburgh economic summit, where the Chinese signed onto the leaders' statement promising that deficit and surplus countries alike would take steps to reduce future imbalances. The remainder of the year, however, did not seem to go so well. The president's November visit to China yielded no major accomplishments, and the press coverage was largely negative. And when he joined the Copenhagen climate summit the next month, his ultimately successful efforts to salvage an acceptable outcome, employing his "formidable interpersonal diplomatic skills," met visible Chinese resistance, including "a finger-wagging lecture by a Chinese official" (Stokes 2010, 25). Ironically, while Beijing rejected a framework that would have committed the country to binding climate targets, its officials did bring to the table a substantial program for lowering Chinese emissions of greenhouse gases.

Both nations' economic imbalances dropped sharply in 2009: China's global current account deficit fell by one-third (the first decline since 2001), and the international trade deficit of the United States fell 45 percent to $381 billion, the lowest since 1999. The bilateral trade imbalance also shrank, albeit by just 15 percent. These salutary developments, however, were generally seen as products of the Great Recession, not reflecting durable shifts in economic policies or structures. And as the year ended, the U.S. monthly trade deficit rebounded to $39.9 billion, the highest figure of the year, and was averaging around $45 billion in mid-2010.[9]

China had weathered the downturn remarkably well. Notwithstanding a sharp drop in exports, the nation's growth rate fell only modestly—from 11.4 percent in 2007 and 9.6 percent in 2008 to an estimated 8 percent in 2009. Washington therefore hoped that Beijing would resume allowing the RMB to rise in value. Otherwise, the long-term international economic rebalancing envisioned at Pittsburgh would simply not happen. There was evidence that China was moving in this direction—given credence when Secretary Geithner announced that Treasury would delay its currency report and then made a brief surprise visit to China in May for talks with top officials. Beijing seemed to respond in late June when Chinese authorities announced a return to greater exchange rate flexibility. But RMB appreciation was miniscule through the summer, and in late September the House passed a bill making an undervalued exchange rate a subsidy subject to imposition of punitive tariffs.

Another way to respond to the China challenge was to develop deeper trade relations with other East Asian nations. Obama took a step in this direction on November 14 when he announced readiness to engage in trade talks with the Trans-Pacific Partnership (TPP), a group of seven Asia-Pacific nations moving toward free trade among themselves.[10] In early 2010, he signaled readiness for further trade movement in his State of the Union address.

> . . . the more products we make and sell to other countries, the more jobs we support right here in America. So tonight, we set a new goal: We will double our exports over the next five years, an increase that will support two million jobs in America. To help meet this goal, we're launching a National Export Initiative that will help farmers and small businesses increase their exports, and reform export controls consistent with national security.
>
> . . . If America sits on the sidelines while other nations sign trade deals, we will lose the chance to create jobs on our shores. But realizing those benefits also means enforcing those agreements so our trading partners play by the rules. And that's why we will continue to shape a Doha trade agreement that opens global markets, and why we will strengthen our trade relations in Asia and with key partners like South Korea, Panama, and Colombia. (Obama 2010c)

Those three countries were, of course, the partners in the three Bush free trade agreements that remained unratified. Obama was not yet ready to move them to Congress for action, but he seemed to signal that might later be possible. This became concrete in June when, after meeting with South Korean president Lee Myung-bak, Obama announced that the two nations' trade officials would work to resolve differences over their FTA in the months leading up to the November 2010 global economic summit to be held in the Korean capital.

Meanwhile, on the other side of the Hill, the House Committee on Ways and Means was getting a new chair. Historically, the committee had been a key partner for presidential free trade initiatives. But Chair Charles Rangel (D-NY), beset with health and ethics problems, had not been in a good position to play this role even if Obama (and Pelosi) had wished it. As the House Ethics Committee completed one chastising report and prepared another, criticism mounted—first from Republicans, then from Democrats worried about being tarred with corruption charges. In early March, Rangel bowed to the inevitable and stepped aside—ostensibly until the problems were resolved. Assuming the role of acting chair was Sander Levin (D-MI), an outspoken critic of Republican trade policies with a mixed voting record on FTAs.

Obama trade policy seemed to be emerging, but very slowly. With ongoing pressure on the international side, movement seemed likely on at least the

Korean free trade agreement and, less certainly, on Doha as well. But perhaps not until the second half of his term. Meanwhile, there were midyear changes in the Obama economic team. CEA chair Romer resigned (amid reports of tensions with NEC director Summers) to be replaced by longtime Obama adviser Austan Goolsbee. OMB director Peter Orzsag had departed also, with his designated successor—Jacob Lew—awaiting Senate confirmation as of early September. Shortly thereafter, Summers announced that he would be departing by year's end to return to Harvard.

Conclusion

There is a long-standing proposition about trade politics that goes by the name of the "bicycle theory." In the words of the man who coined the phrase, C. Fred Bergsten, "trade policy has to either be moving ahead, toward greater liberalization, or it topples in the face of protectionist pressures from individual sectors" (Destler and Noland 2006, 17). Such protectionist pressures are particularly fierce, Bergsten and others would argue, during a severe economic downturn. So by this theory the Obama administration *ought to* have applied its every effort to liberalize trade, lest political-economic forces drive the world toward a repeat of the protectionism that dogged the 1930s.

Instead, the Obama administration largely stood still. It did not initiate serious trade-restrictive measures, and it joined others in inveighing against them. It "did no harm." But it took few positive initiatives. If the theory held, one would have expected a collapse of the global trade regime as nation after nation strove to protect its own production at others' expense. Instead it was the system that held. It bent a bit,[11] but it surely did not break.

The United States is now in the midst of a slow recovery, with production expanding and unemployment bottoming out but remaining high. The Obama administration has suffered politically because the slump has been so deep and because its measures have not achieved more. Democrats appear certain to take a serious hit in the midterm elections, either losing their House and/or Senate majorities or hanging on by very thin margins. In any case, they will no longer possess, in 2011–12, the healthy working majorities they held in Obama's first two years.

The president and Congress will be under pressure to enact measures to counter the long-term fiscal squeeze facing the United States. They will also be looking for other measures consistent with that need, initiatives that do not bear major budgetary costs. Trade initiatives fall into that category. As an internationalist leader seeking action, seeking engagement, Obama began in 2010 to move cautiously in this direction. He is likely to move further in 2011 and thereafter. And this is an issue where more Republicans in Congress would actually improve his chances for achievement.

Notes

1. Saul I. Stern Professor, Maryland School of Public Policy; Fellow, Peterson Institute for International Economics
2. The final estimate of fourth-quarter change in GDP (annual rate equivalent) was even worse—minus 6.8 percent. The figure for the first quarter of 2009 was adjusted downward to minus 4.9 percent (Bureau of Economic Analysis–U.S. Department of Commerce 2010).
3. More precise figures are in Destler, *American Trade Politics* (Institute for International Economics, 4th edition, 2005), pages 45 and 250, taken in turn from statistical tables in *Economic Report of the President* (www.gpoaccess.gov/eop).
4. The Standard & Poor's Case-Shiller national home price index stood at 189.93 in 2Q 2006 (2000 = 100). It fell to 183.16 in 2Q 2007, 155.68 in 2Q 2008, and 111.11 in 2Q 2009 (cited in *Wikipedia*, "Case-Shiller Index" 2010).
5. Just 35 percent found such agreements to be a "good thing."
6. According to a BBC World Service Poll in January 2009, at least 70 percent of British, French, Germans, Italians, and Spanish expected that U.S. world relations would become "better" due to Obama's election. Only 2–4 percent thought they would become worse (see Meunier 2010).
7. These percentages compare the values for July 2008 to those for April 2009. There was recovery thereafter—in December 2009, exports had rebounded to 85 percent of those in July 2008, and imports to 82 percent (U.S. Census Bureau 2010). The nine-month drop exceeded, in percentage terms, that of a comparable period during the Great Depression.
8. For a comprehensive, lively, and critical account of the negotiations through 2008, see Blustein 2009.
9. Chinese data are government statistics; U.S. trade data are from U.S. Census Bureau 2010.
10. The original TPP members were Singapore, Chile, New Zealand, and Brunei. Australia, Peru, and Vietnam have recently joined the negotiations.
11. For a compilation leaning toward pessimism, see Simon J. Evenett, "The G20's Assault on World Trade," September 22, 2009, *Vox,* at www.voxeu.org/index.php?q=node/4008.

CHAPTER 12

U.S. Global Environmental Policy in the Post-Bush Era

Michael E. Kraft

ACTING UNDER COURT order in May 2008, PRESIDENT GEORGE W. BUSH released a new report on global climate change. In contrast to many previous administration reports and announcements on the subject, this one pointed to the substantial and harmful impact that could be expected as a result of human activities that are slowly warming the planet. Most of the findings were well known to scientists and students of climate change policy, and they had been thoroughly documented for years, particularly by the work of the Intergovernmental Panel on Climate Change (IPCC) and especially its fourth assessment report issued in 2007 (IPCC 2007; U.S. Climate Change Science Program 2008).

The administration was forced to release the report after it was sued by environmentalists over its failure to issue periodic climate change assessments as required by law and a federal judge ordered that a comprehensive report on the effects of climate change in the United States be published by the end of May. In a pointed jab at the Bush White House, the climate program director for the lead plaintiff in the suit, the Center for Biological Diversity, argued that the report represented "what federal scientists can and should be doing when they are freed from political interference and allowed to actually do their jobs" (Revkin 2008b). Senator John Kerry (D-MA), the lead author of the 1990 federal law requiring such reports, the Global Change Research Act of 1990, and the Democratic nominee for president in 2004, echoed the sentiment: "The three-year delay of this report," he said, "is sadly fitting for an administration that has wasted several years denying the real threat of global climate change" (Revkin 2008b).

The climate assessment report and reactions to its release illustrate well the concerns long expressed by environmentalists and many students of environmental policy. Since 2001, they had faulted the Bush administration for its seeming indifference to global environmental challenges such as energy use and climate change, protection of biological diversity, and the adverse impacts of population growth and rapid economic development on the world's natural resources and public health. Most of them also were sharply critical of the White House for its tendency to give short shrift to scientific evidence in its policy decisions and to try to keep agency scientists from speaking to the press or public and in other ways to interfere in their work (Union of Concerned Scientists 2009; Vig and Kraft 2010).

The first weeks of the Barack Obama administration brought a strikingly different posture on energy and the environment. In a clear reference to Bush's misuse of science and a statement of changed priorities, the new president said in his inaugural address that he would "restore science to its rightful place" and work to "harness the sun and the winds and the soil to fuel our cars and run our factories" (Obama 2009c). Within days, he sought to overturn the Bush administration's stance on climate change. Most notably, he urged the U.S. Environmental Protection Agency (EPA) to reconsider the Bush administration's denial of California's request for a federal waiver that would allow it—and many other states—for the first time to limit greenhouse gas emissions from automobiles; the Bush White House had long blocked such a waiver (Broder and Baker 2009). As he suggested during his campaign and in his inaugural address, Obama's economic stimulus package approved by Congress in February 2009 aimed to boost the use of green technologies and to create jobs through investment in renewable energy sources.

At the same time, Obama ordered the Department of Energy (DOE) to draft immediately energy efficiency standards for appliances, a requirement on which the Bush administration had made little progress (Broder 2009e). Among other early actions, Obama also reversed a Bush administration ruling that restricted the use of federal money for international family planning organizations that promoted or provided abortions, and he named what the press termed an environmental "dream team" to take charge of energy, environment, and climate change issues in his administration (Baker 2009; Broder and Revkin 2008; Vig and Kraft 2010).

There has been no comparable shift in presidential policy positions on the environment in the last forty years. Yet the change from the Bush administration to the Obama administration is only one element in what will need to be a wholesale reformulation of environmental policy in the years and decades ahead if the United States and other nations are seriously to tackle emerging global challenges such as climate change. The need for such policy change is captured in the imperative to plan for and institute worldwide sustainable development, admittedly a concept of multiple meanings but nonetheless useful for setting out concrete goals (Brown 2008; Hempel 2009; Kraft 2011; Speth 2004, 2008; Starke 2008). It was first pushed on the international scene in the

1980s in a widely read World Commission on Environment and Development report, *Our Common Future* (1987), and it was discussed at length at the United Nations Conference on Environment and Development (the Earth Summit) in 1992, where the 179 nations in attendance agreed to an ambitious and costly program of action for the twenty-first century with sustainable development at its center: Agenda 21 (*Agenda 21* 1993; World Commission on Environment and Development 1987). The goals were reinforced at the International Conference on Population and Development in Cairo, Egypt, in 1994 and at the World Summit on Sustainable Development in 2002, particularly those of committing to alleviate world poverty while also addressing global environmental problems.

Most of the world's nations, however, including the United States, have yet to take sustainable development seriously. Whether they will institute sufficient policy changes toward that end and do so with speed and determination remains to be seen. This chapter offers a brief retrospective examination of the Bush administration's global environmental policy. It begins with a review of contemporary environmental and resource problems and the difficulty of addressing them both domestically and globally. It then turns to the Bush administration and selected actions on global environmental issues over its eight years, both successful and unsuccessful. Finally, it looks ahead to what can be expected over the next few years in the Obama administration.

Global Environmental Challenges of the Twenty-First Century

It is not easy to summarize briefly the daunting array of environmental, energy, and resource problems that the United States and the world face in the decades ahead. In the last twenty years in particular, numerous reports have laid them out for the public and policy makers to consider, and hundreds of scientific studies and assessments continue to be published annually. They are issued by UN agencies, international scientific bodies such as the IPCC, the U.S. National Academy of Sciences, and many other reliable and often authoritative sources. Collectively, they have described in some detail threats to global environmental systems attributable to human population growth and rapid economic development, such as adverse impacts on the world's water supply, air quality, agricultural productivity, oceanic and fresh water fisheries, forests, and critical habitats and ecosystems, as well as the earth's biogeochemical cycles, such as the climate regulation system, on which life depends.

For example, a comprehensive Millennium Ecosystem Assessment released by the World Health Organization in 2005 concluded that 60 percent of critical ecosystem functions are being degraded by human activities. The same study found that about half of the urban population in Asia, Africa, and Latin America suffers from diseases associated with inadequate water and sanitation, leading to some 1.7 million deaths a year. Without greater commitment to alleviating poverty, for example by working toward the UN Millennium Development Goals, environmental and public health conditions like these are likely to deteriorate further (Millennium Ecosystem Assessment 2005; Tobin 2010; United Nations 2007).

Or consider climate change, largely traceable to heavy reliance on the use of fossil fuels in addition to extensive deforestation and other human activities. As noted, the IPPC and other reports suggest severe impacts as the twenty-first century advances, even if most of the anticipated effects have yet to occur. Scientists anticipate a doubling of carbon dioxide levels in the atmosphere over the next 100 years, the consequences of which likely include a climate that is warmer and wetter, with rising sea levels; significant risks of abrupt and unpredictable shifts in weather patterns; and extreme events such as droughts, floods, and more severe tropical storms. Among other effects, there could be catastrophic consequences for agriculture, and thus for the world's food supply, and major risks to ecosystem integrity and biodiversity as well as to human health, particularly in developing nations (DiMento and Doughman 2007; IPCC 2007; Selin and VanDeveer 2010).

Human activities that affect ecosystems and climate are likely to increase over the next 50 to 100 years unless major changes occur in societal values and public policy. For example, the world's population, at more than 6.9 billion in fall 2010, is expected to rise to about 8 billion by 2025 and more than 9 billion by 2050. Unlike most of the world's developed nations, which have exceptionally low rates of growth (about 0.1 to 0.2 percent annually), the United States continues to grow at more than 1 percent a year, or five to ten times as fast. This growth rate will likely take it from its fall 2010 population of more than 310 million to between 420 and 440 million by 2050, an increase of more than 35 percent. While China and India have far larger populations, the United States, because of its affluence and prevailing lifestyle, has a disproportionate impact on global resource use, emissions of greenhouse gases, and release of toxic and hazardous chemicals (Brown 2008; Population Reference Bureau 2010; Tobin 2010). Still, nearly all the anticipated population growth will be in developing nations, and the impacts on land use, agriculture, and water and other natural resources will be most evident there. For example, with a rising population and its needs, the world demand for fresh water is expected to double in the next fifty years (Dugger 2006).

Human demand for energy, currently met largely (about 86 percent) from fossil fuels such as coal, oil, and natural gas, is expected to grow exponentially for years, reflecting expectations for both population and economic growth. The DOE's Energy Information Administration in 2009 projected an increase of nearly 50 percent from 2005 base levels to 2030, with total energy demand in non-OECD (Organisation for Economic Co-operation and Development) countries increasing by 81 percent compared to an increase of 15 percent in OECD countries (U.S. DOE 2009). In its 2009 annual *World Energy Outlook,* the International Energy Agency forecasted that global electricity demand would rise by 76 percent by 2030, much of it generated by burning coal; the agency anticipated a continuing growth in use of coal for such purposes despite its impact on climate change (International Energy Agency 2009).

Before the economic recession of 2008 and 2009, China alone was completing two large coal-fired power plants *every week,* with clear implications for greenhouse gas emissions and urban air pollution. Indeed, although not well recognized, according to the World Health Organization, indoor and outdoor air pollution together cause an estimated 2 to 4 million premature deaths each year worldwide (Kraft 2011). A further concern is that some of the fossil fuels on which the world depends, especially oil, will not last much longer at current rates of use. Projections indicate a peak supply of oil between 2020 and 2030; no nation has yet to prepare for the decline thereafter (Kerr 2008). Taken together, these trends suggest the wisdom of a fairly rapid transition to non–fossil fuel energy sources, and not only because of climate change or air pollution. As demand for oil exceeds supply, we will likely see soaring prices and adverse economic impacts, as was evident worldwide in mid-2008.

Beyond whatever concerns such evidence may prompt, the world also faces glaring inequity, which in turn poses national security challenges (Matthew 2010; Tobin 2010). Much of the developing world, for example, has limited access to clean water, sanitation, and essential health care services. As has long been the case, there are high rates of poverty in Latin America, Africa, and Asia without much chance of short-term improvement despite the international commitments reflected in *Agenda 21* and adoption of the Millennium Development Goals. This means that many of the world's children are at great risk. Richard Tobin captured that grim risk in stark detail:

> Only seven of one thousand American children die before the age of five; in some Asian and African countries as many as 20 to 25 percent do. *Every week* about 190,000 children under age five die in developing countries from diseases that rarely kill Americans. Tetanus, measles, malaria, diarrhea, whooping cough, or acute respiratory infections cause most of these deaths, most of which can be easily and cheaply cured or prevented. (Tobin 2010, 286)

Similar differences between rich and poor nations can be seen in their use of natural resources. For example, Americans "represent less than 5 percent of the Earth's inhabitants, yet they use about one-fifth of the world's energy. On a typical day in 2006, 300 million Americans consumed more petroleum than the 2.9 *billion* people that lived in China, India, Russia, Japan, and Brazil" (Tobin 2010, 299). It is not just oil. The world's wealthier nations consume a far greater share of global resources than their numbers suggest. The richest one-quarter of the world's nations, for example, control about 75 percent of global income and consume a disproportionate share of meat and fish and of energy, paper, chemicals, iron, and steel. They also generate more than 90 percent of hazardous and industrial waste. Americans alone produce about 20 percent of greenhouse gas emissions, and they have by far the highest level of per capita emissions in the world, even if China has now emerged as the larger emitter of greenhouse gases (Brown 2008; Lewis and Gallagher 2011; Starke 2008; Tobin 2010).

What do these various global trends have in common? They are interlinked and reflect the impacts that human behavior and use of damaging technologies, particularly related to consumption of energy and consumer goods, can have on natural systems. There is another set of characteristics shared by climate change, population growth, threats to ecosystems and biodiversity, and related problems. Some analysts refer to these kinds of environmental and resource challenges as "third-generation" problems to distinguish them from the pollution control and land use issues of the 1970s and efficiency-based efforts to reform environmental protection policies in the 1980s and 1990s (Mazmanian and Kraft 2009). The distinguishing characteristics of this new generation of environmental problems can be summarized in this way:

- They are global in their origins and effects as well as national and local.
- Their impacts on society may be observed only in the long term, with the full effects often noticeable only over several generations. The benefits of public policy interventions may also be recognized only in the long term.
- They have low visibility. They are not sensed as readily as air pollution, water pollution, or congestion in national parks. Thus, they are not as likely to be salient to the public.
- They are characterized by some degree of scientific uncertainty. Experts disagree on the magnitude of the problems and often on the timing and location of their effects.
- The decision-making process over how best to address the problems is complex, with diverse policy actors involved in many different institutions in both the public and private sectors and at multiple levels of government, from the local level to international.
- The problems are not easily resolved, in part because the causes are rooted in fundamental social, economic, and political beliefs and behavior, such as a desire to improve people's economic welfare and to protect national sovereignty. Individual changes in attitudes and behavior are necessary on a large scale in contrast to early environmental policy actions that called chiefly for compliance by polluters with technical and legal requirements.
- The solutions may be very costly, and the costs are likely to be imposed in the short term.

One conclusion is that the benefits of acting on these problems tend to be uncertain, long-term, and broadly distributed among the public. Yet the costs of acting on them tend to be more certain, short-term, and, often, concentrated on particular individuals and groups (such as industry). The result is that policy makers face few incentives to act on the problems and few penalties for delaying action. Solving the problems is likely to involve a higher degree of conflict than is the case for many other issues, and thus solutions depend on strong governing capacity and a political process that can resolve conflicts and achieve environmental quality goals. Put otherwise, solving environmental and energy problems requires much more than just better science and engineering, investment in new technologies, or improving management within government agencies. It will take a strong political will to act and creative and effective political leadership to build the coalitions that are essential to approval of the requisite policies.

In this context, several critical questions come to mind. In what ways might the United States use its influence and resources internationally to secure collective action on climate change and other third-generation environmental issues? What are the prospects for serious multilateral coordination on these challenges, and how feasible is it to act on energy use (which may raise energy costs sharply) at a time of severe economic constraints? To address these questions, the chapter turns next to the legacy of the Bush administration and how well it lived up to these expectations and then to what might be expected to change in the Obama administration and beyond.

Addressing Global Challenges: The Bush Years

Presidential administrations may be evaluated on any number of bases, such as personnel appointments; budgetary decisions; legislative initiatives; and use of the unique powers of the presidency to reach out to the public, set the political agenda, and build political support essential for action in the U.S. political system (Vig 2010). Whether presidents make use of these powers to advance environmental and energy policy depends to a great extent on their political philosophy and policy agendas and on their political resources and capacity for leadership. In a number of critical policy areas, George W. Bush chose not to give a high priority to global action on environmental challenges. In many cases, such as climate change and support for family planning, an antigovernment ideology and strategic political calculations about support from social conservatives led to a series of poorly conceived policy responses. As a result, the administration missed the opportunity to leave a lasting imprint on global environmental policy and the campaign against world poverty. Although its record, as is always the case, is mixed, on the whole the Bush administration's chief legacy is one of delayed U.S. action on a range of critical global problems, particularly climate change. Advancement in the next few years depends on the ability of the Obama administration to do a better job of using the United States' distinctive position in the world and its considerable resources to get on with the task.

Several of the Bush administration's most important policy actions merit brief comment. The most widely recognized is its refusal to advance meaningful solutions to climate change beyond funding research programs and touting the value of voluntary initiatives. The U.S. stance has been covered well in many accounts (Betsill 2011; DiMento and Doughman 2007; Selin and VanDeveer 2010; Vig 2010). Two aspects of the Bush policy are especially important for present purposes. One is the administration's rejection of the Kyoto Protocol on climate change, itself part of a pattern of America's isolation from the world community and from other international treaties. By 2010, 194 nations and the European Union had ratified the protocol, and the United States was the only developed nation in the world not to be a party to it. President Bush had called the agreement "fatally flawed," primarily because it failed to include developing nations (especially China and India) in its mandate for reducing greenhouse gas emissions and thus, he said, it would pose an undue economic hardship on the United States. While this criticism of the Kyoto agreement is widely shared, under the Bush administration the United States chose not to exert its leadership to develop an alternative to Kyoto.

The other notable aspect of Bush policy is that the administration spent most of its eight years denying the science of climate change and thus undercutting the reasons for U.S. action beyond research and voluntary steps, as well as misinforming the American public about the very real risks of climate change. One House committee exhaustively examined thousands of pages of documents on climate science and concluded that the administration had mounted a systematic effort to "manipulate climate science and mislead policymakers and the public about the dangers of global warming" (Vig 2010, 87). The strategy seems to have worked as the administration intended, as even by 2010 the public remained poorly informed about climate change and accorded it far less attention than otherwise might have been the case (Guber and Bosso 2010; Revkin 2009a). Those conditions in turn made it difficult for both Congress and the Obama administration to advance climate change policy in 2009 and 2010.

Moreover, intentionally or not, there was a clear disconnect between the administration's proposals for energy use and its eventual acknowledgment that climate change could impose real burdens on the nation and world. Its energy policies consistently favored increased use of fossil fuels with little recognition of the potential contribution of energy efficiency and conservation or of renewable energy sources. Whether the subject was drilling for oil in the Arctic National Wildlife Refuge, from offshore platforms, or on public lands in the west, the clear priority was to increase the supply of U.S. domestic oil, natural gas, and coal. The stance was justified as making the nation less dependent on imported oil. Yet U.S. dependency on that oil remains very high, and increased drilling for domestic oil cannot possibly alter that pattern anytime soon.

Simply put, there is not enough oil to meet current U.S. demand, and the Department of Energy concluded that producing significantly more of it will take at least a decade if not longer (Myers and Hulse 2008; Vig 2010).[1] In addition, the catastrophic oil spill resulting from a blowout of a BP-owned deep-water oil well in the Gulf of Mexico in spring 2010 is certain to affect the nation's willingness to expand offshore drilling going forward. At a minimum, the federal government and the states are likely to require much more extensive environmental and safety reviews before such drilling is permitted.

Another policy area in which there was a comparable tendency of the Bush administration to ignore science and depart from the historical U.S. leadership role is international population assistance. From the mid-1960s in the Johnson administration, the U.S. government saw rapidly growing populations as a major barrier to economic development around the world, and for that reason it contributed strongly to voluntary family-planning programs through both bilateral and multilateral assistance programs. Indeed, the United States was the world's largest contributor to such programs. However, bowing to conservative factions in the Republican Party, in 1984 Ronald Reagan's administration initiated what is called the Mexico City policy, named for an international population conference held that year in Mexico's capital.

The U.S. government's policy had long banned organizations from using U.S. funds overseas for abortion practices. The Mexico City policy went further. It allowed aid only for those organizations that pledged not to perform abortion *or* to promote it as a method of family planning, even if the groups used their own funds, and not U.S. government money, for these purposes— what some groups have called a "global gag rule." Essentially, the United States stopped contributing to the UN Population Fund even though it continued funding for bilateral population assistance (Kraft 1994, 2011). The Mexico City policy was continued during the George H. W. Bush administration and then overturned by President Bill Clinton only days after he took office in 1993. President George W. Bush reinstated the policy on January 22, 2001. In his first week of office, President Obama, like Clinton before him, reversed the ban. His January 23, 2009, executive order left the current funding for these programs (administered by the U.S. Agency for International Development) at $461 million in fiscal 2009, but it significantly expanded the number of groups qualified to receive grants to manage such programs.

On a more positive note, Bush was praised for his commitment to spend $15 billion over five years, beginning in 2004, to fight HIV/AIDS, tuberculosis, and malaria in the developing world. The President's Emergency Program for AIDS Relief (PEPFAR) was widely thought to be successful, and Congress in 2008 authorized an additional $48 billion to continue the program for five more years. Private groups, most notably the Bill and Melinda Gates Foundation, also contributed to the Global Fund to Fight AIDS, Tuberculosis, and Malaria (see Tobin 2010). In addition, the Bush administration raised contributions to the World Bank to a total of $1 billion in 2008 to help replenish the International Development Association for grants and loans to poor nations. American bilateral economic aid remained very low as a percentage of the nation's gross national income (GNI) at 0.16 percent, yet it was still the largest in the world at about $22 billion a year (Kraft 2011; Tobin 2010). However, *Agenda 21* (1993) had called for developed nations to contribute 0.7 percent of GNI to assistance for developing nations, a goal reinforced at the 2002 World Summit on Sustainable Development. Few nations have met that goal, and development assistance from most developed nations remains well short of the target level. Official environmental assistance to developing nations also fails to live up to the promises made in the 1990s and 2000s (MacFarquhar 2008; Roberts et al. 2009).

Meeting Global Environmental Challenges: The Post-Bush Years

Barack Obama's electoral victory in November 2008 reflected broad support and enthusiasm among the American public for a presidency that pledged to offer policy change across a variety of areas and a more accountable and transparent governance process. The president made clear during the campaign and in the early days of his administration that this change would extend to global environmental policy, including energy use, climate change, population policy, and other areas noted earlier.

The change was immediately evident in Obama's selection of his top environmental appointees. In announcing his environmental team on December 15, 2008, Obama hinted at the new policy agenda, for example, by stating his intention to address global warming and America's costly reliance on fossil fuels; he also acknowledged that previous presidents and Congresses had made little headway toward these goals. He promised to press on despite the weak economy, although the extent to which he can do so remained unclear as of fall 2010. "This time must be different," he said. "This will be a leading priority of my presidency and a defining test of our time. We cannot accept complacency, nor accept any more broken promises" (quoted in Broder and Revkin 2008).

The energy and environmental team, and other key science appointees, were impressive by any measure. Obama named John Holdren, former president of the American Association for the Advancement of Science (AAAS), as his science adviser and director of the White House Office of Science and Technology Policy. He named Steven Chu, director of the Lawrence Berkeley National Laboratory and strong supporter of developing renewable energy sources, as his secretary of energy. Jane Lubchenco, another former AAAS president, became administrator of the National Oceanic and Atmospheric

Administration. Lisa Jackson, New Jersey's commissioner of environmental protection, was named as the new EPA administrator, and Carol Browner, EPA head in the Clinton administration, filled a new position as White House coordinator (czar) of energy and climate policy (Broder 2008; Kintisch and Mervis 2009).

Hillary Clinton's appointment as secretary of state is similarly distinctive, particularly because of her statements supporting the use of "smart power" in the exercise of U.S. leadership abroad. By this, she means use of all of the tools of foreign policy, including diplomatic, economic, military, political, legal, and cultural—that is, a combination of hard (military) and soft (diplomatic) power. This approach would distinguish Obama's foreign policy from what had been the pattern under President Bush. The implication of this new emphasis is that only a careful and pragmatic assessment of any given problem can inform the choice of foreign policy instruments, a clear critique of the Bush administration's heavy reliance on the exercise of hard power, especially military intervention or its threatened use. This Clinton view also reflects much new scholarship that has emphasized a broad perspective of how, in a global economy, U.S. and other nations' interests can be furthered by a diversity of economic, intellectual, cultural, technological, and scientific endeavors that go well beyond traditional diplomatic and military policy tools. This new perspective is particularly important for fostering innovations in support of sustainable development (Brown 2008; Friedman 2008; Singh 2009; Speth 2008).

The difference between the two administrations and the implications for global environmental policy could be seen by early February 2009. Two new studies were prominently reported on February 5, just before Clinton was to begin her first trip abroad in her new job; she would make an important stop in China with climate and energy use high on the agenda. The Brookings Institution released a major report on ways to build support for sustained cooperation between the United States and China on cutting greenhouse gas emissions. At the same time, the Pew Center on Global Climate Change, in conjunction with the Asia Society, produced a "road map" for climate cooperation between the two nations. One of the Brookings authors captured the timing of the reports' release and the expectations many held for the new administration: "New leadership and new technologies are creating unprecedented opportunities for action" (quoted in Revkin 2009b; see also Wong and Revkin 2009).

These and other events and proposals of early 2009, as well as events since that time, suggest what some have called a "tipping point" on energy and climate change issues, as scientific evidence of the risk becomes more broadly accepted and public support for policy action grows—even if recent surveys confirm that environmental problems, and climate change in particular, remain low-salience issues at a time when the economic crisis dominates public fears and the current political agenda (Guber and Bosso 2010; Revkin 2009a). In light of the continued low salience of climate change and with the U.S. economy weakened by a severe recession, the trick for members of Congress and the Obama administration is to link action on energy and climate change effectively to an improved economy. They have tried to do so by emphasizing creation of "green jobs" in renewable energy production, energy efficiency, mass transit, and similar programs, although with mixed results. The administration highlighted such investments and included some of them in the massive economic stimulus package Congress debated in early February 2009.

Still, no one has suggested this would be an easy task given the fragile state of the U.S. economy. The prospects for the United States making better use of its predominant influence and resources internationally can be seen in an overview of two fundamental goals: making real progress toward multilateral coordination of action on climate change during a world economic crisis and moving toward the long-term goal of sustainable development.

Climate Change and Energy Use

There are clear opportunities for a substantial change in U.S. climate change policy, even if the political obstacles loom large. President Obama recognizes the scope of the problem, and he has clearly stated his intention to take significant new action, both domestically and internationally. As noted, his new energy and environmental appointees share his concern and intentions. The timing is also fortuitous, as the Kyoto Protocol expires in 2012. The international parties responsible for designing a replacement treaty already had started negotiations by the time Obama took office. They began talking about a follow-up agreement in 2001; met at a UN-sponsored conference in Bali, Indonesia, in December 2007; and met again in Copenhagen, Denmark, in December 2009 (Aldy and Stavins 2008). While more than a thousand U.S. cities have agreed to some form of climate change policy, as have about half of the states, the U.S. government did little during the Bush administration (Betsill 2011; Selin and VanDeveer 2010).

This changed in 2008, when the U.S. Senate held the first real floor debate on climate change policy as a dress rehearsal for what was expected to take place in 2009 and 2010. But sharp partisan conflicts on the issue led to brief and unproductive Senate consideration of the legislation. Climate change legislation fared no better in the House. Yet in 2009 the House narrowly approved the American Clean Energy and Security Act of 2009, which set limits on overall emissions of carbon dioxide (CO_2) while allowing for the buying and selling of permits to release the gas under a cap that is to decline over time. The legislation's goal was to reduce CO_2 emissions by 17 percent below 2005 levels by 2020 and by 83 percent by 2050. In addition, the bill stipulated that 20 percent of the nation's electricity was to come from renewable sources or gains in efficiency by

2020. It also provided billions of dollars for energy research and development in such areas as clean energy technologies for wind and solar generation, greater energy efficiency, the production of hybrid vehicles, and expanded mass transit projects. By most accounts, the legislation would fundamentally transform the way the nation uses energy and, as a result, affect nearly every sector of the economy (Kraft 2010, 2011).

Passage of the complex and convoluted House bill was not easy, and it foreshadowed the battles to come in the Senate. The legislation was strongly opposed by Republicans, who branded it as a "cap-and-tax" measure and vowed to use it against Democrats in the 2010 election campaign. Even the Democrats were deeply divided, and the bill's key sponsors, Reps. Henry Waxman (D-CA) and Edward Markey (D-MA), were forced to negotiate billions of dollars in "special-interest favors" to secure the support of hesitant members. These included major concessions to automakers, steel companies, natural gas drillers, refiners, utilities, and farmers (Broder 2009b, 2009f; Davenport and Palmer 2009; Hulse 2009; Wald 2009). There was no question that domestic politics of this kind would be a major factor in any U.S. action on global climate change (DeSombre 2011; Harrison and Sundstrom 2010).

These compromises left many environmentalists wondering whether the bill merited their support at all, despite the importance they attached to action on climate change. Greenpeace and Friends of the Earth opposed the final measure for that reason, but most other environmental groups agreed that even a watered-down climate bill was better than none at all. Despite its weaknesses, they saw it as the first comprehensive attempt by the nation's top policy makers to mitigate climate change, and they hoped that congressional action would facilitate U.S. leadership when the world's nations gathered in December 2009 to negotiate the next global climate change treaty to replace the Kyoto Protocol. The Obama administration was similarly hopeful that Congress would make enough progress to permit the U.S. representatives at the Copenhagen meeting to announce strong commitments to global action on climate change.

The companion Senate measure was introduced by Senators John Kerry (D-MA) and Barbara Boxer (D-CA) in September 2009, but the Senate made little progress as the ongoing recession pushed members to focus on short-term economic costs (Broder 2009a, 2009c; Samuelsohn 2009). By mid-2010 the Senate made clear that whatever measure might still be considered and approved in that body would not incorporate the House's cap-and-trade structure (Hobson 2010). At the center of debate was a new proposal, the American Power Act, by Senator Kerry and Senator Joseph Lieberman (I-CT), which offered some promise of bipartisan agreement. The bill would establish a national cap on greenhouse gas emissions and reduce them by 17 percent below 2005 levels by 2020, and eventually by 80 percent by 2050. It also sought billions of dollars in loan guarantees for nuclear power plants, for expansion of mass transportation, and for federal investment in clean energy research and development and carbon sequestration technologies. The bill also favored expanded offshore oil and gas drilling although with significant restrictions, which are certain to be tightened even more in light of the BP oil spill in the Gulf of Mexico (Broder 2010b).

In the aftermath of that spill and the extensive media coverage of the environmental and economic damage it caused, combined with public outrage over mismanagement by both BP and the federal government, President Obama again urged Congress to act on energy policy. In a speech at Carnegie Mellon University in June 2010, the president "invoked the spill to pound on Congress about its duty to pass a comprehensive energy bill that addressed oil dependency and global warming" ("The Spill and Energy Bill" 2010). Despite new public concern over energy issues as a result of the spill, congressional action was not assured, as partisan and regional divisions continued.

The failure of Congress to act did not stop the administration from committing the United States to the goals embodied in the House and Senate bills, and it pursued other actions consistent with those commitments (Broder 2009d; Revkin 2009c). One of them occurred in May of 2009 when the Obama White House negotiated a far-reaching agreement with ailing automobile companies on new national fuel economy standards (the final rules for which were announced in April 2010); the new standards call for a fleet average of 35.5 miles per gallon by the 2016 model year. The Obama EPA also issued a critical legal finding in late 2009 that current and projected concentrations of six different greenhouse gases in the atmosphere pose a danger to public health and welfare, thus setting the stage for the agency to regulate large industrial releasers of greenhouse gases under authority granted by the Clean Air Act should Congress not be able to enact a broader climate change policy. In addition, the administration began a new program that mandates reporting of greenhouse gas emissions by large sources within the United States. Collection of data began in 2010, and the first public reports are due in 2011.[2]

Developments at the international level were only slightly more encouraging, and here too prevailing economic conditions constrained meaningful policy action. When world leaders gathered in New York in September 2009 for a high-level conference on climate change as a prelude to the Copenhagen meeting set for December, European representatives expressed continuing doubts about the willingness of the United States to assume a leadership role on climate change. Americans had signaled a reluctance to accept any agreement that would impose mandatory targets for limitation of greenhouse gas emissions (Broder and Kanter 2009). Nonetheless, Secretary of State Clinton stated repeatedly during 2009 that the United States would play such a leadership role: "The United States is fully engaged and determined to lead and make up for lost time both at home and abroad" (quoted in Broder 2009f).

The Copenhagen meeting made very limited progress toward global agreement on a new climate change policy, and the U.S. government continued to disappoint other world leaders. No one thought that such agreement would be easy in light of the profound implications of determined efforts to mitigate climate change. But the conference nonetheless fell well short of expectations, with many attendees suggesting that 2010 might bring more serious efforts to find common ground among the world's nations. Critics of global warming seized upon leaks of e-mail communications among some climate scientists in the United Kingdom as further evidence of the insufficiency of knowledge regarding global warming and its effects and, thus, a reason to delay action (Kintisch 2009; Revkin and Broder 2009; Stokes 2009). Obama called the agreement, the Copenhagen Accord, "an unprecedented breakthrough," but that sentiment was not widely shared as negotiations continued into 2010 and beyond.

Underlying the continuing U.S. political stalemate is a long-standing debate among economists and business leaders over just what the costs of climate change policy might be. As suggested earlier, action on climate change and other third-generation issues is affected by political and economic calculations of short-term costs even when multilateral cooperation on long-term goals is essential. The greatest need to get the process started is agreement among the major emitters of greenhouse gases (the United States, the European Union, China, and India) on specific targets and policy tools. Whereas the Bush administration chose to go its own way and emphasize additional research and voluntary guidelines, Obama engaged the issues more proactively and by cooperating more closely with other nations.

One model that may apply under these circumstances can be found in Richard Benedick's insightful study (1998) of what made the Montreal Protocol so successful—in its initial adoption, modification over the years to keep pace with scientific developments, and actual impact on the production and use of ozone depleting chemicals. Among other key factors, Benedick suggested that the United States can step out ahead of other nations as an example, not wait for agreement to be reached. By setting an example on climate change, the United States could begin re-establishing itself as an international leader on the environment and be at the forefront of developing the technologies that the rest of the world might need in the future, such as techniques for carbon sequestration, more efficient appliances and automobiles, and improved solar panel designs.

Should the United States, perhaps in partnership with other nations, choose to be more proactive and exert stronger international leadership on climate change going forward, recent polls are encouraging. One, released in late 2007, found strong support around the world for decisive action to reduce greenhouse gas emissions (BBC World Service 2007). In 2008 another set of surveys of 21 nations found very strong backing for requirements for using more wind and solar power and for greater energy efficiency, even if doing so increased costs. And in June 2010 a survey of Americans found that just over half felt that Congress and the president should do "more" or "much more" to address global warming (Leiserowitz, Maibach, Roser-Renouf, and Smith 2010).

The timing for a reassertion of U.S. leadership is ripe, with negotiations having been underway for several years already and expectations that 2010 would permit more progress than was evident in Copenhagen in late 2009. So the United States may yet choose a new direction on climate change, and it may find substantial political support both domestically and internationally. News reports as early as December 2008 suggested that the Kyoto parties were waiting for the Obama administration to take office before proceeding further, knowing that negotiations could take on a decidedly different tone with the end of the Bush presidency. By September 2009, journalists began speaking of the many ways in which Clinton was "revolutionizing American foreign policy" by making climate change negotiations a key component of the new administration's global agenda (Rosenthal 2008; Rothkopf 2009b).

Sustainable Development

As noted earlier, the principles and goals for sustainable development were set out at the Earth Summit in 1992, reinforced at the World Summit on Sustainable Development held in Johannesburg, South Africa, in 2002, and incorporated into several international environmental treaties such as the Framework Convention on Climate Change and the Convention on Biological Diversity (CBD). The Framework Convention led to the Kyoto Protocol and is now structuring discussion of its replacement. The CBD was not signed by the United States, but it has been endorsed by more than 191 nations and could be an important set of principles and guidelines for slowing the rate of biodiversity loss around the world, which continues apace (Kraft 2011).[3] The promised assistance from developed countries to help realize sustainable development in poor nations never reached the level that was stipulated in 1992, and prospects for the next few years seem even less encouraging in light of recent economic crises. Yet it would be fair to say that sustainable development remains a contemporary guiding principle for the work of the United Nations, the World Bank, and other international organizations and regimes. Clearly, the UN Millennium Development Goals (ostensibly to be met by 2015) reflect a commitment to these principles (Axelrod, VanDeveer, and Downie 2011). The concept has since been endorsed in a number of other venues, including major corporations, many colleges and universities, and nongovernmental organizations around the world (Mazmanian and Kraft 2009; Vig and Kraft 2010).

The importance of sustainable development was made clear early in the chapter. The world faces a perilous future in light of a rising human population, growth in demand for energy (most of which will be met with fossil fuels), and the environmental and public health impacts of trying to satisfy increasing societal demands. In the poorest of the world's nations, there also are severe threats to agricultural lands, water supplies, forests, fisheries, and ecosystems pressed to their limits (Tobin 2010). Yet current institutional capacity and commitment have proven inadequate to the task. For example, the World Bank and other international lending institutions have long fallen short of the goals of sustainable development aid. Recent studies of World Bank lending found that commitments to sustainability generally were not matched by changes in the lenders' bureaucracies or by actual lending decisions in the field. The implication is that more commitment and meaningful follow-through are needed. The 2008 World Bank *Global Monitoring Report* summed up the challenge: "The report's messages are clear: urgent action is needed to help the world get back on track to achieve the MDGs; and urgent action is also needed to combat climate change that threatens the well-being of all countries, but particularly of poor countries and poor people. The goals of development and environmental sustainability are closely related, and the paths to those goals have important synergies" (World Bank and International Monetary Fund 2008).[4]

Increasingly, scholars also recognize the close connection between sustainable development goals and national security. In prior years, security was defined as a need to create international institutions (such as the United Nations), strengthen international law, form key military alliances, and deter various foreign threats with sufficient military power. Today, many would add the essential tasks of minimizing the risks of climate change; protecting world fisheries and agriculture; ensuring sufficient water and agricultural capacity to feed the world's population; and ensuring that other environmental, energy, and natural resource trends do not adversely affect people's well-being (Dabelko 2008; Matthew 2010). To the extent that such environmental and security goals are linked, presidents might find it easier to build requisite public support for action. The 2008 presidential elections were revealing in this light. Both John McCain and Barack Obama referred to U.S. energy use and reliance on imported oil as a national security threat as well as an economic and environmental problem.

Although it is too early to assess the outcome of Obama's stated commitment to sustainable development, the changes in perspective and priorities compared to the Bush administration are substantial. American policy on biodiversity protection and population programs is likely to be more consistent with contemporary world opinion and UN goals. For example, in remarks on the fifteenth anniversary of the Cairo International Conference on Population and Development in January 2010, Clinton highlighted the Obama administration's renewed funding for reproductive health care through the UN Population Fund. She also launched a new Global Health Initiative that committed the

United States to spending $63 billion over six years to improve global health through investment in maternal and child mortality and prevention of unintended pregnancies, among other goals.[5]

These actions are more urgent than many people may realize, and further delays in making progress come with a very high long-term cost. Action during the next decade is imperative, particularly on climate change, as cuts in greenhouse gas emissions may have to be far stronger by 2050 to head off negative effects. Jeffrey Sachs, a development economist and director of the Earth Institute at Columbia University, has argued that without a new set of energy technologies on a global scale, we cannot achieve the goals of sustainable development (Revkin 2008a; Vig and Kraft 2010). Similarly, former vice president Al Gore in July 2008 called for a complete phase-out in ten years of U.S. reliance on fossil fuels for generating electricity (Stout 2008). For his part, Obama stated a goal of producing 25 percent of U.S. electricity from renewable sources by 2025. He also signed an executive order in October 2009 that set sustainability goals for federal government agencies in many areas of energy conservation.

Conclusion

The chapter has reviewed global environmental challenges, the actions of the Bush administration on them, and some of the policy changes made to date in the Obama administration. Clearly, it is too early to speak with confidence about the outcomes of Obama's efforts in this area given the uncertain constraints he has faced domestically and internationally. His receipt of the Nobel Peace Prize in 2009 was widely seen as an acknowledgment of his potential for advancing global policy reforms on a number of fronts related to environmental policy, most notably climate change. As with so many other assessments of his administration's early actions and achievements, there was little question that Obama departed substantially from the agenda and actions of President George W. Bush.

Two key questions were posed early in this chapter. In what ways might the United States use its influence and resources internationally to secure collective action on climate change and other third-generation environmental issues? And what are the prospects for serious multilateral coordination on these challenges, particularly at a time when weak economies around the world are at the center of attention and limit government resources that might be directed at environmental and energy goals? The answers are tentative and mixed. There are significant opportunities for the Obama administration to return the United States to its historical position of international leadership on global environmental problems. Success in "renewing" U.S. leadership will spur multilateral cooperation and greatly improve the prospects for concrete action on climate change and other urgent issues. Progress, however, will be constrained by economic conditions that preoccupy the public and policy makers around the world today.

As much as global environmental problems require urgent action, the reality is that the United States and other nations will have to build the requisite political support, and doing so will take time. Hence, incremental policy change is far more likely than radical change, even if it produces less adequate action. In his book *Red Sky at Morning*, James Gustave Speth (2004, xiii) offered a suitable perspective on this dilemma: "Some may look at the difficulty of reversing current trends and despair; they are stuck in the abyss. Others may blithely assume that things will work out ('they always do'); they are being wishful. The right answer, I believe, lies at neither extreme. However bad the situation looks, remember: there are solutions." His book and many other treatments of global environmental problems are filled with such solutions. To be adopted, they need a supportive alignment of political forces in the United States and the world over the next few decades. The Obama administration may be able to turn a corner in U.S. foreign policy and help to build such political support.

Notes

1. When Obama announced in 2010 that large areas off the East Coast, in the Gulf of Mexico, and in Alaska would be open to oil and gas leasing, he acknowledged the very limited role that such drilling would play in the larger context of U.S. energy use, and he called for a major push to develop a balanced supply of energy with emphasis on development of renewable sources (Broder 2010a).
2. Details of the program and the related endangerment finding can be found at the EPA website for climate change: www.epa.gov/climatechange/index.html.
3. Development under the climate change convention can be found at www.unfccc.int, and actions taken under the biodiversity convention can be followed at www.cbd.int. The Obama administration may seek Senate approval for the biodiversity treaty, but doing so has not been a priority for the administration.
4. On the critiques of institutional failure to pursue sustainable development sufficiently, see McMichael 2008 and Revkin 2008c.
5. The text of Clinton's speech on the administration's population policy can be found at the website for the ICPD at www.state.gov/secretary/rm/2010/01/135001.htm, as well as the site for the UN Population Fund at www.unfpa.org. However, it received almost no coverage in the nation's mainstream media.

References

$25 billion for Iraq, Afghanistan wars. 2005. In *CQ Almanac 2004*. Washington, D.C.: CQ Press. www.cqpress.com/reference/ (document ID cqa104-836-24361-1085025).

$40 billion emergency bill clears. 2002. In *CQ Almanac 2001*. Washington, D.C.: CQ Press. www.cqpress.com/reference/ (document ID cqa101-106-6382-328588).

$78.5 billion supplemental enacted. 2004. In *CQ Almanac 2003*. Washington, D.C.: CQ Press. www.cqpress.com/reference/ (document ID cqa103-835-24336-1083963).

$430.6 billion enacted for defense. 2008. In *CQ Almanac 2007*. Washington, D.C.: CQ Press. www.cqpress.com/reference/ (document ID cqa107-1006-44911-2047855).

9/11 Public Discourse Project. 2005. *Final report on 9/11 commission recommendations*. www.9-11pdp.org/press/2005-12-05_report.pdf.

Abott, Stephen. 2009. FY 2010 budget request: International affairs. *Budget Insight*, July 1. http://budgetinsight.wordpress.com/2009/07/01/fy-2010-budget-request-international-affairs.

Abrams, Eliot. 1989. Why everyone hates the State Department and what to do about it. *The National Interest* 17 (Fall): 85–88.

Acheson, Dean. 1971. The eclipse of the State Department. *Foreign Affairs* 49 (July): 593–606.

Adams, Gordon. 2008. Establishing the next president's national security agenda: Strengthening the civilian instrument. *Bulletin of the Atomic Scientists,* September 8. www.thebulletin.org/web-edition/columnists/gordon-adams/establishing-the-next-presidents-national-security-agenda-streng.

Agenda 21: The United Nations Programme of Action from Rio. 1993. New York: United Nations Department of Public Information.

Ahrari, Mohammed E., ed. 1987. *Ethnic groups and U.S. foreign policy.* New York: Greenwood.

Aldy, Joseph E., and Robert N. Stavins. 2008. Climate policy architectures for the post-Kyoto world. *Environment* 50 (May/June): 7–17.

Alfano, Sean. 2007. Obama: "Punjab" memo was a "dumb mistake"; Candidate disavows campaign memo that mocked Hillary's India ties. Associated Press/*CBS News,* June 19. www.cbsnews.com/stories/2007/06/19/politics/main2947307.shtml.

AlHajal, Khalil. 2008. Obama taps local woman for state outreach. *Arab American News,* August 29. www.arabamericannews.com/news/index.php?mod=article&cat=Community&article=1430.

Allen, Mike. 2009. Dick Cheney: Barack Obama "trying to pretend." *Politico,* December 30. www.politico.com/news/stories/1209/31054.html.

Ambrosio, Thomas, ed. 2002. *Ethnic identity groups and U.S. foreign policy.* Westport, Conn.: Praeger.

Anderson, Benedict. 1991. *Imagined communities: Reflections on the origins and spread of nationalism.* Rev. ed. London: Verso.

Another war president after all: Barack Obama and terrorism. 2010. *The Economist,* January 9. www.economist.com/node/15213339?story_id=15213339.

Armstrong, Matthew. 2009. Hitting bottom in Foggy Bottom. *Foreign Policy,* September 11. www.foreignpolicy.com/articles/2009/09/11/hitting_bottom_in_foggy_bottom.

Article 15-6 investigation of the 800th Military Police Brigade (Taguba report). 2004 [made public from May 2]. www1.umn.edu/humanrts/OathBetrayed/general-investigations.html.

Asher, Herbert B., and Herbert F. Weisberg. 1978. Voting change in Congress: Some dynamic perspectives on an evolutionary process. *American Journal of Political Science* 22 (2): 391–425.

Associated Press. 2009a. Kal Penn starts job as White House liaison. MSNBC, July 6. www .msnbc.msn.com/id/31765640/ns/entertainment-celebrities.

———. 2009b. Obama's bow in Japan sparks some criticism. MSNBC, November 16. www .msnbc.msn.com/id/33978533.

Avishai, Bernard. 2008. Obama's Jews. *Harper's Magazine,* October. www.harpers.org/ archive/2008/10/0082187.

Axelrod, Regina S., Stacy D. VanDeveer, and David Leonard Downie, eds. 2011. *The global environment: Institutions, law, and policy.* 3rd ed. Washington, D.C.: CQ Press.

Bacevich, Andrew J. 2008. *The limits of power: The end of American exceptionalism.* New York: Holt.

Backward at Bagram [editorial]. 2010. *New York Times,* May 31. www.nytimes.com/2010/ 06/01/opinion/01tue1.html.

Baer, Robert. 2008. With Dennis Blair, don't expect smarter intelligence. *Time,* December 20. www.time.com/time/nation/article/0,8599,1868019,00.html.

Baker, Peter. 2009. Obama reverses rule on U.S. abortion aid. *New York Times,* January 26. www.nytimes.com/2009/01/24/us/politics/24obama.html.

———. 2010a. Obama challenges terrorism critics. *New York Times,* February 7. www .nytimes.com/2010/02/08/us/politics/08terror.html.

———. 2010b. Obama puts his own mark on foreign policy issues. *New York Times,* April 13. www.nytimes.com/2010/04/14/world/14prexy.html.

———. 2010c. Obama's war over terror. *New York Times Magazine,* January 4. www .nytimes.com/2010/01/17/magazine/17Terror-t.html.

Balz, Dan. 2009a. In Oslo, Obama tries to reconcile early antiwar rhetoric with prevailing realities. *Washington Post,* December 11. www.washingtonpost.com/wp-dyn/content/ article/2009/12/10/AR2009121003991.html.

———. 2009b. Partisan divide widens as Obama considers Afghanistan policy. *Washington Post,* November 22. www.washingtonpost.com/wp-dyn/content/article/2009/11/21/ AR2009112101240.html.

Banerjee, Neela. 2007. In Jews, Indian-Americans see a role model in activism. *New York Times,* October 2. www.nytimes.com/2007/10/02/world/americas/02iht-02hindu .7711282.html.

Barber, James David. 1992. *The presidential character.* Upper Saddle River, N.J.: Prentice Hall.

Barry, Ellen. 2009. Putin sounds warning on arms talks. *New York Times*, December 29. www.nytimes.com/2009/12/30/world/europe/30russia.html.

Barston, R. P. 1988. *Modern diplomacy*. New York: Longman.

Bax, Frans R. 1977. The legislative-executive relationship in foreign policy: New partnership or new competition? *Orbis* 20 (Winter): 881–904.

BBC World Service. 2007. *All countries need to take major steps on climate change: Global poll.* www.worldpublicopinion.org/pipa/pdf/sep07/BBCClimate_Sep07_rpt.pdf.

———. 2010. *Global views of United States improve while other countries decline.* www.world publicopinion.org/pipa/pipa/pdf/apr10/BBCViews_Apr10_rpt.pdf.

Becerra won't be Obama's trade rep. 2008. *ABC News: The Note,* December 16. Comments to editorial board of *La Opinion* (Los Angeles). http://blogs.abcnews.com/the note/2008/12/becerra-trade-n.html.

Bell, Daniel. 1960. *The end of ideology: On the exhaustion of political ideas in the fifties.* Glencoe, Ill.: Free Press.

Benedick, Richard Elliot. 1998. *Ozone diplomacy: New directions in safeguarding the planet.* 2nd ed. Cambridge, Mass.: Harvard University Press.

Benjamin, Daniel. 2010. The Obama administration's counterterrorism policy at one year. Keynote address at the CATO Institute, Washington, D.C., January 13. www.state .gov/s/ct/rls/rm/2010/135171.htm.

Bergen, Peter. 2009. Reassessing the evolving al Qaeda threat to the homeland. Testimony before the Homeland Security Committee, Subcommittee on Intelligence, Information Sharing and Terrorism Risk Assessment, U.S. House of Representatives. 111th Cong., 1st sess. http://homeland.house.gov/SiteDocuments/20091119111322-14267 .pdf.

Berggren, D. Jason, and Nicol Rae. 2006. Jimmy Carter and George W. Bush: Faith, foreign policy and an evangelical presidential style. *Presidential Studies Quarterly* 36 (December): 606–632.

Betsill, Michele M. 2011. International climate change policy: Toward the multilevel governance of global warming. In *The global environment: Institutions, law, and policy,* 3rd ed., ed. Regina S. Axelrod, Stacy D. VanDeveer, and David Leonard Downie, 111–131. Washington, D.C.: CQ Press.

Betts, Richard K. 2007. *Enemies of intelligence: Knowledge and power in American national security.* New York: Columbia University Press.

Biden, Joseph. 2009. Remarks by Vice President Biden at 45th Munich Conference on Security Policy, Germany, February 7. www.whitehouse.gov/the_press_office/Remarks byVicePresidentBidenat45thMunichConferenceonSecurityPolicy.

Binder, Sarah A. 2003. *Stalemate: Causes and consequences of legislative gridlock.* Washington, D.C.: Brookings Institution.

Blair, Dennis. 2010. Intelligence reform: The lessons and implications of the Christmas Day attack. Testimony before the Committee on Homeland Security and Governmental Affairs, U.S. Senate. 111th Cong., 2nd sess. www.dni.gov/testimonies/20100120_1_testi mony.pdf.

Blustein, Paul. 2009. *Misadventures of the most favored nations: Clashing egos, inflated ambitions, and the great shambles of the world trade system.* New York: PublicAffairs.

Booth, Ken. 2007. *Theory of world security.* New York: Cambridge University Press.

Boumediene v. Bush, 553 U.S. 723 (2008), U.S. Supreme Court.

Brennan, John O. 2009. A new approach for safeguarding Americans. Address to the Center for Strategic and International Studies (CSIS), Washington, D.C., August 6. http:// csis.org/files/attachments/090806_brennan_transcript.pdf.

———. 2010. Opposing view: We need no lectures. *USA Today,* February 9. http://content .usatoday.com/topics/post/USA+TODAY+editorial/620010086.blog/1.

Broder, John M. 2008. Obama team set on environment. *New York Times,* December 10. www.nytimes.com/2008/12/11/us/politics/11appoint.html.

———. 2009a. Geography is dividing Democrats over energy. *New York Times,* January 26. www.nytimes.com/2009/01/27/science/earth/27coal.html.

———. 2009b. House backs bill, 219–212, to curb global warming. *New York Times,* June 26. www.nytimes.com/2009/06/27/us/politics/27climate.html.

———. 2009c. In Obama's team, two camps on climate. *New York Times,* January 2. www .nytimes.com/2009/01/03/washington/03enviro.html.

——— (with James Kanter). 2009d. Obama offers targets to cut greenhouse gas. *New York Times,* November 26. www.nytimes.com/2009/11/26/us/politics/26climate.html.

———. 2009e. Obama orders new rules to raise energy efficiency. *New York Times,* February 5. www.nytimes.com/2009/02/06/us/politics/06energy.html.

———. 2009f. "U.S. ready to lead on climate pact," Clinton says. *New York Times,* April 27. www.nytimes.com/2009/04/28/science/earth/28climate.html.

———. 2009g. With something for everyone, climate bill passed. *New York Times,* June 30. www.nytimes.com/2009/07/01/us/politics/01climate.html.

———. 2010a. Obama to open offshore areas to oil drilling for first time. *New York Times,* March 31. www.nytimes.com/2010/03/31/science/earth/31energy.html.

———. 2010b. Senate gets a climate and energy bill, modified by a Gulf spill that still grows. *New York Times,* May 12. www.nytimes.com/2010/05/13/science/earth/13climate .html.

Broder, John. M., and Peter Baker. 2009. Obama's order is likely to tighten auto standards. *New York Times,* January 25. www.nytimes.com/2009/01/26/us/politics/26calif.html.

Broder, John M., and James Kanter. 2009. Europeans say U.S. lacks will on climate. *New York Times,* September 20. www.nytimes.com/2009/09/21/world/europe/21climate .html.

Broder, John M., and Andrew C. Revkin. 2008. Hard task for new team on energy and climate. *New York Times,* December 16. www.nytimes.com/2008/12/16/us/politics/ 16energy.html.

Brookings Institution (with Zogby International). 2010. *2010 Arab public opinion poll.* www .brookings.edu/reports/2010/0805_arab_opinion_poll_telhami.aspx.

Brown, Lester. 2008. *Plan B 3.0: Mobilizing to save civilization.* New York: W. W. Norton.

Bruce, Mary. 2009. Obama: Gitmo likely won't close in first 100 days. ABC News, *This Week with Christiane Amanpour,* January 11. http://abcnews.go.com/ThisWeek/Economy/ story?id=6619291.

Brysk, Allison, and Gershon Shafir. 2007. *Human rights and national insecurity: Democracies debate counter terrorism.* Berkeley: University of California Press.

Brzezinski, Zbigniew. 2007. *Second chance.* New York: Basic Books.

———. 2010. From hope to audacity. *Foreign Affairs* 89 (January): 16–30.

Bumiller, Elisabeth. 2007. *Condoleezza Rice: An American life; a biography.* New York: Random House.

———. 2009. In new book, ex-spokesman has harsh words for Bush. *Washington Post,* May 28. http://query.nytimes.com/gst/fullpage.html?res=9A0DE6D81E38F93BA15756C0A96E9C8B63.

Burden, Barry C. 2007. *Personal roots of representation.* Princeton, N.J.: Princeton University Press.

Bureau of Economic Analysis, U.S. Department of Commerce. 2010. Gross domestic product: Second quarter 2010 (second estimate); Corporate profits: Second quarter 2010 (preliminary estimate) [press release]. www.bea.gov/newsreleases/national/gdp/2010/pdf/gdp2q10_2nd.pdf.

Burgin, Eileen. 1997. Assessing Congress' role in the making of foreign policy. In *Congress Reconsidered,* 6th ed., ed. Lawrence C. Dodd and Bruce I. Oppenheimer. Washington, D.C.: CQ Press, 293–324.

Bush, George H. W. 2001. America under attack: Former President Bush speaks out against terrorism [rush transcript]. CNN, September 13. http://edition1.cnn.com/TRANSCRIPTS/0109/13/se.50.html.

Bush, George H. W., and Brent Scowcroft. 1998. *A world transformed.* New York: Vintage.

Bush, George W. 2001. Address to a Joint Session of Congress, Washington, D.C., September 20. http://georgewbush-whitehouse.archives.gov/news/releases/2001/09/20010920-8.html.

———. 2005. President's statement on signing of H.R. 2863, the "Department of Defense, Emergency Supplemental Appropriations to Address Hurricanes in the Gulf of Mexico, and Pandemic Influenza Act, 2006." http://georgewbush-whitehouse.archives.gov/news/releases/2005/12/20051230-8.html.

Bush signs defense authorization, stating some provisions "optional." 2007. In *CQ Almanac 2006,* ed. J. Austin. Washington, D.C.: CQ Press. www.cqpress.com/reference/(document IDcqa106-1421593).

Calabresi, Massimo. 2009. Personal touch: How Obama's hands-on diplomacy helped bring Iran to the table. *Time,* November 2, 14.

Campbell, Colin. 2004. Unrestrained ideological entrepreneurship in the Bush II advisory system. In *The George W. Bush presidency,* ed. Colin Campbell and Bert Rockman, 73–104. Washington D.C.: CQ Press.

Campbell, John Franklin. 1975. The disorganization of State. In *Problems of American foreign policy,* 2nd ed., ed. Martin B. Hickman, 151–170. Beverly Hills, Calif.: Glencoe Press.

Campbell, Kurt M., ed. 2008. *Climatic cataclysm: The foreign policy and national security implications of climate change.* Washington, D.C.: Brookings Institution.

Capps, Ron. 2009. *Drawing on the full strength of America: Seeking greater civilian capacity in U.S. foreign affairs.* Washington, D.C.: Refugees International.

Carter, Ralph G. 1986. Congressional foreign policy behavior: Persistent patterns of the postwar period. *Presidential Studies Quarterly* 16 (2): 329–359.

Carter, Ralph G., and James M. Scott. 2004. Taking the lead: Congressional foreign policy entrepreneurs in U.S. foreign policy. *Politics & Policy* 32 (1): 34–70.

———. 2009. *Choosing to lead: Understanding congressional foreign policy entrepreneurs.* Durham, N.C.: Duke University Press.

Case-Shiller index. 2010. In *Wikipedia, the free encyclopedia*, August 26. http://en.wikipedia .org/wiki/Case–Shiller_index/ (accessed September 12, 2010).

Cave, Damien. 2008. Democrats see Cuba travel limits as a campaign issue in Florida. *New York Times,* June 1. www.nytimes.com/2008/06/01/us/01florida.html.

———. 2009. U.S. overtures find support among Cuban-Americans. *New York Times,* April 20. www.nytimes.com/2009/04/21/us/21miami.html.

Centre for the Study of Political Change. 2006. *European elites survey: Survey of members of the European Parliament and top European Commission officials; key findings 2006.* Siena, Italy: Centre for the Study of Political Change at the University of Siena. www.circap .unisi.it/ees/ees_overview.

Cheney, Richard. 2009. Remarks by Richard B. Cheney. Speech at the American Enterprise Institute for Public Policy Research, Washington, D.C., May 21. www.aei.org/speech/100050.

Chicago Council on Foreign Relations. 2002. *Worldviews 2002: American public opinion and foreign policy.* http://worldviews.org/detailreports/usreport.pdf.

Chicago Council on Global Affairs. 2008. *Global views 2008.* www.thechicagocouncil.org/ pos_overview.php.

———. 2009. *Anxious Americans seek a new direction in United States foreign policy: Results of a 2008 survey of public opinion.* Chicago: Chicago Council on Global Affairs. www .thechicagocouncil.org/UserFiles/File/POS_Topline%20Reports/POS%202008/ 2008%20Public%20Opinion%202008_US%20Survey%20Results.pdf.

Chittick, William O., Keith R. Billingsley, and Rick Travis. 1995. A three-dimensional model of foreign policy beliefs. *International Studies Quarterly* 39: 313–331.

Christensen, Thomas. Posing problems without catching up: China's rise and challenges for U.S. security policy. 2001. *International Security* 25 (Spring): 5–40.

Citizens United v. Federal Election Commission, 558 U.S. 50 (2010).

Clark, Lesley. 2009. Money affects Cuba policy. *Miami Herald,* November 16. www.miami herald.com/news/southflorida/story/1335580.html.

Clarke, Duncan L. 1987. Why State can't lead. *Foreign Policy* 66 (Spring): 128–142.

———. 1989. *American defense and foreign policy institutions: Toward a sound foundation.* Lanham, Md.: University Press of America.

Clarke, Richard. 2004. *Against all enemies.* New York: Free Press.

Cleaning up the leftovers of FY 2007. 2008. In *CQ Almanac 2007.* Washington, D.C.: CQ Press. www.cqpress.com/reference/ (document ID cqa107-1006-44911-2047832).

Clinton, Hillary. 2009a. Foreign policy address at the Council of Foreign Relations, Washington, D.C., July 15. www.state.gov/secretary/rm/2009a/july/126071.htm.

———. 2009b. Town hall on the Quadrennial Diplomacy and Development Review at the Department of State, Washington, D.C., July 10. www.state.gov/secretary/rm/2009a/ july/125949.htm.

Coast Guard enters new phase. 2005. In *CQ Almanac 2004.* Washington, D.C.: CQ Press. www.cqpress.com/reference/ (document ID cqa104-836-24365-1085106).

Cohen, Bernard C. 1973. *The public's impact on foreign policy.* Boston: Little, Brown.

Cohen, Richard. 2009. With friends like Pelosi . . . . *Washington Post,* March 24. www .washingtonpost.com/wp-dyn/content/article/2009/03/23/AR2009032302137.html.

Cohen, Richard E., and Brian Friel. 2010. Politics as usual: 2009 vote ratings. *National Journal,* February 27, 18–60.

Cole, David, and James X. Dempsey. 2006. *Terrorism and the Constitution: Sacrificing civil liberties in the name of national security.* 3rd ed. New York: New Press.

Colvin, Ross, 2009. Obama rights record questioned ahead of Nobel Prize. Reuters, December 9. www.reuters.com/article/idUSTRE5B82TM20091209/.

Commander's Emergency Response Program (CERP). 2008. *Commander's emergency response program smartcard for leaders* (GTA 90-01-017). www.acq.osd.mil/dpap/pacc/cc/jcchb/Contingency%20Model/JCC/JCC%20Tools%20CD/training_smartcard/CERP%20GTA%2090-01-017.pdf.

Congress imposes Syria sanctions. 2004. In *CQ Almanac 2003.* Washington, D.C.: CQ Press. www.cqpress.com/reference/ (document ID cqa103-835-24326-1083619).

Congressional Research Service. 2010. *Security assistance reform: "Section 1206" background and issues for Congress.* http://opencrs.com/document/RS22855.

Congress OKs force after Sept. 11. 2002. In *CQ Almanac 2001.* Washington, D.C.: CQ Press. www.cqpress.com/reference (document ID cqa101-106-6388-328730).

Cooper, Michael. 2008. Campaigns in a skirmish over terrorism and law. *New York Times,* June 18. www.nytimes.com/2008/06/18/us/politics/18mccain.html.

Cordesman, Anthony. 2007. *Salvaging American defense: The challenge of strategic overstretch.* Westport, Conn.: Praeger Security International.

Corwin, Edward. 1957. *The president: Office and powers, 1787–1957.* 4th ed. New York: New York University Press.

Cronin, Thomas E., and Michael A. Genovese. 2004. *The paradoxes of the American presidency.* New York: Oxford University Press.

Crowley, Michael. 2009. The decider: Who runs U.S. foreign policy? *The New Republic,* August 12. www.tnr.com/article/the-decider.

Cuba provisions draw veto threat. 2007. In *CQ Almanac 2006.* Washington, D.C.: CQ Press. www.cqpress.com/reference/ (document ID cqa106-1421463).

Cuba Study Group. 2008. *Lifting restrictions on travel and remittances: A case for unilateral action.* Washington, D.C.: Cuba Study Group. www.cubastudygroup.org/index.cfm/lifting-restrictions-on-travel-and-remittances-to-cuba.

Daalder, Ivo H., and I. M. Destler. 2009. *In the shadow of the Oval Office: Profiles of the national security advisers and the presidents they served—from JFK to George W. Bush.* New York: Simon and Schuster.

Daalder, Ivo H., and James M. Lindsay. 2006. *America unbound: The Bush revolution in foreign policy.* Rev. ed. Washington, D.C.: Brookings Institution.

Dabelko, Geoffrey D. 2008. An uncommon peace: Environment, development, and the global security agenda. *Environment* 50 (May/June): 32–45.

Daniel, Donald C. F., Peter Dombrowski, and Rodger A. Payne. 2005. The Bush Doctrine is dead; long live the Bush Doctrine. *Orbis* 49 (Spring): 199–212.

Davenport, Coral, and Avery Palmer. 2009. A landmark climate bill passes. *CQ Weekly,* June 29, 1516.

Davis, Jack. 1995. A policymaker's perspective on intelligence analysis. *Studies in Intelligence* 38 (5): 7–15.

de la Garza, Paul. 2002. Bush sidesteps Senate, appoints Reich, Scalia. *St. Petersburg Times,* January 12. www.sptimes.com/2002/01/12/Worldandnation/Bush_sidesteps_Senate.shtml.

Deal reached on military tribunals. 2007. In *CQ Almanac 2006.* Washington, D.C.: CQ Press. www.cqpress.com/reference/ (document ID cqa106-1421603).

Democrats yield to President Bush on war funds, domestic spending. 2008. In *CQ Almanac 2007.* Washington, D.C.: CQ Press. www.cqpress.com/reference/ (document ID cqa107-1006-44911-2047830).

Desch, Michael C. 2007–08. America's liberal illiberalism: The ideological origins of over-reaction in U.S. foreign policy. *International Security* 32 (Winter): 7–43.

DeSombre, Elizabeth R. 2011. The United States and global environmental politics: Domestic sources of U.S. unilateralism. In *The Global Environment,* 3rd. ed., ed. Regina S. Axelrod, Stacy D. VanDeveer, and David Leonard Downie, 192–212. Washington, D.C.: CQ Press.

Destler, I. M. 1974. *Presidents, bureaucrats, and foreign policy.* Princeton, N.J.: Princeton University Press.

———. 1996. *The National Economic Council: A work in progress* (Policy Analysis No. 46). Washington, D.C.: Institute for International Economics.

———. 2005. *American trade politics.* Washington, D.C.: Institute for International Economics.

———. 2007. *American trade politics in 2007: Building bipartisan consensus* (policy brief 07-5). Washington, D.C.: Peterson Institute for International Economics.

Destler, I. M., Leslie H. Gelb, and Anthony Lake. 1984. *Our own worst enemy: The unmaking of American foreign policy.* New York: Simon and Schuster.

Destler, I. M., and Marcus Noland. 2006. Constant ends, flexible means: C. Fred Bergsten and the quest for open trade. In *C. Fred Bergsten and the World Economy,* ed. Michael Mussa. Washington, D.C.: Peterson Institute for International Economics.

DeYoung, Karen. 2006a. A fight against terrorism—and disorganization. *Washington Post,* August 9. www.washingtonpost.com/wp-dyn/content/article/2006/08/08/AR2006080800964.html.

———. 2006b. *Soldier: The life of Colin Powell.* New York: Random House.

———. 2009. Obama's NSC will get new power. *Washington Post,* February 8. www.washingtonpost.com/wp-dyn/content/article/2009/02/07/AR2009020702076.html.

DeYoung, Karen, and Glenn Kessler. 2009. As Obama visits State Dept., Clinton announces two special envoys. *Washington Post,* January 23. www.washingtonpost.com/wp-dyn/content/article/2009/01/22/AR2009012203886.html.

DeYoung, Karen, and Michael Leahy. 2009. Warning on Detroit suspect didn't rise above the "noise"; U.S. official says father's tip, like many, included "minimal information." *Washington Post,* December 28. www.washingtonpost.com/wp-dyn/content/article/2009/12/27/AR2009122700279.html.

Dilanian, Ken. 2009a. Clinton adopts low-key style at the State Dept. *USA Today,* June 10. www.usatoday.com/news/world/2009-06-10-hillary-clinton_N.htm.

———. 2009b. Under bills, U.S. would funnel more money into diplomacy. *USA Today,* July 20. www.usatoday.com/news/world/2009-07-19-diplomacy_N.htm.

DiMento, Joseph F. C., and Pamela Doughman, eds. 2007. *Climate change: What it means for us, our children, and our grandchildren.* Cambridge, Mass.: MIT Press.

Director of National Intelligence (DNI). 2008. *Vision 2015: A globally networked and integrated intelligence enterprise.* www.dni.gov/Vision_2015.pdf.

Disputes delay reauthorization of anti-terrorism act provisions. 2006. In *CQ Almanac 2005*. Washington, D.C.: CQ Press. www.cqpress.com/reference/ (document ID cqa105-766-20097-1042102).

Donadio, Rachel. 2009. Italy convicts 23 Americans for C.I.A. renditions. *New York Times,* November 4. www.nytimes.com/2009/11/05/world/europe/05italy.html.

Donnelly, Jack. 2007. *International human rights.* 3rd ed. Boulder, Colo.: Westview Press.

Donohue, Laura K. 2004. Fear itself: Counterterrorism, individual rights, and U.S. foreign relations post 9-11. In *Terrorism and counterterrorism,* ed. Russell D. Howard and Reid L. Sawyer. New York: McGraw-Hill.

Duffield, John, and Peter Dombrowski, eds. 2009. *Balance sheet: The Iraq War and U.S. national security.* Palo Alto, Calif.: Stanford University Press.

Dugger, Celia W. 2006. Need for water could double in 50 years, U.N. study finds. *New York Times,* August 22. www.nytimes.com/2006/08/22/world/22water.html.

Eddy, R. P. 2008. The resilient homeland: How DHS intelligence should empower America to prepare for, prevent, and withstand terrorist attacks. Testimony before the Committee on Homeland Security, Subcommittee on Intelligence, Information Sharing, and Terrorism—Risk Assessment Hearing, U.S. House of Representatives. 110th Cong., 2nd sess. www.manhattan-institute.org/html/testimony_eddy_5-15-08.htm.

Eggen, Dan. 2009. Israel conference to open amid controversy. *Washington Post,* October 29. www.washingtonpost.com/wp-dyn/content/article/2009/10/24/AR2009102400994_pf.html.

Eilperin, Juliet. 2009a. After hard sell in Copenhagen, an even harder sell in the Senate—Obama faces tough fight in delivering on climate pledges made overseas. *Washington Post,* December 26. www.washingtonpost.com/wp-dyn/content/article/2009/12/25/AR2009122501671.html.

———. 2009b. U.S. weighs backing interim international climate agreement. *Washington Post,* November 13. www.washingtonpost.com/wp-dyn/content/article/2009/11/12/AR2009111209127.html.

———. 2010. U.S. to cut greenhouse gas emissions by 17 percent by 2020. *Washington Post,* January 29. www.washingtonpost.com/wp-dyn/content/article/2010/01/28/AR20100 12803632.html.

Eilperin, Juliet, and Anthony Faida. 2009. Ultimate deal falls short of key goal. *Washington Post,* December 19.

Eisler, Peter. 2009. Obama's intelligence pick has range of credentials. *USA Today,* January 9.

Emergency funding softens cuts. 2008. In *CQ Almanac 2007.* Washington, D.C.: CQ Press. www.cqpress.com/reference (document ID cqa107-1006-44911-2047883).

Erdbrink, Thomas, and Glenn Kessler. 2009. Obama's tone in Iran message differs sharply from Bush's. *Washington Post,* March 21. www.washingtonpost.com/wp-dyn/content/article/2009/03/20/AR2009032000398.html.

Erikson, Daniel P. 2008. *Cuba wars: Fidel Castro, the United States, and the next revolution.* New York: Bloomsbury Press.

Feith, Douglas J. 2008. *War and decision: Inside the Pentagon at the dawn of the war on terrorism.* New York: Harper.

Findley, Paul. 1989. *They dare speak out: People and institutions confront Israel's lobby.* Chicago: Lawrence Hill Books.

Fingar, Thomas. 2008. Remarks and Q&A by the deputy director of national intelligence for analysis & chairman, National Intelligence Council. Address to the Council on Foreign Relations, New York, March 18. www.dni.gov/speeches/20080318_speech.pdf.

Fiscal 2006 spending bills finished, plus $200 billion in emergency funds. 2006. In *CQ Almanac 2005*. Washington, D.C.: CQ Press. www.cqpress.com/reference/ (document ID cqa105-766-20104-1042261).

Fisher, Louis. 2008. NSA eavesdropping: Unchecked or limited presidential power? In *Contemporary cases in U.S. foreign policy*, 3rd ed., ed. Ralph G. Carter, 185–215. Washington, D.C.: CQ Press.

Fleshler, Dan. 2009. *Transforming America's Israel lobby: The limits of its power and the potential for change*. Washington, D.C.: Potomac Books.

Flynn, Michael T., Matt Pottinger, and Paul D. Batchelor. 2010. *Fixing Intel: A blueprint for making intelligence relevant in Afghanistan*. Washington, D.C.: Center for a New American Security. www.cnas.org/files/documents/publications/AfghanIntel_Flynn_Jan 2010_code507_voices.pdf.

Fordham, Benjamin O. 2007. Paying for global power: Assessing the costs and benefits of postwar U.S. military spending. In *The long war: A new history of U.S. national security policy since World War II*, ed. Andrew J. Bacevich. New York: Columbia University Press.

Foreign aid bill rewards allies. 2005. In *CQ Almanac 2004*. Washington, D.C.: CQ Press. www.cqpress.com/reference/ (document ID cqa104-836-24361-1084944).

Foreign aid bill sticks to tradition. 2002. In *CQ Almanac 2001*. Washington, D.C.: CQ Press. www.cqpress.com/reference/ (document ID cqa101-106-6382-328475).

Foreign aid enjoys singular boost. 2006. In *CQ Almanac 2005*. Washington, D.C.: CQ Press. www.cqpress.com/reference/ (document ID cqa105-766-20104-1042314).

Forsythe, David P. 2005. *The humanitarians: The International Committee of the Red Cross*. Cambridge, England: Cambridge University Press.

———. 2006. *Human rights in international relations*. New York: Cambridge University Press.

——— (with Baekkwan Park). 2009. Turbulent transition: From the UN Human Rights Commission to the Council. In *The United Nations: Past, present and future*, ed. Scott Kaufman and Alissa Warters. Hauppauge, N.Y.: Nova Science.

———. Forthcoming. *The politics of abuse: The U.S. and enemy prisoners after 9/11*. New York: Cambridge University Press.

Foyle, Douglas C. 2007. The convinced, the skeptical, and the hostile: American and world public opinion on the Bush doctrine. In *Understanding the Bush doctrine: Psychology and strategy in an age of terrorism*, ed. Stanley A. Renshon and Peter Suedfeld, 65–104. New York: Routledge.

———. 2010. Public opinion, foreign policy, and the media: Toward an integrative theory. In *Oxford handbook of American public opinion and the media*, ed. Lawrence R. Jacobs and Robert Y. Shapiro. New York: Oxford University Press.

Franck, Thomas M., and Edward Weisband. 1979. *Foreign policy by Congress*. New York: Oxford University Press.

Friedman, Matti, and Matthew Lee. 2010. Obama and Israeli PM meet amid dispute. Associated Press/*ABC News*, March 23. http://abcnews.go.com/Politics/wireStory?id=10179909.

Friedman, Thomas L. 2006. The bus is waiting. *New York Times*, October 11. http://query
.nytimes.com/gst/fullpage.html?res=9C0CE4DF1030F932A25753C1A9609C8B63.
————. 2008. *Hot, flat, and crowded: Why we need a green revolution—and how it can renew
America.* New York: Farrar, Straus, and Giroux.
Frist pulls foreign relations bill. 2004. In *CQ Almanac 2003*. Washington, D.C.: CQ Press.
www.cqpress.com/reference/ (document ID cqa103-835-24326-1083605).
Fukuyama, Francis. 2006. *America at the crossroads: Democracy, power, and the neoconservative legacy.* New Haven, Conn.: Yale University Press.
Fulbright, J. William. 1966. Fatal arrogance of power. *New York Times Magazine,* May 15,
28–29, 103–105.
Fullilove, Michael. 2009. Send the envoy. *Foreign Affairs,* March 12. www.foreignaffairs
.com/articles/64895/michael-fullilove/send-the-envoy.
Gaddis, John Lewis. 1982. *Strategies of containment.* New York: Oxford University Press.
Gallup Opinion Poll. 2010. World citizens' views on U.S. leadership, pre- and post-Obama.
www.gallup.com/poll/121991/world-citizens-views-leadership-pre-post-obama.aspx.
Gates, Robert, M. 2007. Landon lecture: Remarks as delivered by Secretary of Defense
Robert M. Gates, Manhattan, Kansas, November 26. www.defense.gov/speeches/
speech.aspx?speechid=1199.
Gellman, Barton. 2008. *Angler: The Cheney vice presidency.* New York: Penguin.
Gellner, Ernest. 1998. *Nationalism.* London: Phoenix.
Gelpi, Christopher, Peter D. Feaver, and Jason Reifler. 2009. *Paying the human costs of war:
American public opinion and casualties in military conflicts.* Princeton, N.J.: Princeton
University Press.
Geman, Ben. 2010. Pelosi tells Reid: Immigration bill before climate change is "fine." *The
Hill: E² Wire,* April 21. http://thehill.com/blogs/e2-wire/677-e2-wire/93691-pelosi-to-
reid-immigration-before-climate-is-fine.
George, Alexander L. 1969. The "operational code": A neglected approach to the study of
political leaders and decision-making. *International Studies Quarterly* 13 (2): 190–222.
http://jeffreyfields.net/pols/The%20operational%20code.pdf.
————. 1980. *Presidential decision making in foreign policy.* Boulder, Colo.: Westview Press.
German Marshall Fund. 2009. *Transatlantic trends 2009.* www.gmfus.org/trends.
Gerstein, John. 2009. DNI claims 2-for-3 in oversight scrap. *Politico,* November 18. www
.politico.com/blogs/joshgerstein/1109/DNI_claims_2for3_in_oversight_scrap.html.
Gertz, Bill. 2002. *Breakdown: How America's intelligence failures led to September 11.*
Washington, D.C.: Regnery Press.
————. 2009. Inside the ring. *Washington Times,* September 10. www.gertzfile.com/gertz
file/ring091009.html.
Gettleman, Jeffrey. 2009. Hillary Clinton's folksy diplomacy. *New York Times,* August 16.
www.nytimes.com/2009/08/16/weekinreview/16gettleman.html.
Gharib, Ali. 2010. U.S.: Obama losing control of Iran policy. Inter Press Service, January 29.
http://ipsnews.net/news.asp?idnews=50161.
Ghattas, Kim. 2009. Clinton ready to talk tough with Karzai. *BBC News,* November 18.
http://news.bbc.co.uk/2/hi/south_asia/8367432.stm.
Ghosh, Bobby. 2009. Domestic-terrorism incidents hit a peak in 2009. *Time,* December 23.
www.time.com/time/nation/article/0,8599,1949329,00.html.

Giridharadas, Anand. 2007. Lobbying in U.S., Indian firms present an American face. *New York Times,* September 4. www.nytimes.com/2007/09/04/business/worldbusiness/04 outsource.html.

Glaberson, William. 2008. 5 charged in 9/11 attacks seek to plead guilty. *New York Times,* December 8. www.nytimes.com/2008/12/09/us/09gitmo.html.

Glain, Stephen. 2009. The American leviathan. *The Nation,* September 9. www.thenation .com/article/american-leviathan.

Goldberg, David H. 1990. *Foreign policy and ethnic interest groups: American and Canadian Jews lobby for Israel.* New York: Greenwood Press.

Goldsmith, Jack. 2007. *The terror presidency: Law and judgment inside the Bush administration.* New York: W. W. Norton.

———. 2009. The Cheney fallacy. *New Republic,* May 18. www.tnr.com/article/politics/ the-cheney-fallacy?id=1e733cac-c273-48e5-9140-80443ed1f5e2.

Gottlieb, Stuart. 2008. Three keys to fighting terrorism. *Hartford Courant,* December 5.

———. 2009. Obama's drone-strike counterterrorism policy. *Foreign Policy,* April 7. http:// experts.foreignpolicy.com/blog/5736.

Graham, Bradley. 2009. *By his own rules: The ambitions, successes, and ultimate failures of Donald Rumsfeld.* New York: Public Affairs.

Graham, Carol, and Martin S. Indyk. 2010. *How we're doing in the world.* Washington, D.C.: Brookings Institution. www.brookings.edu/papers/2010/0228_recovery_renewal.aspx.

Graham-Silverman, A. 2008a. 2008 legislative summary: Global AIDS relief. *CQ Weekly,* December 8, 3276.

———. 2008b. Colombian aid gets new cash calculus. *CQ Weekly,* January 28, 239.

Greenberg, Karen, and Joshua Dratel. 2005. *The torture papers: The road to Abu Ghraib.* New York: Cambridge University Press.

Greenstein, Fred. 1982. *The hidden-hand presidency.* New York: Basic Books.

Greenwald, Glenn. 2009. Obama and habeas corpus—then and now. *Salon,* April 11. www .salon.com/news/opinion/glenn_greenwald/2009/04/11/bagram.

Gresser, Edward. 2009. American public opinion on trade has sharply improved this year. *Progressive Policy Institute (PPI) Trade Fact of the Week,* May 13. www.ppionline.org/ ppi_ci.cfm?knlgAreaID=108&subsecID=900003&contentID=254980.

Grunwald, Michael. 2009. Person of the year 2009. *Time,* December 16. www.time.com/ time/specials/packages/article/0,28804,1946375_1947251_1947520,00.html.

Guber, Deborah Lynn, and Christopher J. Bosso. 2010. Past the tipping point? Public discourse and the role of the environmental movement in a post-Bush era. In *Environmental Policy,* 7th ed., ed. Norman J. Vig and Michael E. Kraft, 51–74. Washington, D.C.: CQ Press.

Guttman, Nathan. 2009. Pro-Palestinian advocates sense winds of change in Washington. *Forward,* June 11. http://zogby.com/Soundbites/ReadClips.cfm?ID=18874.

Haass, Richard N. 2008. The age of nonpolarity: What will follow U.S. dominance. *Foreign Affairs* (May/June). www.foreignaffairs.com/articles/63397/richard-n-haass/the-age-of-nonpolarity/.

Hamdi v. Rumsfeld. 542 U.S. 547 (2004). U.S. Supreme Court.

Hamilton, Lee (with Jordan Tama). 2002. *A creative tension: The foreign policy roles of the president and Congress.* Washington, D.C.: Woodrow Wilson Center Press.

Hammond, Susan Webb. 1989. Congressional caucuses in the policy process. In *Congress reconsidered,* 4th ed., ed. Lawrence C. Dodd and Bruce I. Oppenheimer. Washington, D.C.: CQ Press, 351–371.

Haney, Patrick J. 2010. Ethnic lobbying in foreign policy. In *The international studies encyclopedia,* ed. Robert A. Denemark, 1677–1693. London: Wiley-Blackwell.

Haney, Patrick J., and Walt Vanderbush. 1999. The role of ethnic interest groups in U.S. foreign policy: The case of the Cuban American National Foundation. *International Studies Quarterly* 43 (June): 341–361.

———. 2005. *The Cuban embargo: The domestic politics of an American foreign policy.* Pittsburgh, Pa.: University of Pittsburgh Press.

Harrison, Kathryn, and Lisa McIntosh Sundstrom, eds. 2010. *Global commons, domestic decisions: The comparative politics of climate change.* Cambridge, Mass.: MIT Press.

Harrison, Todd. 2010. *Few surprises in the FY 2011 defense budget request.* Center for Strategic and Budgetary Assessments: Washington, D.C. www.csbaonline.org/4Publications/PubLibrary/U.20100201.Few_Surprises_in_t/U.20100201.Few_Surprises_in_t.pdf.

Hartz, Louis. 1955. *The liberal tradition in America.* New York: Harcourt, Brace.

Hastedt, Glenn. 2011. *American foreign policy.* 8th ed. Boston: Longman.

Hedgpeth, Dana, and Sarah Cohen. 2008. Money as a weapon. *Washington Post,* August 11. www.washingtonpost.com/wp-dyn/content/article/2008/08/10/AR2008081002512.html.

Hempel, Lamont C. 2009. Conceptual and analytical challenges in building sustainable communities. In *Toward sustainable communities: Transitions and transformation in environmental policy,* 2nd ed., ed. Daniel A. Mazmanian and Michael E. Kraft, 33–62. Cambridge, Mass.: MIT Press.

Henderson, Nia-Malika. 2009. Hillary Clinton talks tough on North Korea, Iran. *Politico,* June 7. www.politico.com/news/stories/0609/23441.html.

Hermann, Charles F. 1969. International crisis as a situational variable. In *International politics and foreign policy,* rev. ed., ed. James N. Rosenau. New York: Free Press, 409–421.

Herskovitz, Jon. 2009. Obama proposes U.S. liaison in North Korea: Yonhap. Reuters, December 18. www.reuters.com/article/idUSTRE5BF4JS20091218.

Hersman, Rebecca K. C. 2000. *Friends and foes: How Congress and the president really make foreign policy.* Washington, D.C.: Brookings Institution.

Hillary Clinton (D-Punjab)'s personal financial and political ties to India. 2007. *New York Times,* June 16. http://graphics8.nytimes.com/packages/pdf/politics/memo1.pdf.

Hirsh, Michael. 2010. A politically correct war: Nine years after 9/11 we still don't know how to deal with radical Islam. *Newsweek,* June 17.

Hobsbawm, Eric. 1990. *Nations and nationalism since 1780: Programme, myth, reality.* New York: Cambridge University Press.

Hobson, Margaret Kriz. 2010. The wages of inaction. *National Journal,* April 17, 18–23.

Hoffman, David, and Margaret Shapiro. 1985. Reagan flays Congress on Nicaraguan rebel aid. *Washington Post,* May 22.

Hoffmann, Stanley, 2003. The high and mighty. *American Prospect* 13 (January): 157–162.

Holbrooke, Richard. 2008. The next president's daunting agenda. *Foreign Affairs* 87 (September): 2–24.

Holland, Steve. 2009a. Obama breaks silence on Gaza, voices concern. Reuters, January 6. http://uk.reuters.com/article/idUKTRE5055N420090106.

————. 2009b. Obama defends choice of Panetta to head CIA. Reuters, January 6. www .reuters.com/article/idUSTRE5044JS20090106.

Holmes, J. Anthony. 2009. Where are the civilians? How to rebuild the U.S. foreign service. *Foreign Affairs* 88 (1): 148–160. www.foreignaffairs.com/articles/63727/j-anthony-holmes/ where-are-the-civilians.

Holsti, Ole R. 2004. *Public opinion and American foreign policy.* Rev. ed. Ann Arbor: University of Michigan Press.

————. 2008. *To see ourselves as others see us.* Ann Arbor: University of Michigan Press.

Holsti, Ole R., and James N. Rosenau. 1984. *American leadership in world affairs: Vietnam and the breakdown of consensus.* New York: Allen and Unwin.

Homeland department created. 2003. In *CQ Almanac 2002.* Washington, D.C.: CQ Press. www.cqpress.com/reference/ (document ID cqa102-236-10378-664466).

Hook, Steven W., and James M. Scott, eds. 2011. *American renewal? New directions in foreign policy.* Washington, D.C.: CQ Press.

Hook, Steven W., and John Spanier. 2010. *American foreign policy since World War II.* 18th ed. Washington, D.C.: CQ Press.

Howell, William G., and Jon C. Pevehouse. 2007. *While dangers gather: Congressional checks on presidential war powers.* Princeton, N.J.: Princeton University Press.

Hsu, Spencer S. 2010. Senators draft plan to rework U.S. immigration policy. *Washington Post,* March 18. www.washingtonpost.com/wp-dyn/content/article/2010/03/18/AR2010031803762.html.

Hsu, Spencer S., and Joby Warrick. 2009. Obama's battle against terrorism to go beyond bombs and bullets. *Washington Post,* August 6. www.washingtonpost.com/wp-dyn/content/article/2009/08/05/AR2009080503940.html.

Hufbauer, Gary Clyde, and Jeffrey J. Schott. 2009. *Buy American: Bad for jobs; worse for reputation* (policy brief 09-2). Washington, D.C.: Peterson Institute for International Economics.

Hughes, John. 2009. Obama soars abroad, but America's PR doesn't. *Christian Science Monitor,* July 2. www.csmonitor.com/Commentary/Opinion/2009/0702/p09s01-coop.html.

Hulse, Carl. 2009. In climate change bill, a political message. *New York Times,* June 27. Available at www.nytimes.com/2009/06/28/us/politics/28cong.html.

Human Rights Watch. 2010. *Counterterrorism and human rights: A report card on President Obama's first year.* Washington, D.C.: Human Rights Watch. www.hrw.org/en/news/2010/01/14/us-obama-s-first-year-record-counterterrorism-reform-mixed.

Ignatieff, Michael, ed. 2005. *American exceptionalism and human rights.* Princeton, N.J.: Princeton University Press.

Ikenberry, G. John. 2001. *After victory: Institutions, strategic restraint, and the rebuilding of order after major wars.* Princeton, N.J.: Princeton University Press.

Ikenberry, G. John, and Marie Slaughter. 2006. *Forging a world of liberty under law: U.S. national security in the 21st century.* Princeton, N.J.: Princeton Project on National Security, Princeton University.

Independent Panel to Review Department of Defense Detention Operations. 2004. *Final report of the Independent Panel to Review Department of Defense Detention Operations* (Schlesinger report). http://fl1.findlaw.com/news.findlaw.com/wp/docs/dod/abughrai brpt.pdf.

India nuclear deal goes forward. 2007. In *CQ Almanac 2006*. Washington, D.C.: CQ Press. www.cqpress.com/reference/ (document ID cqa106-1421143).

Intelligence bill creates 9/11 panel. 2003. In *CQ Almanac 2002*. Washington, D.C.: CQ Press. www.cqpress.com/reference/ (document ID cqa102-236-10378-664498).

Intelligence bill enhances FBI powers. 2004. In *CQ Almanac 2003*. Washington, D.C.: CQ Press. www.cqpress.com/reference/ (document ID cqa103-835-24326-1083627).

Intelligence overhaul enacted. 2005. In *CQ Almanac 2004*. Washington, D.C.: CQ Press. www.cqpress.com/reference/ (document ID: cqa104-836-24353-1084600).

Intergovernmental Panel on Climate Change (IPCC). 2007. *Synthesis report: Contribution of Working Groups I, II and III to the fourth assessment report of the Intergovernmental Panel on Climate Change*. Ed. R. K. Pachauri and A. Reisinger. Geneva, Switzerland: IPCC. www.ipcc.ch.

International Committee of the Red Cross. 2007. *ICRC report on the treatment of fourteen high value detainees in CIA custody*. Given to Mark Danner and posted via *New York Review of Books* 56 (7; April 30, 2009). www.nybooks.com/articles/archives/2009/apr/09/us-torture-voices-from-the-black-sites.

International Energy Agency. 2009. *World energy outlook 2009*. Paris: International Energy Agency. www.worldenergyoutlook.org.

International Monetary Fund (IMF). (2009). *World economic outlook: Crisis and recovery*. Washington, D.C.: International Monetary Fund. www.imf.org/external/pubs/ft/weo/2009/01/index.htm.

Iran-Libya sanctions extended. 2002. In *CQ Almanac 2001*. Washington, D.C.: CQ Press. www.cqpress.com/reference/ (document ID: cqa101-106-6373-328147).

Jaben-Eilon, Jan. 2009. Vying for Obama's ear [extract]. *Jerusalem Post,* January 18. www.jpost.com/Home/Article.aspx?id=129836.

Jha, Lalit K. 2009. Obama administration changing the course of the UN: Rice. *Business Standard,* September 19. www.business-standard.com/india/news/obama-administration-changingcourseun-rice/21/46/73881/on.

Johnson, Carrie, and Ellen Nakashima. 2009. White House seeks renewal of surveillance laws, perhaps with tweaks. *Washington Post,* September 16. www.washingtonpost.com/wp-dyn/content/article/2009/09/15/AR2009091503182.html.

Johnson, Carrie, and Julie Tate. 2009. New interrogation details emerge: As it releases Justice Dept. memos, administration reassures CIA questioners. *Washington Post,* April 17. www.washingtonpost.com/wp-dyn/content/article/2009/04/16/AR2009041602768.html.

Johnson, M. M. 2008. 2008 legislative summary, Homeland Security appropriations. *CQ Weekly,* December 8, 3248.

Johnson, Richard Tanner. 1974. *Managing the White House.* New York: Harper Row.

Johnston, Alastair Ian. Is China a status quo power? 2003. *International Security* 27 (Spring): 5–56. http://belfercenter.ksg.harvard.edu/publication/301/is_china_a_status_quo_power.html.

Jones, Anthony R., and George R. Fay. 2004. *AR 15-6 investigation of the Abu Ghraib Prison and 205th Military Intelligence Brigade, and AR 15-6 investigation of the Abu Ghraib Detention Facility and the 205th Military Intelligence Brigade* (Fay-Jones Report). http://fl1.findlaw.com/news.findlaw.com/hdocs/docs/dod/fay82504rpt.pdf.

Jones, Christopher M. 2006. The other side of Powell's record. *American Diplomacy* (Winter): 1–16. www.unc.edu/depts/diplomat/item/2006/0103/jone/jonesc_powell .html.

Jones, Jeffrey M., Frank Newport, and Lydia Saad. 2009. The decade in review: Four key trends. www.gallup.com/poll/124787/Decade-Review-Four-Key-Trends.aspx.

Kagan, Robert. 2010a. Allies everywhere feeling snubbed by President Obama. *Washington Post,* March 17. www.washingtonpost.com/wp-dyn/content/article/2010/03/16/ AR2010031603322.html.

———. 2010b. Bipartisan spring. *Foreign Policy*, March 3. www.foreignpolicy.com/articles/ 2010/03/03/bipartisan_spring.

Kamdar, Mira. 2007. Forget the Israel lobby. The Hill's next big player is made in India. *Washington Post,* September 30. www.washingtonpost.com/wp-dyn/content/article/ 2007/09/28/AR2007092801350.html.

Kamen, Al. 2009. The end of the global war on terror. *Washington Post,* March 24. http:// voices.washingtonpost.com/44/2009/03/23/the_end_of_the_global_war_on_t.html.

Kampeas, Ron. 2008. Obama team opens a wide door to Jewish groups. *Baltimore Jewish Times,* December 29. www.jewishtimes.com/index.php/jewishtimes/news/jt/national_ news/obama_team_opens_a_wide_door_to_jewish_groups.

———. 2009. Waiting for Obama to fill out the Mideast policy machine. JTA, January 20. http://jta.org/news/article/2009/01/20/1002393/waiting-for-obama-to-fill-out-the- mideast-policy-machine.

Kantor, Jodi, and Charlie Savage. 2010. After 9/11 trial plan, Holder hones political ear. *New York Times,* February 14. www.nytimes.com/2010/02/15/us/politics/15holder.htm.

Kaplowitz, Donna R. 1998. *Anatomy of a failed embargo: U.S. sanctions against Cuba.* Boul- der, Colo.: Lynne Rienner.

Karon, Tony. 2010. Why Obama defaulted to Bush foreign policies. *Time*, January 4. www .time.com/time/world/article/0,8599,1950827,00.html.

Kelly, Raymond. 2009. *The post-9/11 NYPD: Where are we now?* [rush transcript]. Address to the Council on Foreign Relations, New York, April 22. www.cfr.org/publication/19198/ post911_nypd.html.

Kelman, Steven. 1987. *Making public policy: A hopeful view of American government.* New York: Basic Books.

Kennedy, Paul. 1987. *The rise and fall of the great powers: Economic change and military conflict from 1500 to 2000.* New York: Random House.

Kent, Sherman. 1949. *Strategic intelligence for American world policy.* Princeton, N.J.: Princeton University Press.

Kerr, Richard A. 2008. World oil crunch looming? *Science* 322 (November 21): 1178–1179. www.sciencemag.org/cgi/content/summary/322/5905/1178.

Kessler, Glenn. 2009a. On Clinton's travels, a duality in style. *Washington Post,* March 8. www .washingtonpost.com/wp-dyn/content/article/2009/03/07/AR2009030701765.html.

———. 2009b. U.S. urges "multi-partner world": Secretary seeks to define approach. *Wash- ington Post,* July 16. www.washingtonpost.com/wp-dyn/content/article/2009/07/15/AR 2009071503163.html.

———. 2010. For some, a disquieting shift in U.S.-Israel ties. *Washington Post,* March 24. www.washingtonpost.com/wp-dyn/content/article/2010/03/23/AR2010032304312.html.

Kettle, Donald. 2007. *System under stress: Homeland security and American politics.* 2nd ed. Washington, D.C.: CQ Press.

Kiger, Patrick J. 1997. *Squeeze play: The United States, Cuba, and the Helms-Burton Act.* Washington, D.C.: The Center for Public Integrity.

Kilcullen, David, and Andrew Exum. 2009. Death from above, outrage down below. *New York Times,* May 16. www.nytimes.com/2009/05/17/opinion/17exum.html.

Kintisch, Eli. 2009. Stolen e-mails turn up heat on climate change rhetoric. *Science* 326 (December 4): 1329.

Kintisch, Eli, and Jeffrey Mervis. 2009. Holdren named science adviser, Varmus, Lander to co-chair PCAST. *Science* 323 (January 2): 22–23.

Kirk, Jason A. 2008. Indian-Americans and the U.S.-India nuclear agreement: Consolidation of an ethnic lobby? *Foreign Policy Analysis* 4: 275–300.

Kirk, Ron. 2009. Ambassador Kirk announces new initiatives for trade enforcement. Address at Mon Valley Steel Works, Edgar Thomson Plant, Pittsburgh, Pennsylvania, July 16. www.ustr.gov/about-us/press-office/speeches/transcripts/2009/july/ambassador-kirk-announces-new-initiatives-trade.

Kissinger, Henry, et al. 2009. U.S. must deploy more foreign diplomacy personnel. *Politico,* June 25. www.politico.com/news/stories/0609/24159.html.

Klare, Michael. 2002. *Resource wars: The new landscape of global conflict.* New York: Holt.

Klein, Aaron. 2010. Report: Obama undermines State in Syria talks. *WorldNetDaily,* July 19. www.wnd.com/index.php?pageId=104430.

Klein, Joe. 2009. Hillary's moment. *Time,* November 16, 24–33.

Klonsky, Joanna. 2009. Dennis C. Blair, director of national intelligence. *Council on Foreign Relations,* February 9. www.cfr.org/publication/18189/dennis_c_blair_director_of_national_intelligence.html.

Koger, Gregory. 2003. Position taking and cosponsorship in the U.S. House. *Legislative Studies Quarterly* 28 (2): 225–246.

Koh, Harold. 1990. *The national security Constitution.* New Haven, Conn.: Yale University Press.

Kornblut, Anne, Scott Wilson, and Karen DeYoung. 2009. Obama pressed for faster surge. *Washington Post,* December 6. www.washingtonpost.com/wp-dyn/content/article/2009/12/05/AR2009120501376.html.

Kovach, Gretel C. 2008. Five convicted in terrorism financing trial. *New York Times,* November 24. www.nytimes.com/2008/11/25/us/25charity.html.

Kraft, Michael E. 1994. Population policy. In *Encyclopedia of policy studies,* 2nd ed., ed. Stuart S. Nagel, 617–642. New York: Marcel Dekker.

———. 2010. Environmental policy in Congress. In *Environmental policy,* 7th ed., ed. Norman J. Vig and Michael E. Kraft, 99–124. Washington, D.C.: CQ Press.

———. 2011. *Environmental policy and politics.* 5th ed. New York: Pearson Longman.

Krauthammer, Charles. 2001. The Bush doctrine. *Weekly Standard,* June 4.

———. 2009. Travesty in New York. *Washington Post,* November 20. www.washingtonpost.com/wp-dyn/content/article/2009/11/19/AR2009111903434.html.

Krepinevich, Andrew, and Barry Watts. 2009. Lost at the NSC. *The National Interest* 99 (January): 63–72.

Kull, Steven, Clay Ramsay, Stephen Weber, and Evan Lewis. 2009. *America's global image in the Obama era.* Washington, D.C.: World Public Opinion.org. www.worldpublicopinion.org/pipa/pdf/jul09/WPO_USObama_Jul09_packet.pdf.

Kupchan, Charles, and Peter Trubowitz. 2007. Dead center: The demise of liberal internationalism in the United States. *International Security* 32 (Fall): 7–44.

Kurien, Prema. 2007. Who speaks for Indian Americans? Religion, ethnicity, and political formation. *American Quarterly* 59 (3): 759–783.

Lamb, Ramdas. 2010. Terrorism, fear and political correctness. *Washington Post*, July 21. http://newsweek.washingtonpost.com/onfaith/panelists/ramdas_lamb/2010/07/terrorism_fear_and_political_correctness.html.

Landler, Mark. 2009a. Appointing emissaries, Obama and Clinton stress diplomacy. *New York Times*, January 23. www.nytimes.com/2009/01/23/washington/23diplo.html.

———. 2009b. Clinton paints China policy with a green hue. *New York Times*, February 21. www.nytimes.com/2009/02/22/world/asia/22diplo.html.

———. 2009c. Reshaping diplomacy by tossing the script. *New York Times*, February 20. www.nytimes.com/2009/02/21/world/asia/21diplo.html.

———. 2010. Clinton pleads for patience at U.S.-Islamic World Forum. *New York Times*, February 14. www.nytimes.com/2010/02/15/world/middleeast/15diplo.html.

Landler, Mark, and Helene Cooper. 2010. After a bitter campaign, forging an alliance. *New York Times*, March 18. www.nytimes.com/2010/03/19/us/politics/19policy.html.

Laqueur, Walter. 1999. *The new terrorism: Fanaticism and the arms of mass destruction.* New York: Oxford University Press.

Last-minute disputes slow defense bill. 2006. In *CQ Almanac 2005.* Washington, D.C.: CQ Press. www.cqpress.com/reference/ (document ID cqal05-766-20104-1042287).

Layman, Geoffrey C., Thomas M. Carsey, and Juliana Menasce Horowitz. 2006. Party polarization in American politics: Characteristics, causes, and consequences. *Annual Review of Political Science* 9: 83–110.

Leaders' statement: The Pittsburgh summit. 2009. www.pittsburghsummit.gov/mediacenter/129639.htm.

Leahy, Michael, and Spencer S. Hsu. 2009. Nigerian arrested in failed jet attack; suspect claims Al Qaeda link; White House calls incident an attempted act of terrorism. *Washington Post*, December 26.

Lebovic, James, and Erik Voeten. 2006. The politics of shame. *International Studies Quarterly* 50 (4): 861–888.

Leffler, Melvyn P. 1992. *A preponderance of power: National security, the Truman administration, and the Cold War.* Stanford, Calif.: Stanford University Press.

———. 2004. Think again: Bush's foreign policy. *Foreign Policy*, September 1. www.foreignpolicy.com/articles/2004/09/01/think_again_bushs_foreign_policy/.

Leiserowitz, Anthony, Edward Maibach, Connie Roser-Renouf, and Nicholas Smith. 2010. *Climate change in the American mind: Public support for climate & energy policies in June 2010.* New Haven, Conn.: Yale Project on Climate Change Communication. http://environment.yale.edu/climate/files/PolicySupportJune2010.pdf.

Levy, Philip I. 2009. When it comes to trade, talk is not cheap. *The Enterprise Blog*, May 12. http://blog.american.com/?p=466.

Lewis, Joanna I., and Kelly Sims Gallagher. 2011. Energy and environment in China: Achievements and enduring challenges. In *The global environment: Institutions, law, and policy,* 3rd ed., ed. Regina S. Axelrod, Stacy D. VanDeveer, and David Leonard Downie, 259–284. Washington, D.C.: CQ Press.

Lindsay, James M. 1993. Congress and foreign policy: Why the Hill matters. *Political Science Quarterly* 107 (Winter): 607–628.

———. 1994. Congress, foreign policy, and the new institutionalism. *International Studies Quarterly* 38 (June): 281–304.

———. 2000. The new apathy: How an uninterested public is reshaping foreign policy. *Foreign Affairs* 79 (September/October): 2–8. www.foreignaffairs.com/articles/56425/james-m-lindsay/the-new-apathy-how-an-uninterested-public-is-reshaping-foreign-p/.

———. 2002. Getting Uncle Sam's ear: Will ethnic lobbies cramp America's foreign policy style? *Brookings Review* (Winter): 37–40. www.brookings.edu/articles/2002/winter_diplomacy_lindsay.aspx.

Lipset, Seymour Martin. 1996. *American exceptionalism: A two-edged sword.* New York: W. W. Norton.

Lizza, Ryan. 2004. Havana John. *The New Republic,* July 26, 10–11. www.tnr.com/article/havana-john.

———. 2009. Inside the crisis: Larry Summers and the White House economic team. *New Yorker,* October 12.

Lobe, Jim. 2010. Sanctions, "regime change" take centre stage. Inter Press Service, January 27. http://ipsnews.net/news.asp?idnews=50131.

The London Summit 2009. 2009. *Global plan for recovery and reform: The communiqué from the London Summit.* www.londonsummit.gov.uk/en/summit-aims/summit-communique.

Longmyer, Kenneth. 1985. Black Americans' demands. *Foreign Policy* 60: 3–18.

Loomis, Burdett A., and Wendy J. Schiller. 2005. *The contemporary Congress.* 5th ed. Belmont, Calif.: Wadsworth.

Lowenthal, Mark M. 2009. *Intelligence: From secrets to policy.* Washington, D.C.: CQ Press.

MacEachin, Douglas J. 1997. The record versus the charges: CIA assessments of the Soviet Union. *Studies in Intelligence* 40 (5): 57–65. https://www.cia.gov/library/center-for-the-study-of-intelligence/kent-csi/vol40no5/pdf/v40i5a08p.pdf.

MacFarquhar, Neil. 2008. Donors' aid to poor nations declines, U.N. reports. *New York Times,* September 4. www.nytimes.com/2008/09/05/world/05nations.html.

Maltzman, Forrest. 1998. Maintaining congressional committees: Sources of member support. *Legislative Studies Quarterly* 23 (May): 197–218.

Mandelbaum, Michael, 2005. *The case for Goliath: How America acts as the world's government in the 21st century.* New York: Public Affairs.

Mann, James. 2004. *The rise of the Vulcans: The history of Bush's war cabinet.* New York: Viking.

Marrar, Khalil. 2009. *The Arab lobby and U.S. foreign policy.* New York: Routledge.

Martins, Mark S. 2005. The Commander's Emergency Response Program. *Joint Forces Quarterly* 37 (April): 46–52.

Matthew, Richard A. 2010. Environmental security. In *Environmental policy,* 7th ed., ed. Norman J. Vig and Michael E. Kraft, 327–348. Washington, D.C.: CQ Press.

Mayer, Jane. 2008. *The dark side: The inside story of how the war on terror turned into a war on American ideals.* New York: Doubleday.

———. 2010. The trial. *New Yorker,* February 15.

Mayhew, David R. 2005. Actions in the public sphere. In *The legislative branch*, ed. Paul J. Quirk and Sarah A. Binder. New York: Annenberg Foundation Trust at Sunnylands/ Oxford University Press.

Mazmanian, Daniel A., and Michael E. Kraft, eds. 2009. *Toward sustainable communities: Transitions and transformation in environmental policy.* 2nd ed. Cambridge, Mass.: MIT Press.

Mazzetti, Mark (with Charlie Savage and Jeff Zeleny). 2009a. Obama seeks to mend a party rift over Panetta. *New York Times,* January 7. http://query.nytimes.com/gst/fullpage .html?res=9405E0DA153DF934A35752C0A96F9C8B63&ref=stephen_r_kappes.

———. 2009b. Panetta open to tougher methods in some C.I.A. interrogation. *New York Times,* February 5. www.nytimes.com/2009/02/06/us/politics/06cia.html.

Mazzetti, Mark, and Carl Huse. 2009. Panetta chosen as chief of C.I.A. in surprise step. *New York Times,* January 6. http://query.nytimes.com/gst/fullpage.html?res=9B01E4D6123 CF935A35752C0A96F9C8B63.

McClellan, Charles. 2009. *What happened.* New York: Public Affairs.

McLaughlin, John. 2008. Serving the national policymaker. In *Analyzing intelligence: Origins, obstacles, and innovations,* ed. Roger Z. George and James B. Bruce, 71–81. Washington, D.C.: Georgetown University Press.

McManus, Doyle. 2010. Broken "engagement" in the Middle East. *Los Angeles Times,* February 21. http://articles.latimes.com/2010/feb/21/opinion/la-oe-mcmanus21-2010feb21.

McMichael, Anthony J. 2008. Population, human resources, health, and the environment: Getting the balance right. *Environment* 50 (January/February): 46–59.

McNearney, Michael J. 2005. Stabilization and reconstruction in Afghanistan: Are PRTs a model or a muddle? *Parameters* 35 (Winter): 32–46.

Meacham, Jon. 2009. The interviews: Hillary Clinton and Henry Kissinger. *Newsweek,* December 28, 41–49. www.newsweek.com/2009/12/20/meeting-of-the-diplomats. html.

Mead, Walter Russell. 2010. "Bush did it too." What does it mean? What does it prove? [post in The Arena]. *Politico,* February 11. www.politico.com/arena/archive/bush-did-it-too .html.

Mearsheimer, John J., and Stephen M. Walt. 2007. *The Israel lobby and U.S. foreign policy.* New York: Farrar, Straus, and Giroux.

Melanson, Richard. 2005. *American foreign policy since the Vietnam War: The search for consensus from Richard Nixon to George W. Bush.* 4th ed. Armonk, N.Y.: M. E. Sharpe.

Mendes, Elizabeth. 2009. Prior to bomb scare, worry about terrorism at 39%. Gallup .org, December 29. www.gallup.com/poll/124892/Prior-Bomb-Scare-Worry-Terrorism .aspx.

Mercado, Stephen C. 2004. Sailing the sea of OSINT in the Information Age. *Studies in Intelligence* 48 (3): 45–56. https://www.cia.gov/library/center-for-the-study-of-intelligence/csi-publications/csi-studies/studies/vol48no3/article05.html.

Meunier, Sophie. 2010. Anti-Americanism and the financial crisis. Paper presented at the meeting of the International Studies Association, New Orleans, Louisiana, February 19.

Millennium Ecosystem Assessment. 2005. *Ecosystems and human well-being: General synthesis.* Washington, D.C.: Island Press. www.millenniumassessment.org/en/Synthesis .aspx.

Miller, Greg. 2009a. Interrogation documents provide fodder to both sides: Key intelligence was obtained from terror suspects, but whether harsh CIA methods helped isn't clear. *Los Angeles Times,* August 26. http://articles.latimes.com/2009/aug/26/nation/na-cia26/.

———. 2009b. The nation: CIA spy missions will be reviewed. *Los Angeles Times,* November 17. http://articles.latimes.com/2009/nov/17/nation/na-cia17/.

Morley, Morris H., and Christopher McGillion. 2002. *Unfinished business: America and Cuba after the Cold War, 1989–2001.* New York: Cambridge University Press.

Mueller, John E. 1973. *War, presidents, and public opinion.* New York: Wiley.

Mullen, Michael G. 2009. Remarks by Adm. Mike Mullen, Chairman of the Joint Chiefs of Staff. Address at Princeton University, Woodrow Wilson School of Public and International Affairs, Princeton, New Jersey, February 5. www.jcs.mil/speech.aspx?ID=1041.

———. 2010. Admiral Mullén's speech on Military Strategy. Address at Kansas State University, Fort Leavenworth, March. www.cfr.org/publication/21611/admiral_mullens_speech_on_military_strategy_ft_leavenworth_march_2010.html.

Murdock, Clark A., Michèle A. Flournoy, Christopher A. Williams, and Kurt M. Campbell (with Michael A. Coss, Adam N. Marks, and Richard W. Weitz). 2004. *Beyond Goldwater-Nichols Project: Defense reform for a new strategic era; Phase I report.* http://csis.org/publication/beyond-goldwater-nichols-phase-i-report.

Murray, Shailagh. 2008. Obama joins fellow senators in passing new wiretapping measure. *Washington Post,* July 10. www.washingtonpost.com/wp-dyn/content/story/2008/07/09/ST2008070902472.html.

Myers, Steven Lee, and Carl Hulse. 2008. Bush lifts moratorium on offshore drilling. *New York Times,* July 14. www.nytimes.com/2008/07/14/washington/14drillcnd.html.

Nathan, James A., and James K. Oliver. 1994. *Foreign policy making and the American political system.* Baltimore, Md.: Johns Hopkins University Press.

National Commission on Terrorist Attacks Upon the United States. 2004. *The 9/11 Commission report.* New York: W. W. Norton.

National security strategy. 2010. Washington, D.C.: The White House. www.whitehouse.gov/sites/default/files/rss_viewer/national_security_strategy.pdf.

The national security strategy of the United States of America. 2002. Washington, D.C.: The White House. http://georgewbush-whitehouse.archives.gov/nsc/nss/2002/.

The national strategy for combating terrorism. 2006. Washington, D.C.: The White House. http://georgewbush-whitehouse.archives.gov/nsc/nsct/2006.

Nau, Henry R. 1990. *The myth of America's decline.* New York: Oxford University Press.

NBC News' *Meet the Press.* 2001. Dick Cheney on *Meet the Press*: Transcript for Sept. 16 [rush transcript]. www.freerepublic.com/focus/f-news/525111/posts.

Neustadt, Richard A. 1960. *Presidential power: The politics of leadership.* New York: John Wiley.

New York Times Editorial Board. 2009. Obama's outreach to Muslims [editorial]. *New York Times* The Board, January 28. http://theboard.blogs.nytimes.com/2009/01/28/obamas-outreach-to-muslims.

Nielsen, Kirk. 2004. Politics and policy: With its severe new Cuba regulations, the Bush administration alienated some Miami exiles, but not the ones who matter. *Miami New Times,* July 29. www.miaminewtimes.com/2004-07-29/news/politics-and-policy.

Noftsinger, John B., Jr., Kenneth F. Newbold Jr., and Jack K. Wheeler. 2007. *Understanding homeland security: Policy, perspectives, and paradoxes.* New York: Palgrave Macmillan.

Nokken, Timothy P. 2000. Dynamics of congressional loyalty: Party defection and roll-call behavior, 1947–97. *Legislative Studies Quarterly* 25 (August): 417–444.

Norwegian Nobel Committee. 2009. Announcement: Nobel Peace Prize for 2009. http:// nobelpeaceprize.org/en_GB/home/announce-2009.

NSA program prompts flurry of bills. 2007. In *CQ Almanac 2006*. Washington, D.C.: CQ Press. www.cqpress.com/reference/ (document ID cqa106-1421234).

Nye, Joseph S., Jr. 1994. *Soft power: The means to success in world politics.* New York: Public Affairs.

Obama, Barack. 2007a. Renewing American leadership. *Foreign Affairs* 86 (July/August): 2–16.

———. 2007b. The war we need to win. Remarks at the Woodrow Wilson Center, Washington, D.C., August 1. www.barackobama.com/2007/08/01/the_war_we_need_to_win.php.

———. 2009a. Address to Joint Session of Congress, Washington, D.C., February 24. www.whitehouse.gov/the_press_office/Remarks-of-President-Barack-Obama-Address-to-Joint-Session-of-Congress.

———. 2009b. Executive order: Ensuring lawful interrogations. www.whitehouse.gov/ the_press_office/Ensuring_Lawful_Interrogations.

———. 2009c. Inaugural address, Washington, D.C., January 21. www.whitehouse.gov/ blog/inaugural-address.

———. 2009d. 2009. Interview by Chris Wallace, *Fox News Sunday*. February 3. www .foxnews.com/story/0,2933,487865,00.html.

———. 2009e. Was C. News conference, ExCel Center, London, England, April 2. www .whitehouse.gov/the_press_office/News-Conference-by-President-Obama-4-02-09.

———. 2009f. The president on preliminary findings regarding the attempted terrorist attack. Remarks at Kaneohe Bay Marine Base in Kaneohe, Hawaii, December 29. www .whitehouse.gov/blog/2009/12/29/president-preliminary-findings-regarding-attempted-terrorist-attack.

———. 2009g. Presidential policy directive (PPD) 1. www.fas.org/irp/offdocs/ppd/ppd-1. pdf.

———. 2009h. Remarks by President Obama at Strasbourg Town Hall, Strasbourg, France, April 3. www.whitehouse.gov/the_press_office/Remarks-by-President-Obama-at-Strasbourg-Town-Hall.

———. 2009i. Remarks by President Barack Obama, Hradcany Square, Prague, Czech Republic, April 5. www.whitehouse.gov/the_press_office/Remarks-By-President-Barack-Obama-In-Prague-As-Delivered.

———. 2009j. Remarks by President Obama to the Turkish Parliament, Ankara, Turkey, April 6. www.whitehouse.gov/the_press_office/Remarks-By-President-Obama-To-The-Turkish-Parliament.

———. 2009k. Remarks by the president at the acceptance of the Nobel Peace Prize, Oslo, Norway, December 10. www.whitehouse.gov/the-press-office/remarks-president-acceptance-nobel-peace-prize.

———. 2009l. Remarks by the president at the New Economic School Graduation, Gostinny Dvor, Moscow, Russia, July 7. www.whitehouse.gov/the_press_office/remarks-by-the-president-at-the-new-economic-school-graduation.

————. 2009m. Remarks by the president at the United Nations Security Council summit on nuclear non-proliferation and nuclear disarmament, New York, September 24. www.whitehouse.gov/the_press_office/Remarks-By-The-President-At-the-UN-Sec urity-Council-Summit-On-Nuclear-Non-Proliferation-And-Nuclear-Disarmament.

————. 2009n. Remarks by the president in address to the nation on the way forward in Afghanistan and Pakistan. Address at the U.S. Military Academy at West Point, West Point, New York, December 1. www.whitehouse.gov/the-press-office/remarks-president-address-nation-way-forward-afghanistan-and-pakistan.

————. 2009o. Remarks by the president on a new beginning. Address at Cairo University, Cairo, Egypt, June 4. www.whitehouse.gov/the-press-office/remarks-president-cairo-university-6-04-09.

————. 2009p. Remarks by the president to the Ghanaian Parliament, Accra, Ghana, July 11. www.whitehouse.gov/the_press_office/Remarks-by-the-President-to-the-Ghanaian-Parliament.

————. 2009q. Remarks on national security. Address at the National Archives, Washington, D.C., May 21. www.whitehouse.gov/the_press_office/Remarks-by-the-President-On-National-Security-5-21-09.

————. 2009r. Statement of President Barack Obama on release of OLC memos, April 16. Washington, D.C.: White House, Office of the Press Secretary. www.whitehouse.gov/the_press_office/Statement-of-President-Barack-Obama-on-Release-of-OLC-Memos.

————. 2009s. Videotaped remarks by the president in celebration of Nowruz, Washington, D.C., March 20. www.whitehouse.gov/the_press_office/Videotaped-Remarks-by-The-President-in-Celebration-of-Nowruz.

————. 2010a. Remarks by the president in address to the nation on the end of combat operations in Iraq, Oval Office, White House, Washington, D.C., August 31. www .whitehouse.gov/the-press-office/2010/08/31/remarks-president-address-nation-end-combat-operations-iraq.

————. 2010b. Remarks by the president on strengthening intelligence and aviation security, Washington, D.C., January 7. www.whitehouse.gov/the-press-office/remarks-president-strengthening-intelligence-and-aviation-security.

————. 2010c. State of the Union address. Address to U.S. Congress, Washington, D.C., January 27. www.whitehouse.gov/the-press-office/remarks-president-state-union-address.

O'Donnell, Pierce. 2005. *In time of war.* New York: New Press.

Office of the U.S. Trade Representative. 2010. U.S.-Canada joint statement on government procurement. www.ustr.gov/about-us/press-office/press-releases/2010/february.

Omnibus bill wraps up 2004. 2005. In *CQ Almanac 2004.* Washington, D.C.: CQ Press. www.cqpress.com/reference (document ID cqa104-836-24361-1084891).

Open Secrets. 2010. [Search U.S.-Cuba Democracy PAC]. www.opensecrets.org/pacs/look up2.php?strID=C00387720&cycle=2010.

Ornstein, Norman J. 2010. A very productive Congress, despite what the approval ratings say. *Washington Post,* January 31. www.washingtonpost.com/wp-dyn/content/article/2010/01/29/AR2010012902516.html.

Otterman, Sharon. 2009. U.S. opens way to ease sanctions against Syria. *New York Times,* July 28. www.nytimes.com/2009/07/29/world/middleeast/29syria.html.

Page, Benjamin, and Marshall M. Bouton. 2006. *The foreign policy disconnect.* Chicago: University of Chicago Press.

Paletta, Damian, and Jonathan Weisman (with David Wessel). 2010. Proposal set to curb bank giants. *Wall Street Journal,* January 21. http://online.wsj.com/article/SB10001424 052748704320104575015910344117800.html.

Patrick, Stewart, and Kaysie Brown. 2007. *The Pentagon and global development: Making sense of DoD's expanding role* (working paper 131). Washington, D.C.: Center for Global Development. www.cgdev.org/content/general/detail/14815.

Patriot Act renewed after skirmish. 2007. In *CQ Almanac 2006.* Washington, D.C.: CQ Press. www.cqpress.com/reference/ (document ID cqa106-1421258).

Paul, David M., and Rachel Anderson Paul. 2009. *Ethnic lobbies and U.S. foreign policy.* Boulder, Colo.: Lynne Rienner.

Peck, Edward. 2007. Chief-of-mission authority: A powerful but underused tool. *Foreign Service Journal* 84 (December): 29–32.

Peleg, Ilan. 2009. *The legacy of George W. Bush's foreign policy.* Boulder, Colo.: Westview.

Perine, Keith. 2010. Bush-era terrorism law gets Obama-era support. *CQ Weekly,* February 1.

Perle, Richard. 2002. Why the West must strike first against Saddam Hussein. *Daily Telegraph,* August 9. www.telegraph.co.uk/comment/personal-view/3580181/Why-the-West-must-strike-first-against-Saddam-Hussein.html.

Pew Global Attitudes Project. 2004. A year after Iraq War: Mistrust of America in Europe ever higher, Muslim anger persists. http://people-press.org/report/206/a-year-after-iraq-war.

———. 2007. *Global unease with major world powers.* Washington, D.C.: The Pew Global Attitudes Project. http://pewglobal.org/files/pdf/256.pdf.

———. 2009. *Confidence in Obama lifts U.S. image around the world.* Washington, D.C.: The Pew Global Attitudes Project. http://pewglobal.org/files/pdf/264.pdf.

Pew Research Center for the People & the Press. 2008a. Declining public support for global engagement, even as optimism about Iraq surges. http://people-press.org/report/453/declining-public-support-global-engagement.

———. 2008b. *Obama image slips, his lead over Clinton disappears; public support for free trade declines* (Section 4: Trade and the economy). http://people-press.org/report/414/obamas-image-slips-his-lead-over-clinton-disappears.

——— (with the Council on Foreign Relations). 2009a. *America's place in the world 2009: An investigation of public and leadership opinion about international affairs.* Washington, D.C.: The Pew Research Center for the People & the Press. http://people-press.org/reports/pdf/569.pdf.

———. 2009b. Support for free trade recovers despite recession. http://people-press.org/report/511/free-trade-support-recovers.

———. 2010. Public remains conflicted over Islam. http://pewresearch.org/pubs/1706/poll-americans-views-of-muslims-object-to-new-york-islamic-center-islam-violence.

Pfiffner, James P. 2009. *Torture as public policy: Restoring U.S. credibility on the world stage.* Boulder, Colo.: Paradigm.

Pillar, Paul R. 2004. *Terrorism and U.S. foreign policy.* Washington, D.C.: Brookings Institution.

Pincus, Walter. 2009a. Foreign policy beyond the Pentagon. *Washington Post,* February 9. www.washingtonpost.com/wp-dyn/content/article/2009/02/08/AR2009020801852 .html.

———. 2009b. Intelligence pick blames "Israel lobby" for withdrawal. *Washington Post,* March 12. www.washingtonpost.com/wp-dyn/content/article/2009/03/11/AR200903110 4308.html.

———. 2009c. Settling an intelligence turf war. *Washington Post,* November 17. www.washing tonpost.com/wp-dyn/content/article/2009/11/16/AR2009111603636.html.

Pious, Richard M. 1979. *The American presidency.* New York: Basic Books.

———. 2008. *Why presidents fail.* Lanham, Md.: Rowman and Littlefield.

Pollack, Kenneth M. 2010. Five myths about the Iraq troop withdrawal. *Washington Post,* August 22. www.washingtonpost.com/wp-dyn/content/article/2010/08/19/AR20100 81905642.html.

Pollard, Vincent Kelly. 2004. *Globalization, democratization and Asian leadership: Power sharing, foreign and society in the Philippines and Japan.* London: Ashgate.

PollingReport.com. 2010a. *Afghanistan: CNN/Opinion Research Corporation poll, Sept. 1–2, 2010.* www.pollingreport.com/afghan.htm.

———. 2016. *Iraq: CNN/Opinion Research Corporation poll, Sept. 1–2, 2010.* www.polling report.com/iraq.htm.

Pomfret, John. 2010. China's lobbying efforts yield new influence, openness on Capitol Hill. *New York Times,* January 9. www.washingtonpost.com/wp-dyn/content/article/2010/ 01/08/AR2010010803710.html.

Population Reference Bureau. 2010. *2010 world population data sheet.* www.prb.org/ pdf10/10wpds_eng.pdf.

Posen, Barry. 2003. Command of the commons: The military foundation of U.S. hegemony. *International Security* 28 (Summer): 5–46.

Posner, Richard A. 2006. *Not a suicide pact: The Constitution in a time of national emergency.* New York: Oxford University Press.

Powlick, Philip J., and Andrew Z. Katz. 1998. Defining the American public opinion/foreign policy nexus. *Mershon International Studies Review* 42 (May): 29–61.

Prashad, Vijay. 2007. Obama and outsourcing. *Counterpunch,* July 4. www.counterpunch .org/prashad07042007.html.

President prevails on Iraq War policy. 2008. In *CQ Almanac 2007.* Washington, D.C.: CQ Press. www.cqpress.com/reference (document ID cqa107-1006-44915-2048031).

Priest, Dana. 2004. *The mission: Waging war and keeping peace with America's military.* New York: W. W. Norton.

———. 2009. Bush's "war" on terror comes to a sudden end. *Washington Post,* January 23. www.washingtonpost.com/wp-dyn/content/article/2009/01/22/AR2009012203929. html.

Pringle, Robert. 1977–78. Creeping irrelevance at Foggy Bottom. *Foreign Policy* 29 (Winter): 129–139.

Quinnipiac University Polling Institute. 2010. *February 10, 2010.* www.quinnipiac.edu/x1295 .xml?ReleaseID=1422.

Radelet, Steven. 2003. Bush and foreign aid. *Foreign Affairs* 82 (September/October): 104–117.

Rademaker, Stephen G. 2010. This is no way to approve the New START treaty. *Washington Post*, August 20. www.washingtonpost.com/wp-dyn/content/article/2010/08/19/AR 2010081905214.html.

Rasul v. Bush. 542 U.S. 466 (2004).

Rasul v. Myers. 130 S. Ct. 1013 (2009).

Reidel, Bruce. 2009. *White paper of the Interagency Policy Group's report on U.S. policy toward Afghanistan and Pakistan.* www.whitehouse.gov/assets/documents/afghanistan_pakistan_ white_paper_final.pdf.

Renan, Ernst. 1996. What is a nation? In *Becoming national: A reader,* ed. Geoff Eley and Ronald Grigor Suny, 41–55. New York: Oxford University Press.

Renshon, Jonathan. 2008. Stability and change in belief systems: The operational code of George W. Bush. *Journal of Conflict Resolution* 52 (December): 820–849.

Renshon, Stanley. 2008. Psychological reflections on Barack Obama and John McCain: Assessing the contours of a new presidential administration. *Political Science Quarterly* 123 (Fall): 391–433.

Revkin, Andrew C. 2008a. Shift in the debate over global warming. *New York Times,* April 6. www.nytimes.com/2008/04/06/weekinreview/06revkin.html.

———. 2008b. Under pressure, White House issues climate change report. *New York Times,* May 30. www.nytimes.com/2008/05/30/washington/30climate.html.

———. 2008c. World Bank criticized on environmental efforts. *New York Times,* July 22. www.nytimes.com/2008/07/22/science/earth/23enviro.html.

———. 2009a. Environment issues slide in poll of public's concerns. *New York Times,* January 23. www.nytimes.com/2009/01/23/science/earth/23warm.html.

———. 2009b. First trip for Clinton aims at China, climate. *New York Times Dot Earth,* February 4. http://dotearth.blogs.nytimes.com/2009/02/04/first-trip-for-clinton-aims-at-china-climate.

———. 2009c. Obama aide concedes climate law must wait. *New York Times,* October 2. www.nytimes.com/2009/10/03/us/politics/03climate.html.

Revkin, Andrew C., and John M. Broder. 2009. Facing skeptics, climate experts sure of peril. *New York Times,* December 6. www.nytimes.com/2009/12/07/science/earth/07climate .html.

Richardson, Bill. 1985. Hispanic American concerns. *Foreign Policy* 60 (Autumn): 30–39.

Richey, Warren. 2009. Obama's Guantánamo, counterterror policies similar to Bush's? *Christian Science Monitor,* October 16. www.csmonitor.com/USA/2009/1016/p02s07-usgn.html.

Richter, Paul. 2009. Hillary Clinton's star power overshadowed, analysts say. *Los Angeles Times,* July 16. http://articles.latimes.com/2009/jul/16/world/fg-clinton16.

Rieff, David. 2008. Will Little Havana go blue? *New York Times Magazine,* July 13. www .nytimes.com/2008/07/13/magazine/13CUBANS-t.html.

Rieselbach, Leroy N. 1995. *Congressional politics: The evolving legislative system.* 2nd ed. Boulder, Colo.: Westview.

Ripley, Randall B., and Grace A. Franklin. 1990. *Congress, the bureaucracy, and public policy.* 5th ed. Boston: Houghton Mifflin.

Ripley, Randall B., and James M. Lindsay. 1993. Foreign and defense policy in Congress: An overview and preview. In *Congress resurgent: Foreign and defense policy on Capitol*

Hill, ed. Randall B. Ripley and James M. Lindsay. Ann Arbor: University of Michigan Press, 3–14.

Roberts, J. Timmons, Bradley C. Parks, Michael J. Tierney, and Robert L. Hicks. 2009. Has foreign aid been greened? *Environment* 51 (January/February): 8–19. www.environ mentmagazine.org/Archives/Back%20Issues/January-February%202009/RobertsParks TierneyHicks-full.html.

Rockman, Bert A. 1981. America's Departments of State: Irregular and regular syndromes of policy making. *American Political Science Review* 75 (December): 911–927.

Rohde, David W. 2005. Committees and policy formulation. In *The legislative branch,* ed. Paul J. Quirk and Sarah A. Binder. New York: Oxford University Press, 201–223.

Rosati, Jerel A., and James M. Scott. 2010. *The politics of United States foreign policy.* 5th ed. New York: Cengage.

Rosen, Steven J. 2009. Puneet Talwar to head NSC Near East Affairs; was Elliot Abrams. *Middle East Forum,* January 12. www.meforum.org/blog/obama-mideast-monitor/ 2009/01/puneet-talwar-to-head-nsc-near-east-affairs.html.

Rosenbach, Eric. 2008. The incisive fight: Recommendations for improving counterterror- ism intelligence. *Annals of the American Academy of Political and Social Science* 618: 133–147.

Rosenthal, Elizabeth. 2008. U.S. transition hampers talks on climate change. *New York Times,* December 10. www.nytimes.com/2008/12/11/world/europe/11climate.html.

Roth, Kenneth. 2010. Obama's hesitant embrace of human rights. *New York Times,* March 3. www.nytimes.com/2010/03/04/opinion/04iht-edroth.html.

Rothkopf, David J. 2005. *Running the world: The inside story of the National Security Council and the architects of American power.* New York: Public Affairs.

———. 2009a. A thousand envoys bloom. *The National Interest* 101 (May): 15–26.

———. 2009b. Forget the 3 a.m. phone call: Hillary Clinton is quietly revolutionizing Amer- ican foreign policy. *Washington Post National Weekly Edition,* August 31–September 6, 25–26.

———. 2009c. It's 3 a.m. Do you know where Hillary Clinton is? *Washington Post,* August 23. www.washingtonpost.com/wp-dyn/content/article/2009/08/21/AR2009082101772 .html.

Rozen, Laura. 2009a. India's stealth lobbying against Holbrooke's brief. *Foreign Policy,* Janu- ary 24. http://thecable.foreignpolicy.com/posts/2009/01/23/india_s_stealth_lobbying_ against_holbrooke.

———. 2009b. Obama White House pow-wow with American Jewish groups. *Foreign Policy,* July 13. http://thecable.foreignpolicy.com/posts/2009/07/13/obama_white_ house_powwow_with_american_jewish_groups.

———. 2009c. Puneet Talwar to NSC. *Foreign Policy,* February 10. http://thecable.foreign policy.com/posts/2009/02/09/puneet_talwar_to_nsc.

———. 2010. Appointments: NSC South Asia senior director. *Politico,* January 8. http:// dyn.politico.com/blogs/laurarozen/index.cfm/category/India.

Rubenzer, Trevor. 2008a. Campaign contributions and U.S. foreign policy outcomes: An analysis of Cuban-American and Armenian-American interests. Paper presented at the annual meeting of the International Studies Association, San Francisco, California, March 29.

—————. 2008b. Ethnic minority interest group attributes and U.S. foreign policy influence: A qualitative comparative analysis. *Foreign Policy Analysis* 4: 169–185.

Rubin, Barry. 1987. *Secrets of State: The State Department and the struggle over U.S. foreign policy.* New York: Oxford University Press.

Ruggie, John Gerard. 2006. Doctrinal unilateralism and its limits: America and global governance in the new century. In *American foreign policy in a globalized world,* ed. David P. Forsythe, Patrice C. McMahon, and Andrew Wedeman, 31–50. New York: Routledge.

Sadd, David J., and G. Neal Lendenmann. 1985. Arab American grievances. *Foreign Policy* 60: 17–30.

Samuelsohn, Darren. 2009. Boxer, Kerry set to introduce climate bill in Senate. *New York Times,* September 28. www.nytimes.com/cwire/2009/09/28/28climatewire-boxer-kerry-set-to-introduce-climate-bill-in-43844.html.

Sands, Amy. 2005. Integrating open sources into transnational threat assessments. In *Transforming U.S. intelligence,* ed. Jennifer E. Sims and Burton Gerber, 63–78. Washington, D.C.: Georgetown University Press.

Sands, Philippe. 2008. *Torture team: Rumsfeld's memo and the betrayal of American values.* New York: Palgrave Macmillan.

Savage, Charlie. 2007. *Takeover: The return of the imperial presidency and the subversion of American democracy.* New York: Little, Brown.

—————. 2009. To critics, new policy on terror looks old. *New York Times,* July 1. www .nytimes.com/2009/07/02/us/02gitmo.html.

Schatz, J. J. 2008. 2008 legislative summary, free-trade agreements. *CQ Weekly,* December 8, 3285.

Scherer, Michael. 2009a. At home abroad. *Time,* April 20, 23.

—————. 2009b. The deference debate. *Time,* November 30, 18.

Schiffer, Adam J. 2006. Blogswarms and press norms: News coverage of the Downing Street memo controversy. *Journalism and Mass Communication Quarterly* 83 (3): 496–512.

—————. 2007. Between pajamas and Pulitzers: Distributed gatekeeping and the potential of blogs as news media. Address to the Annual Meeting of the American Political Science Association, Chicago, August 30. www.allacademic.com/meta/p208737_index .html.

Schlesinger, Arthur M., Jr. 1973. *The imperial presidency.* Boston: Houghton Mifflin.

—————. 2004. *The imperial presidency* (with new introduction). Boston: Mariner Books/ Houghton Mifflin.

Schmitt, Eric, and Mark Mazzetti. 2009. U.S. relies more on allies in questioning terror suspects. *New York Times,* May 23. www.nytimes.com/2009/05/24/world/24intel .html.

Schneider, William. 1983. Conservatism, not interventionism: Trends in foreign policy opinion. In *Eagle defiant: United States foreign policy in the 1980s,* ed. Kenneth A. Oye, Robert J. Leiber, and Donald Rothchild, 33–64. Boston: Little, Brown.

—————. 1987. "Rambo" and reality: Having it both ways. In *Eagle resurgent? The Reagan era in American foreign policy,* ed. Kenneth A. Oye, Robert J. Leiber, and Donald Rothchild, 41–74. Boston: Little, Brown.

—————. 2001. Elián González defeated Al Gore. *The Atlantic,* May. www.theatlantic.com/ politics/nj/schneider2001-05-02.htm.

Schoultz, Lars. 2009. *The United States and the Cuban revolution: That infernal little Cuban republic.* Chapel Hill: University of North Carolina Press.

Schulz, William F. 2008. *U.S. policy for a new era: The future of human rights.* Philadelphia: University of Pennsylvania Press.

Scott, Andrew M. 1975. The problem of the State Department. In *Problems of American Foreign Policy*, 2nd ed., ed. Martin B. Hickman, 143–151. Beverly Hills: Glencoe Press.

Scott, James M. 1997. In the loop: Congressional influence in American foreign policy. *Journal of Political and Military Sociology* 25 (Summer): 47–76.

Scott, James M., and Ralph G. Carter. 2002. Acting on the Hill: Congressional assertiveness in U.S. foreign policy. *Congress & the Presidency* 29 (2): 151–169.

Selin, Henrik, and Stacy D. VanDeveer. 2010. Global climate change: Kyoto and beyond. In *Environmental policy,* 7th ed., ed. Norman J. Vig and Michael E. Kraft, 265–285. Washington, D.C.: CQ Press.

Sewell, Dan. 2009. Indian-American profile up, from politics to film. Associated Press, February 28. Available at http://seattletimes.nwsource.com/html/nationworld/2008797104_aphighprofileindians.html.

Shane, Scott. 2009. Shadow of 9/11 is cast again. *New York Times,* December 30. www.nytimes.com/2009/12/31/us/31intel.html.

Shapiro, Ari. 2010. Roadblocks may keep Guantánamo prison open. *NPR News: All Things Considered,* February 2. www.npr.org/templates/transcript/transcript.php?storyId=123268250.

Shaughnessy, Larry. 2008. CIA, FBI push "Facebook for Spies." *CNN.com*, September 5. http://articles.cnn.com/2008-09-05/tech/facebook.spies_1_facebook-social-networking-site-space?_s=PM:TECH.

Sheridan, Mary Beth. 2009. Clinton: U.S. drug policies failed, fueled Mexico's drug wars. *Washington Post,* March 26. www.washingtonpost.com/wp-dyn/content/article/2009/03/25/AR2009032501034.html.

Sherman, Jack. 2010. Boehner: Obama has "pre-9/11 mentality." *Politico,* February 4. www.politico.com/news/stories/0210/32536.html.

Sidoti, Liz. 2009. AP-GfK poll: Gains for Obama, not his Afghan plans. Associated Press, December 16. Available at http://abcnews.go.com/Politics/wireStory?id=9353716.

Silber, Mitchell D., and Arvin Bhatt. 2007. *Radicalization in the West: The homegrown threat.* New York: New York Police Department. www.nypdshield.org/public/SiteFiles/documents/NYPD_Report-Radicalization_in_the_West.pdf.

Silverstein, Gordon. 1994. Judicial enhancement of executive power. In *The president, the Congress, and the making of foreign policy,* ed. Paul E. Peterson. Norman: University of Oklahoma Press, 23–45.

Simon, James Monnier, Jr. 2005. Managing domestic, military, and foreign policy requirements: Correcting Frankenstein's blunder. In *Transforming U.S. intelligence,* ed. Jennifer E. Sims and Burton Gerber, 149–161. Washington, D.C.: Georgetown University Press.

———. 2010. Lecture at Georgetown University, Washington, D.C., February 29.

Simon, Steven. 2008. The price of the surge. *Foreign Affairs* (May/June). www.foreignaffairs.com/articles/63398/steven-simon/the-price-of-the-surge.

Simpson, Glenn R., and Amy Chozick. 2008. Obama's Muslim-outreach adviser resigns. *Wall Street Journal,* August 6. http://online.wsj.com/article/SB121797906741214995.html.

Sims, Jennifer E. 2005. Transforming U.S. espionage: A contrarian's approach. *Georgetown Journal of International Affairs* 6 (1): 53–59.

———. 2006. Foreign intelligence liaison: Devils, deals, and details. *International Journal of Intelligence and Counter Intelligence* 19 (2): 195–217.

———. 2009. A theory of intelligence and international politics. In *National intelligence systems: Current research and future prospects,* ed. Gregory F. Treverton and Wilhelm Agrel, 58–92. Cambridge, UK: Cambridge University Press.

Sims, Jennifer, and Burton Gerber, eds. 2009. *Vaults, mirrors and masks: Rediscovering U.S. counterintelligence.* Washington, D.C.: Georgetown University Press.

Sinclair, Barbara. 1993. Congressional party leaders in the foreign and defense policy arena. In *Congress resurgent: Foreign and defense policy on Capitol Hill,* ed. Randall Ripley and James Lindsay. Ann Arbor: University of Michigan Press, 207–233.

———. 2005. Parties and leadership in the House. In *The legislative branch,* ed. Paul J. Quirk and Sarah A. Binder. New York: Oxford University Press, 224–254.

Singh, J. P. 2009. *Negotiation and the global information economy.* New York: Cambridge University Press.

Slaughter, Anne-Marie. 2009. America's edge: Power in the networked century. *Foreign Affairs* 88 (January/February): 94–113.

Smith, Hedrick. 1988. *The power game: How Washington works.* New York: Random House.

Smith, Jonathan C. 1998. Foreign policy for sale? Interest group influence on President Clinton's Cuba policy, August 1994. *Presidential Studies Quarterly* 28: 207–220.

Smith, R. Jeffrey 2009. Obama taps CIA veteran as adviser on terror; Brennan has drawn fire on interrogations. *Washington Post,* January 9. www.washingtonpost.com/wp-dyn/content/article/2009/01/08/AR2009010804108.html.

Smith, Steven S. 1994. Congressional party leaders. In *The president, the Congress, and the making of foreign policy,* ed. Paul E. Peterson. Norman: University of Oklahoma Press, 129–160.

———. 2005. Parties and leadership in the Senate. In *The legislative branch,* ed. Paul J. Quirk and Sarah A. Binder. New York: Oxford University Press, 255–279.

Smith, Tony. 1994. *America's mission: The United States and the worldwide struggle for democracy in the twentieth century.* Princeton, N.J.: Princeton University Press.

———. 2000. *Foreign attachments: The power of ethnic groups in the making of American foreign policy.* Cambridge, Mass.: Harvard University Press.

Snyder, Jack, Robert Y. Shapiro, and Yaeli Bloch-Elkon. 2009. Free hand abroad, divide and rule at home. *World Politics* 61 (January): 155–187.

Solomon, Deborah. 2010. Bailout anger undermines Geithner. *Wall Street Journal,* February 21. http://online.wsj.com/article/SB10001424052748703798904575069610953163620.html.

Sorensen, Theodore C. 1963. *Decision-making in the White House: The olive branch or the arrows.* New York: Columbia University Press.

———. 1987–88. The president and the secretary of state. *Foreign Affairs* 66 (Winter): 231–248.

Spaulding, Suzanne E. 2008. Restoring the rule of law. Testimony before the Committee on the Judiciary, U.S. Senate. 110th Cong., 2nd sess. http://judiciary.senate.gov/hearings/testimony.cfm?id=3550&wit_id=7415.

Speth, James Gustave. 2004. *Red sky at morning: America and the crisis of the global environment.* New Haven, Conn.: Yale University Press.

———. 2008. *Bridge at the edge of the world: Capitalism, the environment, and crossing from crisis to sustainability.* New Haven, Conn.: Yale University Press.

The spill and energy bill [editorial]. 2010. *New York Times,* June 4. www.nytimes.com/2010/06/05/opinion/05sat1.html.

Spiro, Peter J. 2000. The new sovereigntists: American exceptionalism and its false prophets. *Foreign Policy* (November/December): 9–15.

Starke, Linda, ed. 2008. *State of the world 2008: Innovations for a sustainable economy.* New York: W. W. Norton.

The state-secrets privilege, tamed [editorial]. 2009. *New York Times,* April 29. www.nytimes .com/2009/04/30/opinion/30thu1.html.

Steele, Robert David Steele. 2001. *On intelligence: Spies and secrecy in an open world.* Fairfax, Va.: AFCEA International Press.

Stephens, Bret. 2009. Does Obama believe in human rights? *Wall Street Journal,* October 19. http://online.wsj.com/article/SB10001424052748704500604574481341183751038.html.

Stokes, Bruce. 2009. Countdown to Copenhagen. *National Journal,* October 31, 22–43.

———. 2010. Chinese checkers. *National Journal,* February 20.

Stone, Geoffrey R. 2004. *Perilous times.* New York: W. W. Norton.

Stout, David Stout. 2008. Gore calls for carbon-free electric power. *New York Times,* July 18. www.nytimes.com/2008/07/18/washington/18gorecnd.html.

Subcommittee on International Organizations, Human Rights, and Oversight of the House Committee on Foreign Affairs. 2008. *The decline in America's reputation: Why?* Washington, D.C.: U.S. Government Printing Office. http://hcfa.house.gov/110/42566 .pdf.

Sullivan, Andy. 2008. Arab Americans support Obama, Democrats: Poll. Reuters, September 18. www.reuters.com/article/idUSN1718128820080918.

Suskind, Ron. 2006. *The one percent solution: Deep inside America's pursuit of its enemies since 9/11.* New York: Simon and Schuster.

Swanson, Ian. 2007. Hard-line Cuba PAC makes inroads with House freshmen. *TheHill. com,* September 21, 1–3.

Taleb, Nassim. 2007. *The black swan: The impact of the highly improbable.* New York: Random House.

Taylor, Stuart. 2010. A course correction on terrorism. *National Journal,* February 6.

Teibel, Amy. 2009. Palestinian memo: hopes in Obama "evaporated" after "Zionist lobby" pressure. Associated Press, October 13. Found at www.huffingtonpost.com/2009/10/13/ palestinian-memo-hopes-in_n_318333.html.

Tenet, George. 2007. *At the center of the storm.* New York: HarperCollins.

Tharoor, Ishaan. 2009. Singh in Washington: Making the case for India. *Time,* November 24. www.time.com/time/world/article/0,8599,1942511,00.html.

Theriault, S. 2009. Party polarization in the 111th Congress. In *Legislative Studies Section Newsletter,* ed. R. M. Peters Jr. Norman: University of Oklahoma, Carl Albert Center. Legislative Studies Section Newsletter Online Edition: www.apsanet.org/~lss/Newsletter/ jan2009/Theriault.pdf.

Third-world mobile telecoms. 2008. *TheEconomist.com,* May 29. www.economist.com/display Story.cfm?story_id=11465558.

Thomma, Steven. 2009. Obama's no. 1—Most foreign travel by first year president. McClatchy Newspapers, October 7. www.mcclatchydc.com/2009/10/07/v-print/ 76725/obamas-no-1-most-foreign-travel.html.

Thompson, Ginger, and Ron Nixon. 2009. Leader ousted, Honduras hires U.S. lobbyists. *New York Times,* October 7. www.nytimes.com/2009/10/08/world/americas/08honduras .html.

Tobin, Richard J. 2010. Environment, population, and the developing world. In *Environmental policy,* 7th ed., ed. Norman J. Vig and Michael E. Kraft, 286–307. Washington, D.C.: CQ Press.

Torres, Maria de los Angeles. 2001. *In the land of mirrors: Cuban exile politics in the United States.* Ann Arbor: University of Michigan Press.

Trade Policy Study Group. 2008. *A report to the president-elect and the 111th Congress: A new trade policy for the United States.* Washington, D.C.: Peter G. Peterson Institute for International Economics. www.piie.com/publications/papers/20081217presidentmemo.pdf.

Traub, James. 2009. The new Israel lobby. *New York Times Magazine,* September 9. www.nytimes.com/2009/09/13/magazine/13JStreet-t.html.

Treverton, Gregory F. 2008. Intelligence analysis: Between "politicization" and irrelevance. In *Analyzing intelligence: Origins, obstacles, and innovations,* ed. Roger Z. George and James B. Bruce, 91–104. Washington, D.C.: Georgetown University Press.

Trubowitz, Peter. 1998. *Defining the national interest: Conflict and change in American foreign policy.* Chicago: University of Chicago Press.

Tully, Andrew. 2009. What's behind the tough U.S. talk on Iran, North Korea? Radio Free Europe/Radio Liberty Transmission. www.rferl.org/content/Whats_Behind_The_Tough_US_Talk_On_Iran_North_Korea_/1784419.html.

Tyson, Ann Scott. 2008. Gates warns of militarized policy. *Washington Post,* July 16. www.washingtonpost.com/wp-dyn/content/article/2008/07/15/AR2008071502777.html.

Union of Concerned Scientists. 2009. Scientific integrity and the presidential transition. www.ucsusa.org/scientific_integrity/solutions/big_picture_solutions/transition-main-page.html.

United Nations. 2007. *UN global environment outlook 4 (GEO-4): Environment for development.* New York: United Nations. www.unep.org/geo/geo4/media.

U.S. Census Bureau. 2010. U.S. international trade in goods and services, July 2010 [press release]. www.bea.gov/newsreleases/international/trade/2010/pdf/trad0710.pdf.

U.S. Climate Change Science Program. 2008. *U.S. climate change science program revised research plan: An update to the 2003 strategic plan.* Washington, D.C., May 29, available at www.climatescience.gov.

U.S. Congress. Senate. Select Committee on Intelligence. 2004. *9/11 Commission recommendations on intelligence reform.* 108th Cong., 2nd sess. S. Hrg. 108–835.

U.S. Department of Defense. 2005. *Department of Defense directive, number 3000.05—Military support for stability, security, transition, and reconstruction (SSTR) operations.* www.globalsecurity.org/military/library/report/2006/sigir-jan06_appdx-k.pdf.

———. 2009. *Department of Defense instruction, number 3000.05—Stability operations.* www.dtic.mil/whs/directives/corres/pdf/300005p.pdf.

———. 2010a. *Nuclear posture review report.* www.defense.gov/npr/docs/2010%20nuclear%20posture%20review%20report.pdf.

———. 2010b. *Quadrennial defense review report.* www.defense.gov/qdr/QDR%20as%20of%2026JAN10%200700.pdf.

U.S. Department of Energy. 2009. *International energy outlook 2009.* Washington, D.C.: Energy Information Administration. www.eia.doe.gov/oiaf/ieo/ieorefcase.html.

U.S. Department of Homeland Security. 2008. *Brief documentary history of the Department of Homeland Security, 2001–2008.* www.dhs.gov/xlibrary/assets/brief_documentary_history_of_dhs_2001_2008.pdf.

U.S. Department of Justice. 2009. Special task force on interrogations and transfer policies issues its recommendations to the president. www.justice.gov/opa/pr/2009/August/09-ag-835.html.

U.S. Department of State. 2009. Country reports on terrorism, 2008. www.state.gov/s/ct/rls/crt/2008/122436.htm.

———. 2010. Our employees at work. http://careers.state.gov/general/about-us.html.

Uslander, Eric M. 1995. All politics are global: Interest groups in the making of foreign policy. In *Interest group politics,* 4th ed., ed. Allan J. Cigler and Burdett A. Loomis, 369–391. Washington, D.C.: CQ Press.

U.S. Navy, U.S. Marine Corps, and U.S. Coast Guard. 2007. *A cooperative strategy for 21st-century seapower.* Washington, D.C.: U.S. Navy. www.navy.mil/maritime/Maritime Strategy.pdf.

U.S. Office of the Director of National Intelligence (ODNI). 2008. *United States intelligence community information sharing strategy.* www.dni.gov/reports/IC_Information_Sharing_Strategy.pdf.

———. 2009a. Dennis C. Blair: Director of national intelligence. www.dni.gov/blair_bio.html.

———. 2009b. DNI names Robert Bryant new national counterintelligence executive (news release no. 31-09). www.ncix.gov/about/20090918_NewNCIX.pdf.

U.S. Senate, Committee on Armed Services. 2009. *Inquiry into the treatment of detainees in U.S. custody* (Levin report). http://levin.senate.gov/newsroom/supporting/2009/SASC.DetaineeReport.042209.pdf.

Vargas, Jose Antonio. 2008. Obama defends compromise on new FISA bill. *Washington Post,* July 4. www.washingtonpost.com/wp-dyn/content/article/2008/07/03/AR2008070303 623.html.

Vig, Norman J. 2010. Presidential powers and environmental policy. In *Environmental policy,* 7th ed., ed. Norman J. Vig and Michael E. Kraft, 75–98. Washington, D.C.: CQ Press.

Vig, Norman J., and Michael E. Kraft, eds. 2010. *Environmental policy.* 7th ed. Washington, D.C.: CQ Press.

Wald, Matthew L. 2009. Debate on clean energy leads to regional divide. *New York Times,* July 13. www.nytimes.com/2009/07/14/science/earth/14grid.html.

Walt, Stephen M. 2002. Keeping the world off-balance: Self-restraint and U.S. foreign policy. In *America unrivaled: The future of the balance of power,* ed. G. John Ikenberry. Ithaca, N.Y.: Cornell University Press, 121–154.

———. 2005. *Taming American power: The global response to U.S. primacy.* New York: W. W. Norton.

The war on terror's legal battle [editorial]. 2010. *Los Angeles Times,* February 3. http://articles.latimes.com/2010/feb/03/opinion/la-ed-trial3-2010feb03.

A war within. 2010. *Newsweek,* September 12. www.newsweek.com/2010/09/12/what-gates-plans-to-do-before-he-leaves-office.html.

Ward, Jon. 2009. Obama's term "empire of envoys." *Washington Times,* August 25. www.washingtontimes.com/news/2009/aug/25/obamas-empire-of-envoys/.

Warshaw, Shirley Anne. 2009. *The co-presidency of Bush and Cheney.* Stanford, Calif.: Stanford University Press.

Watanabe, Paul Y. 1984. *Ethnic groups, Congress, and American foreign policy: The politics of the Turkish arms embargo.* Westport, Conn.: Greenwood.

Wax, Emily. 2008. In India, a world of hurt over a perceived Obama slight. *Washington Post,* November 13. www.washingtonpost.com/wp-dyn/content/article/2008/11/12/AR2008 111201655.html.

———. 2009. U.S. removes Kashmir from envoy's mandate; India exults. *Washington Post,* January 30. www.washingtonpost.com/wp-dyn/content/article/2009/01/29/AR20090 12903737.html.

Weaver, Ole. 1995. On securitization and desecuritization. In *On security,* ed. Ronnie D. Lipshutz, 46–86. New York: Columbia University Press.

Weich, Ronald. 2009. Letter from Assistant Attorney General Ronald Weich to Chairman Patrick Leahy, U.S. Senate Committee on the Judiciary. http://judiciary.senate.gov/ resources/documents/111thCongress/upload/091409WeichToLeahy.pdf.

Weissman, Stephen R. 1995. *A culture of deference: Congress's failure of leadership in foreign policy.* New York: Basic Books/HarperCollins.

Wessel, David. 2009. *In Fed we trust: Ben Bernanke's war on the Great Panic; how the Federal Reserve became the fourth branch of government.* New York: Crown.

The White House. 2010. Foreign policy. www.whitehouse.gov/issues/foreign-policy.

The White House, Office of the Press Secretary. 2010. Key facts about the National Security Summit. www.whitehouse.gov/the-press-office/key-facts-about-national-security-summit.

Wildavsky, Aaron. 1966. The two presidencies. *TRANS-action* 4: 7–14.

Williams, Rebecca. 2009. FY 2010 defense and foreign affairs spending allocations. *Budget Insight,* July 1. http://budgetinsight.wordpress.com/2009/07/01/fy-2010-defense-and-foreign-affairs-spending-allocations.

Wills, Garry. 2009. Entangled giant. *New York Review of Books,* September 10. www.nybooks .com/articles/archives/2009/oct/08/entangled-giant.

Wilson, Scott. 2009a. Afghan strategy divides lawmakers—Obama tells bipartisan meeting he has no plans to lower troop levels. *Washington Post,* October 7. www.washington post.com/wp-dyn/content/article/2009/10/06/AR2009100603817.html.

———. 2009b. On war, Obama could turn to GOP: Democrats oppose larger Afghan effort. *Washington Post,* October 1. www.washingtonpost.com/wp-dyn/content/article/ 2009/09/30/AR2009093005114.html.

———. 2009c. Shared interests define Obama's world. *Washington Post,* November 2. www .washingtonpost.com/wp-dyn/content/article/2009/11/01/AR2009110102604.html.

Wittes, Benjamin. 2008. *Law and the long war.* New York: Penguin Press.

Wittkopf, Eugene. 1990. *Faces of internationalism: Public opinion and American foreign policy.* Durham, N.C.: Duke University Press.

Wolfers, Arnold. 1962. *Discord and collaboration.* Baltimore, Md.: Johns Hopkins University Press.

Wong, Edward, and Andrew C. Revkin. 2009. Experts in U.S. and China see a chance for cooperation against climate change. *New York Times,* February 4. www.nytimes.com/ 2009/02/05/world/asia/05china.html.

Woodward, Bob. 2002. *Bush at war.* New York: Simon and Schuster.

———. 2004. *Plan of attack.* New York: Simon and Schuster.

———. 2008. *The war within: A secret White House history, 2006–2008.* New York: Simon and Schuster.

World Bank and International Monetary Fund (IMF). 2008. *Global monitoring report 2008: MDGs and the environment; agenda for inclusive and sustainable development.* Washington, D.C.: World Bank.

World Commission on Environment and Development. 1987. *Our common future.* New York: Oxford University Press.

World Public Opinion.org. 2006. World public says Iraq War has increased global terrorist threat. Washington, D.C.: World Public Opinion, Global Public Opinion on International Affairs. www.worldpublicopinion.org/pipa/articles/international_security_bt/172.php.

———. 2009a. Obama rockets to top of poll on global leaders. www.worldpublicopinion.org/pipa/articles/views_on_countriesregions_bt/618.php.

———. 2009b. Though Obama viewed positively, still much criticism of US foreign policy: Global poll. www.worldpublicopinion.org/pipa/articles/views_on_countriesregions_bt/623.php.

———. 2010. Global views of United States improve while other countries decline. www.worldpublicopinion.org/pipa/articles/views_on_countriesregions_bt/660.php.

Wright, John R. 2000. Interest groups, congressional reform, and party government in the United States. *Legislative Studies Quarterly* 25 (May): 217–235.

Yoo, John. 2004. Terrorists have no Geneva rights. *Wall Street Journal,* May 26. http://online.wsj.com/article/SB108552765884721335.html.

———. 2005. *The powers of war and peace.* Chicago: University of Chicago Press.

———. 2010a. *Crisis and command.* New York: Kaplan.

———. 2010b. Executive powers, civil liberties, and security: Constitutional trade-offs in fighting global terrorism. In *Debating terrorism and counterterrorism: Causes, contexts, and responses,* ed. Stuart Gottlieb, 339–352. Washington, D.C.: CQ Press.

Zakaria, Fareed. 2008. *The post-American world.* New York: W. W. Norton.

Zartman, I. William, ed. 2009. *Imbalance of power: US hegemony and international order.* Boulder, Colo.: Lynne Riener.

Zeleny, Jeff. 2007. A new kind of politics closely resembles the old. *New York Times,* June 16. www.nytimes.com/2007/06/16/us/politics/16obama.html.

Zeleny, Jeff, and Helene Cooper. 2010. Obama says U.S. failed to understand intelligence on terror plot. *New York Times,* January 5. www.nytimes.com/2010/01/06/us/politics/06obama.html.

Zeller, Shawn. 2007. Who's in charge here? *Foreign Service Journal* 84 (December): 20–28.

———. 2008. Five questions for Babak Hoghooghi, Public Affairs Alliance of Iranian Americans executive director. *Congressional Quarterly Weekly Reports,* June 2, 1457.

Zengerle, Jason. 2009. Clinton's tough talk on Pakistan. *New Republic,* October 29. www.tnr.com/blog/the-plank/clintons-tough-talk-pakistan.

Zoll, Adam, and Steve Layton. 2010. Graphic: A well-traveled first year. *Chicago Tribune,* January 20. http://articles.chicagotribune.com/2010-01-20/news/1001200107_1_2nd-visit-tobago-saudi-arabia.

Index